WORLD ECONOMIC OUTLOOK

May 1995

**A Survey by the Staff of the
International Monetary Fund**

INTERNATIONAL MONETARY FUND
Washington, DC

World economic outlook (International Monetary Fund)
World economic outlook: a survey by the staff of the International
Monetary Fund.—1980– —Washington, D.C.: The Fund, 1980–

v.; 28 cm.—(1981–84: Occasional paper/International Monetary Fund
ISSN 0251-6365)
Annual.
Has occasional updates, 1984–
ISSN 0258-7440 = World economic and financial surveys
ISSN 0256-6877 = World economic outlook (Washington)
1. Economic history—1971– —Periodicals. I. International
Monetary Fund. II. Series: Occasional paper (International Monetary
Fund)
HC10.W7979   84-640155
                              338.5'443'09048--dc19
                                        AACR 2 MARC-S

Library of Congress   8507

Published biannually.
ISBN 1-55775-468-3

*The cover, charts, and interior of this publication
were designed and produced by the IMF Graphics Section*

Price: US$34.00
(US$23.00 to full-time faculty members and
students at universities and colleges)

Please send orders to:
International Monetary Fund, Publication Services
700 19th Street, N.W., Washington, D.C. 20431, U.S.A.
Tel.: (202) 623-7430   Telefax: (202) 623-7201
Internet: publications@imf.org

recycled paper

Contents

	Page
Assumptions and Conventions	**vii**
Preface	**ix**
Chapter I. Economic Prospects and Policies	**1**
Industrial Countries	2
Developing Countries	5
Countries in Transition	7
Adequacy of World Saving	7
Chapter II. Policies for Sustained Growth in Industrial Countries	**9**
Cyclical Developments and Stance of Monetary Policies	10
Foreign Exchange and Financial Markets	17
Need to Safeguard Reasonable Price Stability	20
Urgency of Fiscal Consolidation	22
Structural Policies to Strengthen Employment and Productivity	26
Convergence in the European Union	33
Chapter III. Policy Challenges Facing Developing Countries	**35**
Recent Developments and Short-Term Prospects	35
Foreign Exchange and Financial Markets	39
External Payments, Financing, and Debt	40
Capital Flows and Economic Performance	41
Medium-Term Outlook and Policy Challenges	45
Chapter IV. Disinflation, Growth, and Foreign Direct Investment in Transition Countries	**52**
Financial Stabilization and Growth	52
External Viability and Capital Flows	58
Foreign Direct Investment and Macroeconomic Performance	60
Policy Issues Related to Foreign Direct Investment	61
Chapter V. Saving in a Growing World Economy	**67**
Trends in Saving Patterns	67
Important Questions About Saving	69
Key Factors Affecting Saving	72
Future Supply of Saving	77
Limits on Borrowing the Saving of Others	79
Global Real Interest Rate as an Indicator of Saving Adequacy	83
World Economic Performance Under Different Saving Scenarios	86
Conclusions and Policy Considerations	88

Page

Annexes

I Factors Behind the Financial Crisis in Mexico — **90**
Developments During 1988–93 — 90
Developments in 1994 — 91
Factors Behind the Crisis — 94

II Adjustment in Sub-Saharan Africa — **98**
Overview, 1980–94 — 98
Adjustment, 1986–94 — 101
Strong Adjusters — 104
Slow Adjusters — 104
CFA Franc Countries — 105
Challenges for the Period Ahead — 106

III Structural Fiscal Balances in Smaller Industrial Countries — **108**

Statistical Appendix — **112**

Output (Tables A1–A7) — 121
Inflation (Tables A8–A13) — 132
Financial Policies (Tables A14–A21) — 140
Foreign Trade (Tables A22–A26) — 149
Current Account Transactions (Tables A27–A32) — 156
External Financing (Tables A33–A37) — 167
External Debt and Debt Service (Tables A38–A43) — 178
Flow of Funds (Table A44) — 188
Medium-Term Baseline Scenario (Tables A45–A46) — 192

Boxes
Chapter

II   1. Macroeconomic Impact of the Japanese Earthquake — 16
2. Can Fiscal Contraction Be Expansionary in the Short Run? — 24
3. New Zealand's Structural Reforms and Economic Revival — 30
4. Capital Formation and Employment — 32

III   5. Brazil and Korea — 48
6. North-South R&D Spillovers — 50

IV   7. Price Convergence in Transition Economies — 54
8. The Output Collapse in Russia — 57
9. Foreign Direct Investment in Estonia — 63

V   10. Saving and Real Interest Rates in Developing Countries — 75
11. Pension Reform in Developing Countries — 76
12. Cross-Border Capital Flows and Capital Market Integration — 80
13. Effects of Increased Government Debt: Illustrative Calculations — 86

Tables
Chapter

I   1. Overview of the *World Economic Outlook* Projections — 3

II   2. Industrial Countries: Real GDP, Consumer Prices, and Unemployment Rates — 9
3. Industrial Countries: Inflation Objectives — 21
4. Industrial Countries: General Government Fiscal Balances and Debt — 26
5. Industrial Countries: Medium-Term Fiscal Objectives — 28
6. European Union: Convergence Indicators for 1995 and 1996 — 29

		Page
III	7. Selected Developing Countries: Real GDP, Consumer Prices, and Current Account Balance	37
	8. Selected Developing Countries: Macroeconomic Indicators	44
	9. Developing Countries: Medium-Term Projections	46
IV	10. Selected Countries in Transition: Growth, Inflation, Unemployment, and Fiscal Balance	53
	11. Countries in Transition: Indicators of External Viability, 1994	59

Annex

I	12. Mexico: Selected Economic Indicators	92
	13. Mexico: Quarterly Economic Indicators	93
II	14. Sub-Saharan Africa: Growth, Inflation, and Fiscal Performance	99
	15. Sub-Saharan Africa: External Sector Performance	100
	16. Sub-Saharan Africa: Saving and Investment	101
III	17. Selected Smaller Industrial Countries: Potential Output	109
	18. Selected Smaller Industrial Countries: Cyclical Responsiveness of General Government Budget	109
	19. Selected Smaller Industrial Countries: General Government Structural Balances, Actual Balances, and Output Gaps	110

Box

1	Simulated Macroeconomic Impact of Earthquake	16
12	Cross-Border Securities Transactions	80
	Government Debt Held by Foreign Investors	81
13	Estimates of Long-Run Effects of a Change in Government Debt from an Initial Steady State Debt-to-GDP Ratio of 40 Percent	86

Charts
Chapter

I	1. World Indicators	1
	2. World Saving and Real Long-Term Interest Rate	8
II	3. Major Industrial Countries: Real GDP	10
	4. Major Industrial Countries: Output Gaps	11
	5. Selected Industrial Countries: Policy-Related Interest Rates and Ten-Year Government Bond Rates	12
	6. Selected Industrial Countries: Short-Term Interest Rates and Yield Curves	13
	7. Major Industrial Countries: Nominal and Real Effective Exchange Rates	18
	8. Selected Industrial Countries: Exchange Rates and Long-Term Interest Rate Differentials	19
	9. Selected Industrial Countries: Inflation and Real Short-Term Interest Rates in the Recovery	22
	10. Major Industrial Countries: General Government Budget Balances	23
III	11. Developing Countries: Real GDP	35
	12. Commodity Prices	36
	13. Mexico: Financial Indicators	39
	14. Selected Developing Countries: Equity Prices	40
	15. Developing Countries: Net Capital Flows	41
	16. Developing Countries: Balances on Current Account and Reserves	42
	17. Developing Countries: External Debt and Debt Service	43
IV	18. Selected Countries in Transition: Consumer Prices	56
	19. Selected Countries in Transition: Foreign Direct Investment, 1992–94	61
	20. Countries in Transition: Foreign Investment Projects by Host Country, 1990–93	62

		Page
21.	Countries in Transition: Foreign Investment Projects, 1990–93	64
22.	Countries in Transition: Foreign Investment Projects by Target Industry, 1990–93	65

V 23. World Saving Rate — 68
24. Major Industrial Countries: Gross National Saving Rates — 68
25. Saving Rates — 69
26. Gross National Saving Rates and Per Capita Income Levels — 70
27. Share of World Output and Saving, 1993 — 71
28. Saving Rate and Per Capita Real GDP Growth — 72
29. Japan and Korea: Growth and Saving Rates — 73
30. Highest- and Lowest-Saving Economies — 74
31. Dependency Rates — 78
32. Largest Suppliers and Users of Net Capital Flows, 1989–93 — 83
33. Global Short-Term and Long-Term Real Interest Rates — 84
34. The Effects of a Lower Saving Rate in Japan: A Simulation Exercise — 88

Annex

I 35. Mexico: Nominal Exchange Rate — 94
36. Mexico: Inflation, Interest Rates, and Public Debt — 95

II 37. Sub-Saharan Africa: Terms of Trade and Real Effective Exchange Rates — 102
38. Sub-Saharan Africa: Real GDP and Per Capital Income — 103

Box

2 Denmark and Ireland: GDP Growth and General Government Structural Balance — 25
4 The European Union and the United States: Output, Capital, Employment, and Wages — 32
5 Brazil and Korea — 49
7 Czech Republic and Russia: Price Levels and Real Exchange Rates — 54
8 Russia: Indicators of Real Economic Activity — 57
9 Estonia: Fully or Partially Owned Foreign Companies — 63
13 Industrial Countries: Net Public Debt — 87

Assumptions and Conventions

A number of assumptions have been adopted for the projections presented in the *World Economic Outlook*. It has been assumed that average real effective exchange rates will remain constant at their March 1–24, 1995 levels except for the bilateral rates among the exchange rate mechanism (ERM) currencies, which are assumed to remain constant in nominal terms; that "established" policies of national authorities will be maintained; that the average price of oil will be $16.90 a barrel in 1995 and 1996, and remain unchanged in real terms over the medium term; and that the six-month U.S. dollar London interbank offered rate (LIBOR) will average 6¾ percent in 1995 and 7 percent in 1996. These are, of course, working hypotheses rather than forecasts, and the uncertainties surrounding them add to the margin of error that would in any event be involved in the projections. The estimates and projections are based on statistical information available on April 10, 1995.

The following conventions have been used throughout the *World Economic Outlook*:

. . .   to indicate that data are not available or not applicable;

—   to indicate that the figure is zero or less than half the final digit shown;

–   between years or months (for example, 1993–94 or January–June) to indicate the years or months covered, including the beginning and ending years or months;

/   between years or months (for example, 1993/94) to indicate a fiscal or financial year.

"Billion" means a thousand million; "trillion" means a thousand billion.

"Basis points" refer to hundredths of 1 percentage point (for example, 25 basis points are equivalent to ¼ of 1 percentage point).

Minor discrepancies between constituent figures and totals are due to rounding.

*   *   *

As used in this report, the term "country" does not in all cases refer to a territorial entity that is a state as understood by international law and practice. As used here, the term also covers some territorial entities that are not states but for which statistical data are maintained on a separate and independent basis.

Preface

The projections and analysis contained in the *World Economic Outlook* are an integral element of the IMF's ongoing surveillance of economic developments and policies in its member countries and of the global economic system. The IMF has published the *World Economic Outlook* annually from 1980 through 1983 and biannually since 1984.

The survey of prospects and policies is the product of a comprehensive interdepartmental review of world economic developments, which draws primarily on information the IMF staff gathers through its consultations with member countries. These consultations are carried out in particular by the IMF's area departments together with the Policy Development and Review and Fiscal Affairs Departments.

The country projections are prepared by the IMF's area departments on the basis of internationally consistent assumptions about world activity, exchange rates, and conditions in international financial and commodity markets. For approximately 50 of the largest economies—accounting for 90 percent of world output—the projections are updated for each *World Economic Outlook* exercise. For smaller countries, the projections are based on those prepared at the time of the IMF's regular Article IV consultations with member countries or in connection with the use of IMF resources; for these countries, the projections used in the *World Economic Outlook* are incrementally adjusted to reflect changes in assumptions and global economic conditions.

The analysis in the *World Economic Outlook* draws extensively on the ongoing work of the IMF's area and specialized departments, and is coordinated in the Research Department under the general direction of Michael Mussa, Economic Counsellor and Director of Research. The *World Economic Outlook* project is directed by Flemming Larsen, Senior Advisor in the Research Department, together with David T. Coe, Chief of the World Economic Studies Division.

Primary contributors to the current issue are Francesco Caramazza, Staffan Gorne, Robert F. Wescott, Vincent Koen, Mahmood Pradhan, Paula De Masi, Alexander Hoffmaister, Hossein Samiei, and Cathy Wright. Other contributors include Sheila Bassett, Robert Feldman, Thomas Helbling, Douglas Laxton, Guy Meredith, Anton Op de Beke, Jonathan Ostry, Todd Smith, Anthony G. Turner, and David Weil. The authors of the annexes are indicated in each case. The Fiscal Analysis Division of the Fiscal Affairs Department computed the structural budget and fiscal impulse measures. Sungcha Hong Cha and Toh Kuan provided research assistance. Shamim Kassam, Allen Cobler, Nicholas Dopuch, Gretchen Gallik, Yasoma Liyanarachchi, and Subodh Raje processed the data and managed the computer systems. Susan Duff, Margarita Lorenz, and Nora Mori-Whitehouse were responsible for word processing. Juanita Roushdy of the External Relations Department edited the manuscript and coordinated production of the publication; Tom Walter assisted in the manuscript preparation.

The analysis has benefited from comments and suggestions by staff from other IMF departments, as well as by Executive Directors following their discussion of the *World Economic Outlook* on April 5 and 7, 1995. However, both projections and policy considerations are those of the IMF staff and should not be attributed to Executive Directors or to their national authorities.

I

Economic Prospects and Policies

The world economy registered important progress on a number of fronts in 1994, indicating the start of a new expansion following the 1990–93 global slowdown (Chart 1). Growth was stronger than expected and inflation was contained in the industrial countries—often at levels closer to price stability than seen in three decades. Among the developing countries, the buoyant expansion in Asia continued while countries in other regions witnessed an encouraging strengthening of their economic performance and prospects. And an increasing number of transition economies in central and eastern Europe began to see positive growth. Despite continued financial instability in Russia and many of the neighboring transition countries, world growth last year was in line with its long-term trend of 3½ to 4 percent while world trade expanded by an impressive 9½ percent, well above its long-term average growth rate.

Recent changes in financial market sentiment toward some emerging market countries, together with turmoil in exchange markets more generally, have cast a shadow on the otherwise encouraging picture. The global flight to quality, which had already begun prior to the financial crisis in Mexico, has led to a substantial slowdown in the large flows of capital to developing countries witnessed during 1990–93. A key factor behind these earlier capital flows was the encouraging long-term growth prospects of many of the recipient countries. Cyclical factors, notably weak growth and investment demand in the industrial countries and associated low or declining interest rates, also played an important role. In addition to substantial inflows of foreign direct investment, large short-term portfolio investments also flowed into many developing countries, including some where the fundamentals may not have fully warranted the enthusiasm of foreign investors.

Since early 1994, the pickup in global activity has increased demand for funds and put upward pressure on interest rates. Meanwhile, investors appear to have become more cautious. Among the industrial countries, these developments were reflected in a sharp rise in risk premiums for countries with relatively weak anti-inflation credentials and large fiscal imbalances. At the same time, portfolio flows to the developing countries began to ease and equity prices in these markets generally declined. In Mexico, concerns about the external current account deficit and political developments contributed to substantial reserve losses at

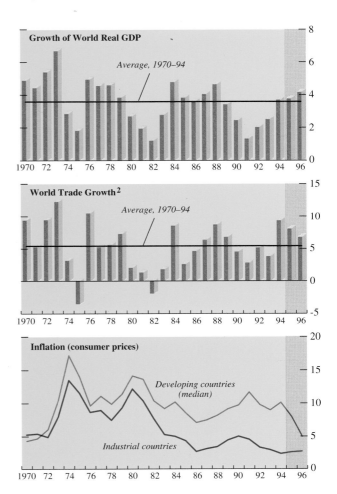

Chart 1. World Indicators[1]
(In percent)

Growth of World Real GDP

Average, 1970–94

World Trade Growth[2]

Average, 1970–94

Inflation (consumer prices)

Developing countries (median)

Industrial countries

[1]Blue shaded areas indicate IMF staff projections.
[2]Excluding trade among the Baltic countries, Russia, and the other countries of the former Soviet Union.

1

times during 1994, eventually leading to the devaluation of the new peso in December and triggering a severe crisis of confidence. Contagion effects were felt in asset markets in other emerging market countries, especially in Latin America, as well as in some industrial countries.

This episode serves as a powerful reminder for all economies of the speed with which perceptions about a country's situation can change, and of the heavy costs of allowing economic imbalances to persist until financial markets force the necessary policy adjustments. The resolution of the current crisis has necessitated a tightening of financial policies in Mexico and several other countries. Some other emerging market economies also need to strengthen their fundamentals. Conditional financial assistance from multilateral and bilateral sources should facilitate orderly adjustment in Mexico and help to contain the systemic repercussions of the crisis. Nevertheless, in the short run it seems likely that portfolio capital flows to many of the emerging market countries will remain volatile and may well decline, perhaps significantly.

Another key development since the beginning of 1995 has been the sharp weakening of the U.S. dollar and many other currencies against the yen, the deutsche mark and closely linked currencies, and the Swiss franc. At the same time, exchange market pressures within Europe have prompted a number of countries to raise official interest rates; most of the countries that have seen their currencies weaken are characterized by relatively large budget deficits. These developments threaten to exacerbate inflationary pressures in the United States, risk weakening the expansion in Europe, and could jeopardize recovery in Japan.

The recent decisions by Germany and Japan to lower official interest rates should help to counter these threats. It would be appropriate for the Federal Reserve to reinforce the actions by the Bundesbank and the Bank of Japan by raising short-term interest rates in the United States. This would help to strengthen the dollar, which is important in view of its role as the key international currency and is consistent with the need to contain domestic inflationary pressures associated with a weak exchange rate. Broader policy actions are also needed to foster greater exchange rate stability. In the United States, more ambitious fiscal consolidation efforts are required to raise the relatively low level of national saving and thereby reduce the external current account deficit. In Europe, fiscal consolidation should also be given greater priority during this period of economic recovery. Stronger efforts at deregulation and market opening in Japan are necessary to increase the exposure of the domestic economy to the benefits of international competition and thereby reduce the pressure on the yen.

Although the economic outlook for several countries has been adversely affected by the turbulence in financial markets, growth in the world economy is still expected to remain fairly robust during the period ahead. For many industrial countries, the strong growth momentum seen recently and still-large margins of slack may even suggest some upside potential in the near term. And for those developing countries that continue to face substantial demand pressures, a moderation of capital inflows may actually help some countries to prevent overheating and, hence, to sustain a satisfactory growth performance. At the same time, however, the recent events have underscored the downside risks to the projections, especially the danger of market volatility that may exacerbate, and expose, fragilities in the financial system. To reduce such risks, and to strengthen their economic potential, all countries need to act expeditiously to meet critical policy challenges, as emphasized in the Interim Committee's Declaration on "Cooperation to Strengthen the Global Expansion" adopted at its last meeting in Madrid.

Industrial Countries

With buoyant economic conditions in North America and the United Kingdom, recoveries in continental Europe, and a modest pickup in economic activity in Japan, output in the industrial countries advanced by 3 percent in 1994. This is the highest growth rate in five years and, except for Japan, uniformly stronger than expected six months ago (Table 1). Although the pattern of growth across countries is likely to change, average growth is projected to remain close to 3 percent in 1995–96. However, unemployment is likely to remain high in many countries, particularly in Europe. Looking further ahead, there is scope for output to continue to expand at a rate of 2½ to 3 percent, but both the level and the sustainability of growth and gains in employment will depend on the resolve of policymakers to contain inflationary pressures as the expansion matures, to restore greater balance in public finances, and to address important structural rigidities. (The projections were finalized in early April and reflect average exchange rates in the first three weeks of March.)

The reduction of inflation to only 2½ percent in 1994 in the industrial countries as a whole stands out as a major achievement. To reduce the risk of an early repetition of the often-experienced inflation-recession cycle, and because of the relatively long lags in the effects of policy action, it is necessary to allow a gradual tightening of monetary conditions well before rates of capacity utilization and unemployment return to levels at which inflation begins to pick up. The monetary authorities in a number of countries have already demonstrated by their actions their commitment to contain inflationary pressures. At the same time, however, differences in cyclical conditions continue to warrant somewhat differentiated policy stances.

Table 1. Overview of the *World Economic Outlook* Projections

(Annual percent change, unless otherwise noted)

	1993	1994	Current Projections		Differences from October 1994 Projections	
			1995	1996	1994	1995
World output	**2.5**	**3.7**	**3.8**	**4.2**	**0.3**	**—**
Industrial countries	1.2	3.0	3.0	2.7	0.3	0.3
United States	3.1	4.1	3.2	1.9	0.3	0.8
Japan	−0.2	0.6	1.8	3.5	−0.4	−0.7
Germany	−1.1	2.9	3.2	3.3	0.6	0.4
France	−1.0	2.5	3.2	3.0	0.6	0.2
Italy	−0.7	2.5	3.0	3.0	1.0	0.2
United Kingdom	2.2	3.8	3.2	2.8	0.5	0.3
Canada	2.2	4.5	4.3	2.6	0.4	0.5
Seven countries above	1.4	3.1	3.0	2.6	0.3	0.3
Other industrial countries	0.2	2.8	3.3	3.1	0.5	0.2
Memorandum						
European Union[1]	−0.4	2.8	3.2	3.1	0.6	0.2
Developing countries	6.1	6.3	5.6	6.1	0.5	−0.1
Africa	0.7	2.7	3.7	5.3	−1.0	−0.8
Asia	8.7	8.6	7.6	7.3	0.5	0.3
Middle East and Europe	3.7	0.7	2.9	4.7	−0.6	0.4
Western Hemisphere	3.2	4.6	2.3	3.7	1.8	−1.0
Countries in transition	−9.2	−9.4	−3.8	3.5	−1.5	−3.2
Central and eastern Europe	−6.2	−3.8	0.4	3.5	0.9	−1.3
Excluding Belarus and Ukraine	−2.0	2.7	3.6	4.3	1.1	0.4
Russia	−12.0	−15.0	−9.0	4.5	−3.0	−5.1
Transcaucasus and central Asia	−11.9	−14.9	−5.7	—	−8.3	−6.1
World trade volume	**3.8**	**9.4**	**8.0**	**6.8**	**2.2**	**2.1**
Import volume						
Industrial countries[2]	1.5	10.5	7.8	5.0	3.3	3.0
Developing countries	10.4	8.7	8.6	11.2	1.6	0.7
Export volume						
Industrial countries[2]	1.5	8.6	8.0	4.8	2.6	3.2
Developing countries	9.0	10.4	9.1	10.7	1.3	0.4
Commodity prices						
Oil[3]	−11.5	−4.1	9.3	—	1.9	9.3
In U.S. dollars a barrel	16.13	15.47	16.90	16.90	0.31	1.75
Nonfuel[4]	−3.7	12.3	8.0	−1.1	−1.2	1.5
Consumer prices						
Industrial countries	3.0	2.4	2.6	2.7	—	—
Developing countries	43.0	48.0	17.5	8.9	3.6	4.7
Countries in transition	675.1	295.2	126.9	18.9	−18.5	38.5
Six-month LIBOR (in percent)[5]						
On U.S. dollar deposits	3.4	5.1	6.8	7.0	—	0.8
On Japanese yen deposits	3.0	2.4	2.0	3.0	—	−0.8
On deutsche mark deposits	6.9	5.3	5.4	5.9	0.2	0.6

Note: Real effective exchange rates are assumed to remain constant at the levels prevailing during March 1–24, 1995, except for the bilateral rates among ERM currencies, which are assumed to remain constant in nominal terms.

[1]Fifteen current members of the European Union.

[2]Information on 1993 trade may understate trade volume because of reduced data coverage associated with the abandonment of customs clearance of trade within the European Union. Similarly, the strong rebound in trade volumes in 1994 may partly reflect improved data coverage.

[3]Simple average of the U.S. dollar spot prices of U.K. Brent, Dubai, and Alaska North Slope crude oil; assumptions for 1995 and 1996.

[4]Average, based on world commodity export weights, of U.S. dollar prices.

[5]London interbank offered rate.

In the group of countries where the expansion has progressed the most—the United States, the United Kingdom, Australia, and New Zealand—monetary conditions have firmed appropriately during the past year. There are only a few signs so far in these countries of a pickup in broader indicators of inflation. Nevertheless, their rate of economic growth has remained well above potential for some time, there are signs of strains on capacity in some markets for labor and intermediate inputs, and it is not yet clear that short-term interest rates have been raised sufficiently to slow activity to a more sustainable pace, partly in view of the expected strengthening of foreign demand as economic recovery gains momentum in other industrial countries.

To ensure that inflation does not accelerate, the need for a moderation of growth is particularly pressing in the United States, where economic slack has been fully absorbed. Monetary stimulus was gradually withdrawn during 1994 in the face of increasing capacity constraints, including rapidly tightening labor market conditions. While the economy still appears to be operating at or above potential, there are signs that growth is slowing toward more sustainable levels. In the United Kingdom, the strong upswing during 1994 has raised concerns about inflation even though some economic slack remains to be absorbed. Monetary policy has begun to tighten and ongoing fiscal consolidation efforts should also help to contain demand, but underlying inflation appears to have already bottomed out and inflation expectations have remained well above official medium-term objectives. In both countries, the tightening of monetary policy that has occurred already will be felt to its full extent only gradually, but the asymmetric nature of the risks warrants a monetary stance that errs on the side of caution. The recent weakness of the U.S. dollar and of sterling against other major currencies argues for earlier steps to raise interest rates further than would have been required otherwise.

In Canada, Italy, Sweden, and Spain, monetary policy has also been tightened during the past year, at least partly in response to persistent downward pressure on their exchange rates stemming from concerns in financial markets about the fiscal situation and outlook. Economic recovery is now under way in all four cases—most strongly in Canada—but margins of slack are still significant, and the main immediate threat to inflation is the weakness of these countries' currencies. The difficult dilemma this situation poses for monetary policy can only be resolved through stronger efforts to reduce fiscal imbalances. Such action is particularly urgent in Italy and Sweden.

The pace of recovery has been disappointing so far in Japan, where the rate of capacity utilization remains quite low. With weak short-term growth prospects, prices stable or even falling in some sectors, and in view of the excessive strength of the yen, a relatively easy stance of monetary policy is warranted for the time being. The further reduction of official interest rates in mid-April is consistent with both domestic requirements and the need to counter exchange market pressures.

In Germany, inflation is within the authorities' objectives and there is scope for growth to continue at the pace seen recently without any immediate threat to price performance. The strength of the deutsche mark and the sluggish growth of M3 together with other indicators justified the recent further decline in official interest rates. At some point, however, a firming of monetary conditions will be needed. Among the other countries participating in the European exchange rate mechanism, the decision to raise official interest rates in Denmark and Ireland in early March was consistent with their cyclical positions. For France and other European countries with high levels of unemployment and generally large margins of slack, recent increases in short-term interest rates, while justified by the need to resist exchange market pressures, were not warranted by their fundamentals. These interest rate hikes have subsequently been reversed to a significant extent. Although this episode is unlikely to derail the recovery in continental Europe, it has accentuated the downside risks for countries with particularly large interest risk premiums.

Progress with fiscal consolidation would help to alleviate the burden on monetary policy as the expansion matures. The reduction of budgetary imbalances is also essential in order to raise saving available to finance investment and employment growth in the private sector, to reduce the reliance on foreign saving in some countries, and to lessen the risk of instability in foreign exchange and financial markets. The robust growth seen recently and expected to continue in the near term presents an excellent opportunity to sharply reduce fiscal deficits.

Unfortunately, although the industrial countries all agree on the need to better balance public budgets, existing consolidation plans remain too modest in most cases. Absorption of economic slack will reduce the cyclical components of budget deficits, but relatively large structural imbalances are likely to persist in the absence of stronger deficit reduction efforts. In view of the sharp buildup of public debt during the past two decades, an appropriate objective would be not only to stabilize debt-to-GDP ratios but also to substantially curtail the accumulation of debt over the business cycle and ensure a clearly declining trend in debt ratios in the future.

Germany, the United Kingdom, Denmark, and New Zealand appear to be well on the way in current fiscal consolidation plans to permit some reduction in debt ratios before the end of the decade. In the United States, following significant progress in 1993–94, the structural deficit is estimated at about 2½ percent of GDP in 1995–96 (on a general government basis).

But, without policy changes, the deficit is expected to increase again over the medium term. In Japan, while the active use of fiscal policy to counter the recent recession was appropriate, the authorities need to improve substantially the fiscal position over the medium term. Although the overall budgetary balance at present is only showing a small structural deficit of $\frac{3}{4}$ of 1 percent of GDP, the structural deficit excluding social security—which is of particular interest in view of Japan's rapidly aging population and the resulting need to build up assets in the pension system—is estimated at almost 5 percent of GDP.

In France and several other members of the European Union, including Austria, Belgium, Finland, the Netherlands, Portugal, and Spain, measures taken so far imply a very slow reduction of underlying fiscal imbalances over the medium term. Their public debt ratios are therefore expected to remain at relatively high levels. For all of these countries, increases in interest rates or a cyclical downturn could easily compromise their objective of bringing fiscal deficits within the Maastricht convergence criterion of 3 percent of GDP—already a modest goal that risks becoming a floor rather than a ceiling. As indicated by the large risk premiums on interest rates, the fiscal situation and outlook are of particular concern in Italy, Sweden, and Greece, where gross debt ratios are close to or well over 100 percent of GDP and still rising. In Canada, the fiscal outlook has improved with the recent budget, but further action is needed to reduce significantly the high level of public debt.

In view of the large requirements for fiscal consolidation, it is reasonable to consider whether a general tightening of fiscal policies would entail risks for the economic expansion. A withdrawal of fiscal stimulus can normally be expected to have some adverse short-run effects on activity, with positive effects on investment and growth emerging only after one or two years. Under current circumstances, however, it is unlikely that any short-run adverse effects would be very large. The upward pressure on world real interest rates experienced since early 1994 provides an indication of growing tension between private sector demand for investment funds and government borrowing needs. Private demand can therefore be expected to crowd in relatively quickly as fiscal stimulus is withdrawn, as already has been experienced in the United States, the United Kingdom, and Germany. Even if consumers and investors might respond with a delay in some cases, this would not be a serious problem since the need to tighten monetary policy during the expansion would diminish correspondingly. In countries that have large risk premiums on real interest rates, serious efforts at fiscal consolidation hold the promise of reducing these premiums, with additional beneficial effects on business and consumer confidence; in such cases, the economic impact could conceivably be positive even in the short run. On balance, concern about the short-term effects on activity should not be a reason for postponing needed fiscal consolidation during a generally robust economic expansion. By contrast, if action on fiscal consolidation were delayed until the next economic slowdown, both the short-term and the longer-run costs would be considerable.

Achieving a better fiscal balance will require deep-rooted reforms to control the level and growth of public expenditures. Additional revenues may be necessary in some cases, but significant further increases in already very high levels of taxation, particularly in Europe and Canada, may have adverse effects on productivity and employment. User fees for some types of public services and better targeted support programs to meet the legitimate needs of low-income groups will need to be considered, together with labor market reforms to reduce structural unemployment and the associated burden on government budgets. Reforms will also be needed to alleviate future budgetary strains resulting from aging populations.

As has already occurred in the United States, continued recovery can also be expected to reduce cyclical unemployment in other industrial countries. The monetary and fiscal policies to foster a sustained expansion as previously discussed will be essential in this regard. However, average unemployment in Europe is still expected to be around 10 percent of the labor force by the end of 1996, only $1\frac{1}{2}$ percentage points lower than today, with relatively little scope for cyclical forces alone to bring unemployment much below $8\frac{1}{2}$ to 9 percent as the expansion matures. To tackle the very high level of structural unemployment in Europe, there remains a need for fundamental reform of labor market and social policies aimed at strengthening incentives for firms to increase employment and for the unemployed to accept job offers. Such reforms, which may need to include appropriate changes in tax and transfer policies, should not be viewed as a setback to long-standing, legitimate social objectives, but rather as critical to better achieving such objectives without harmful effects on unemployment. In the United States, labor markets are more flexible and structural unemployment has shown little long-run trend increase. However, there remains a key challenge to strengthen education and training policies in order to raise productivity and real wages, especially for low-income groups.

Developing Countries

The recent turmoil in some emerging country financial markets should not detract from the fundamental improvements that have occurred in recent years in economic policies and performances in most of the developing world. These improvements have allowed the developing countries to experience average growth of almost 6 percent during 1991–94, well above the average growth rate of about 4 percent in the decade to 1990. The prospects for sustained gains in output and living standards in the future are also better than they have been for a long time. Despite a likely slowdown in net capital inflows and a significant downward revision of the short-term growth estimates for Mexico and several other emerging market countries, the staff's projections point to sustained growth in most developing countries during the period ahead. However, developing country growth could be more adversely affected in the short run if the contagion effects from the Mexican crisis were to result in a collapse of confidence in the prospects for the emerging market countries, with a large and sudden slowdown in capital flows.

The strengthening of economic conditions in many developing countries during the past decade has resulted from determined efforts at stabilization and economic reform. Moderate inflation and a lowering of budget deficits have helped to maintain or restore financial stability and to foster a favorable business climate. And market-oriented structural reforms have reduced distortions and stimulated incentives and competition through price liberalization, privatization, and opening to trade and foreign direct investment. The benefits from such policies and reforms have so far been most striking in the developing countries in Asia. But fundamental changes in economic policies have also occurred, or are under way, in Latin America, Africa, and the Middle East. The number of successfully reforming countries has been growing steadily year by year throughout the developing world.

With success comes new challenges and risks of policy mistakes. The surges in capital flows to developing countries in recent years have complicated policymaking and in some cases have led to excessive liquidity expansion and upward pressures on real exchange rates. The resulting widening of current account deficits might appear to be of little concern as long as foreign capital keeps flowing. The recent events in Mexico, however, have illustrated the limits to the sustainability of external imbalances and the dangers stemming from excessive real exchange rate appreciation. In some countries, financial market pressures have also highlighted the fragility of banking systems in the face of capital outflows and greater monetary restraint. The problems experienced in Mexico are closely related to the country's very low private saving rate, which will require a strengthening of the public sector's contribution to national saving, as well as measures to stimulate private saving. Countries with a stronger saving performance and greater success in managing the surge in capital inflows are generally less vulnerable to shifts in market sentiment, although they have not been immune to contagion effects from the crisis in Mexico.

The rapid growth in many developing countries in recent years has also increased the risk of overheating, especially in some southeast Asian countries and in China. For these countries, just as for the industrial countries, it will be essential to prevent the buildup of inflationary pressures through gradual policy adjustments *before* a more drastic adjustment is required. Appropriate responses may need to involve both monetary and fiscal policy changes in order to avoid destabilizing short-term capital inflows that may be attracted by high levels of interest rates; for some countries it may also be appropriate to allow nominal exchange rates to appreciate somewhat. In China, in addition to a cautious stance of macroeconomic policies, it is necessary to strengthen financial discipline in the state-owned enterprise sector.

Improvements in policies and in economic performance are still relatively recent in many cases, and many tasks remain to avoid a re-emergence of macroeconomic imbalances and to establish a higher sustainable growth path. In Brazil, for example, the recent stabilization plan has reduced inflation substantially; to ensure that this progress is not jeopardized, the authorities will need to strengthen public finances, which will also help to contain the balance of payments deficit. In India, where the dismantling of controls on private industrial activity has been extensive, relatively high trade barriers and slow public sector reform continue to impede competition and productivity. India, together with the Philippines, will also need to step up fiscal consolidation efforts to alleviate inflationary pressures, strengthen national saving, and reduce the burden on monetary policy. In Egypt, there is a similar need to change the policy mix to establish a solid base for the resumption of growth. Among the large oil exporting countries in the Middle East, the decline in oil revenues since the mid-1980s, which has not yet been fully reflected on the expenditure side of public budgets, will require greater efforts at fiscal consolidation in coming years.

The low-income countries of Africa are increasingly seeking to address the causes of their protracted poor growth performance, and prospects for stronger economic growth are improving. But progress is uneven and there are risks of setbacks linked to political uncertainties. The recent recovery of commodity prices should help to strengthen the external position of a number of countries. In the CFA countries, despite policy slippages in some cases, reform efforts have been stepped up considerably and much of the gain in external competitiveness following the January 1994 devaluation has been maintained. In Kenya, fiscal and monetary policies have been tightened and have helped to restore macroeconomic stability, while both current and capital account transactions have been liberalized. For a number of the highly indebted countries in the region, however, debt burdens continue to dampen growth prospects despite their strengthened adjustment efforts. For these countries, it is essential that external creditors provide adequate financial assistance, including significant debt relief in some cases. Recent enhancements of debt-restructuring terms by Paris Club creditors, which involve an increase in the level of concessionality and greater flexibility with respect to debt rescheduling, should help to reduce debt and debt-service payments of low-income countries to more sustainable levels.

Countries in Transition

Half a decade has elapsed since the process of transition began. All of the former centrally planned economies have implemented market-oriented reforms, some early on and boldly, others more recently or tentatively. Relatively favorable initial conditions have contributed to success in some instances. It is also clear, however, that comprehensive liberalization coupled with financial discipline and broad-based institutional reforms shortens the transitional period and lowers the costs of economic transformation. Vigorous economic growth resumed within three years of the initiation of the more radical stabilization and reform programs. By contrast, measured output continues to decline in those transition countries that have followed a less comprehensive strategy.

In countries such as Albania, Estonia, Latvia, Lithuania, Poland, the Slovak Republic, and Slovenia, growth is projected to reach or exceed 5 percent in 1995, and open unemployment is declining or stabilizing. Moreover, despite the ongoing process of convergence of the domestic price structure toward world market prices, inflation continues to fall or is contained in all of these countries. In the Czech Republic, the pace of the recovery has been somewhat more subdued but macroeconomic performance has been outstanding in other respects. In countries such as Bulgaria, Romania, and the Transcaucasian and central Asian countries, where the pace and scope of reforms have been less bold, disinflation and the turnaround of output have been slower to materialize or are still elusive. Confronted with the social and political costs of drawn-out output slumps and hyperinflation, and the realization that there is nothing to be gained by delay, most of the countries that had postponed decisive reforms have now begun serious adjustment efforts.

Russia has made significant progress in structural reform and, in the summer of 1994, appeared to be within striking distance of macroeconomic stabilization. During the second half of the year, however, fiscal adjustment efforts were relaxed, reversing much of the progress that had been made toward disinflation, and the government's commitment to the privatization program and other aspects of structural reform was put in doubt. The privatization program now appears to be back on track, and the economic program for 1995 sets both fiscal and monetary policy on a course consistent with rapid macroeconomic stabilization. The prospects for a turnaround in activity as indicated by the staff's projections depend on the successful implementation of this program.

At the start of the transformation process, many observers expected that substantial capital inflows would be one of the engines of economic recovery. Foreign direct investment, in particular, was expected to play a critical role in the transfer of market-oriented technologies and business practices to the countries in transition. Although there are strong incentives for foreign enterprises to invest in the transition countries and there has been a substantial increase in foreign direct investment to some countries, the overall level of capital inflows remains modest in most cases. Foreign investors have been deterred by macroeconomic instability, by uncertainties about the pace of and commitment to structural reforms, and by the lack of transparent and stable legal structures.

Many of the countries in transition have made extraordinary efforts. In some, there have been remarkable achievements in the critical areas of macroeconomic stabilization and structural and institutional reform. Considerable challenges remain, particularly in the area of enterprise reform, but the process of transformation to market economies now appears to be irreversible in virtually all cases. As the reform process continues, there should be scope for larger flows of foreign direct investment. The relatively low level of capital inflows thus far, however, underscores the experience of other countries that most investment needs will have to be financed domestically. This highlights the need for adequate incentives for private saving, for the establishment of an environment that does not encourage capital flight, and for macroeconomic policies that contain inflation and limit the absorption of private saving to finance excessive budget deficits. It is vital that the international community continue to support the transition process in those countries that implement and persevere with appropriate stabilization and reform policies.

Adequacy of World Saving

The high level of world real interest rates that has persisted since the early 1980s is prima facie evidence of strong demand for investment funds relative to the supply of world saving (Chart 2). Taken together with the decline in the world saving rate during the same period, it is reasonable to ask whether the high level of real interest rates implies a suboptimal supply of saving that adversely affects world growth and economic welfare. With the substantial investment needs of the countries in transition, and in light of the large capital flows to many developing countries in recent years,

Chart 2. World Saving and Real Long-Term Interest Rate

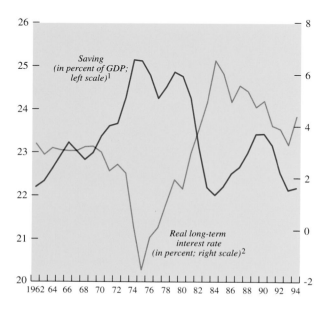

¹Three-year centered moving average. Data before 1970 represent less than complete country coverage.

²GDP-weighted average of real ten-year (or nearest maturity) government bond rates for the United States, Japan, Germany, the United Kingdom, Canada, Belgium, the Netherlands, and Switzerland.

this question leads to another: Is there a risk of further upward pressure on global real interest rates as demands for funds intensify?

It is debatable whether the level of private saving in the world economy is inadequate. There is ample evidence, however, to suggest that world growth and economic welfare are adversely affected by the strong pressures on the available level of financial resources. This is mainly due to the persistent absorption of private sector saving to finance fiscal imbalances in the industrial countries, which accounts for the bulk of the decline in the world saving rate since the 1970s. The supply of private saving may well be higher than otherwise in response to public sector deficits, but empirical evidence suggests that the degree of "offset" is little more than about half, on average. Notwithstanding conflicting results in the economic literature, this is consistent with analyses that have found a close relationship between the need to finance the accumulation of public debt in the industrial countries and the increase in global real interest rates since the 1960s. Overall, there is little doubt about the key responsibility of the industrial countries to address their fiscal imbalances and thereby alleviate pressure on global real interest rates.

It is less clear that real interest rates are likely to rise further because of the investment needs of the emerging market economies in the developing world and among the transition countries. The experience of both the industrial countries and the most successful developing countries suggests that the growing number of emerging market countries are likely to register substantial increases in domestic saving as economic performance strengthens, creating a virtuous circle between growth, saving, and investment. These countries may also contribute toward alleviating pressure on global interest rates by mobilizing domestic saving, by reducing the reliance on foreign saving, and by permitting greater international portfolio diversification by domestic investors. Indeed, while some countries will continue to attract net capital flows from abroad, others may become net suppliers of capital. Finally, experience suggests clear limits on the extent to which world financial markets can be expected to finance persistent external imbalances, especially when a heavy reliance on foreign saving becomes a substitute for adequate domestic saving. Overall, it seems unlikely that the potentially rapid catching up of these countries will seriously aggravate pressures on global saving.

II

Policies for Sustained Growth in Industrial Countries

The achievement of reasonable price stability in most industrial countries under circumstances of generally robust growth is a particular cause for satisfaction. The near-term outlook is for continued solid economic expansion in most countries and for a gradual absorption of cyclical unemployment in countries where labor market slack remains large. But many challenges continue to confront policymakers, including the need to safeguard progress on the inflation front, restore fiscal balance and reduce debt-to-GDP ratios, and improve the functioning of labor markets. Meeting these objectives is essential to strengthening the medium-term outlook for growth and employment.

The industrial countries have generally adopted price stability as a medium-term policy objective, but the real test of the commitment to price stability will come in the years ahead, when the expansion matures and countries have absorbed the slack generated in the last recession. Thus far, signs have been encouraging (Table 2). The countries most advanced in the cycle, such as the United States, the United Kingdom, Australia, and New Zealand, have acted to raise interest rates to dampen demand, even as inflation was falling. While further moderate tightenings may prove necessary, these actions have demonstrated strong resolve to prevent an acceleration of inflation. As for

Table 2. Industrial Countries: Real GDP, Consumer Prices, and Unemployment Rates

(Annual percent change and percent of labor force)

	Real GDP				Consumer Prices				Unemployment Rates			
	1993	1994	1995	1996	1993	1994	1995	1996	1993	1994	1995	1996
Industrial countries	**1.2**	**3.0**	**3.0**	**2.7**	**3.0**	**2.4**	**2.6**	**2.7**	**8.1**	**8.1**	**7.6**	**7.4**
Major industrial countries	1.4	3.1	3.0	2.6	2.8	2.2	2.5	2.7	7.3	7.2	6.7	6.6
United States[1]	3.1	4.1	3.2	1.9	3.0	2.6	3.1	3.5	6.8	6.1	5.5	5.7
Japan	−0.2	0.6	1.8	3.5	1.3	0.7	0.3	0.7	2.5	2.9	2.9	2.8
Germany	−1.1	2.9	3.2	3.3	4.7	3.1	2.0	2.0	8.8	9.6	9.1	8.6
West Germany	−1.7	2.3	2.6	2.8	4.1	3.0	2.0	2.0	7.3	8.3	8.1	7.7
France	−1.0	2.5	3.2	3.0	2.1	1.7	2.0	2.0	11.6	12.6	12.1	11.4
Italy	−0.7	2.5	3.0	3.0	4.4	4.0	5.2	4.2	10.2	11.3	11.3	10.6
United Kingdom[2]	2.2	3.8	3.2	2.8	3.0	2.4	2.9	2.8	10.3	9.3	8.3	8.1
Canada	2.2	4.5	4.3	2.6	1.8	0.2	2.0	1.9	11.2	10.4	9.2	9.0
Other industrial countries	0.2	2.8	3.3	3.1	3.7	3.2	3.4	3.0	12.2	12.6	12.1	11.6
Spain	−1.0	1.9	3.0	3.0	4.6	4.7	4.1	3.5	22.7	24.2	24.0	23.5
Netherlands	0.4	2.4	3.0	2.7	2.6	2.8	2.5	2.3	7.7	8.8	8.8	8.5
Belgium	−1.7	2.3	3.0	2.9	2.8	2.4	2.3	2.3	9.4	10.1	9.8	9.3
Sweden	−2.1	2.2	2.4	2.6	4.6	2.2	3.2	3.4	8.2	7.9	7.3	6.9
Austria	−0.1	2.8	3.0	2.8	3.6	3.0	2.5	2.7	4.3	4.1	4.0	4.0
Denmark	1.4	4.6	3.6	2.5	1.3	2.0	2.5	2.5	12.2	12.1	10.3	10.0
Finland	−1.6	3.9	5.2	4.8	2.2	1.1	2.3	2.8	17.9	18.5	16.5	14.0
Greece	−0.5	1.5	1.8	2.3	14.5	10.9	8.6	7.3	9.8	10.0	10.3	10.2
Portugal	−1.0	1.0	3.5	4.5	6.5	5.2	4.5	4.0	5.5	6.8	5.8	5.7
Ireland	4.0	5.2	6.2	4.9	1.4	2.5	2.5	2.5	15.7	14.8	13.8	13.5
Luxembourg	2.8	2.8	3.0	3.3	3.6	2.3	2.2	2.3	2.1	2.8	3.0	2.6
Switzerland	−0.9	2.0	2.3	3.2	3.3	0.8	2.5	1.5	4.6	4.8	4.3	3.4
Norway	2.3	5.5	3.6	1.7	2.3	1.4	2.5	3.0	6.0	5.5	5.0	4.5
Iceland	0.9	2.0	2.1	1.5	4.1	1.5	2.0	2.5	4.4	4.8	4.6	4.9
Australia	3.7	4.7	4.4	3.8	1.8	2.4	4.0	3.0	10.9	9.9	8.9	8.3
New Zealand	4.1	4.8	4.4	3.3	1.3	1.8	3.8	1.8	9.4	8.2	7.2	6.8
Memorandum												
European Union	−0.4	2.8	3.2	3.1	3.8	3.1	3.1	2.8	11.0	11.6	11.1	10.6

[1]The projections for unemployment have been adjusted to reflect the new survey techniques adopted by the U.S. Bureau of Labor Statistics in January 1994.

[2]Data for consumer prices are based on the retail price index excluding mortgage interest.

Chart 3. Major Industrial Countries: Real GDP[1]

(Percent change from four quarters earlier)

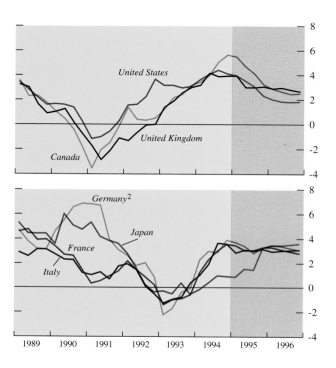

[1]Blue shaded areas indicate IMF staff projections; data for Italy for the fourth quarter of 1994 are also projected.

[2]Through 1991, west Germany only; thereafter, IMF staff estimates for unified Germany.

countries where increases in official interest rates have not yet been called for, such as Germany and Japan, their well-established anti-inflation record suggests that they too can be expected to act on a timely basis.

In the area of fiscal policy the picture is much less satisfactory, which has been an important contributing factor behind recent exchange market pressures and the rise in risk premiums on interest rates in many countries during the past year. While a few countries have embarked on meaningful fiscal adjustment programs, the pace of consolidation in most countries remains inadequate. Governments are generally taking insufficient advantage of the economic expansion to accelerate fiscal consolidation. Greater progress is also needed in the structural policy area. Although some countries have committed themselves to structural reforms, many have yet to announce and implement specific proposals. Selective measures to address the high levels of structural unemployment in Europe, in particular, have been ineffective in most cases, and only a few countries have undertaken the broad-based labor and product market reforms necessary to tackle the problem. Progress has also been limited in containing health care costs and with respect to pension reform. Success has been greater with privatization of state enterprises and deregulation.

Cyclical Developments and Stance of Monetary Policies

Economic recovery is now under way in all industrial countries. As a group, they achieved a growth rate of 3 percent in 1994 and output is projected to expand by 3 percent again this year before slowing slightly in 1996. There are important differences in cyclical positions across countries, however (Chart 3). For countries that are well into their third or fourth year of expansion, including the United States, Canada, the United Kingdom, Australia, and New Zealand, growth is expected to moderate this year and next. For most of the continental European countries and Japan, which emerged from the recession only in 1994, growth is expected to remain high or to strengthen further. Inflation may edge up slightly on average but should remain relatively low, reflecting the pre-emptive tightening of monetary policy in the countries most advanced in the cycle, and the continuing existence of significant margins of slack in continental Europe and Japan (Chart 4).

Underpinned by strong domestic demand, the economic expansion in the *United States* accelerated in 1994. Real GDP grew by 5 percent in the fourth quarter and by 4 percent for the year as a whole. Business investment was particularly buoyant and more than offset a drop-off in residential investment. Capacity utilization has reached its highest level since 1979, while unemployment has dipped below most estimates of the natural rate of unemployment. Meanwhile, inflation has remained relatively subdued; but survey evidence of shortages of skilled workers and rising crude and intermediate goods prices point to incipient price pressures in some sectors and the likelihood of somewhat higher inflation during the period ahead. The weakness of the dollar is an additional reason to expect somewhat stronger price increases this year and next.

Growth in the U.S. economy is projected to moderate to about 3¼ percent in 1995 and to slow further in 1996 in response to tighter monetary conditions. The projected slowdown in demand and activity should permit inflation to level off at about 3½ percent in 1996. Following a sharp rise in the current account deficit to an estimated $156 billion (or 2¼ percent of GDP) in 1994, the external deficit is expected to widen somewhat further in the near term, and to remain at about 2¼ percent of GDP into the medium term. Mexico's financial crisis is expected to reduce exports in the short run, but the medium-term impact on the U.S. economy is likely to be small.

In response to the rapid pace of economic growth, monetary policy has become progressively less accommodating since February 1994. The federal funds rate has been raised by 3 percentage points, to 6 percent, and real short-term interest rates have risen by a similar amount. Long-term interest rates rose by about 1½ percentage points in the early months of 1994 and by a further 1 percentage point in the second half of the year, but have since declined to their fall 1994 levels (Chart 5). The flattening of the yield curve at both ends of the maturity spectrum suggests that most of the needed adjustment of monetary conditions may already have occurred (Chart 6). But some further tightening would be warranted if the underlying momentum in economic activity and the downward pressure on the dollar do not abate sufficiently. In the staff's projections, short-term interest rates are expected to rise to 6¾ percent by the end of 1995.

Canada's exports and growth have been buoyed by robust U.S. growth, strong markets for commodities throughout the past year, and the weakness of the Canadian dollar. The strength of foreign demand was particularly marked in the second half of the year, but the recovery in final domestic demand has slowed, partly in response to higher interest rates. The current account deficit narrowed by about 1 percent of GDP. The relatively strong expansion brought the unemployment rate down by over 1½ percentage points since early 1994 to 9.7 percent in March 1995, which nevertheless remains above estimates of the natural rate. Real GDP growth is projected to moderate to 4¼ percent in 1995 and to 2½ percent in 1996, reflecting a weaker U.S. economy and the effects of high real interest rates. The still-large output gap is projected to

Chart 4. Major Industrial Countries: Output Gaps[1]
(Actual less potential, as a percent of potential)

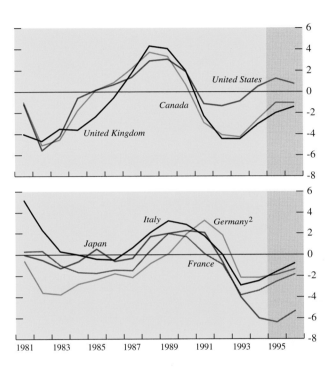

[1]Blue shaded areas indicate IMF staff projections. The gap estimates are subject to a significant margin of uncertainty. For a discussion of the approach to calculating potential output, see the October 1993 *World Economic Outlook,* p. 101.

[2]Data through 1990 apply to west Germany only.

Chart 5. Selected Industrial Countries: Policy-Related Interest Rates and Ten-Year Government Bond Rates[1]

(In percent a year)

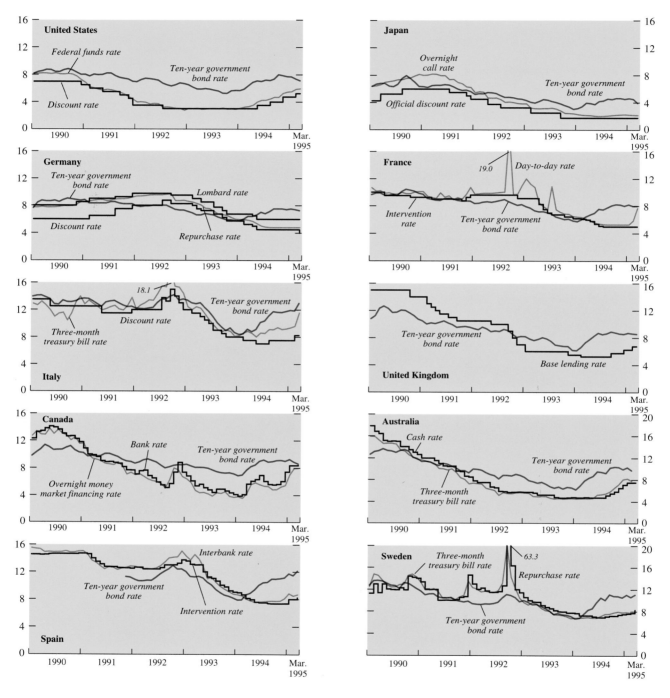

[1]The U.S. federal funds rate, Japanese overnight call rate, German repurchase rate, Italian treasury bill rate, Australian cash rate, and all ten-year government bond rates are monthly averages. The Canadian bank rate and overnight money market financing rate are those of the last Wednesday of each month. All others are end of month.

close gradually over the medium term, thus keeping core inflation under control, even though the recent exchange rate depreciation is likely to raise inflation temporarily.

Interest rates in Canada have been strongly influenced by exchange market developments and by investor concerns about public finances and political uncertainty over Quebec. Thus, in spite of weak labor market conditions, significant margins of slack, and very low inflation, real interest rates have risen to relatively high levels across all maturities. The new budget announced in February helped to reduce long-term premiums somewhat, but greater progress on fiscal consolidation is necessary to relieve the pressure on monetary policy and to allow a more balanced expansion.

In *Japan*, the recovery that began in early 1994 has been weak and erratic. It has been underpinned by private consumption, which was buoyed by the income tax cut in June. Residential and government investment have also been strong, and business investment rose in the third quarter of 1994 for the first time in three years. The recovery marked time in the fourth quarter as a sharp fall in private consumption and a steep decline in residential investment contributed to almost a 1 percent contraction in real GDP. Business investment, however, continued to rise. Because of the unexpectedly weak fourth quarter, Japan was the only major industrial country for which 1994 GDP growth was weaker than had been projected in the October 1994 *World Economic Outlook*. Net exports made a negative contribution to growth during the past year: imports surged, while the effects on exports of the global recovery have been blunted by the approximately 33 percent real appreciation of the yen since mid-1992. For 1995, moderate growth of 1¾ percent and a decline in inflation to ¼ of 1 percent is projected; the large output gap is not expected to begin to decline until 1996, as growth gradually accelerates.

The strength of Japan's recovery remains uncertain, however. There are some recent indications of a pause in the strong growth of household consumption. Low capacity utilization and the lagged effects of the yen's continued appreciation may also have a dampening effect on investment. On the positive side, the unemployment rate has stabilized, and indicators of business confidence have improved as the recovery in profits observed in 1994 is expected to continue this year. The January earthquake should not impede the recovery beyond the very short run: although economic activity in the first quarter of 1995 is likely to have been affected by the disruption of production and transportation, output in subsequent quarters is expected to be boosted by higher spending for reconstruction (Box 1).

As in other industrial countries, monetary policy in Japan has been supportive of the recovery, although the stimulative effects of low nominal interest rates

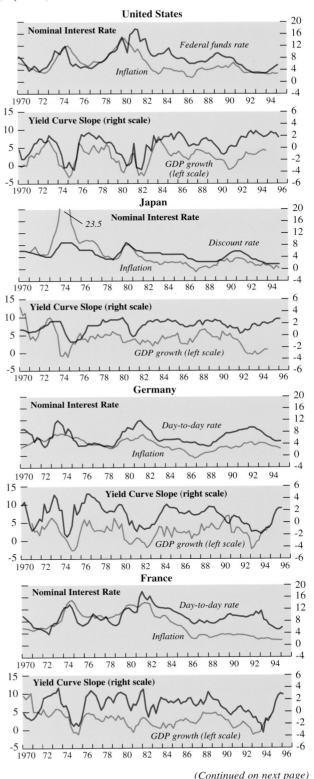

Chart 6. Selected Industrial Countries: Short-Term Interest Rates and Yield Curves[1]
(In percent)

(Continued on next page)

have been partly offset by the appreciation of the yen and lower inflation. Money supply growth has picked up over the past year, reflecting the strengthening of activity. Short-term interest rates rose slightly in late summer of 1994 and remained relatively stable, with three-month rates at about 2¼ percent through early 1995. At the end of March, the Bank of Japan signaled an easing of monetary policy, resulting in a decline in both the overnight call rate and other short-term interest rates of about 50 basis points, and the discount rate was cut by 75 basis points to 1 percent in mid-April. The stability of prices, the large output gap, and the excessive strength of the yen argue for a continued accommodative monetary policy stance for the time being.

The pace of economic activity in the *United Kingdom* picked up in 1994. Real GDP grew by 3¾ percent, with net exports contributing approximately 1 percentage point. Until early 1994, the recovery was sustained mainly by private consumption, which was financed largely by a sharp decline in the household saving rate and in mortgage interest payments following earlier interest rate reductions. During the year, consumption growth slowed in response to tax increases, but this was more than offset by a surge in both oil and non-oil exports. The current account deficit as a proportion of GDP narrowed by 1¾ percentage points during 1994 to a position of approximate balance. With real GDP growth in 1994 well above trend, the output gap narrowed considerably, and the unemployment rate declined steadily to 8½ percent in February 1995 from 9¾ percent a year earlier. Underlying inflation (retail prices excluding mortgage payments) fell to 2 percent in the fall of 1994, but subsequently picked up to 2¾ percent in early 1995, in part reflecting higher indirect taxes but also an increase in retail price margins. Private consumption is projected to remain subdued in 1995–96, in response to the already scheduled fiscal tightening and recent interest rate increases, but growth will be underpinned by strong exports and rising investment.

Monetary conditions in the United Kingdom began to be tightened in the second half of 1994 with a view to slowing the rate of economic expansion to a more sustainable pace. Base rates were raised in two 50-basis-point steps in September and December. With most indicators of inflation rising and with the growth of M0 remaining well above its target range, base rates were raised by a further 50 basis points to 6¾ percent in February. The yield curve has flattened considerably since mid-1994, but still remains rather steep. A further firming of monetary conditions may soon be required to achieve the medium-term inflation target.

In continental Europe, the recovery has been stronger than earlier anticipated and consumer confidence remains high. In *Germany*, the upswing was initially export led but it has now become more broadly

Chart 6 *(continued)*

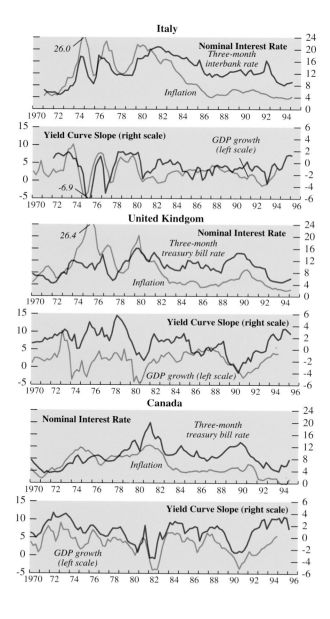

based. Business fixed investment has strengthened whereas private consumption has been affected by tax increases. Real GDP grew by 3 percent in 1994 and is expected to rise by 3¼ percent this year. Inflation has declined to about 2¼ percent in the 12 months to March, and although some pressures are apparent in producer prices and wage demands, a renewed upsurge in inflation is unlikely in the short run, especially in light of the appreciation of the deutsche mark.

Short-term interest rates in Germany continued to decline in the first half of 1994 and stabilized at between 5 percent and 5¼ percent until the end of March 1995, when they declined by about 50 basis points following a similar reduction in the discount rate. The yield curve has started to level off in recent months, while the growth of M3 decelerated sharply during the second half of 1994 and came within the official target range at the end of the year.[1] The stance of monetary policy has helped the recovery to become firmly established, and although the expansion is expected to remain strong, a number of factors suggest that monetary conditions remain broadly appropriate: the output gap is projected to close only gradually, unit labor costs are declining, fiscal consolidation is proceeding at an appropriate pace, and the continuing decline in inflation is resulting in a firming of real interest rates. Excessive upward pressure on the deutsche mark justified the recent further easing of official interest rates. Nonetheless, a gradual tightening of monetary conditions will probably need to begin toward year-end, especially if economic activity shows signs of being much stronger than expected.

Growth has also firmed in *France*, where real GDP rose by 2½ percent in 1994 and is projected to accelerate to 3¼ percent this year as both domestic and foreign demand continue to strengthen. Inflation has declined further and is expected to remain low in view of the persistence of a significant output gap and provided wage cost pressures can be contained. The unemployment rate, which was at 12.5 percent until September 1994, has eased only marginally despite a pickup in employment. The projected pickup of growth, however, should permit a gradual reduction in labor market slack.

The stance of monetary policy has also been supportive of recovery in France. Short-term interest rates declined in the first half of 1994 and subsequently stabilized at around 5¾ percent until the end of February 1995, some 60 to 70 basis points above comparable German rates. In March, however, short-term rates rose by about 2 percentage points in the wake of exchange market tensions; by early April about half of this increase had been reversed. Largely reflecting de-

<hr>

[1]The monetary target for 1994 was a rate of expansion for M3 of 4 to 6 percent between the fourth quarter of 1993 and the fourth quarter of 1994. This target range has been maintained for 1995.

Chart 6 *(concluded)*

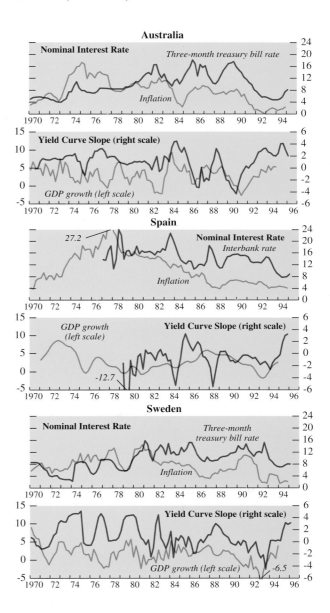

[1]Yield curve slope is lagged one year with respect to GDP growth.

Box 1. Macroeconomic Impact of the Japanese Earthquake

Damage from the earthquake that struck the Kansai region of Japan on January 17 was centered on Kobe, a city of 1.5 million people. The area accounts for slightly less than 5 percent of Japan's industrial output, while the port, the nation's second busiest, handles about 10 percent of foreign trade. In addition to the tragic loss of over 5,000 lives, initial estimates of the total material damage center on about ¥6 trillion (or $60 billion), equivalent to 1¼ percent of Japan's GDP. This estimate is substantially larger than the damage of about $20 billion resulting from the 1994 earthquake in California. The initial reaction of financial markets was mixed. The stock market fell by about 6½ percent in the week following the earthquake, reflecting, inter alia, investors' uncertainty about the extent of the damage.[1] Bond and foreign exchange markets, by contrast, were little affected. The Bank of Japan increased market liquidity, and overnight interest rates declined slightly.

The earthquake will affect economic activity in various ways. The reduction in Japan's capital stock—estimated at about ½ of 1 percent of the total existing stock—will tend to reduce output through supply effects, while reconstruction spending will raise aggregate demand. In the very short run, the supply effect is likely to dominate, and economic growth in the first quarter of 1995 is expected to be reduced from what would otherwise have been observed. In addition, Japan's external trade has been adversely affected in the near term given Kobe's importance as a transportation center. Over time, the effect of the aggregate demand stimulus on output will become more important, especially as the Japanese economy is currently operating at well below its longer-run capacity.

The government has declared Kobe and the surrounding area a "special" disaster zone, making it eligible for additional national assistance. The authorities have also decided to take a liberal approach in applying the Disaster Relief Law, allowing the central government to shoulder an increased share of financing rescue work and reconstruction costs. In addition, new legislation has been introduced to facilitate the restoration of transportation infrastructure, as well as to provide tax concessions for enterprises and individuals. As there is little room for new earthquake-related claims in the existing budget, additional fiscal measures will be necessary: the govern-

Simulated Macroeconomic Impact of Earthquake

	Deviation from Baseline			
	1995	1996	1997	2000
Real GDP (level in percent)	0.2	0.4	0.3	–0.1
Potential GDP (level in percent)	–0.2	–0.1	—	—
GDP deflator (growth rate)	0.1	0.2	0.2	–0.2
Long-term interest rate (percentage points)	0.2	0.2	0.1	—
Current account (percent of GDP)	—	–0.1	–0.1	—

ment has passed a supplementary budget for FY 1994 of about ¥1 trillion to deal with immediate needs. A supplementary FY 1995 budget containing a comprehensive reconstruction plan will be introduced in the months ahead.

To illustrate the possible macroeconomic impact of the earthquake over the medium term, a simulation was performed using the staff's simulation model (MULTIMOD). The simulation incorporates a drop in capacity output starting in 1995 due to capital destruction of the amount discussed above, as well as an equivalently sized demand stimulus arising from reconstruction. For this exercise, it was assumed that the reconstruction spending would be spread over the period 1995–97, with the effect in 1995 being somewhat smaller than in the latter two years owing to the initial dislocation caused by the earthquake.

In the simulation, potential output falls by about ¼ of 1 percent in 1995 relative to its baseline level, while actual GDP rises by a similar amount, reflecting higher investment spending. In 1996, the effect on GDP rises to almost ½ of 1 percent given the assumed scaling up of the reconstruction process and the induced effects on other components of demand, while potential GDP converges to its baseline level. Inflation is raised by less than ¼ of 1 percentage point during 1995–97, reflecting the large margins of excess capacity in the Japanese economy. Increased capital demands put modest upward pressure on long-term interest rates, while the current account surplus falls by 0.1 percent of GDP in 1996 and 1997 in response to higher domestic demand. These results, of course, are sensitive to both the assumed size and timing of the reconstruction expenditures, which remain uncertain. Nevertheless, they suggest that the earthquake should not have a large impact on Japan's medium-term economic prospects.

---

[1]The market decline implies an estimated loss of ¥12 trillion in the (noncorporate) shareholder value in the first section of the Tokyo stock exchange, twice the estimated damage caused by the earthquake.

velopments in international bond markets, long-term interest rates rose through November to around 8¼ percent before declining to 8 percent in February and March. The yield curve has been positively sloped since March 1994, and both short- and long-term real interest rates appear high in view of the impressive inflation performance and the remaining margins of slack. Nevertheless, barring significant adverse effects

on business and consumer confidence, the rise in short-term interest rates prompted by recent exchange market tensions is unlikely to derail the recovery.

The economic upswing gathered momentum in *Italy* in 1994, with a continuing strong export performance and a resurgence of domestic demand. Business investment began to recover, aided by improved profitability and notwithstanding relatively high real interest rates. Unemployment has not yet shown any decline from the high levels reached during the recession, however, and a substantial degree of slack remains to be absorbed. The projections show a strengthening of growth to 3 percent in 1995. But there are risks of setbacks to the recovery process stemming from political instability and the resulting skepticism about the political system's ability to reduce the level of public debt over the medium term. Inflation is expected to rise to 5¼ percent in 1995. As in Canada and Sweden, recent increases in official interest rates were linked to downward pressure on the exchange rate and the resulting risk of a pickup in inflation.

In *Spain* and *Portugal*, the recovery has been led by strong export growth, which was spurred by the depreciations of the peseta and the escudo in the past couple of years. Domestic demand started picking up in 1994 and is expected to sustain the expansion in 1995 and 1996. In Spain, stronger growth, together with the effects of labor market reforms that entered into force in 1994, should help to reduce the very high level of unemployment. Inflation will be adversely affected temporarily by the value-added-tax increase in 1995 and by the further adjustment of the peseta within the ERM in early 1995. The recovery has proceeded at a moderate pace in *Austria, Belgium,* the *Netherlands,* and *Switzerland* as private consumption and business investment have gradually gathered strength. The pace of economic activity has been more brisk in *Ireland, Denmark*, and *Norway.* In Ireland, the confidence engendered by low inflation and relatively low interest rates has encouraged domestic spending. In Denmark, domestic demand has reacted strongly to a temporary relaxation of the fiscal stance and the improved international environment. Booming exports have pulled *Finland* and *Sweden* out of their deep recessions. The recovery remains very uneven in Finland, however, but domestic demand should begin to strengthen as the consolidation of financial positions by households and the sheltered sector nears completion. In Sweden, the rapid accumulation of public sector debt has increased risk premiums on long-term interest rates, which have retarded the pickup of domestic demand and, as in Italy, poses risks for the recovery. In *Greece*, economic activity has remained weak, and only a modest recovery is expected, reflecting the very slow progress in tackling the large budget deficit and in reducing inflation.

Growth in *Australia* and *New Zealand* accelerated markedly in 1994 as robust domestic spending boosted activity. Both countries have allowed monetary conditions to firm significantly, despite low rates of inflation. In Australia, the current account deficit deteriorated sharply in 1994 to an estimated 4½ percent of GDP. Although consumer spending and investment growth are expected to moderate, the current account deficit is projected to remain relatively large.

Inflation is expected to rise in 1995, but should moderate subsequently on the assumption that the monetary tightening that has already occurred, and any additional measures that may be taken, will be sufficient to slow the pace of expansion.

Monetary policy in Australia was tightened on three occasions in the second half of 1994, raising the official cash rate by a cumulative 2 ¾ percentage points to 7½ percent in December. Long-term government bond rates rose steeply through 1994, with the differential against U.S. rates widening by about 200 basis points. The yield curve has flattened slightly in recent months but remains steep. Concerns about inflation are also reflected in the high yields on index-linked bonds. The extent of further monetary tightening that may be necessary will depend in part on the degree of fiscal consolidation undertaken in the 1995/96 budget (to be presented in May 1995). In New Zealand, the Reserve Bank has allowed short-term interest rates to rise by about 4½ percentage points during the past year to 9½ percent in early 1995.

Foreign Exchange and Financial Markets

The U.S. dollar has weakened sharply so far in 1995, reaching record lows against the Japanese yen and the deutsche mark. Through February 1995, the U.S. dollar was still above its lows for the 1990s against the industrial country currencies on both a nominal (and real) effective basis (Chart 7). The weakening of the U.S. dollar against the yen and the deutsche mark was offset by its strength against the Canadian dollar and some European currencies. On a broader effective basis, which takes into account key developing country trading partners, the U.S. dollar also benefited from its strength against the Mexican peso in particular. However, in considering the role of the U.S. dollar as the world's leading reserve and financial currency, its value against the other key currencies—in particular, the deutsche mark and the yen—should be assigned a larger importance than trade weights alone might suggest. From the end of 1994 to April 10, 1995, the U.S. dollar declined by 17 percent against the Japanese yen and by 10 percent against the deutsche mark.[2] The declines since the end of February were 14 percent and 4 percent, respectively. Moreover, these latter developments brought the dollar on an effective basis near its lows of recent years, in circumstances where, with the U.S. economy operating at or above full capacity, a weakened dollar heightened concerns about future inflationary pressures. The U.S. dollar steadied against the deutsche mark after the Bundesbank lowered official interest

---

[2]Based on London noon quotations.

rates on March 30, but continued to decline against the yen, even after the Bank of Japan guided the call money interest rate lower in late March.

As a counterpart to the dollar's weakness, both the deutsche mark and the Japanese yen have strengthened significantly in recent months. The appreciation of the deutsche mark reflected not only its rise against the U.S. (and Canadian) dollar, but also increases against several European currencies affected by political uncertainties or fiscal difficulties, or both, including especially the lira, the peseta, the krona, and sterling; the French franc and the Belgian franc were affected to a lesser extent. Accompanying pressures on the exchange rate mechanism (ERM) of the European Monetary System resulted in the devaluation of the central parity of the Spanish peseta by 7 percent and of the Portuguese escudo of 3½ percent during the first weekend of March. In the week that followed, currency pressures were also reflected in increased official interest rates in a number of European countries. The Japanese yen appreciated across a range of currencies, including the deutsche mark and the Swiss franc.

It is always difficult to explain with any degree of precision the movements in exchange rates, or other financial variables for that matter, but several factors are particularly relevant to the recent developments in key currencies. First, Japan's large current account surpluses and concerns over recent and prospective U.S. current account deficits and their financing would seem to have been a positive force on the yen and a negative one on the dollar. Indeed, in the United States, the persistence of current account deficits has resulted in a gradual and continuing buildup of net foreign liabilities that has underscored the need for further fiscal consolidation and higher domestic saving. In these circumstances, the poor prospects of further reductions in the U.S. budget deficit seem to have contributed to a weaker dollar. Despite mixed indications of the extent of a slowdown in U.S. growth, there also appeared to be a growing perception in the market that U.S. short-term interest rates were near their peak in this cycle. And the continuing economic crisis in Mexico and worries in the market about the situation in the rest of Latin America weighed adversely on the U.S. currency. Efforts to support the dollar by coordinated central bank intervention appeared to have had little lasting impact; there was little expectation that intervention would be backed by interest rate adjustments by the leading central banks, or by more fundamental policy changes.

In Europe, with several countries beset by political uncertainties and fiscal difficulties, the deutsche mark (and the Swiss franc) benefited considerably from increased demand from risk conscious investors. Indeed, market perceptions of weak fiscal fundamentals, associated concerns about inflation and public debt positions, and political uncertainties have con-

Chart 7. Major Industrial Countries: Nominal and Real Effective Exchange Rates

(1980 = 100; logarithmic scale)

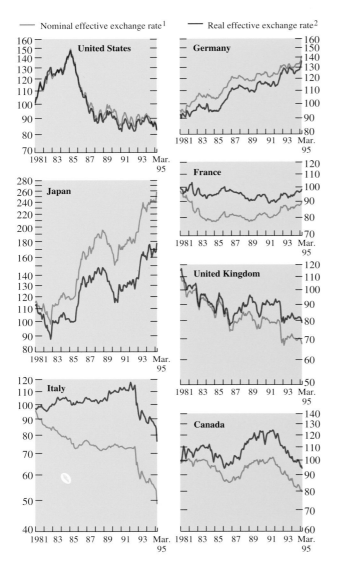

[1]Constructed using 1989–91 trade weights.

[2]Defined in terms of relative normalized unit labor costs in manufacturing, as estimated by the IMF's Competitiveness Indicators System, using 1989–91 trade weights.

tributed during the past year to periodic bouts of downward pressures on the Italian lira, the Spanish peseta, and the Swedish krona. The Canadian dollar has been in a similar situation (Chart 8). These circumstances have been reflected in substantial risk premiums on long-term interest rates and have prompted these countries to increase policy-related short-term interest rates. General nervousness related to developments in several emerging markets may also have played a role through flight-to-quality effects.

An important additional factor until late March was the strengthening expansion in Germany, along with high wage demands and recent wage settlements in some sectors. These considerations had contributed to expectations that the Bundesbank was more likely to tighten—or less likely to ease—and perhaps sooner than might be warranted in some of Germany's trading partners. In the event, in late March the Bundesbank lowered official interest rates in light of domestic considerations, in particular the slow growth in its main monetary aggregate, and the effective tightening of monetary conditions implied by the appreciation of the mark. The monetary easing in Germany helped to relieve currency pressures in Europe and facilitated a lowering of official interest rates in several countries.

The deutsche mark appreciated by 10 percent against the U.S. dollar and by 4 percent in nominal effective terms from the end of 1994 to April 10, 1995. The krona, the peseta, the lira, and sterling fell to record lows against the deutsche mark. The French franc, amid election uncertainties, fell well below the central rate in the ERM although it remained quite strong in real effective terms; however, three-month interest rate differentials with respect to Germany rose to over 3 percentage points in March before narrowing somewhat in early April. The Japanese yen appreciated by 17 percent against the U.S. dollar, and by 16 percent in nominal effective terms from the end of 1994 to April 10, 1995.

In government bond markets, much of the general rise in long-term interest rates in the largest industrial countries during the past year or so was attributable to the strengthening of growth prospects and inflation expectations. More recently, long-term interest rates in several of the larger countries—the United States, Japan, Germany, France, and the United Kingdom— have declined, as the credibility of commitments to resist inflationary pressures appears to have strengthened. For the United States and the United Kingdom, where the expansions are more advanced and where pre-emptive actions have been taken to firm monetary conditions, yield curves have leveled on both ends. More generally, from their peaks in the fall, long-term interest rates have declined by about 90 basis points in the United States and by 60 to 70 basis points in France, Germany, and the United Kingdom. Recently, long-term interest rates in Japan have declined by

Chart 8. Selected Industrial Countries: Exchange Rates and Long-Term Interest Rate Differentials

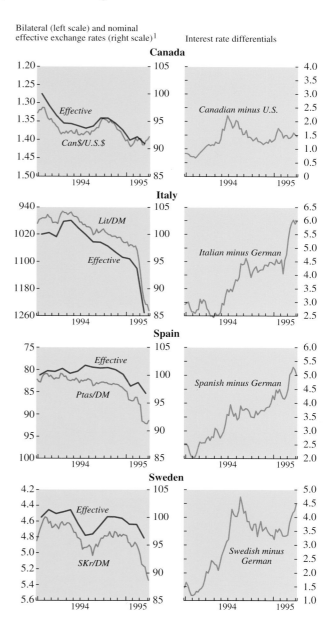

Bilateral (left scale) and nominal effective exchange rates (right scale)[1]

Interest rate differentials

[1]Nominal effective exchange rates are based on 1980 = 100.

about 125 basis points, apparently in the expectation of a cut in the official discount rate.

Under the weight of rising long-term interest rates, and their offset to the impact on stock markets of the buoyancy of growth and generally strong profits, equity prices in the major markets fell in the latter half of 1994. With the main exception of U.S. equity prices, they have remained at comparatively low levels into 1995. From August 1994 through April 10, 1995, equity prices have declined on balance by 8 to 16 percent in Germany, France, and Italy. Over the same period, the Nikkei in Japan was down almost 22 percent, 16 percent of which has been since the earthquake. The recent strength of the deutsche mark and the yen appears to have had a negative effect on share prices in Germany and Japan. Share prices in the United Kingdom and Canada increased by 1 to 3 percent, while equity prices in the United States have recently rebounded markedly to test new highs.

Need to Safeguard Reasonable Price Stability

A key policy lesson of the past two decades has been that the costs of allowing inflation to rise are very high and that deep and protracted recessions have typically been required to subdue the inflationary forces generated during booms. This experience suggests an asymmetric relationship between inflation and economic activity whereby excess demand has a much stronger effect in raising inflation than excess supply has in reducing inflation.[3] The implication for monetary policy of this asymmetry, and the long lags in the effects of policy action, is the need to pre-empt inflationary pressures before they build so as to avoid having to respond more forcefully later to economic overheating. Failure to respond promptly is costly, as it raises the cumulative loss of output and adds to structural unemployment due to persistence effects. In contrast, policies that prevent overheating and thereby reduce fluctuations of output around its long-run trend can be expected to raise the average level of output and employment.

In accordance with this experience, monetary policies in the industrial countries have become increasingly focused on the goal of price stability. A growing number of countries are making this goal operational by adopting formal targets for inflation, or at least implicit medium-term objectives (Table 3). In a number of countries, the exchange rate or a monetary aggregate continues to serve as the intermediate target of monetary policy. To strengthen the credibility of inflation objectives, a number of countries have recently revised central bank legislation and practices to enhance the independence of their central banks. This strong commitment to safeguard price stability comes at a time when actual inflation in industrial countries is at 30-year lows, and most countries have either attained or are within reach of their medium-term inflation objective; only Greece and, to a lesser extent, Italy, Portugal, and Spain, have some distance to go.

To some extent, of course, the recent favorable inflation performance has reflected the existence of considerable economic slack in a number of countries. As slack is absorbed, monetary policy faces the challenge of avoiding a re-emergence of inflationary pressures through timely adjustments of monetary conditions. The degree to which official interest rates will have to be tightened and the timing of policy actions will vary across countries depending importantly on the evolution of the cycle and the stance of fiscal policy. Countries with weak anti-inflation credentials will need to pay particular attention to market expectations about future inflation and to exchange market developments. So far, however, there are encouraging signs that monetary authorities are responding with greater determination than in the past.

Will the strong commitment of monetary authorities be able to ensure a "soft landing" and prevent the excesses often experienced in the past? Although a soft landing is indeed assumed in the staff's projections, it cannot be taken as a foregone conclusion. It is important to recall that forecasters have typically underestimated the strength of economic recoveries just as they have tended to underestimate the severity of economic downturns. In fact, this was again the case in 1994, when the growth momentum was stronger than expected in most industrial countries. Looking ahead, it is possible that the strength of activity will continue to exceed expectations in the United States and other countries that are advanced in the cycle. The likely degree of underestimation, however, would probably be smaller than in 1994, in light of the pre-emptive tightenings of monetary policy that have occurred. In continental Europe, by comparison, the possibility of a stronger-than-projected outlook is probably somewhat greater at this stage in the expansion although there is also a risk of setbacks in the recovery process, at least in some countries. For Japan, the risks appear to be more evenly balanced.

While it is difficult to assess the degree of monetary tightening consistent with a soft landing, it is important to consider whether the adjustments in monetary conditions that have occurred so far appear to be more timely than in the past. Such an analysis is, of course, mainly relevant for those countries, such as the United States, the United Kingdom, Australia, and New Zealand, where recovery from the recent recessions is already complete or well advanced.

---

[3]Evidence on asymmetries in the relationship between economic activity and inflation in the major industrial countries is presented in Douglas Laxton, Guy Meredith, and David Rose, "Asymmetric Effects of Economic Activity on Inflation: Evidence and Policy Implications," IMF Working Paper 94/139 (November 1994).

Table 3. Industrial Countries: Inflation Objectives

Country	Inflation Rate, 1994[1]	Target Rate and Period	Comments
	In percent		
United States	2.6	—	No quantified target. Federal Reserve sets target growth rates for M2 and M3 and a monitoring range for domestic debt.
Japan	0.7	—	No quantified target.
Germany	3.1	less than 2 percent medium term	Implicit objective derived from money growth target and output and velocity assumptions.
France	1.7	less than 2 percent medium term	
Italy	4.0	2 percent medium term	Inflation target of 2.5 percent in 1995 and 2 percent in 1996 and 1997 in government's three-year fiscal plan. Price index: private consumption index.
United Kingdom[2]	2.4	1–4 percent and 1–2½ percent by spring 1997	Objective is for underlying inflation (RPIX) to be in lower half of the 1–4 percent range by end of current Parliament (spring 1997 at the latest). Price index: retail price index excluding mortgage interest payments (RPIX).
Canada[2]	0.2	1–3 percent through 1998	Price index: CPI. The measure of underlying inflation used by the Bank of Canada for operational purposes is the CPI excluding food, energy, and the effect of indirect tax changes. On this measure, the inflation rate in 1994 was 1.7 percent.
Australia	2.4	2–3 percent medium term	Reserve Bank's publicly stated goal for underlying inflation to be achieved on average over the cycle. Price index: CPI, excluding the impact of interest rates on mortgage and other interest payments, indirect tax changes, and certain other volatile price items.
Austria	3.0	—	No quantified target.[3]
Belgium	2.4	—	No quantified target.[3]
Denmark	2.0	—	No quantified target.[3]
Finland[2]	1.1	about 2 percent in 1995 and beyond	Price index: CPI excluding indirect taxes, government subsidies, house prices, and mortgage interest payments.
Greece	10.9	4 percent by 1997	Objective in revised convergence program. Price index: GDP deflator.
Iceland	1.5	—	No quantified target.
Ireland	2.5	—	Objective is price stability, viewed as the achievement of low inflation comparable with rate prevailing in the group of low inflation countries in recent years, which has averaged about 3 percent.
Netherlands	2.8	—	No quantified target.[3]
New Zealand[2]	1.8	0–2 percent for 1995 through 1998	Price index: CPI adjusted for, among other things, significant price effects resulting from changes in the terms of trade, interest rates, and indirect taxes.
Norway	1.4	—	No quantified target.
Portugal	5.2	3–4¼ percent in 1995–97	Inflation objective in convergence program. Price index: CPI.
Spain	4.7	less than 3 percent by 1997	Bank of Spain's stated target. Price index: CPI.
Sweden[2]	2.2	1–3 percent by 1995	Price index: CPI.
Switzerland	0.8	less than 1 percent medium term	Implicit objective derived from money growth target and output and velocity assumptions.

[1]Consumer prices; for the United Kingdom, retail price index excluding mortgages.
[2]Countries with formal inflation targets.
[3]Under the Maastricht Treaty convergence criteria, the inflation rate should not exceed that of the three best performing members of the European Union by more than 1½ percentage points.

Chart 9. Selected Industrial Countries: Inflation and Real Short-Term Interest Rates in the Recovery
(Horizontal scale indicates number of quarters from cyclical trough for GDP)

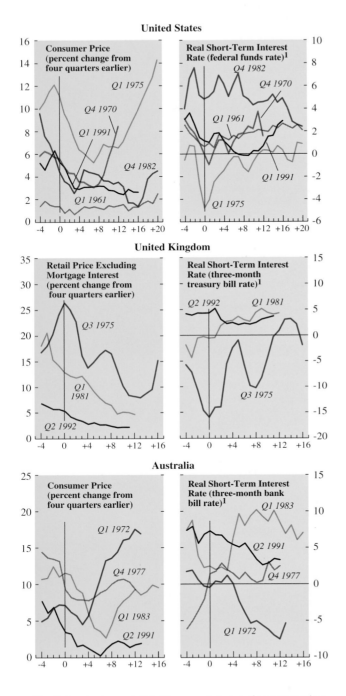

[1]Real interest rates are deflated by percent change of consumer prices from four quarters earlier.

In the United States and the United Kingdom, both nominal and real short-term interest rates were lower in the early stages of this recovery, relative to their values at the troughs of the cycles, than at similar stages in previous recoveries (Chart 9). Furthermore, yield curves have been fairly steep, indicating continued monetary support for the economic expansions. These developments reflect the fact that at the cyclical troughs the levels of real interest rates were relatively high, while in the early stage of the current recovery output growth was comparatively weaker and the pressure on resources has been less intense. The major difference, however, has been that the monetary authorities raised short-term interest rates at the first signs of incipient price pressures in the current recovery even though *actual inflation* was still declining and was generally at the lowest sustained levels in decades. In Australia, the situation has been similar. While monetary conditions have been tightened, underlying inflation has remained at around 2 percent. In New Zealand, actual inflation has remained subdued so far, but the monetary authorities have allowed short-term interest rates to rise sharply in anticipation of inflation pressures stemming from rapid economic growth. Overall, the prompt monetary policy actions, together with the nonsynchronized business cycles in the United States and the United Kingdom as compared with continental Europe and Japan, suggest that the cyclical upturn in inflation in industrial countries may prove to be more short-lived in the present upswing than in the past. Interest rates may not have to rise as much in the future, and yield curves may not become as sharply inverted as in previous cycles. This would help to ensure longer-lasting economic expansions with inflation peaking at relatively low levels.

Urgency of Fiscal Consolidation

Almost all of the industrial countries have entered the second half of the 1990s with large fiscal imbalances. In part, these reflect the effects of the cyclical downturn on actual balances, which will be reversed as the expansion proceeds. But they also reflect the persistence of large structural budget deficits in a large number of countries (Chart 10). The structural deficit averaged 2½ percent of GDP in 1994 for the seven major industrial countries, and it was somewhat higher in the group of smaller industrial countries (Table 4).[4] Reflecting the large fiscal imbalances, government debt has continued to rise sharply, with general government gross debt now averaging 70 percent of GDP. The high levels of government debt are a key contributing factor behind the high level of real inter-

---

[4]Estimates of structural budget deficits in the smaller industrial countries are presented in Annex III.

est rates. They have also reduced the ability of fiscal policy to respond to cyclical downturns. The notable exception is Japan, where the successful fiscal consolidation strategy of the 1980s allowed the adoption of stimulative fiscal measures during the past couple of years.

Governments have generally recognized the need for fiscal consolidation, and a number have announced medium-term deficit-reduction objectives (Table 5). However, while a few countries are making considerable progress, most others will need to put in place additional measures in order to ensure a significant decline in budget deficits and debt ratios. The need to strengthen the pace of fiscal consolidation is all the more pressing for several reasons. First, the envisaged progress toward fiscal consolidation is generally based on medium-term scenarios that assume robust growth and declining long-term interest rates. If growth turns out to be weaker than expected, or interest rates higher, progress in reducing deficits and debt ratios could easily be reversed. Second, levels of public debt in 1994 are already very high in absolute terms and relative to the last cyclical peak. The high debt ratios put into question the sustainability and credibility of fiscal policies, contributing to large risk premiums on interest rates in some countries. Third, aging populations and the existence of large unfunded liabilities in public pension systems risk exacerbating public finances in the future in the absence of reforms aimed at controlling the level and growth of public expenditures. Finally, the present cyclical situation presents the best possible circumstances to make significant inroads into the large deficits. Postponing the necessary actions until the next economic slowdown would exacerbate any short-term loss of output and employment associated with a withdrawal of fiscal stimulus. In some countries, fiscal retrenchment may actually help to strengthen economic performance even in the short run (Box 2).

The *United States* has made substantial progress in the past two years toward the medium-term objective of fiscal consolidation. The August 1993 budget legislation, the robust economic expansion, and net sales of assets of failed thrift institutions have helped reduce the deficit of the federal government on a unified basis. However, the administration's February budget proposal implies little further progress toward deficit reduction in the foreseeable future. The staff's projections suggest that the federal deficit and the debt-to-GDP ratio will begin to rise again after FY 1995. Even assuming that effective measures to curtail health care costs and other entitlements are adopted, it would be difficult to achieve the necessary further improvement in the fiscal balance in the medium term. Fiscal policy should focus on measures to contain the growth of spending, and also on measures to raise federal revenues as expenditure restraint alone is unlikely to bring about the needed consolidation. The relatively

Chart 10. Major Industrial Countries: General Government Budget Balances[1]
(In percent of GDP)

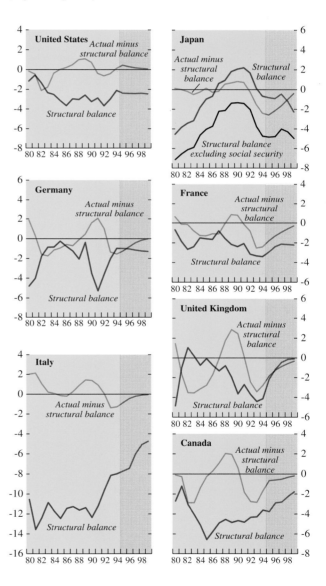

[1]Blue shaded areas indicate IMF staff projections.

Box 2. Can Fiscal Contraction Be Expansionary in the Short Run?

Policymakers are often reluctant to implement significant reductions in government deficits because of a perception that withdrawing fiscal stimulus might lower aggregate demand and jeopardize growth. This view is rooted in the standard fiscal multiplier analysis that has influenced economic policy thinking in many countries during the postwar period. According to this analysis, increases in government expenditures are transmitted through a positive fiscal multiplier into increases in aggregate demand, at least for a year or two after the fiscal expansion. Beyond the initial positive impact, many models, including the staff's multicountry econometric model MULTIMOD, which incorporates forward-looking expectations, show a declining multiplier that eventually turns negative because of crowding out effects on investment and on the capital stock. The standard analysis also suggests that the effects of a fiscal contraction would be broadly symmetric to those of a fiscal expansion.

This traditional view concerning the effects of reductions in budget deficits may not apply to countries with very large budgetary imbalances, especially if financial markets are internationally integrated. In such economies, the multiplier may be negative even in the short run—that is, a fiscal contraction may *increase* economic activity in both the short and the longer run. The possibility of a negative short-run multiplier rests on the central role played by expectations about future policy actions and interest rates. The basic argument is as follows. Suppose that the government in a country with a very large and rapidly growing budget deficit and a high level of government debt makes a firm commitment to significantly reduce its budget deficit. Provided that financial market participants regard the policy measures as fully credible, the pressure on long-term interest rates is likely to abate very quickly. The reason is that a credible policy announcement will be viewed as reducing the danger of rising inflation and of future financial instability. As a result, the risk premium in long-term interest rates will tend to decline, perhaps significantly.

In such a scenario, the reduction in long-term interest rates would have expansionary effects on both demand and supply. It would lower the cost of capital and increase investment and the capital stock. The debt-servicing burden of households, firms, and the public sector would ease, particularly in economies with large public and private debt overhangs, and the adjustment of balance sheets would be facilitated. Diminished uncertainty about the sustainability of the budgetary situation should also help to boost confidence of investors and consumers. To the extent that the reduction in public debt-servicing payments would lower budgetary pressures and expected future tax rates, consumption and investment would be further stimulated. These expansionary effects might well outweigh the traditional negative short-term impulse from fiscal consolidation.[1]

There is evidence of a negative fiscal multiplier from the experience of the 1983–86 Danish stabilization program and the 1987–89 Irish stabilization.[2] In both cases, the fiscal imbalances before the intensification of consolidation efforts were clearly unsustainable, and risk premiums on interest rates were extremely high. Following

---

[1]For a theoretical derivation of the negative multiplier, see Giuseppe Bertola and Allan Drazen, "Trigger Points and Budget Cuts: Explaining the Effects of Fiscal Austerity," *American Economic Review*, Vol. 83 (March 1993), pp. 11–26. For a survey, see Frank Barry and Michael Devereux, "The Macroeconomics of Government Budget Cuts: Can Fiscal Contractions Be Expansionary?" in *Deficit Reduction: What Pain, What Gain?* ed. by William Robson and William Scarth (Toronto: C.D. Howe Institute, 1994).

[2]Ireland had undertaken an earlier, less successful, fiscal adjustment program in 1982–84 that had relied mainly on higher discretionary taxes, rather than on lower government expenditures, and did not go far enough in reducing budgetary imbalances to reverse the rising trend in the debt-to-GDP ratio. The coexistence of robust growth during periods of fiscal contraction in a number of developing and transition countries also suggests the possibility of a negative fiscal multiplier.

---

low saving rate in the United States underscores the need for strengthened efforts at fiscal consolidation so that the burden of adjustment of the external imbalance does not fall on investment.

Germany and the *United Kingdom* have begun to reduce large underlying deficits through expenditure restraint and higher taxes, and are in a good position to achieve their medium-term fiscal consolidation objectives if the announced medium-term plans are fully carried out. In Germany, the general government budget deficit is projected to decline as a proportion of GDP for the second successive year in 1995 and should be within the target of less than 2 percent in 1996. In the United Kingdom, current policies, if fully implemented, would stabilize the debt-to-GDP ratio in 1995/96 and eliminate the structural deficit by the end

of the decade, mainly through expenditure restraint. However, lower-than-anticipated inflation in 1994 resulted in less real spending restraint than initially envisaged, and much of the planned spending restraint lies in the future.

A number of other countries, including Australia, France, Denmark, the Netherlands, Norway, Spain, and Switzerland, have also announced fiscal objectives that should result in some improvement over the medium term. Some progress has been made in containing the growth of public expenditures, but further measures will be necessary in most cases. In *France*, the fiscal situation is improving mainly as a result of the recovery, and it will be important to put in place specific measures also to achieve a reduction of the underlying fiscal deficit in 1996/97. Further reform of

the adoption of front-loaded fiscal consolidation programs, which relied on expenditure reductions, both countries rapidly experienced an improvement in economic performance, with stronger growth and declining unemployment (*see chart*).[3]

The views and responses of investors have come to play a crucial role in countries with large budget deficits and public debts. This is illustrated by the sharp widening of interest differentials among the industrial countries during the past year and by the downward pressure on the exchange rates of some currencies. By requiring higher yields on government debt, financial markets have frequently signaled that the lack of credible fiscal austerity programs is economically costly. At least for some countries, the "macroeconomic model" used by market participants appears to be consistent with the existence of a negative multiplier. Governments need to exploit these market sentiments in a constructive way. Under current circumstances, this would seem to apply particularly to Italy, Greece, and Sweden. For other countries with large fiscal imbalances and high levels of public debt, such as Canada, Belgium, Finland, and Spain, the economic outlook would also be strengthened, even in the relatively near term, by the adoption of stronger deficit reduction measures. In all cases, the credibility of the fiscal adjustment program would be enhanced by front-loaded action to achieve the necessary degree of medium-term fiscal consolidation.

---

[3]The growth in output cannot be ascribed solely to fiscal retrenchment; other factors such as favorable real wage developments, robust external demand, and the effects of exchange rate policy on interest risk premiums, also contributed. The experience of Denmark and Ireland is analyzed in Francesco Giavazzi and Marco Pagano, "Can Severe Fiscal Contractions Be Expansionary? Tales of Two Small European Countries," in *NBER Macroeconomics Annual,* ed. by Olivier Blanchard and Stanley Fischer (Cambridge, Massachusetts: MIT Press, 1990).

Denmark and Ireland: GDP Growth and General Government Structural Balance[1]
(In percent and percent of potential GDP, respectively)

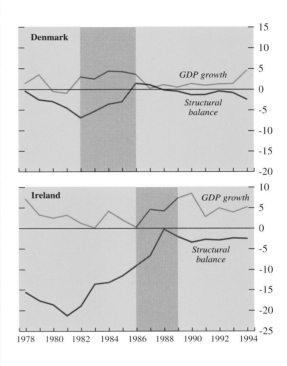

[1]The structural budget balance is the budgetary position that would be observed if output was at its potential level. For Ireland, it is based on the public sector borrowing requirement. Blue shaded areas indicate fiscal consolidation periods.

social security is needed to contain the growth of outlays, even though deficits are expected to decline in the next few years as revenues recover. *Australia* has announced that measures will be introduced in the 1995/96 Commonwealth budget to move the budget into surplus in 1996/97, although the exact measures are as yet unspecified. In *Denmark*, much of the improvement in the fiscal balance aimed at over the medium term hinges on an optimistic assumption of a decline in structural unemployment.

In Canada, Greece, Italy, and Sweden, the high levels of public debt make fiscal adjustment programs very susceptible to derailment by adverse shocks, including higher-than-anticipated interest rates. In Belgium, the very high debt-to-GDP ratio also constitutes an element of vulnerability. In all of these countries, and most urgently in Italy and Sweden, there is a need for more ambitious fiscal adjustment plans and efforts. In *Italy*, despite a robust recovery and some progress in deficit reduction, the large structural fiscal imbalance has resulted in a rapid buildup of public debt. In combination with political uncertainties, this has tended to undermine confidence in the lira and push up the level of interest rates. To correct the situation, the government of Prime Minister Dini introduced a supplementary budget at the end of February. But much stronger measures are required in coming years to substantially reduce the budget deficit and place the debt-to-GDP ratio on a clearly declining trend. In *Canada*, the federal government tabled a budget for the 1995/96 fiscal year at the end of February that is set to achieve its medium-term tar-

Table 4. Industrial Countries: General Government Fiscal Balances and Debt[1]

(In percent of GDP)

	1981–90	1991	1992	1993	1994	1995	1996	2000
Major industrial countries								
Actual balance	-2.9	-2.6	-3.6	-4.1	-3.5	-3.2	-2.9	-2.4
Output gap	-0.1	0.1	-1.1	-2.4	-1.8	-1.3	-1.1	—
Structural balance	-2.8	-2.8	-3.1	-2.9	-2.4	-2.4	-2.3	-2.4
United States								
Actual balance	-2.5	-3.2	-4.3	-3.4	-2.0	-1.9	-2.1	-2.5
Output gap	-0.2	-1.2	-1.4	-0.9	0.5	1.2	0.8	0.1
Structural balance	-2.4	-2.9	-3.7	-3.0	-2.1	-2.4	-2.4	-2.5
Net debt	36.7	49.8	53.8	56.5	56.0	55.7	55.9	56.1
Gross debt	50.5	63.7	66.8	68.8	68.3	67.9	68.1	68.3
Japan								
Actual balance	-1.1	3.0	1.5	-1.4	-3.0	-3.4	-3.0	-3.4
Output gap	0.3	2.0	-0.7	-4.0	-6.0	-6.4	-5.3	-0.1
Structural balance	-1.2	2.2	1.7	0.1	-0.7	-0.8	-0.9	-3.3
Net debt	20.9	5.3	4.4	4.8	7.8	11.0	13.6	21.1
Gross debt	66.7	67.7	71.2	76.6	83.7	89.7	93.0	99.7
Memorandum								
Actual balance excluding social security	-4.0	-0.7	-2.3	-5.2	-6.9	-7.1	-6.7	-5.6
Structural balance excluding social security	-4.1	-1.4	-2.0	-3.8	-4.7	-4.8	-4.8	-5.6
Germany[2]								
Actual balance	-2.1	-3.2	-2.6	-3.3	-2.5	-2.2	-1.8	-1.2
Output gap	-1.4	3.3	1.9	-2.1	-2.1	-1.8	-1.3	—
Structural balance	-1.8	-5.3	-3.6	-2.0	-1.0	-1.0	-1.0	-1.2
Net debt	20.6	21.4	27.7	35.1	38.4	45.4	44.9	42.1
Gross debt	39.8	41.1	43.7	47.7	51.0	58.0	57.5	54.7
France								
Actual balance	-2.0	-2.2	-3.9	-5.8	-5.8	-4.7	-3.7	-2.2
Output gap	-0.1	0.1	-0.9	-3.8	-3.4	-2.5	-1.8	—
Structural balance	-1.7	-2.1	-3.1	-3.3	-3.4	-2.9	-2.4	-2.2
Net debt[3]	22.0	27.2	30.2	34.3	40.3	43.1	44.7	46.9
Gross debt	29.6	35.4	39.4	44.4	48.8	50.7	51.8	53.0

get of limiting the federal deficit to 3 percent of GDP by 1996/97. However, additional efforts are necessary to lower the high debt-to-GDP ratio over the medium term and to lessen the vulnerability of the fiscal position to a cyclical downturn and financial market disturbances. *Sweden*'s fiscal position has also deteriorated rapidly in the past few years. Gross public debt to GDP has doubled from 45 percent of GDP in 1990 to 92 percent of GDP in 1994. The 1995/96 budget presented in January proposed new savings geared to the medium-term objective of stabilizing the debt ratio by 1998. But the budget was not well received in financial markets and stronger efforts are likely to be necessary to restore confidence of financial investors and improve the fiscal and overall economic outlook.

In *Japan*, a succession of fiscal packages has provided desirable support to economic activity. Supplementary spending for reconstruction following the earthquake will provide further support to activity this year. However, the flexible use of fiscal policy has led to a marked deterioration in the fiscal position. Starting in 1996, there will be a need to resume fiscal consolidation. The government has passed a tax reform package and approved a pension reform bill that should go some way toward deficit reduction, but further significant measures appear necessary to achieve long-run fiscal sustainability.

Structural Policies to Strengthen Employment and Productivity

The importance of broad-based structural reforms for improving economic performance is clearly illustrated by the impressive recent and prospective performance of New Zealand, the country that has made most progress in implementing such reforms (Box 3). In Europe and Canada, the most pressing structural

Table 4 *(concluded)*

	1981–90	1991	1992	1993	1994	1995	1996	2000
Italy[4]								
Actual balance	−10.9	−10.2	−9.5	−9.5	−9.2	−8.5	−7.9	−4.5
Output gap	2.1	1.7	—	−2.9	−2.5	−1.6	−0.8	−0.1
Structural balance	−11.8	−11.2	−9.6	−8.1	−8.0	−7.7	−7.4	−4.4
Net debt	81.7	96.2	103.0	111.2	112.9	112.2	110.7	107.8
Gross debt	80.7	105.8	113.3	122.4	124.2	123.5	121.8	118.6
United Kingdom								
Actual balance	−2.0	−2.6	−6.1	−7.8	−6.9	−4.0	−2.4	−0.3
Output gap	−0.6	−2.3	−4.4	−4.4	−3.0	−2.0	−1.4	—
Structural balance	−1.3	−2.7	−3.7	−4.4	−4.1	−2.2	−1.2	−0.2
Net debt	40.3	26.7	28.1	32.5	37.7	41.7	41.9	36.7
Gross debt	48.0	33.6	34.9	40.4	46.0	48.2	48.4	43.2
Canada								
Actual balance	−4.5	−6.6	−7.1	−7.1	−5.3	−4.4	−3.5	−1.4
Output gap	−0.2	−2.9	−4.0	−4.2	−2.5	−1.0	−1.0	−0.3
Structural balance	−4.3	−4.8	−4.3	−4.3	−3.6	−3.8	−2.9	−1.2
Net debt	30.1	49.8	57.1	62.0	64.2	65.0	65.6	63.4
Gross debt	60.9	80.1	87.5	92.2	95.2	95.4	95.6	91.0
Other industrial countries[5]								
Actual balance	−2.1	−3.7	−4.8	−6.1	−5.2	−4.6	−3.9	−3.0
Output gap	−0.1	−0.3	−1.6	−3.5	−2.9	−1.9	−1.3	0.1
Structural balance	−2.5	−3.7	−3.6	−3.3	−2.8	−2.9	−2.6	−2.8

[1]The output gap is actual less potential output, as a percent of potential output. Structural balances are expressed as a percent of potential output. The structural budget balance is the budgetary position that would be observed if the level of actual output coincided with potential output. Changes in the structural budget balance consequently include effects of temporary fiscal measures, the impact of fluctuations in interest rates and debt-service costs, and other noncyclical fluctuations in the budget balance. The computations of structural budget balances are based on IMF staff estimates of potential GDP and revenue and expenditure elasticities (see the October 1993 *World Economic Outlook*, Annex I). Net debt is defined as gross debt less financial assets, which include assets held by the social security insurance system. Estimates of the output gap and of the structural budget balance are subject to significant margins of uncertainty.

[2]Data before 1990 refer to west Germany. For net debt, the first column refers to 1986–90. Beginning in 1995 the debt and debt-service obligations of the Treuhandanstalt (and of various other agencies) are to be taken over by the general government. This debt is equivalent to 8 percent of GDP, and the associated debt service to ½ of 1 percent of GDP.

[3]Figure for 1981–90 is average of 1983–90.

[4]Net debt includes tax refund liabilities. Net debt figure for 1981–90 is for 1984–90.

[5]Includes Australia, Austria, Belgium, Denmark, Finland, Ireland, the Netherlands, New Zealand, Norway, Spain, and Sweden. See Annex III.

problem is the high level of unemployment. In Australia and New Zealand, unemployment also remains at the top of the political agenda, although the recovery has already made substantial inroads into cyclical unemployment, especially in New Zealand. Double-digit unemployment rates are now the norm in Europe. The recent recessions have played a part, but the bulk of unemployment appears to be structural, implying enormous economic and social costs that will persist beyond the cyclical recovery.

Most economists and policymakers have more or less the same diagnosis of the structural unemployment problem, although specific causes vary from country to country.[5] Many would agree, for example, that unemployment benefit systems as currently structured discourage people from seeking work and con-

tribute to high levels of long-duration unemployment; that high payroll taxes and social insurance contributions discourage employers from seeking employees, particularly low-wage employees; that school systems generally do not adequately prepare students for the requirements of the labor market and that public sector training programs are inadequate and often ineffective; that insufficiently competitive product and housing markets restrain the demand for workers and reduce mobility; and that union power, collective bargaining systems, minimum wages, job security legislation, and barriers to labor mobility insulate incumbent employees from the forces of demand and supply, make wages less responsive to market forces, prevent wage differentials from reflecting productivity differentials, and encourage the substitution of capital for labor (Box 4).

Reflecting the broad consensus about the structural nature of the unemployment problem, most governments have made attempts at labor market reform dur-

---

[5]*OECD Jobs Study: Evidence and Explanations* (Paris, 1994) contains a comprehensive survey of these issues.

Table 5. Industrial Countries: Medium-Term Fiscal Objectives

	General Government Budget Balance, 1994	Objectives
	As a percent of GDP	
United States	−2.0	Fiscal policy at the federal level is constrained by the Omnibus Budget Reconciliation Act of 1993, which places nominal limits extending to FY 1998 on discretionary spending, and requires that legislation affecting entitlement programs or tax revenues not increase the deficit over a five-year horizon. Many state governments are subject to balanced budget requirements.
Japan	−3.0	Two principal guidelines: to reduce the central government bond-financing ratio to 5 percent or lower by the year 2000; and the continued implementation of the planned public investment outlays of ¥630 trillion over the period 1995–2004.
Germany	−2.5	To reduce the budget deficit to a sustainable level while allowing, through expenditure restraint, for a reduction in the tax burden. The general government budget deficit is to be limited to 2 percent of GDP by 1996 and be near balance by 1998.
France	−5.8	To reduce the central government deficit to 2½ percent in 1997 and the general government deficit to 2 percent. Central government total expenditures are to remain constant in real terms. The debt-to-GDP ratio is to remain below 50 percent and decrease from 1997 onwards.
Italy	−9.2	To stabilize the debt-to-GDP ratio by 1996, while maintaining the tax burden at the 1994 level and limiting the increase in primary expenditure to the target rate of inflation.
United Kingdom	−6.9	The medium-term objective is to bring the public sector borrowing requirement back to balance. Tax increases have contributed to the early phase of the adjustment; over the medium term an important role is to be played by expenditure restraint: total public real expenditure is to grow at a slower rate than potential output.
Canada	−5.3	To reduce the federal budget deficit to 3 percent of GDP in 1996/97.
Australia	−2.7	To move the Commonwealth government budget into surplus in 1996/97.
Austria	−4.0	To reduce the federal budget deficit to less than 3 percent of GDP by 1998.
Belgium	−5.4	To achieve a 3 percent general government budget deficit in 1996, and a sufficiently large primary surplus to substantially lower the debt ratio over the medium term.
Denmark	−4.3	To achieve fiscal balance by 1998. The objective is to run a budgetary surplus on average over the business cycle with a view to reducing (as a share of GDP), and eventually eliminating, the net public debt.
Finland	−5.5	To keep central government expenditures constraint in real terms from 1995 onward.
Greece	−12.9	To reduce the general government budget deficit to 4.2 percent of GDP in 1997 and to 2.4 percent in 1998. The debt-to-GDP ratio is to be stabilized by 1996 and reduced thereafter.
Iceland	−4.0	To achieve a balanced budget by 1998.
Ireland	−2.5	To rapidly lower the debt-to-GDP ratio.
Netherlands	−3.5	To reduce general government expenditure by 0.7 percent per year on average in real terms during 1995–98, while keeping the central government deficit under annual ceilings that fall to 2.9 percent of GDP in 1998.
New Zealand	0.3	To reduce public debt to prudent levels by achieving operating surpluses, maintain debt at these levels by balancing the budget over the cycle, and achieve levels of public sector net worth that provide a buffer against adverse shocks (Fiscal Responsibility Act 1994). The net public debt is to be reduced to below 30 percent of GDP by 1997.
Norway	−3.1	To restrict growth in government real expenditure to 1 percent a year, below the trend growth of mainland GDP of about 2¼ percent, while keeping the burden of taxation unchanged.
Portugal	−6.5	To eliminate the primary deficit on average in 1995–96, and reduce the overall deficit to 2¼ percent of GDP on average in 1995–99.
Spain	−6.7	To reduce the overall fiscal deficit to 4.4 percent of GDP in 1996 and to 3 percent of GDP by 1997, mainly through expenditure control.
Sweden	−11.4	To stabilize the ratio of gross public debt to GDP at about 100 percent by 1998.
Switzerland	−4.5	To reduce the federal government deficit by Sw F 4 billion, to ½ of 1 percent of GDP, by 1998, through tax increases and expenditure reductions in equal measure.

Table 6. European Union: Convergence Indicators for 1995 and 1996
(In percent)

	1994 GDP Weights[1]		Consumer Price Inflation		General Government Balance/GDP		Gross Government Debt/GDP[2]		Long-Term Interest Rates[3]
	In EU	In world	1995	1996	1995	1996	1995	1996	March 1995
Germany	23.8	5.0	2.0	2.0	−2.2	−1.8	58.0	57.5	7.4
France	17.0	3.6	2.0	2.0	−4.7	−3.7	50.7	51.8	8.1
Italy	16.0	3.4	5.2	4.2	−8.5	−7.9	123.5	121.8	13.1
United Kingdom[4]	15.7	3.4	2.9	2.8	−4.0	−2.4	48.2	48.4	8.7
Largest four countries[5]	72.6	15.3	2.9	2.6	−4.6	−3.7	68.6	68.4	9.1
Spain	8.1	1.7	4.1	3.5	−5.9	−5.8	64.8	67.0	11.6
Netherlands	4.2	0.9	2.5	2.3	−3.2	−3.0	79.7	79.0	7.6
Belgium	3.1	0.6	2.3	2.3	−4.4	−4.2	134.5	131.8	8.3
Sweden	2.3	0.5	3.2	3.4	−10.1	−6.8	99.1	102.7	10.8
Austria	2.4	0.5	2.5	2.7	−4.5	−3.7	64.4	64.6	7.7
Denmark[6]	1.6	0.3	2.5	2.5	−2.5	−1.6	78.9	76.8	8.9
Finland	1.2	0.3	2.3	2.8	−5.5	−4.1	65.9	68.5	10.2
Greece[7]	1.4	0.3	8.6	7.3	−11.5	−10.0	123.8	126.2	19.5
Portugal	1.8	0.4	4.5	4.0	−6.0	−5.5	70.6	70.0	11.5
Ireland	0.8	0.2	2.5	2.5	−2.5	−2.5	83.7	79.1	8.8
Luxembourg	0.2	—	2.2	2.3	1.0	1.0	9.8	9.9	8.3
Smallest eleven countries[5]	27.3	5.7	3.5	3.2	−5.5	−4.8	82.3	82.6	10.3
All EU[5]	100.0	21.0	3.1	2.8	−4.8	−4.0	72.3	72.3	9.4
Maastricht convergence criteria reference range/value	. . .	. . .	**3.5–3.7**	**3.5–3.8**	**−3.0**	**−3.0**	**60.0**	**60.0**	**9.4–10.1**

Sources: National sources; and IMF staff projections.

Note: The table shows the convergence indicators mentioned in the Maastricht Treaty. The relevant convergence criteria are (1) consumer price inflation must not exceed that of the three best performing countries by more than 1½ percentage points; (2) interest rates on long-term government securities must not be more than 2 percentage points higher than those in the same three member states; (3) the currency must have been held within the normal fluctuation margins of the ERM for two years without a realignment at the initiative of the member state in question; and (4) the financial position must be sustainable, which is defined as a general government deficit no greater than 3 percent of GDP and a public debt-to-GDP ratio of not more than 60 percent. For countries that do not satisfy the fiscal criteria, the Treaty requires a substantial and continuous decline of fiscal deficits toward the reference value, and the debt-to-GDP ratio must be approaching the benchmark at a "satisfactory pace." See "The Maastricht Agreement on Economic and Monetary Union," Annex II in the May 1992 *World Economic Outlook*, pp. 52–55. The fiscal projections are based on current policies and do not take into account further consolidation measures that are planned in accordance with countries' convergence programs.

[1]The GDP shares are based on the purchasing power parity (PPP) valuation of country GDPs.

[2]Debt data refer to end of year. They relate to general government but may not be consistent with the definition agreed at Maastricht.

[3]Ten-year government bond yield or nearest maturity.

[4]Retail price index excluding mortgage interest.

[5]Average weighted by 1994 GDP shares.

[6]The debt-to-GDP ratio would be below 60 percent if certain items acknowledged by ECOFIN as warranting separate consideration are deducted.

[7]General government balance includes capitalized interest; long-term interest rate is 12-month treasury bill rate.

ing the 1980s and early 1990s.[6] These reforms do not appear to have had much of an impact on unemployment, however, except perhaps in the United Kingdom and New Zealand, where changes in the system of industrial relations appear to have led to more flexible wages and employment. There are three factors suggesting that broad-based, fundamental labor and product market reforms, as opposed to the relatively modest reforms adopted in the past, will be needed if European unemployment is to be reduced on a durable basis.

- First, there is no single, well-defined cause of the dramatic rise of European unemployment from the early 1970s to the early 1980s, or of the current high level. If reform is to succeed, it will have to address the myriad of institutions and policies that contribute to high unemployment.

[6]See Box 5 in the May 1994 *World Economic Outlook*, and Dennis J. Snower, "Evaluating Unemployment Policies: What Do the Underlying Theories Tell Us?" IMF Working Paper 95/7 (January 1995).

Box 3. New Zealand's Structural Reforms and Economic Revival

New Zealand has been enjoying rapid economic growth accompanied by low inflation and strong employment growth since 1993. This success has followed a decade of far-reaching structural reforms. The reforms followed mounting frustration over poor economic performance in the wake of a long-term decline in the country's terms of trade and inadequate policy responses. The reforms radically reversed past policies, simultaneously improving microeconomic efficiency and restoring macroeconomic balance.[1] The general approach was a rapid launch of reforms across a wide front, with sequencing decided both by economic imperatives and political feasibility.

Immediately upon taking office in 1984, an exchange market crisis forced the Labor Government to turn its attention to *financial reforms*, accelerating the reform program generally. The New Zealand dollar was devalued by 20 percent in July 1984 before it was set on a free float in March 1985. At the same time, the capital account was completely liberalized and the foreign exchange market deregulated. Monetary control was simplified by replacing reserve requirements, interest rate controls, and credit guidelines with a market-based system for limiting banking system liquidity. Competition in banking was promoted by equalizing the legal status of financial institutions, lifting ownership limitations, and allowing free entry for foreign banks. Bank supervision was introduced in 1985 and recently underwent an innovative reform aimed at allowing market discipline to play a greater role. Financial liberalization together with tight monetary but relaxed fiscal policies contributed to a 25 percent real appreciation of the currency between 1984 and 1988.

By 1987, price stability became the overriding objective of monetary policy, after more than a decade of double-digit inflation. This was formalized with the passage of the *Reserve Bank Act 1989*, which stipulated that price stability was the Reserve Bank of New Zealand's sole monetary policy objective. The act granted the Bank complete independence in the use of its instruments, enhanced monetary policy transparency, and placed accountability with its Governor. In recognition of the government's ultimate responsibility for monetary policy, the act provided for a Policy Targets Agreement between the Minister of Finance and the Governor of the Reserve Bank to define price stability. The current agreement, signed in December 1992 and valid through 1998, obliges the Bank to maintain 12-month increases in the CPI within zero and 2 percent, inflation having been brought down to that range already by the end of 1991. The policy target agreement allows inflation to depart temporarily from its target zone to accommodate relative price movements resulting from specific shocks defined in the agreement. The Bank is obliged to submit to Parliament a Monetary Policy Statement twice a year that contains, inter alia, the two-year inflation forecast, which plays a central role in guiding monetary policy.

Public sector reforms came in two waves, the first directed at eliminating the role of Government in the provision of commercial goods and services, and the second at raising the efficiency of the "core government." Government commercial activities, which were equivalent to about 12 percent of GDP in 1984, were first organized in state-owned enterprises. These enterprises and other government-owned industries (mostly in the utility, transport, and finance sectors) were then corporatized by restructuring them into limited liability companies to be run on a commercial basis. Usually, the privileges these enterprises had enjoyed in legislation (monopoly powers) or practice (subsidies) were removed. Finally, many of these enterprises were privatized with the proceeds from the asset sales largely used to repay public sector debt.

To improve the efficiency of *core government* functions, a financial management reform was launched in 1988 that introduced "performance contracting" deep into the civil service. Department heads became responsible for the delivery of well-defined "outputs," such as vehicle inspections, with ministers retaining responsibility for "outcomes," such as traffic safety. To accomplish this, department heads were given large discretion in the management of budgets and labor inputs. The accounting system was shifted from a cash to an accruals basis in line with generally accepted accounting practice to provide the information needed under the new management system.

The core government reforms culminated in 1994 in the *Fiscal Responsibility Act*. Without setting specific fiscal targets, the act codified disclosure and accounting practices that had gradually been introduced, aiming for maximum transparency about fiscal strategies, outcomes, and forecasts. It prescribed "principles" for responsible fiscal management, such as the requirement to reduce debt to "prudent levels" and, once achieved, to keep it there by balancing operating expenditures and expenses "over a reasonable period of time." Temporary depar-

---

[1]For a summary of the reforms, including their "new microeconomic" theoretical foundations, see Alan Bollard, *New Zealand: Economic Reforms, 1984–1991*, Country Studies No. 10 (San Francisco, California: International Center for Economic Growth, 1992).

- Second, rigidities can be mutually reinforcing. Re-forms that allow real wages to better reflect differences in productivity across regions, for example, would be more effective if accompanied by reforms to housing markets to improve geographic mobility and reforms to enhance the portability of pensions.
- Third, high levels of unemployment have become such a standard feature of the economic landscape in many countries that only a regime change is

tures from these principles were permitted, provided that the government explain why and how it plans to return to the principles. For maximum transparency, the Fiscal Responsibility Act imposed generally accepted accounting practices for all budget statements and introduced a series of new disclosure requirements.

The tax system in New Zealand prior to 1985 was highly distortionary and inequitable. It relied heavily on taxation of labor (60 percent of revenues), with high marginal rates and many tax incentives and expenditures. A comprehensive package of *tax reforms*, announced in 1984, set out to broaden the tax base, lower marginal rates, generate more revenue, and shift the tax mix from income to consumption. Reform of the personal income tax between 1984 and 1990 reduced the number of tax brackets from five, with rates ranging from 20 to 66 percent, to two of 24 and 33 percent, with the top rate aligned with the company tax rate. In 1986, a 10 percent flat-rate value-added tax on all goods and services replaced the wholesale tax and a range of other indirect taxes; the rate was raised to 12½ percent in 1989.

Tax reforms were followed in 1991 by complementary reforms of the *welfare system* to cut costs and improve financial incentives to beneficiaries. By 1994, expenditures on social welfare had been reduced by 2 percent of GDP by paring down most welfare programs, including unemployment benefits, and lowering superannuation payments. Moreover, the eligibility age for superannuation was raised from 60 to 65 phased in over ten years starting in 1992.

Trade liberalization had perhaps the largest immediate impact of all the reforms. New Zealand had developed a system of import licenses and tariffs that implied an average effective rate of protection for the manufacturing sector estimated at 60 to 70 percent. While intended to shelter domestic production, the high level of protection seriously distorted resource allocation, impeded productivity, and hampered external competitiveness. Although trade liberalization had started already in the 1970s and a free trade agreement with Australia was concluded in 1983, the pace of liberalization quickened after 1984 as trade policy sought to derive the maximum benefit for the domestic economy from world competition. By 1988, all import licenses had been abolished and, by 1992, a unilateral program had reduced tariffs to a nominal average rate of 10 percent (compared with 27 percent in the mid-1980s). All export incentives were abolished, including subsidies to agriculture, which had reached the equivalent of 33 percent of output in 1985. Present policies call for a further one-third reduction in tariffs by 1996, at which time protection in New Zealand would be

at a level comparable with the average among industrial countries, leaving only a few sectors, such as textiles, footwear, and motor vehicles, with high effective protection. Further tariff reductions have already been announced for after 1996. The initial effect on manufacturing of the removal of trade protection, along with the real appreciation of the currency, was a sharp decline in manufacturing output and employment. However, international competitiveness has since improved, and manufacturing output and exports have been strong since 1992.

Industrial relations were reformed radically in 1991 with the Employment Contracts Act.[2] The old system was rigid and complex, dominated by "occupational awards" that comprehensively set working conditions for specific occupations across whole industries. Although compulsory arbitration was abolished in 1985, government intervention in the wage bargaining process was still pervasive. The act introduced the legal framework for a highly decentralized, enterprise-level bargaining system. It abolished all awards by turning them into individual employment contracts. This had a profound impact on both unions and employers: the former saw their role reduced to that of freely chosen bargaining agents, and the latter were forced to take responsibility for wage negotiations and labor management generally. Early indications are that the Employment Contracts Act has brought more flexibility in working hours and patterns, and in remuneration practices, while the impact on the level of wages has been limited to a reduction in overtime and weekend pay.

There are a number of reasons for the success of New Zealand's reform program: a strong, popular mandate for change, an exchange market crisis that catalyzed the reform process, strong political support and vision, a coherent agenda, a rapid and comprehensive approach that thwarted opposition from vested interests, and a political system and tradition prone to quick decision taking.[3] The positive supply effects of the reforms took quite a number of years to materialize, but as illustrated by the recent excellent economic performance, the reforms together with the attainment of macroeconomic stability have positioned New Zealand well for sustained, high growth over the medium term.

[2]For an analysis of the genesis and implications of the act, see Raymond Harbridge, ed., *Employment Contracts: New Zealand Experiences* (Wellington: Victoria University Press, 1993).

[3]See Alan Bollard's chapter on New Zealand in *The Political Economy of Policy Reform*, ed. by John Williamson (Washington: Institute for International Economics, 1994).

likely to change entrenched practices and reduce unemployment substantially.

Progress in this important area of public policy will require a greater willingness to tackle sensitive issues

and acknowledgment that some social policies and labor market practices that were intended to protect economically vulnerable groups have had the unacceptable side effect of excluding large segments of the population from productive activity. Despite the broad

Box 4. Capital Formation and Employment

The increase in real GDP in the United States and in the European Union since 1970 has been remarkably similar, as has the increase in the capital stock (*see chart*). The growth of employment, on the other hand, has been very different. Employment in the United States was about 60 percent higher in 1994 than in 1970. In the European Union, by contrast, employment was essentially stagnant in the two decades after 1970, and the uptick in 1991 was mainly due to the inclusion of the eastern Länder into unified Germany.

This combination of developments suggests that the relatively poor employment performance of the European Union compared with the United States cannot be blamed on insufficient demand or on "capital shortage."[1] A more plausible explanation is to be found in the types of investment in the two regions. In Europe, investment was capital *deepening* as indicated by the sharp rise in the capital-labor ratio. With more capital for each worker, the increase in output came about primarily through higher labor productivity rather than through higher employment. In this sense, investment appears to have been primarily directed toward substituting increases in capital for increases in employment. In the United States, on the other hand, the growth of the capital-labor ratio was much more modest, indicating that investment was more capital *widening*.[2]

The relatively small rise in the capital-labor ratio in the United States, and the smaller increase in labor productivity, resulted in increases in employment that kept pace with the growth of the labor supply, and hence the equilibrium level of unemployment was largely unchanged from 1970 to 1994.[3] This was not, however, the case in Europe. The much larger increases in the capital-labor ratio and in labor productivity in Europe were reflected in only modest gains in employment that did not keep pace with the growth in labor supply. Abstracting from cyclical effects, the equilibrium unemployment rate appears to have increased by a staggering 7 or 8 percentage

[1]See Charles Bean, "Capital Shortage and Persistent Unemployment," *Economic Policy*, Vol. 8 (April 1989), pp. 11–53.

[2]Capital widening refers to an increase in the capital stock with an unchanged capital-labor ratio.

[3]The equilibrium level of unemployment was also relatively stable in Japan, although the 1970–94 increase in output, capital, and capital-labor ratios were far higher than in the United States or Europe.

The European Union and the United States: Output, Capital, Employment, and Wages
(1970 = 100, unless noted otherwise)

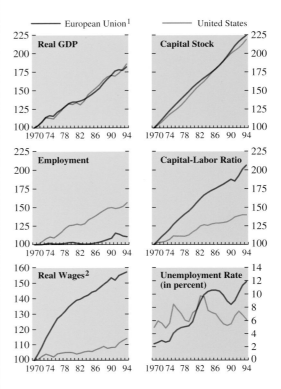

Sources: OECD, analytical data base; and IMF staff estimates.

[1]Excluding Luxembourg and Portugal. Real GDP, capital stocks, and real wages are calculated using PPP-based weights.

[2]National accounts compensation per employee deflated by the GDP deflator.

consensus about the causes of high and persistent unemployment, however, social concerns continue to delay the adoption of appropriate reforms. To address such concerns, and to the extent that labor market reforms have unfavorable distributional consequences, the reforms should be complemented with appropriately designed, well-targeted transfer programs operating through the tax system in the short run, and with improvements in training and education to increase

labor productivity and real wages in the medium to long run.

In the United States, the level of structural unemployment has been relatively stable. The most pressing structural issues are to increase the productivity of unskilled or displaced workers through better training and education, and to increase the efficiency of the health care sector in order to reduce fiscal pressures and to improve equity in the supply of medical ser-

points in Europe.[4] The contrast is even more striking given the relatively modest increase in the labor force in Europe compared with the United States.

Increases in real wages in Europe and the United States were broadly consistent with developments in capital intensity, productivity, and employment. Compared with the United States, the larger increases in capital-labor ratios and labor productivity in Europe supported a bigger rise in real wages. The higher real wages, of course, benefited a declining share of the European labor force. Indeed, many low-paying jobs have effectively disappeared in Europe, which helps to explain the heavy concentration of unemployment among unskilled, low-productivity workers.[5] Average real wages grew much less in the United States, which encouraged the larger increase in employment. The much smaller rise in average real wages in the United States than in Europe also reflected, of course, the fact that much, but not all, of the increase in U.S. employment was for jobs that paid relatively low wages, many of which were in the service sector. The increase in wage inequality in the United States compared with Europe partly reflects this larger increase in employment at the low end of the wage distribution.

Entrepreneurs' investment decisions are based on many factors, including existing and prospective labor market regulations and institutions. Relatively rigid labor markets in Europe have encouraged capital deepening investments that have effectively substituted more capital for labor. Relatively flexible labor markets in the United States, on the other hand, have encouraged much less substitution of capital for labor, and the equilibrium level of unemployment has remained broadly stable. This suggests an urgent need for European governments to adopt fundamental structural reforms to increase labor market flexibility and reduce the cost of labor—broadly defined to include, for example, the costs of hiring and firing—and thereby encourage investments consistent with higher levels of employment. In addition, both the United States and Europe need to strengthen education and training to boost productivity and real wages at the lower end of the skill and income distributions.

---

[4]See the May 1994 *World Economic Outlook*, pp. 34–41.

[5]See Jacques Drèze and Edmond Malinvaud, "Growth and Employment: The Scope of a European Initiative," *European Economic Review*, Vol. 38 (April 1994), pp. 489–504.

vices. Reforms to contain the costs of health care and alleviate future fiscal pressures associated with population aging are also necessary in most other industrial countries. The principal structural issues in Japan are deregulation of the distribution system, telecommunications, finance, housing, and land. Greater progress in these areas would help to increase economic efficiency and allow consumers to benefit fully from their strong purchasing power in world markets.

Convergence in the European Union

The second stage of Economic and Monetary Union (EMU) came into force on January 1, 1994. According to the Treaty on European Union (The Maastricht Treaty), it must be determined not later than the end of December 1996 whether a majority of member states of the European Union (EU) meet the conditions for participation in the third, and final, stage of EMU.[7] To qualify for the third stage, countries must meet convergence criteria for inflation, government budget deficits and debt, long-term interest rates, and exchange rate stability within the ERM. Although most countries meet or are close to meeting the inflation and long-term interest rate criteria, significant reductions in government budget deficits and debt-to-GDP ratios, or both, are needed in most EU members to meet the fiscal criteria (see Table 6, p. 29). The latter will pose a serious obstacle for a number of countries. Fiscal consolidation has not proceeded at a fast enough pace, and countries risk taking insufficient advantage of the recovery to reduce their fiscal imbalances. In 1996, EU budget deficits are expected to average over 4 percent of GDP on current policies, well above the Maastricht reference value of 3 percent, while the gross debt-to-GDP ratio is projected to exceed the 60 percent criterion in all but four or five countries.

According to the Treaty, the debt criterion may be considered satisfied, however, if the debt ratio is sufficiently diminishing and approaching the reference value at a satisfactory pace. On this basis, the EU Council of Ministers has taken the position that Ireland meets the debt criterion, even though Ireland's debt-to-GDP ratio is still relatively high. On current policies, only Germany, the United Kingdom, Denmark, Ireland, Luxembourg, and the Netherlands are likely to meet the deficit criterion in 1996. However, France would be within striking distance (½ of 1 percent of GDP), while Belgium, Austria, and Finland would need a somewhat larger, though still feasible, effort (on the order of 1 to 1¼ percent of GDP). Portugal and Spain, which are committed to reducing their fiscal deficits substantially during the period ahead, face more significant adjustment needs. Italy, Sweden, and Greece are still a long way from meeting the deficit criterion. Although it would seem possible for a majority to satisfy the deficit conver-

---

[7]If a majority of the member countries fulfill the convergence criteria, the Council, meeting at the level of Heads of State or Government, must also decide by that date whether it is appropriate to enter the third stage and, if so, set the date for the beginning of the third stage. If by the end of 1997 the date for the beginning of the third stage has not been set, the third stage shall start on January 1, 1999 (Treaty on European Union, Article 109j (4)). The Treaty does not require that a majority of member countries meet the convergence criteria in order for the third stage to start in 1999.

gence criterion by 1996, and probably also most other criteria, the slow pace of fiscal consolidation may delay the third stage of EMU until 1999.[8]

The convergence criteria set out in the Maastricht Treaty were conceived as minimum requirements aimed at ensuring a high degree of financial discipline and stability in the monetary union. In light of recent EU surveillance activities, including the first excessive budget deficit procedure in the fall of 1994, it appears that the EU intends to apply the convergence requirements strictly. However, beyond meeting the agreed ceilings on budget deficits, a broader question concerns the appropriate degree of fiscal balance that members of the EU should strive for over the medium term. Simply meeting the 3 percent deficit target by the latter part of this decade would still leave signifi-

cant underlying imbalances, since it might well coincide with a relatively high level of capacity utilization as the current expansion matures. Both the Council and the Commission have stressed that deficits will need to be much lower than the Maastricht reference value, and perhaps close to balance by the end of the century. Nevertheless, existing deficit reduction plans of most member states remain relatively unambitious.

There is also reason for concern about the aggregate stance of fiscal policy across the members of the monetary union. A bias toward easy fiscal policy and tight monetary conditions would hamper growth and complicate external exchange rate policy vis-à-vis other major currency areas. In order to ensure the highest possible degree of macroeconomic balance and an appropriate macroeconomic policy mix, it will be important for the members of the prospective monetary union to pursue more stringent objectives for fiscal deficits than seem to be required by the provisions of the Maastricht Treaty.

---

[8]There is some uncertainty as to how the criterion of exchange rate stability within the ERM will be assessed given the wide fluctuation margins that have been in place since August 1993.

III

Policy Challenges Facing Developing Countries

The substantial progress made by many developing countries in fostering macroeconomic stability and in their pursuit of structural reform is expected to sustain robust growth in the period ahead. The Mexican financial crisis and its repercussions on other economies have clouded the short-term outlook for some countries, but longer-term prospects remain promising. All developing countries, however, will have to respond both to the challenges posed by large and potentially reversible capital flows and to many other policy challenges. For the strongest performers, these challenges include the need to avoid overheating and to strengthen efforts in the areas of deregulation and privatization. For many other countries whose performance has not been so strong, trade liberalization and structural reform need to be speeded up to enhance resource allocation, while fiscal and monetary policies should consolidate progress toward greater macroeconomic stability. Progress in these areas would strengthen domestic saving, investment, and long-term growth. Stronger domestic adjustment and reform efforts in the poorest countries will need to be supported by the international community through timely financial assistance and external debt restructuring on appropriate terms.

Recent Developments and Short-Term Prospects

Growth in the developing countries as a group is projected to slow slightly in 1995–96 under the influence of somewhat tighter policies and a decline in portfolio capital flows from the high levels experienced in recent years (Chart 11). In some cases, this tightening of policies reflects responses to contagion effects in the wake of the Mexican financial crisis. In others, it represents an effort to avoid overheating. Among the different regions, the projections show the most pronounced slowdown in the Western Hemisphere, a moderation in the strong pace of economic expansion in Asia, and some strengthening of growth in Africa and the Middle East as a result of the recent intensification of adjustment and reform efforts. In the event of a very sharp and sudden decline in capital flows, activity in the developing world would slow more significantly because of the resulting need to tighten economic policies and reduce do-

Chart 11. Developing Countries: Real GDP[1]
(Annual percent change)

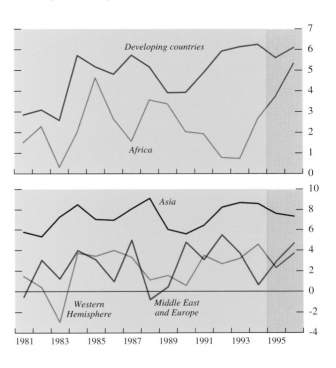

[1]Blue shaded areas indicate IMF staff projections.

mestic demand and imports. Some countries might be able to cushion the adverse impact by drawing on their reserves in the short run, but they would eventually need to adjust.[9]

The cyclical recovery of commodity prices is one factor underlying the improved outlook for countries heavily dependent on commodity exports. Prices of non-oil commodities increased substantially during 1994 as a result of the global recovery, and in February this year, the IMF's world export-weighted index was 10 percent higher than a year earlier. Coffee prices increased sharply in 1994 for the year as a whole owing to adverse weather in Brazil, although they dropped somewhat in December. Prices of copper, nickel, and other metals were up markedly in 1994. Strong demand in the United States has been a major cause of the marked rise in copper prices. The assumption of some rise in oil prices to about $16.90 a barrel in 1995–96, based in part on oil futures market prices in late January, will help to improve the terms of trade of fuel-exporting countries in 1995–96. Oil prices declined from over $17 a barrel in July 1994 to $15.75 in December, reflecting a significant increase in world production and a decline in purchases due to unseasonably warm weather in the Northern Hemisphere (Chart 12). In early 1995, prices picked up somewhat as demand from the United States and Asia increased substantially.

Following the financial crisis in Mexico and the repercussions on a number of countries in the region, average growth in the countries of the *Western Hemisphere* is projected to slow to 2¼ percent in 1995—only half the pace of 1994—and then pick up to 3¾ percent in 1996 (Table 7). Output in Mexico is expected to fall by 2 percent this year, but as financial conditions stabilize, activity is assumed to rise again in 1996. Following a substantial increase in prices in the first quarter of 1995 due to the sharp depreciation of the peso, a tight fiscal stance and a strict incomes policy are expected to contain inflation to just over 30 percent on a year-over-year basis, with a considerably lower rate in 1996. In Brazil, the current stabilization program has reduced monthly inflation from more than 40 percent in June 1994 to an average of less than 1½ percent a month in the first quarter of 1995, despite a sharp expansion of domestic demand. Output growth, which exceeded 5 percent in 1994, is expected to remain robust as monetary and fiscal policies are adjusted to consolidate progress toward greater financial stability. Growth in Argentina is expected to slow significantly in 1995–96, to around 3 percent, partly as a result of a decline in capital inflows. In Peru, following a sharp surge in output in

Chart 12. Commodity Prices
(1980 = 100)

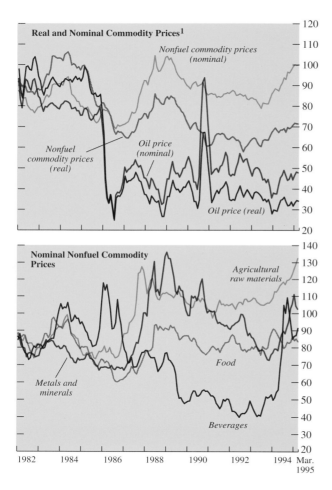

[1]The nonfuel commodity price index is an export-weighted average of 35 prices denominated in U.S. dollars. The oil price is an equally weighted average of the U.S. dollar spot prices of U.K. Brent, Dubai, and Alaska North slope crude oil. The real indices are deflated by the unit value of manufactures in industrial countries.

---

[9]An alternative scenario illustrating the consequences of a sharp reduction in the level of capital flows was discussed in the October 1994 *World Economic Outlook*, pp. 61–64.

Table 7. Selected Developing Countries: Real GDP, Consumer Prices, and Current Account Balance
(Annual percent change, unless otherwise noted)

	Real GDP			Consumer Prices			Current Account[1]		
	1993	1994	1995	1993	1994	1995	1993	1994	1995
Developing countries	**6.1**	**6.3**	**5.6**	**43.0**	**48.0**	**17.5**	**−2.1**	**−1.8**	**−1.5**
Median	**3.2**	**3.5**	**4.5**	**9.0**	**10.1**	**8.0**	**−4.2**	**−3.8**	**−3.3**
Africa	**0.7**	**2.7**	**3.7**	**26.8**	**33.6**	**21.4**	**−2.4**	**−3.4**	**−3.4**
Algeria	−2.2	−0.2	4.3	20.5	29.0	22.6	1.6	−4.3	−6.4
Cameroon	−2.2	−3.8	4.0	−3.7	12.7	27.8	−5.6	−3.3	−2.2
Côte d'Ivoire	−0.8	1.7	6.4	2.1	25.8	8.0	−10.1	−2.4	−2.2
Ghana	5.0	3.8	5.0	25.0	24.8	29.0	−9.2	−4.9	−3.7
Kenya	0.1	3.0	4.9	46.0	28.8	3.2	1.8	1.6	0.8
Morocco	−1.1	11.8	−4.0	5.2	5.0	6.0	−2.1	−2.5	−3.1
Nigeria	1.6	0.6	4.0	57.2	57.5	58.3	−2.9	−3.6	−0.9
South Africa	1.1	2.3	3.0	9.7	9.0	10.8	1.5	−0.5	−1.5
Sudan	7.6	5.5	7.2	111.0	101.0	56.0	−23.3	−23.5	−21.1
Tanzania	5.1	5.0	5.0	23.5	25.1	20.6	−10.0	−8.1	−6.7
Tunisia	2.1	4.4	6.3	4.0	4.7	4.5	−8.1	−7.1	−4.4
Uganda	5.1	7.0	5.5	16.1	7.5	5.0	−2.5	−1.2	−2.0
SAF/ESAF countries[2]	0.8	3.6	5.3	17.5	24.6	8.9	−6.9	−5.5	−4.6
Asia	**8.7**	**8.6**	**7.6**	**9.4**	**13.5**	**9.9**	**−0.7**	**−0.5**	**−0.8**
Bangladesh	4.9	5.0	5.0	1.6	2.9	4.0	1.0	0.6	0.2
China	13.7	12.0	8.9	13.0	21.7	13.0	−2.0	0.4	—
Hong Kong	5.8	5.7	5.7	8.5	8.0	8.5	8.3	6.3	6.3
India	3.8	4.9	5.8	7.9	10.1	9.5	−0.6	−0.7	−1.4
Indonesia	6.5	7.0	7.3	9.7	8.5	9.6	−1.9	−2.1	−2.8
Korea	5.5	8.3	7.4	4.8	6.3	5.5	0.1	−1.3	−1.5
Malaysia	8.3	8.5	8.7	3.6	4.1	5.4	−3.9	−6.4	−6.6
Pakistan	2.5	4.1	5.7	10.5	12.8	10.5	−4.9	−3.6	−3.5
Philippines	2.1	4.5	5.5	7.6	9.1	6.5	−6.0	−4.7	−3.9
Taiwan Province of China	6.1	6.2	6.5	2.9	4.1	3.5	3.1	2.5	2.8
Thailand	8.2	8.5	8.4	3.3	5.0	6.0	−5.4	−5.7	−6.6
Viet Nam	8.1	8.7	8.0	5.2	14.4	7.0	−6.8	−4.1	−4.5
Middle East and Europe	**3.7**	**0.7**	**2.9**	**24.5**	**32.3**	**22.5**	**−3.6**	**−2.1**	**−1.8**
Egypt	1.5	1.3	1.5	12.0	8.1	7.5	3.3	0.2	0.9
Iran, Islamic Republic of	1.8	1.9	5.0	22.9	35.0	20.0	−5.5	7.0	4.0
Israel	3.5	6.8	4.0	10.9	12.3	11.0	−2.1	−6.0	−2.9
Jordan	5.8	5.7	6.1	3.3	3.6	4.5	−12.5	−9.6	−8.7
Kuwait	33.6	7.8	3.0	0.5	0.5	0.5	28.2	18.9	18.6
Saudi Arabia	0.5	0.3	1.4	0.8	0.8	2.4	−11.6	−10.7	−9.5
Turkey	7.5	−5.6	3.0	66.1	106.3	70.6	−3.7	1.9	0.6
Western Hemisphere	**3.2**	**4.6**	**2.3**	**212.3**	**225.8**	**36.1**	**−3.3**	**−3.0**	**−1.9**
Argentina	6.0	7.1	2.5	10.6	4.1	4.3	−2.9	−3.6	−2.0
Brazil[3]	4.3	5.7	4.5	2,103.3	2,407.3	...	−0.2	−0.3	−2.2
Chile	6.3	4.2	5.5	12.7	11.4	8.4	−4.6	−1.4	−0.8
Colombia	5.3	5.3	5.5	22.4	22.6	19.2	−4.2	−4.2	−4.4
Dominican Republic	3.0	5.0	5.0	4.8	4.6	3.5	−3.8	−2.1	−1.4
Ecuador	1.7	3.2	4.2	45.0	25.5	14.8	−3.3	−3.2	−4.7
Guatemala	4.0	5.0	5.0	13.5	10.0	5.0	−3.9	−3.3	−2.9
Mexico	0.6	3.5	−2.0	9.8	7.0	30.6	−6.5	−8.0	−0.9
Peru	6.5	12.9	4.5	48.6	23.7	10.8	−5.6	−5.6	−5.3
Uruguay	1.7	2.1	2.6	54.1	42.1	30.0	−3.0	−2.1	−1.5
Venezuela	−0.4	−3.3	−2.0	38.1	60.8	64.8	−3.7	6.5	3.9

[1]In percent of GDP.

[2]African countries that had arrangements, as of the end of 1994, under the IMF's structural adjustment facility (SAF) or enhanced structural adjustment facility (ESAF).

[3]From December 1993 to June 1994, consumer prices in Brazil rose 763 percent. Following the introduction of the real on July 1, 1994, monthly inflation fell to 5½ percent in July. From June 1994 to December 1994, consumer prices increased by 17 percent. From December 1994 to December 1995, consumer prices are projected to increase by about 30 percent.

1994, growth is also expected to moderate in 1995–96, while inflation is projected to continue its downward trend. Chile, which has been less affected by the crisis in Mexico, is expected to see continued solid growth. In Venezuela, the earlier financial crisis and the exchange and price controls that were imposed in mid-1994 have had negative effects on private sector confidence and investment. A further decline in output is expected in 1995.

Average growth in *Asia* was stronger than expected in 1994, with a number of economies beginning to overheat. With some slowdown in portfolio capital flows to the region, and in view of a tightening of financial policies in response to capacity constraints, growth is projected to slow to 7½ percent in 1995 from about 8¾ percent in 1993–94. In China, output growth moderated slightly in 1994, to 12 percent, while inflation jumped to over 20 percent, partly reflecting adjustments in administered food prices. A strengthening of stabilization efforts is projected to slow growth to a more sustainable pace of 9 percent in 1995 and to reduce inflationary pressures. In Korea, sharp increases in investment demand boosted real GDP by over 8 percent in 1994. Strong investment demand, resulting in large increases in foreign direct investment, also contributed to buoyant growth and emerging inflationary pressures in Malaysia, the Philippines, and Thailand in 1994. Growth in these countries is expected to be sustained at or close to current levels in 1995–96, but some tightening of macroeconomic policies may be necessary to contain inflationary pressures.

In India, the recovery gathered momentum in 1994 as the economy expanded by 5 percent. Efforts to bring down inflation were thwarted by a substantial increase in money growth, induced partly by capital inflows. Continued fiscal consolidation is required to reduce the burden on monetary policy of containing inflationary pressures, to lower public indebtedness, and to bolster national saving. Despite a cotton virus and a drought, real GDP in Pakistan increased by over 4 percent in 1994. Further deregulation in the industrial and services sector, and favorable external conditions should lift growth further in 1995. In Bangladesh, despite lower-than-expected growth in the industrial sector, growth was sustained at 5 percent in 1994, the average of recent years.

The outlook for *Africa* has continued to improve with the recent implementation of structural reforms and stabilization programs in a number of countries.[10] Assuming prudent macroeconomic policies and continuing reforms, output growth in the continent is projected to rise to 3¾ percent in 1995. But the risks of setbacks are considerable, and economic conditions

---

[10]See Annex II for a detailed analysis of adjustment efforts and prospects in sub-Saharan Africa.

remain difficult in many countries. In South Africa, for example, although GDP grew by only 2¼ percent in 1994, the external current account deteriorated dramatically. Growth is projected to average 3 percent in 1995–96, but the problem of high unemployment remains a major policy challenge over the medium term. In Nigeria, the economic and financial situation deteriorated further in 1994, owing to large fiscal imbalances and the maintenance of the exchange rate and interest rates at unrealistic levels. There is a danger of further fiscal slippages if a budgeted increase in oil revenues does not materialize. In Algeria, activity in 1994 was weaker than anticipated, in part due to continuing political instability, but also reflecting strong stabilization efforts and a decline in agricultural production as the drought continued for a second year. However, further trade and foreign exchange market reforms are expected to raise Algeria's growth in 1995–96 to around 5 percent, while tight financial policies should help reduce inflation after a temporary increase stemming from the 1994 devaluation.

Many countries of the CFA franc zone are now beginning to see the benefits from the much-needed currency adjustment in early 1994 and the accompanying reform efforts. One of the most important benefits is that opportunities for investment and exports have increased. With support from multilateral and bilateral donors, and continued efforts to prevent inflation from eroding competitiveness, growth is expected to reach an average of 5 percent in 1995–96, a dramatic change after a decade of stagnation. The overall outlook among the African countries that had arrangements at the end of 1994 under the IMF's structural adjustment facility (SAF) or enhanced structural adjustment facility (ESAF) remains positive. Growth in these countries is expected to average 5½ percent in 1995–96, while inflation is expected to fall to below 10 percent. Kenya, for example, has made great strides in restoring macroeconomic stability, with output growth resuming in 1994 and inflation falling. The current recovery in Kenya is expected to strengthen in 1995–96 as macroeconomic policies strengthen further.

Growth in the *Middle East* and *Europe* declined to only ¾ of 1 percent in 1994, largely as a result of developments in Turkey, but is projected to recover to 3 percent in 1995 and to 4¾ percent in 1996. The severe financial crisis in Turkey during the first half of 1994 contributed to a sharp decline of output. The outcome of the stabilization program adopted in mid-1994 has so far been mixed: external performance has improved but inflation has returned to monthly rates of 5–6 percent, indicating that a further strengthening of stabilization policies is needed. Economic prospects for the oil exporting countries in the region continue to be heavily dependent on oil market developments. Oil prices fell in 1994, but the assumed strengthening in 1995 should help to ease fiscal and external imbalances in some of the larger oil exporting countries.

The favorable impact on the terms of trade will be mitigated, however, by the depreciation of the dollar against other major currencies and by increases in non-oil commodity prices. In the Islamic Republic of Iran, economic activity remained subdued in 1994, in part due to continued financial constraints that have limited imports.

Foreign Exchange and Financial Markets

The Mexican foreign exchange crisis in December 1994 exacerbated exchange market pressures that had been building in a number of Latin American countries during 1994. Cyclical developments, especially the rise in interest rates in the United States and other industrial countries, also played a role in the changing pattern of portfolio investments. In Mexico, the exchange rate vis-à-vis the U.S. dollar, which had already suffered from intermittent bouts of heavy selling earlier in 1994, in part related to political factors, has depreciated particularly sharply since December 1994. By the end of March this year, the new peso had fallen by almost 50 percent in foreign currency terms since the exchange rate was allowed to float in December 1994 (Chart 13). A number of other currencies in the region have also weakened, albeit to a much smaller extent. The Chilean peso was much less affected by events in Mexico, reflecting the country's strong economic fundamentals. In Venezuela, following its own financial crisis and the sharp depreciation of its currency in the first half of 1994, the exchange rate was fixed at 170 Venezuelan bolívares per U.S. dollar on June 27, and a series of foreign exchange restrictions were imposed. These restrictions are expected to be lifted gradually during 1995.

The contagion effects from Mexico have had only limited effects on foreign exchange markets in other developing country regions. On the basis of the official exchange rate, the Chinese renminbi depreciated by about 24 percent in real effective terms for the year as a whole. However, since a large proportion of transactions were already taking place at the swap market rate in 1993, the real exchange rate measured as a weighted average of the official and swap market rate was broadly stable in 1994. The Indian rupee was also relatively stable during 1994, helped by central bank interventions to stem upward pressure associated with substantial foreign equity investments. Following the large depreciation early in 1994 linked to concerns about the rising rate of inflation and uncertainties about fiscal policy, pressures on the Turkish lira have diminished and the external position has improved. In marked contrast to the trend toward exchange market liberalization in Africa, Nigeria abolished the free exchange rate in the foreign exchange bureaus and fixed the rate well below market clearing levels; for 1995, the authorities have announced the introduction of a

Chart 13. Mexico: Financial Indicators
(January 1994 = 100, unless otherwise noted)

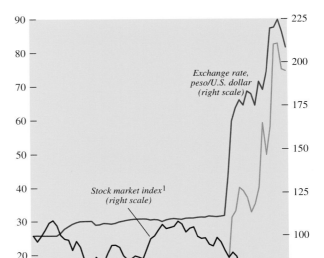

Source: Bloomberg Financial Markets.

[1]The Mexican Bolsa index, consisting of 38 shares weighted by market capitalization.

[2]The yield on Cetes, which are 28-day treasury bills issued by the Mexican government.

dual exchange rate system, in which the official exchange rate will apply to government transactions and an autonomous rate will apply to all other transactions.

Equity markets in the emerging market economies have experienced substantial reversals of the 1990–93 increases in prices. Stock prices, which had already adjusted downward during most of 1994 as interest rates in the industrial countries continued to increase, fell sharply after the Mexican devaluation (Chart 14). Mexican equity prices, measured in U.S. dollars (by the IFC investable index), dropped by over 25 percent by the end of December 1994, and by the end of March 1995 had fallen by another 40 percent. As mentioned earlier, contagion or spillover effects of the crisis were stronger in Latin American countries than in other emerging markets. Stock markets in Argentina and Brazil were hardest hit: in Argentina the IFC index fell by over 13 percent in U.S. dollar terms in the second half of December 1994 and continued to decline in January and February 1995, although prices recovered by over 10 percent in March. In Brazil stock prices fell by almost 40 percent between mid-December 1994 and the end of March 1995. The spillover effects on Asian stock markets were relatively short-lived; by the end of February, a number of markets had recovered most of the initial losses.

External Payments, Financing, and Debt

The large increases in capital flows to developing countries in recent years, mainly to Asian and Latin American countries, have been associated with widening current account deficits in most regions, although many countries have been relatively successful in sterilizing a substantial proportion of the capital inflows and building up reserves (Charts 15 and 16). During the period ahead, net portfolio capital flows to developing countries seem likely to decline considerably, but the strong fundamentals and solid long-term growth prospects of most countries suggest little reason to expect any substantial downward shift in foreign direct investment flows. Among individual regions, net capital flows to the Western Hemisphere are expected to slow the most, largely owing to the crisis in Mexico. There may well be some lag in trade flows, however, and projections for current account deficits do not fully offset the likely decline in capital flows.

Recent increases in commodity prices and strengthened competitiveness are important factors in the current account improvements projected for African countries. These improvements are especially significant for the CFA countries, where progress in controlling domestic price inflation has helped maintain competitiveness following the January 1994 devaluation. In Côte d'Ivoire the current account deficit is expected to narrow by over 2 percent of GDP in 1995–96. The

Chart 14. Selected Developing Countries: Equity Prices

(In U.S. dollars; January 1994 = 100)

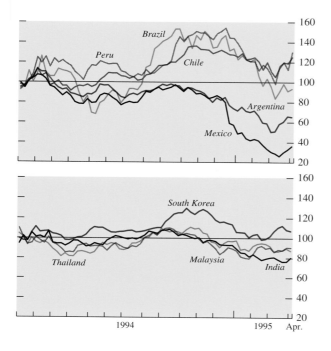

Source: International Finance Corporation, Emerging Markets data base.

external surplus in Egypt is expected to decline further in 1995–96, reflecting in part a real appreciation of the currency. The strengthening of oil prices in 1995 and stronger fiscal adjustment efforts should also contribute to improvements in external positions among the oil exporting countries, especially for the larger oil exporting countries.

The increase in interest rates during 1994 has been reflected in a rise in debt-service ratios for sub-Saharan Africa and for countries in the Middle East and Europe (Chart 17). A more flexible approach to official bilateral debt reduction for low-income countries by the Paris Club, under the "Naples" terms agreed in December 1994 and consistent with the Interim Committee's Madrid Declaration, is expected to reduce debt burdens for low-income countries. Cambodia was the first country to be offered a 67 percent net present value reduction in eligible debt service by the Paris Club in January 1995; subsequently a number of other countries, Chad, Guinea-Bissau, and Togo, in February, and Bolivia and Nicaragua in March, were offered similar terms, whereas Guinea received a 50 percent reduction in January. Furthermore, in February, Uganda was the first country to receive a stock-of-debt operation under Naples terms involving a 67 percent reduction in the net present value of eligible debt. Concessional terms such as these should help reduce debt and debt-service payments of most low-income countries to more sustainable levels, provided that new debt instruments offered to these countries contain similar concessional elements.

In the past six months, progress has continued to be made with debt-restructuring agreements in connection with the London Club and on a bilateral official basis. These include the commercial bank restructuring agreement with Ecuador involving $4.5 billion commercial bank debt and $2.9 billion in interest arrears. Algeria is also negotiating with commercial banks to restructure $4.2 billion debt. Haiti has settled its debt arrears to multilateral lenders, but arrears to the United States and other bilateral lenders remain to be cleared, and South Africa wrote off a $200 million debt owed by Namibia. Talks with regard to the commercial bank debt of Peru and Panama are continuing. Negotiations are also continuing with Nigeria and Venezuela regarding arrears and the management of outstanding debt.

Capital Flows and Economic Performance

In the aftermath of the Mexican financial crisis, equity markets in a number of developing countries experienced significant increases in volatility, raising concerns about the potential contagion effects that could result from a general reappraisal of developing country investments. Policymakers in many of the countries that have witnessed large capital inflows

Chart 15. Developing Countries: Net Capital Flows[1]
(In billions of U.S. dollars)

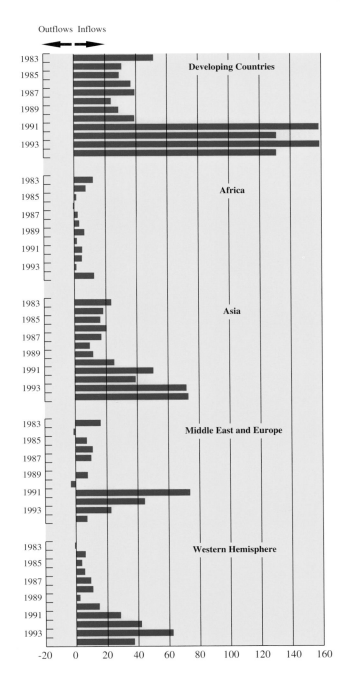

[1]Net capital flows comprise net direct investment, net portfolio investment, and other long- and short-term net investment flows, including official and private borrowing.

face a difficult task of managing the impact of these inflows, especially in limiting the potential adverse consequences on real exchange rates and the buildup of inflationary pressures. In the current environment, they need to guard against the risk of sudden reversals of capital flows. These risks are likely to be particularly acute in countries where the capital inflows are primarily short term.

There are important differences between the recent surge in capital inflows to developing countries and the experience of the late 1970s and early 1980s, when capital inflows consisted largely of bank lending to public sector borrowers. In Asia and in some Latin American countries, such as Chile, the rising share of foreign direct investment and portfolio investments in emerging stock markets has helped to reduce reliance on debt-creating flows. The October 1994 issue of the *World Economic Outlook* focused on many of the factors that have contributed to the increase in private capital flows, including the effect of the recent recessions and the associated decline in interest rates in the industrial countries, and discussed the policy response in some of the large recipient countries.[11] The rise in interest rates in the industrial countries since early 1994 and the strengthening of the recovery have resulted in some moderation of portfolio capital flows to developing countries, but domestic factors such as macroeconomic stability and the sustainability of external balances are still likely to be the key determinants of the sustainability of capital flows. The crisis in Mexico, however, will undoubtedly lead to a period of increased vigilance in financial markets. Even though the longer-term move toward greater international portfolio diversification for industrial country investors can be expected to continue, albeit at a much slower rate, foreign investors are likely to be more selective with regard to developing country investments.

Significant progress in implementing structural reforms and fostering macroeconomic stability, particularly in Latin America and Asia, has generally played a key role in attracting capital inflows. Nevertheless there have been marked differences in macroeconomic performance and in how the recent capital inflows have been utilized (Table 8). Capital inflows have raised aggregate expenditures in all countries. In the Asian countries, however, the ratio of private consumption expenditure to GDP declined by over 4 percentage points in the early 1990s compared with the mid-to-late 1980s, and the ratio of investment to GDP

Chart 16. Developing Countries: Balances on Current Account and Reserves[1]

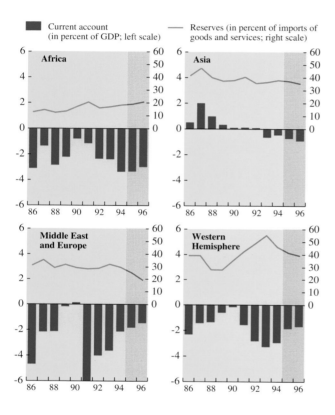

■ Current account
(in percent of GDP; left scale)

— Reserves (in percent of imports of goods and services; right scale)

[1]Blue shaded areas indicate IMF staff projections.

---

[11]There have been a number of other recent studies that examine the causes and effects of large capital inflows. See, for example, Guillermo A. Calvo, Leonardo Leiderman, and Carmen Reinhart, "Capital Inflows and Real Exchange Rate Appreciation in Latin America: The Role of External Factors," *Staff Papers* (IMF), Vol. 40 (March 1993), pp. 108–51; and Susan Schadler, Maria Carkovic, Adam Bennett, and Robert Kahn, *Recent Experiences with Surges in Capital Inflows*, IMF Occasional Paper 108 (December 1993).

rose by almost 5 percentage points. In the Latin American countries, by contrast, the ratio of consumption to GDP increased by over 3½ percentage points in the early 1990s compared with the 1980s, while the investment ratio was only marginally higher.[12] For Latin America, this suggests that the capital inflows have tended to become a substitute for private sector saving. Although these countries have made substantial progress in reducing fiscal deficits, the improvement in public saving has been insufficient to offset the decline in private saving. In several of these countries, stronger programs of fiscal consolidation and structural reform would help to strengthen domestic saving, in line with the experience of Chile.

During the early years of the recent surge in capital inflows, most countries attempted to intervene in foreign exchange markets to limit the appreciation of their nominal exchange rates, to reduce the impact of capital flows on money and credit growth, and to lessen the vulnerability of the financial system in the event of a sudden reversal of capital flows. The Asian countries were relatively successful in sterilizing the monetary effects of the rise in foreign exchange reserves. This helped to contain pressures on domestic inflation and to maintain relatively stable exchange rates. Among the Latin American countries, foreign exchange intervention was limited, and real exchange rates generally appreciated. In many cases, financial markets are not sufficiently well developed for central banks to sterilize the magnitude of capital flows that have been attracted in recent years. However, even when financial markets are relatively developed, sterilization is likely to be effective only in the short term and may not be sufficient to resist persistent pressures on the exchange rate. A particularly important drawback with sterilization is that it tends to raise domestic interest rates, which may attract more short-term capital flows. Even in countries such as Chile, where sterilization has been relatively successful, net costs to the central bank—the difference between domestic interest rates and the return on foreign currency reserves—have been substantial. In Chile, these quasi-fiscal costs were estimated to be around ¾ of 1 percent of GDP in 1991.[13]

The inability to sterilize the effects of the inflows played an important role in Mexico's financial crisis. Since the late 1980s, the Mexican economy has attracted substantial capital inflows, accounting for over 40 percent of total flows to all Latin American countries during 1990–93. These large inflows, including

Chart 17. Developing Countries: External Debt and Debt Service[1]

(In percent of exports of goods and services)

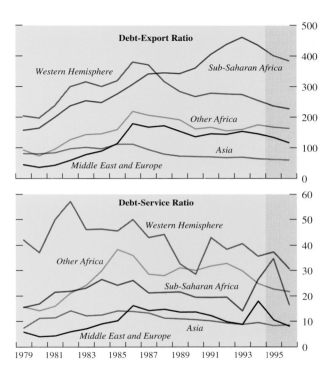

[1]Debt service refers to actual payments of interest on total debt plus actual amortization payments on long-term debt. The projections (blue shaded areas) incorporate the impact of exceptional financing items.

[12]The average figures for Latin American countries as a group mask some important differences between countries; investment rates in Chile, for example, have risen consistently over the recent period.

[13]See Miguel Kiguel and Leonardo Leiderman, "On the Consequences of Sterilized Intervention in Latin America" (unpublished; Washington: World Bank, 1993).

Table 8. Selected Developing Countries: Macroeconomic Indicators

(Annual averages; in percent of GDP, unless otherwise noted)

	1983–89	1990–94	1990	1991	1992	1993	1994
Asia[1]							
Real GDP[2]	6.2	5.5	7.2	5.1	5.1	5.4	6.5
Consumer prices[2]	6.9	8.4	8.7	10.6	8.0	6.9	8.1
Money growth[2]	20.0	18.1	19.8	19.7	16.3	18.6	18.0
Private consumption	62.8	58.5	58.8	58.6	57.5	57.5	60.0
Private saving[3]	16.8	22.4	22.7	22.2	22.9	22.2	22.2
Fiscal balance[4]	–4.8	–2.8	–3.3	–2.8	–2.5	–2.7	–2.6
Current account balance	–1.9	–2.7	–3.7	–3.5	–2.2	–1.9	–2.4
Real effective exchange rate[2]	–6.3	–3.0	–5.0	–6.4	–6.8	–0.4	1.9
Total net capital inflow	2.0	4.1	3.9	4.7	4.1	4.4	3.6
Change in reserves	0.4	1.9	1.2	1.6	2.2	2.9	1.7
Total saving	24.0	28.0	28.4	28.2	27.9	27.5	27.7
Total investment	25.9	30.7	32.1	31.7	30.2	29.4	30.1
Latin America[5]							
Real GDP[2]	3.1	3.5	—	3.1	2.2	3.6	5.3
Consumer prices[2]	193.7	222.9	601.1	152.0	192.5	276.7	291.8
Money growth[2]	200.5	258.1	388.3	207.6	271.1	345.3	223.4
Private consumption	64.4	68.0	66.7	69.2	68.6	68.1	67.5
Private saving	18.6	13.5	14.4	12.8	13.8	12.7	13.9
Fiscal balance[4]	–5.6	0.1	–0.6	0.4	–0.2	0.6	—
Current account balance	–0.9	–2.4	–1.1	–1.5	–2.2	–3.2	–3.6
Real effective exchange rate[2]	0.8	4.3	11.7	–0.6	1.5	8.4	8.1
Total net capital inflow	–1.7	1.4	–0.1	1.4	2.0	3.7	–0.1
Change in reserves	0.3	1.2	1.2	1.5	2.4	1.7	–0.6
Total saving	19.2	18.6	19.6	18.3	18.3	17.9	18.6
Total investment	20.1	20.9	20.7	19.9	20.6	21.2	22.3

[1]India, Indonesia, Korea, Malaysia, the Philippines, and Thailand.

[2]Annual percent change.

[3]For Indonesia, data for private saving are only available from 1986 onward. The data reported for 1983–89 are for 1986–89.

[4]Reflects only central government expenditures and revenues, and therefore the fiscal balance does not equal net public sector saving.

[5]Argentina, Brazil, Chile, Colombia, Mexico, and Peru.

significant increases in foreign direct investment, were attracted by prudent macroeconomic policies, privatization and extensive structural reforms, and the country's promising long-term prospects, not least in the light of the North American Free Trade Agreement. The large capital inflows, however, coupled with the quasi-fixed exchange rate system, also resulted in a substantial appreciation of the real exchange rate and a sharp increase in the external current account deficit. Much of this deficit reflected higher consumption expenditure and a substantial decline in private savings. Against this background, and because of adverse political events, foreign investors' concerns about the sustainability of the current account deficit began to increase during 1994. At the same time, significant increases in liquidity ran counter to the need to tighten domestic monetary conditions in order to stem the capital outflows. (See Annex I for a detailed discussion of factors behind Mexico's financial crisis.)

Concerns about the potential instability of capital flows, especially of portfolio investment in stock and bond markets, have led a number of countries to impose a variety of restrictions to deter short-term inflows, while still maintaining convertibility for longer-term capital account transactions. Among the more common measures are restrictions or ceilings on foreign borrowing by domestic enterprises and high reserve requirements on foreign currency deposits. Chile, for example, has limited the inflows of capital by imposing reserve requirements of 30 percent on all foreign currency credits. The Indian authorities have recently raised reserve requirements on foreign currency deposits to discourage new inflows. Such restrictions tend to raise the cost of finance for domestic firms and reduce the efficiency of the financial system. Nevertheless, in the short term they may help to limit the potential destabilizing effects of capital inflows on real exchange rates and provide policymakers time to address weaknesses in financial markets and to improve macroeconomic fundamentals. It is particularly important to limit the foreign exchange exposure of the banking system, which may exacerbate difficulties in the event of a sudden reversal of capital flows. This may require more effective bank regulations that limit potential mismatches of maturities and currency denominations of bank assets and liabilities, particularly in countries where low-cost deposit insurance encourages excessive risk exposure. Such prudential controls should be distinguished from broader controls on international capital flows, which are rarely effective in stemming either capital inflows or capital outflows over the longer term, especially when they become a substitute for efforts to address macroeconomic imbalances and to correct unsustainable exchange rates.

For countries that are confronted with shifts in market sentiment, the Mexican episode underscores two important policy principles. First, in order to restore confidence and relieve exchange market pressures in a crisis situation, domestic and external macroeconomic imbalances have to be addressed forcefully, and as quickly as possible. In the short term, the appropriate measures should include a tightening of monetary conditions through increases in domestic interest rates as well as fiscal adjustments. Fiscal action may be needed even when the initial imbalances emanate from the private sector. Over the longer term, governments must address the underlying causes of external imbalances and low saving, including structural measures to correct relative price distortions. A second policy lesson concerns the potentially difficult decision regarding exchange rate regimes. Where countries have adopted nominal exchange rate anchors as part of a wider inflation stabilization strategy, the initial response to exchange market pressures should consist primarily of monetary tightening. However, under circumstances of sustained pressures, accepting a devaluation or abandoning a fixed exchange rate parity may be the only credible policy response. In order to limit the inflationary impact of the devaluation, the transition to a new parity or a floating exchange rate regime needs to be accompanied by supporting measures that include tight monetary and credit policy, as well as a fiscal stance that is consistent with the new policy regime.

Medium-Term Outlook and Policy Challenges

In recent years, the aggregate growth performance of developing countries has been sustained at remarkably high levels despite periods of protracted weakness in the industrial countries. In large part, this resilience to weak external conditions has been due to the strong macroeconomic stabilization and structural reform programs in a number of countries. But high aggregate growth rates also mask considerable differences among individual countries and regions. Although these divergences in growth rates are expected to narrow over the medium term, as policies and reform efforts strengthen in some of the weaker performing countries—primarily in Africa, but also in

other parts of the developing world—significant disparities are likely to persist (Table 9).

The divergences in performance and stages of development give rise to very different priorities and policy challenges across individual countries, even though the basic requirements of market-oriented, outward-looking policies are common to all countries. In addressing the policy challenges facing developing countries, it is useful to classify countries into three broad categories: strong performers that are characterized by substantial high growth and rapid improvements in living standards; moderate performers that are catching up more slowly; and countries that have experienced negative growth over the recent past and where living standards continue to decline.

The *strong performers* comprise countries that have managed to sustain a rapid pace of economic growth. Several of these now have high per capita incomes, while others are rapidly catching up from relatively low-income levels. Singapore's per capita growth rate, for example, has averaged over 7 percent a year over the past thirty years; measured at purchasing-power-parity exchange rates, per capita income in Singapore now exceeds that of many industrial countries.[14] A number of countries in Asia, including Korea and Malaysia, have recorded similar strong growth performances. Many of these countries are confronted with policy challenges that are similar to those faced by industrial countries: sustaining growth while minimizing the risk of overheating. Some countries, such as Chile, China, Korea, Malaysia, and Thailand, are experiencing relatively tight conditions in labor markets and capacity constraints arising from the slower pace of improvements in infrastructure. For these countries, it is important to ensure that macroeconomic policies, particularly financial conditions, are adjusted appropriately in light of the strength of economic performance. In China, for example, growth rates of around 13 percent in 1992 and 1993 could not be sustained, and resulted in inflationary pressures. This required the adoption of stabilization measures to slow aggregate demand. In Korea, the authorities have faced similar difficulties in recent years.

Higher investment in infrastructure to keep pace with growth represents a major challenge for these countries.[15] In China, weaknesses in intercity transport systems have adversely affected the supply of coal, which is used to meet a large proportion of the country's rapidly growing electricity needs. In Thailand, the concentration of growth in Bangkok has placed increasing strains on infrastructure in and

---

[14]Per capita incomes in the Bahamas, Cyprus, Hong Kong, Israel, Korea, Taiwan Province of China, and a number of oil exporting countries are also similar to those of many industrial countries; see World Bank, *World Development Report 1994* (Oxford and New York: Oxford University Press for the World Bank, 1994), Table 30.

[15]See World Bank, *World Development Report 1994.*

Table 9. Developing Countries: Medium-Term Projections

(Average annual percent change, unless otherwise noted)

	1975–82	1983–89	1990–94	1995–2000
Developing countries				
Real GDP	4.7	4.7	5.4	6.2
Per capita GDP	2.0	2.5	3.5	4.2
Consumer prices	21.7	38.4	44.1	8.0
Saving[1]	25.3	22.9	23.3	24.7
Investment[1]	25.9	23.9	25.0	25.6
Current account balance[1]	–0.5	–1.0	–1.6	–0.9
Africa				
Real GDP	2.6	2.6	1.6	4.5
Per capita GDP	–0.2	–0.3	–1.1	1.9
Consumer prices	16.1	16.0	26.1	8.5
Saving[1]	25.2	18.7	17.8	20.5
Investment[1]	29.0	20.8	21.1	22.3
Current account balance[1]	–3.8	–2.2	–3.4	–1.8
Asia				
Real GDP	6.1	7.6	7.5	7.4
Per capita GDP	4.0	5.8	5.8	5.8
Consumer prices	7.3	7.9	8.8	6.0
Saving[1]	24.9	29.8	30.9	30.4
Investment[1]	26.5	28.9	31.4	30.9
Current account balance[1]	–1.6	0.9	–0.6	–0.5
Middle East and Europe				
Real GDP	2.6	2.6	1.6	4.5
Per capita GDP	–0.2	–0.3	–1.1	1.9
Consumer prices	18.9	22.3	26.0	10.5
Saving[1]	31.5	19.3	16.3	18.4
Investment[1]	24.4	21.5	19.5	18.8
Current account balance[1]	7.2	–2.1	–3.2	–0.4
Western Hemisphere				
Real GDP	4.2	2.0	2.9	4.2
Per capita GDP	1.6	–0.1	0.9	2.3
Consumer prices	47.0	150.0	216.6	12.3
Saving[1]	20.8	19.2	17.7	21.2
Investment[1]	24.3	20.2	20.5	22.3
Current account balance[1]	–3.5	–1.0	–2.7	–1.2

[1]Percent of GDP.

around the city. Other strong performers, such as Indonesia, Korea, Malaysia, and the Philippines, are experiencing increasing demands for public utilities and transportation systems. The challenge for many of these countries is to address their infrastructure needs, including environmental requirements, without putting undue strains on public finances or on their external positions. To this end, a number of countries have implemented large-scale privatization programs. Malaysia has successfully privatized a container port, telecommunications, and electricity supply; and privatization has played a significant role in eliminating chronic power shortages in the Philippines. Korea and Thailand, on the other hand, are encouraging private participation in infrastructure development. Several large public and private utility companies in Latin America, particularly in Argentina, Chile, and Mexico, have been able to finance infrastructure investment through foreign direct investment. Many of

the infrastructure projects under consideration will require large-scale investments. There is often a presumption that such investments necessarily require foreign financing, but policies in a number of Asian countries are appropriately geared toward mobilizing domestic saving to help meet much of the financing for these projects.

In the group of countries characterized by *relatively moderate economic performance*, many weaknesses remain to be addressed to consolidate important initial achievements. A number of countries with moderate growth performance have attracted substantial capital flows, in part due to greater openness and liberalization of trade and payments systems. Many of these countries have also attained a fair degree of macroeconomic stability, although in comparison with the strong performers macroeconomic stability still appears fragile in some cases. Nevertheless, fiscal deficits—often the underlying reason for wider macroeconomic and external imbalances—are now significantly lower than in the late 1980s in many countries in Latin America and among the moderate performers in Asia, such as Bangladesh, India, and Pakistan. This is an important reason for the improved outlook for many of the moderate performers: the contrast between Brazil, a moderate performer, and Korea, a strong performer, whose per capita incomes were broadly comparable in 1960, provides a stark illustration of the value of stable macroeconomic conditions, outward orientation, and structural reform (Box 5).

Where fiscal deficits are still large, inflation reduction has often been achieved primarily through monetary restraint, which has often given rise to capital inflows attracted by relatively high short-term interest rates. Aside from concerns about vulnerability to changes in investor sentiment, such flows may not necessarily finance capital outlays and investment rates have remained relatively low in countries such as Egypt, Pakistan, and Turkey. As emphasized earlier, the pattern of investment and saving behavior among many of the moderate performers stands in sharp contrast to that observed in economies such as Indonesia, Malaysia, and Singapore, where investment-to-GDP ratios have consistently averaged around 30 percent over the last decade. Indeed, this is one of the key factors that has contributed to high growth in the successful Asian economies.

Although a low saving rate may be explained in part by demographic developments and a country's level of development, it also may reflect the lack of sufficient progress with structural reform, especially financial sector reform. In many countries, public sector deficits are financed mainly by domestic banking systems, often at below market interest rates. Moreover, state-owned banks often provide subsidized credit to public and quasi-public enterprises. Governments that have resorted to directed credit programs may subsequently be faced with the challenge of dealing with a high proportion of nonperforming loans. In Bangladesh, banks have enlarged lending margins in an attempt to restore profitability, with the result that credit growth to the private sector has been constrained. Other countries have experienced similar difficulties. In Nigeria, Uganda, and many countries of the African franc zone, governments have had to assume a large part of the obligations of banks and public enterprises, and this has put added strain on their fiscal policies. Directed credit programs have also resulted in other inefficiencies. By subsidizing the cost of capital over that of labor, there is a risk of encouraging the use of less labor-intensive technologies in economies that have a surplus of labor relative to capital.

The experience of several countries that have recently taken measures to liberalize their financial systems, including a number of countries in Latin America and Africa, suggests that the removal of controls has to be accompanied by the establishment of effective supervisory systems and appropriate legal and accounting frameworks. In a number of countries, there is also a need to restructure banks and develop financial market infrastructure to enhance the operation of monetary policy via the use of indirect instruments.[16] A further important prerequisite for successful liberalization is the reduction of macroeconomic imbalances. The Philippines, for example, attempted financial liberalization during the 1980s before addressing macroeconomic imbalances; subsequent banking crises and a sharp recession ultimately led to a partial reversal of the reforms.[17]

The poor growth performance of many oil exporting developing countries is attributable in large part to delays in rolling back the scale of public sector involvement in economic activity. During much of the 1970s and early 1980s, substantial oil revenues enabled these countries to finance large government expenditure programs that are no longer viable given the substantial declines in oil revenue.[18] These countries are now faced with fiscal deficits that are not sustainable even under reasonably optimistic long-term projections for oil prices, and notwithstanding efforts to raise more revenue from non-oil taxes. Declining oil revenues have also exposed a number of structural weaknesses, including the limited development of non-oil sectors, in large part due to extensive controls on private sector economic activity.

A large number of developing countries have made substantial progress in adopting outward-oriented trade policies. In many instances, however, there are still significant barriers to trade, especially in sectors where domestic producers were originally granted protection on the assumption that they would be able to compete internationally if given time to develop. There is little theoretical or empirical evidence to support this "infant-industry" argument, however, and there is now a widespread consensus that trade liberalization is vital for growth. In this context, it is particularly worth emphasizing the evidence on the role of international R&D spillovers (Box 6).

Despite the positive effects that can be expected from trade opening, many countries are removing

---

[16]For an extensive discussion of the relative merits of direct and indirect instruments of monetary policy, see William E. Alexander, Charles Enoch, and Tomás J. T. Baliño, *The Adoption of Indirect Instruments of Monetary Policy*, IMF Occasional Paper 126 (forthcoming, 1995).

[17]For a detailed discussion of the weaknesses in banking supervision systems in Latin American countries, see Liliana Rojas-Suarez and Steven R. Weisbrod, "Financial Market Fragilities in Latin America: From Banking Crisis Resolution to Current Policy Challenges," IMF Working Paper 94/117 (October 1994).

[18]See Claire Liuksila, Alejandro García, and Sheila Bassett, "Fiscal Policy Sustainability in Oil Producing Countries," IMF Working Paper 94/137 (November 1994).

Box 5. Brazil and Korea

A comparison of the economic performance of Brazil and Korea over the past thirty years provides a powerful illustration of the contribution that stable macroeconomic policies, structural reforms, and outward orientation can make toward sustaining high growth. During the 1960s and 1970s, per capita incomes were broadly similar and GDP growth averaged about 9 percent a year in both countries. Trade policies were also similar in the late 1960s and early 1970s when both countries promoted their export sectors and experienced substantial increases in exports.[1] Starting in the early 1980s, however, their growth rates diverged, and over the past ten years real GDP in Korea has grown more than twice as fast as in Brazil (see chart). As a result, per capita incomes in Korea are now almost twice as high as in Brazil.

In response to the first oil price shock in the early 1970s, both countries increased protection for domestic industry and pursued expansionary policies in an attempt to moderate the impact on output. The results were similar—inflation increased, export growth declined as real exchange rates appreciated, and current account deficits widened to more than 5 percent of GDP in 1979. After the second oil price shock in the late 1970s, external imbalances forced a rethinking of strategy in both countries. Korea implemented a comprehensive stabilization program, while Brazil gave priority to expenditure and credit expansion to finance investment in the agricultural and energy sectors.[2] In Korea, the rapid tightening of macroeconomic policies, and adoption of outward-ori-

ented trade policies to improve competitiveness, gave rise to higher investment and saving rates that allowed the economy to benefit from the improved external environment in the latter part of the 1980s. Brazil also attempted to restore external competitiveness, primarily through large devaluations, but persistent fiscal imbalances in the context of pervasive indexation led to an acceleration of inflation, the crowding out of private investment, and stagnation.

Following the decisive adjustment of 1979–80, Korea pursued moderately countercyclical macroeconomic policies during the 1980s, while maintaining a relatively stable exchange rate to control inflation, especially since the mid-1980s. In Brazil, after the stop-and-go policies of the first half of the 1980s, several heterodox stabilization plans were attempted, largely based on price and wage freezes. These efforts were not supported by sufficiently tight policies, however, and proved unsuccessful in controlling inflation, which reached four-digit levels by 1989. External conditions were broadly similar in Brazil and Korea in the 1980s, although Latin American countries as a group suffered larger terms of trade shocks than east Asian countries.[3] Higher national saving and larger current account surpluses during the mid-1980s also sheltered Korea from the debt crisis.

In addition to the role of macroeconomic policy, differences in productivity growth explain much of the divergence in GDP growth over the recent past. Korea's annual productivity growth increased sharply during the past two decades, from about 1 percent in the 1960s and 1970s to 2½ percent in the 1980s.[4]

[1]See Eliana Cardoso, "From Inertia to Megainflation: Brazil in the 1980s," in *Lessons of Economic Stabilization and Its Aftermath*, ed. by Michael Bruno, Stanley Fischer, Elhanan Helpman, and Nissan Liviatan (Cambridge, Massachusetts: MIT Press, 1991); and Vittorio Corbo and Sang-Mok Suh, *Structural Adjustment in a Newly Industrialized Country: The Korean Experience* (Baltimore: Johns Hopkins, 1992).
[2]Angus Maddison and associates, *Brazil and Mexico: The Political Economy of Poverty, Equity and Growth* (Oxford and New York: Oxford University Press, 1992).

[3]See Jeffrey Sachs, "External Debt and Macroeconomic Performance in Latin America and East Asia," *Brookings Papers on Economic Activity: 2* (1985), pp. 523–64.
[4]See Alwyn Young, "The Tyranny of Numbers: Confronting the Statistical Realities of the East Asian Growth Experience," NBER Working Paper 4680 (Cambridge, Massachusetts: National Bureau of Economic Research, March 1994).

trade barriers only gradually. In India, where deregulation of the industrial licensing system has been extensive since the beginning of the reform efforts in 1991, tariffs on most imports, including many capital goods, are still at the maximum rate of 65 percent, while imports of consumer goods are still largely prohibited. In Egypt, although there have been significant reductions in the general level of tariffs, maximum tariff rates remain relatively high. Such restrictions, together with pervasive nontariff barriers in many developing countries, have often constrained the growth of export sectors. To fully benefit from the Uruguay Round trade agreement, a number of developing countries will need to accelerate and pursue more ambitious trade and other structural reform programs. Some develop-

ing countries will lose preferential access to industrial country markets and will need to adjust to greater competition from other low-cost producers.

Developing countries that have barely grown over the last five to ten years face by far the most daunting policy challenges. A large number of countries in this *falling behind* category have experienced declining real per capita incomes, sometimes exacerbated by unsustainable population growth. In Zaïre, for example, per capita incomes have fallen by over 5 percent a year over the past decade. Other broader indicators of economic development such as infant mortality have also worsened dramatically. Many countries in this category, especially countries in sub-Saharan Africa, are highly dependent on exports of primary commodi-

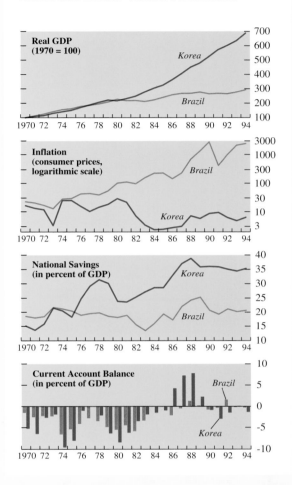

Brazil and Korea: Selected Indicators

Estimates of productivity growth for Brazil, by contrast, suggest that it fell from about 2 percent a year in the period 1940–80 to a negative ¾ of 1 percent during the 1980s.[5]

A recent study provides some evidence on the sources of these productivity differences.[6] The results suggest that economic performance in both Brazil and Korea reflected primarily domestic rather than external factors. Korea's strong economic performance can be attributed mainly to macroeconomic stability and the gradual implementation of structural reforms that enhanced the country's long-run growth potential. The opening up of the Korean economy, combined with financial policies geared toward maintaining a stable macroeconomic environment, allowed Korea to take full advantage of the favorable external environment during the latter part of the 1980s. In contrast, Brazil's less outward-oriented economic strategy—as reflected in substantial import restrictions—and the lack of structural reforms reduced competitive pressures and diminished the benefits from international integration and the strong expansion of world trade.

In Brazil, there has been an important turning point in economic strategy since 1990. Emphasis is now firmly placed on macroeconomic stability and market-oriented structural reforms, including currency reform and trade liberalization. Sustained implementation of these types of policies should help Brazil to maintain low inflation on a durable basis and to sustain stronger growth in the medium term.

---

[5]See Victor Elias, "Sources of Growth: A Study of Seven Latin American Economies" (San Francisco: Institute for Contemporary Studies Press, 1992).

[6]See Alexander Hoffmaister and Jorge Roldós, "The Sources of Macroeconomic Fluctuations in Developing Countries: Brazil and Korea," IMF Working Paper (forthcoming, 1995).

---

ties, making them particularly vulnerable to fluctuations in their terms of trade. The declining long-term trend in real world commodity prices has led to a large cumulative decline in the terms of trade facing many African countries. For sub-Saharan African countries as a group, the terms of trade loss since the mid-1980s has amounted to over 30 percent, with some countries, such as the Congo and Zaïre, experiencing even steeper declines.

Notwithstanding these adverse external developments, economic conditions have begun to improve in recent years in countries that have undertaken comprehensive domestic policy reforms. It is noteworthy that those sub-Saharan African countries that have experienced positive per capita growth since the mid-

1980s have suffered larger terms of trade losses than countries with negative per capita growth (see Annex II). Among the African countries with flexible exchange rate regimes, real exchange rate depreciations have helped to offset much of the negative impact on the external current account resulting from the decline in their terms of trade.[19] By contrast, in the CFA countries, prior to the recent devaluation, real exchange

---

[19]For a detailed analysis of the economic performance of sub-Saharan African countries, see Michael T. Hadjimichael, Dhaneshwar Ghura, Martin Mühleisen, Roger Nord, and E. Murat Uçer, *Sub-Saharan Africa: Growth, Savings, and Investment, 1986–93*, IMF Occasional Paper 118 (January 1995).

Box 6. North-South R&D Spillovers

Research and development (R&D) in the world economy is almost entirely concentrated in the industrial countries. This high concentration of an activity that leads to the development of new technologies, products, materials, and manufacturing techniques raises the question of whether the benefits of R&D are limited to the countries that carry it out. Theoretical and empirical research suggests that the answer is no: a country's productivity depends not only on its own investment in research and development, which may be small or nonexistent, but also on the R&D done by its trade partners. R&D spillovers are thus another aspect of economic linkages among industrial countries and from industrial to developing countries, one that supplements and complements the more traditional channels of trade, commodity prices, interest rates, and financial flows.

There are a number of channels through which the productivity of countries are interrelated.[1] First, international trade enables a country to employ a larger variety of intermediate products and capital equipment, which enhances the productivity of its own resources. Second, international trade and foreign direct investment provide channels of communication that stimulate cross-border learning of production methods, product design, organizational methods, and market conditions. Each one of these helps to employ domestic resources more efficiently and to adjust the mix of products so as to obtain more value added per unit of input. Third, international contacts enable a country to copy foreign technologies and adjust them to domestic use. Imitation is widespread and it has played a major role in the growth of high-performing economies such as Japan and the newly industrializing economies of east Asia.[2] Finally, international trade and foreign direct investment can raise the ability of a country to develop its own new technologies, or to imitate foreign technologies more efficiently, thereby indirectly affecting productivity in the entire economy.

The extent to which a developing country will benefit from foreign trade in these ways depends on the ability of its trade partners to provide it with products and information in which it is in short supply. Both depend on the trade partners' accumulated knowledge that is embodied in products, technologies, and organizations. By trading with an industrial country that has a larger "stock of knowledge," a developing country stands to gain more in terms of both the products it can import and the direct knowledge it can acquire than it would by trading with a country with a smaller stock of knowledge.

Recent research has examined the empirical significance of these R&D spillovers.[3] The results suggest that a developing country's total factor productivity is larger the larger is the R&D capital stock of its trade partners—which is used as a proxy for the stock of knowledge embodied in the country's trade composition—the more open is it to foreign trade with industrial countries, and the more educated is its labor force.[4] An additional implication is that a developing country whose trade is directed toward industrial countries that have large cumulative experiences in R&D has higher productivity. Moreover, a developing country's productivity may primarily be affected by foreign R&D capital through its imports from the industrial countries. This implies that a developing country that is more open to trade with industrial countries derives a larger marginal benefit from foreign R&D; likewise a developing country whose trade is mainly with industrial countries that have heavily invested in R&D will tend to have a larger impact on productivity from a marginal increase in imports from these countries.

The sensitivity of total factor productivity in developing countries with respect to the R&D capital stock of industrial countries is estimated to be large. On average, a 1 percent increase in the R&D capital stock of the industrial countries increases total factor productivity in the developing countries by about 0.1 percent. Increases in the R&D capital stock of the United States, which has by far the largest domestic R&D stock, has the largest impact on productivity in the developing countries as a group. There are, however, substantial differences across countries depending upon bilateral trade patterns between the developing countries and the industrial countries. The substantial rates of return to industrial country R&D, measured in terms of the resulting increase in developing country output, are consistent with other studies that have found much higher rates of return on R&D than on investment in structures, machines, and equipment.[5]

---

[1]See Gene Grossman and Elhanan Helpman, *Innovation and Growth in the Global Economy* (Cambridge, Massachusetts; London: MIT Press, 1991).

[2]For a discussion of the importance of direct learning channels in Japan when it opened up to the rest of the world in the post-Meiji era, see William W. Lockwood, *The Economic Development of Japan: Growth and Structural Change 1868–1938* (Princeton, New Jersey: Princeton University Press, 1954), Chapter 6; and in Korea during its industrialization process, see Yung Whee Rhee, Bruce Ross-Larson, and Garry Pursell, *Korea's Competitive Edge: Managing the Entry into World Markets* (Baltimore: Johns Hopkins University Press for the World Bank, 1984). See also Edward M. Graham, "Foreign Direct Investment in the World Economy," IMF Working Paper (forthcoming, 1995).

[3]See David T. Coe, Elhanan Helpman, and Alexander W. Hoffmaister, "North-South R&D Spillovers," IMF Working Paper 94/144 (December 1994). Evidence of the importance of R&D spillovers among industrial countries is presented in David T. Coe and Elhanan Helpman, "International R&D Spillovers," IMF Working Paper 93/84 (November 1993).

[4]The R&D capital stock is calculated as a weighted average of the domestic R&D capital stocks of its industrial country trade partners, with bilateral import shares serving as weights. The R&D capital stock of the industrial country trade partner is computed as cumulative real R&D spending, with an allowance made for depreciation.

[5]For a review of the literature, see Zvi Griliches, "Productivity, R&D, and the Data Constraint," *American Economic Review*, Vol. 84 (March 1994), pp. 1–23.

rates were maintained at unrealistic levels that impeded adjustment to terms of trade losses.

For many commodity-based countries, policy measures to enhance the efficiency of their agricultural sectors will be critical in the period ahead. Whereas in the past, commodity price booms may have concealed inefficiencies in agriculture, including those resulting from government policies, the generally weak outlook for real commodity prices over the longer term makes it essential that countries implement policies to increase productivity in agriculture and to ensure that domestic producers are in a position to utilize fully the increased access to industrial country markets resulting from the Uruguay Round trade agreement. A number of countries in Africa, such as Zambia and Zimbabwe, have recognized the importance of relaxing price controls in agriculture and liberalizing the marketing and distribution of agricultural products.

Further structural reform and macroeconomic stabilization will be essential to improve living standards and alleviate poverty in the long term. In the short run, however, reform programs may well entail adverse outcomes for some sections of society. The reform efforts therefore need to include well-targeted and affordable social assistance programs, such as the food distribution and income supplement program in Mozambique and the food stamp program implemented in Sri Lanka. General consumption subsidies are not efficient or effective to achieve distributional objectives, and are too costly. Increasing spending on health and education programs in rural areas would help enhance longer-term growth prospects for many countries. Weak growth performance may also reflect political and social instability, however, and in countries that have recently experienced wars, such as Afghanistan, Angola, Ethiopia, Mozambique, Somalia, and Rwanda, growth prospects have been set back by extensive damage to basic infrastructure. Unfortunately, economic performance in some countries has suffered as a result of poor governance and a widespread lack of accountability in the public sector that have tended to limit popular support for stabilization and reform efforts.

Many low-growth countries are highly indebted. Despite debt-relief efforts, debt burdens continue to increase; for some countries in sub-Saharan Africa, debt-service ratios have doubled during the past decade, reaching 400 percent in 1994. For a large number of countries, even under favorable conditions, external viability is unlikely to be attained in the foreseeable future. Countries such as Angola, Central African Republic, Mozambique, and Zaïre, among others, will require timely financial support on concessional terms, including in some cases significant further debt reduction. To support and promote stronger reform efforts in a number of African countries, official and private creditors will need to ensure that excessive debt-service obligations do not weaken incentives to strengthen reforms and stabilization programs.

*   *   *

In recent years a large number of developing countries have enjoyed sustained periods of high growth. For many of these countries, success has brought new policy challenges. Their strong performance and growth potential have attracted substantial capital flows from investors in industrial countries, giving rise in some countries to macroeconomic imbalances and financial market instability. A key policy challenge for a number of these countries is to ensure that domestic saving is sufficient to meet a large part of their financing requirements. Although capital inflows often have beneficial effects, they cannot be a substitute for adequate levels of domestic saving. For countries where growth performance has been modest, the problem of low saving rates will need to be addressed by stronger fiscal adjustment efforts and structural reforms to mobilize and enhance private saving. Further trade liberalization and structural reforms will also be necessary to take full advantage of the opportunities offered by the Uruguay Round agreement, especially the increased access to industrial country markets.

IV

Disinflation, Growth, and Foreign Direct Investment in Transition Countries

Virtually all countries in transition have now embarked on serious stabilization and reform efforts. Early and bold reformers, such as Albania, the Baltic countries, the Czech Republic, Mongolia, Poland, the Slovak Republic, and Slovenia, have witnessed rapid disinflation and a resumption of growth. These countries are currently expanding at a pace approaching or exceeding average growth in the European Union. Despite a head start, performance has been mixed in Hungary. Those countries that initiated reforms later or more timidly have either only recently begun to recover—Bulgaria, the former Yugoslav Republic of Macedonia, and Romania—or have not yet seen a turnaround in measured output—Kazakhstan, Moldova, the Kyrgyz Republic, and Ukraine. In most of these countries, however, disinflation is proceeding or at least being attempted in earnest. Russia made substantial progress toward stabilization during the first half of 1994, but performance deteriorated later in the year. Several countries, including Croatia and the Federal Republic of Yugoslavia, and, more recently, Armenia and Georgia, experienced armed conflicts and hyperinflation before adopting significant adjustment measures. Azerbaijan, Belarus, Tajikistan, Turkmenistan, and Uzbekistan are still at a very preliminary stage of market reforms.

The reversal of capital flight and inflows of private capital in countries in transition has been associated with macroeconomic stabilization and progress with institutional and structural reforms. Except for a few cases, however, the scale of private capital inflows has been modest thus far. While the external viability of the transition mainly hinges on sustained domestic adjustment and reform efforts, foreign direct investment can enhance the pace and quality of growth in the transition economies. However, the scale of foreign direct investment, which is long term and non-debt-generating, will only become significant once a stable, market friendly macroeconomic and institutional environment is in place.

Financial Stabilization and Growth

In the countries that are the most advanced in the transition process, rates of economic growth have picked up and are projected to approach or exceed 5 percent in 1995 (Table 10). Fiscal performance indicators have improved considerably in some cases, although fiscal imbalances remain relatively large. Inflation is nearing the levels recorded in the high-inflation countries of the EU, despite large ongoing relative price adjustments (Box 7). Open unemployment is dropping or stabilizing below the levels prevailing in several countries of the EU.

While these are genuine achievements, several caveats are in order. Brisk growth rates may, to some extent, reflect a temporary rebound from the previous collapse of output. In some countries, relatively small fiscal deficits coexist with large quasi-fiscal deficits stemming from the off-budget financing of the losses of public enterprises. And modest public debt ratios may hide substantial contingent liabilities associated with unfunded pension liabilities or insolvent enterprises and banks. If these hidden fiscal problems were to result in excessive credit creation, disinflation might be rapidly reversed. Finally, hidden unemployment remains substantial even in some of the more successful transition countries, and open unemployment may yet rise further or anew as restructuring deepens, particularly in the large enterprise sector.

The Czech Republic is one of the few transition countries where all the main macroeconomic indicators are favorable and improving further. It now confronts the types of policy challenges faced by the industrial countries and the successful developing countries. Large capital inflows have put strong upward pressure on the exchange rate, highlighting the dilemmas associated with real exchange rate appreciation and progress toward full convertibility. While the foundations of a market economy are securely in place in the Czech Republic, further structural adjustments are needed, including by newly privatized enterprises where excess labor, weak balance sheets, and deficient corporate governance mechanisms remain widespread. The Slovak economy has now also registered an impressive turnaround. Inflation was nearly halved to 13 percent in 1994, output rose by over 5 percent, unemployment stopped rising, the current account swung into a surplus exceeding 5 percent of GDP, and the fiscal deficit declined by almost 5 percentage points to under 3 percent of GDP. Growth is projected to slow only marginally in 1995, and there is scope for further disinflation provided fiscal consolidation is continued. The dynamism of the recovery would have been even more remarkable had it not

Table 10. Selected Countries in Transition: Growth, Inflation, Unemployment, and Fiscal Balance

(Annual percent change, unless specified otherwise)

	Estimates		Projections	
	1993	1994	1995	1996
Real GDP growth				
All countries in transition	**–9.2**	**–9.4**	**–3.8**	**3.5**
Albania	11.0	7.4	6.0	5.5
Czech Republic	–0.9	2.6	3.8	4.9
Estonia	–6.6	6.0	6.0	5.3
Hungary	–2.3	2.6	0.2	1.5
Latvia	–14.8	2.0	4.6	5.0
Lithuania	–16.5	1.5	6.7	4.0
Poland	3.8	6.0	5.0	5.0
Slovak Republic	–4.1	5.3	4.0	4.0
Slovenia	1.3	5.0	5.0	5.0
Memorandum				
European Union	–0.4	2.8	3.1	3.1
CPI inflation				
All countries in transition	**675**	**295**	**127**	**19**
Albania	85	23	11	9
Czech Republic	21	10	8	7
Estonia	89	48	26	21
Hungary	22	19	28	17
Latvia	109	36	19	11
Lithuania	410	72	30	26
Poland	35	32	25	12
Slovak Republic	23	13	10	6
Slovenia	32	20	5	3
Memorandum				
European Union	3.8	3.1	3.1	2.8
Open unemployment (percent, end of year)				
Albania	30	21		
Czech Republic	3½	3		
Estonia[1]	9	8		
Hungary	12½	10½		
Latvia	6	6½		
Lithuania	4	4		
Poland	16½	16		
Slovak Republic	14½	15		
Slovenia[2]	9	9		
Memorandum				
European Union (year average)	11.1	11.6		
Fiscal balance (percent of GDP)				
Albania	–16.2	–13.4	–12.7	–12.0
Czech Republic	0.8	0.8	–0.1	0.7
Estonia[3]	–0.7	—	–2.3	–3.5
Hungary	–7.5	–6.0	–6.5	–7.5
Latvia[3]	0.6	–4.1	–2.2	–1.0
Lithuania[3]	–5.1	–4.4	–3.8	–3.5
Poland	–3.4	–3.0	–3.3	–2.8
Slovak Republic	–2.3	–2.3	–2.7	–2.6
Slovenia	0.5	0.5	–1.0	–0.6
Memorandum				
European Union	–5.9	–5.2	–4.2	–3.6

[1]Period average, based on household survey.
[2]Based on labor force survey.
[3]Includes net lending.

Box 7. Price Convergence in Transition Economies

The liberalization of the price system and the move away from the highly distorted price structure that prevailed under central planning are key steps in moving to a market economy. In virtually all the transition countries, there has been considerable progress toward formal price liberalization. For an overall domestic price measure such as the CPI, however, convergence toward market economy price levels will be a prolonged process for most countries. An important policy implication is that the gradual process of price convergence will continue to exert pressure on inflation or on the nominal exchange rate, and contribute to real exchange rate appreciation.

Following large-scale price liberalization, the prices of many tradables rose fairly rapidly toward international levels.[1] This was mostly so for nonfood products, and especially for durables, because geographical arbitrage is more difficult for perishable foods and because many staples continued to be subsidized or subject to trade restrictions. But even for basic foodstuffs, prices generally moved closer to international levels following liberalization.[2]

For nontradables and particularly for services, price convergence is taking more time.[3] Increases in the prices of services typically lagged adjustments in the prices of goods prior to broad-based liberalization, partly reflecting deliberate pricing policies, but also because price controls were easier to enforce for services than for goods (*see chart*). The initial price jump associated with large-scale price decontrol in many cases entailed a further, sharp drop in the relative price of services, as many of them remained administered and were only partially adjusted. There was a subsequent catch-up as some subsidies were reduced and as structural reforms diminished the role of the public sector in areas such as child and health care and housing. In Russia, for example, the prices of paid services rose seven times more than the overall CPI in the first three years of the transition. A very significant catch-up also occurred in Armenia, Azerbaijan, the Baltic countries, Ukraine, Kazakhstan, the Kyrgyz Republic, and Tajikistan. It was less pronounced in the Czech Republic, Hungary, and Poland, possibly because of a less distorted starting position.

In most transition economies, the depreciation of the real exchange rate in the wake of price and exchange rate liberalization went far beyond what productivity differ-

Czech Republic and Russia: Price Levels and Real Exchange Rates

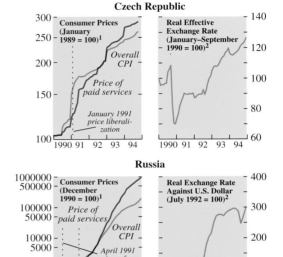

[1]Logarithmic scales.
[2]Based on consumer price indices.

entials would imply.[4] The initial depreciation, however, was typically followed by a rapid real appreciation, reflecting nominal appreciation in some cases as well as high inflation relative to trading partners. In the process, the large initial gap between domestic and international price levels narrowed significantly, although it has remained considerable three or four years into the transition in many countries.[5] As a result, and even in the presence of appropriately tight financial policies, substantial inflationary pressures persist. The implied real appreciation, which so far has not prevented rapid export growth,[6] will be sustainable if it is supported by sufficiently large productivity gains in the tradable sector.

---

[1]The prices of some commodities, including energy carriers, were often not fully liberalized and hence remained well below international levels.

[2]See Paula De Masi and Vincent Koen, "Relative Price Convergence in Russia," IMF Working Paper (forthcoming, 1995).

[3]The same phenomenon occurs in developing countries. See Bela Balassa, "The Purchasing Power Parity Doctrine: A Reappraisal," *Journal of Political Economy*, Vol. 72 (December 1964), pp. 584–96; and Paul Samuelson, "Theoretical Notes on Trade Problems," *Review of Economics and Statistics*, Vol. 46 (May 1964), pp. 145–54.

[4]See László Halpern and Charles Wyplosz, "Exchange Rate Policies in Transition Economies: In Search of Equilibrium," IMF Working Paper (forthcoming, 1995).

[5]See, for example, Anthony Richards and Gunnar Tersman, "Growth, Nontradables, and Price Convergence in the Baltics," IMF Working Paper 95/47 (April 1995).

[6]The latter also reflects the reorientation of trade once interstate trade agreements no longer constrained exports.

been for uncertainty regarding the pace of structural reforms. Privatization virtually came to a halt in late 1994 and decisions to dispose of state property have been reversed on several occasions.

Macroeconomic performance in the Baltic countries has also remained impressive.[20] The recovery of output is now well under way, with real GDP projected to grow by 5 percent or more in 1995 in all three countries. Nevertheless, large-scale privatization needs to be completed and financial sector reform accelerated, as evidenced by the failure of two large banks in Estonia. Moreover, as in other transition economies, widespread tax evasion and underground activities undermine fiscal revenues and raise equity issues.

Growth strengthened in Poland in 1994, reaching 6 percent, and is expected to remain robust during the period ahead. Exports expanded rapidly, contributing to a narrowing of the trade deficit. Labor productivity gains were substantial in the rapidly expanding private sector and also in the state sector, as a result of labor shedding in the latter. The unemployment rate, though still high at around 16 percent, has started to decline. Prices increased more than targeted in 1994, but inflation remained on a downward trend. Perseverance with a prudent fiscal and monetary stance is required to ensure further disinflation in 1995, especially in light of the pervasiveness of indexation.[21] In Slovenia, as well, growth picked up in 1994, fueled by dynamic private small and medium-sized firms. While privatization is proceeding slowly, enterprise restructuring has been relatively extensive, thus laying the foundations for a durable expansion.

In contrast to most other transition countries of central and eastern Europe, growth is expected to slow in Albania and Hungary in 1995. In Albania, the pace of expansion is likely to remain above 5 percent, notwithstanding delays in the next steps in privatization, banking reform, and the creation of a land market. Hungary stood out among centrally planned economies as a pioneer of market reforms until the late 1980s, but macroeconomic performance has not been as good as in some countries that started later. Inflation remains relatively high, in the neighborhood of 20 percent, and the recovery of output that occurred in 1994 appears to be faltering. The persistence of large fiscal and current account deficits points to the need for decisive measures to bolster domestic saving and alleviate pressure on already high real interest rates. The March 1995 devaluation and the associated fiscal package constitute an important step in that direction. Further measures will nevertheless be needed,

including a broadening of the income tax base, a reduction of the burden of the pension system, and an acceleration of privatization.

The costs of partial and inadequate reform efforts are visible in Romania and Bulgaria. In Romania, inflation slowed substantially in 1994 and output continued a gradual recovery. Privatization and structural reforms, however, have continued to lag; monetary control has been threatened by an expansion of subsidized lending to agriculture; and progress generally remains fragile. Output finally bottomed out in 1994 in Bulgaria, but prospects for a recovery of investment are poor owing to the lack of industrial restructuring. The fiscal deficit was reduced from over 17 percent of GDP in 1993 to 7½ percent in 1994, still a highly inflationary level.

In Mongolia, output turned around in 1994, and growth is expected to approach 5 percent by 1996. Inflation is slowing but has remained high. In Croatia, the stabilization program launched in the fall of 1993 has succeeded in arresting inflation, even causing a decline in the overall price level. Real GDP grew by 1¾ percent in 1994, and is projected to rise by 4½ percent in 1995. Maintaining macroeconomic stability will require restricting credit to loss-making enterprises, including by eliminating the control of banks by borrowers. The economic outlook for Croatia is also dependent on the security situation in the region. Substantial progress with stabilization has recently been achieved in the former Yugoslav Republic of Macedonia. Despite externally imposed restrictions on foreign trade, the output decline has bottomed out. However, about one third of the labor force is unemployed or on involuntary leave, and privatization has barely begun. In the Federal Republic of Yugoslavia (Serbia/Montenegro), an exchange rate based stabilization program put a sudden end to extreme hyperinflation in early 1994, but growing fiscal and quasi-fiscal imbalances spurred renewed high open inflation in late 1994.

Financial instability continued in Russia into the early part of 1995.[22] Stabilization seemed within reach in 1994, as the fall in industrial output bottomed out during the year and inflation declined to mid-single-digit levels by the summer. Financial stabilization failed, however, as the fiscal deficit widened and inflation picked up to some 17 percent a month—or over 500 percent at an annualized rate—by the end of the year (Chart 18). The loosening of financial policies that caused the resurgence of inflation stemmed from growing sectoral spending pressures and from the erosion of government revenues associated with tax arrears, numerous exemptions and deferrals, and

---

[20]See Tapio O. Saavalainen, "Stabilization in the Baltic Countries: A Comparative Analysis," IMF Working Paper 95/44 (April 1995).

[21]On January 1, 1995, the zloty was redenominated. While this has no direct economic impact, it reflects the resolve to consolidate disinflation and is a prelude to enhanced convertibility.

[22]See Vincent Koen and Michael Marrese, "Stabilization and Structural Change in Russia, 1992–94," IMF Working Paper 95/13 (January 1995).

Chart 18. Selected Countries in Transition: Consumer Prices

(Annualized monthly percent change)

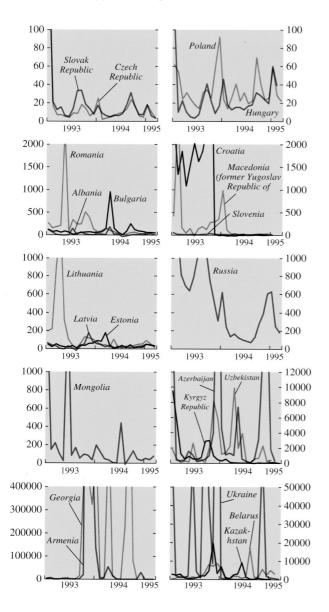

dwindling taxpayer compliance. It was also due to the unsustainable nature of some of the adjustment measures, including an excessive reliance on expenditure sequestration and arrears. The inflationary impact of the deterioration of the fiscal situation was postponed, however, by a sharp drawdown in foreign exchange reserves during the summer. The October exchange rate crisis partly reflected the market's realization that the depletion of reserves was not sustainable.[23] The breakout of open conflict in Chechnya in December 1994 added further pressures to an already difficult fiscal position. Real GDP is reported to have shrunk by another 15 percent in 1994 and is projected to decline further in 1995, although the official statistics probably exaggerate the degree of contraction (Box 8). The pace of structural change remained disappointingly slow, despite a brief pickup with the initiation of cash auctions of enterprise shares in July. Policy intentions with regard to privatization and the liberalization of external trade have at times been hard to decipher. The authorities' program for 1995, however, involves an invigoration of privatization and liberalization efforts this year, including the removal of restrictions on oil exports.

Inflation rebounded in Ukraine in September 1994, partly for the same reasons as in Russia, but also as the result of large and overdue adjustments in administered prices. From its pre-transition peak to 1994, registered output had dropped as much as in Russia while prices had risen over ten times more, mainly reflecting looser financial policies. Determined fiscal adjustment and resolute liberalization and privatization will be needed to achieve stabilization in 1995. In Belarus, some market-oriented reform measures were implemented in 1994, but several were reversed and, in contrast to neighboring countries, near-hyperinflationary conditions prevailed throughout the year. As in Ukraine and Belarus, recorded output in Kazakhstan is projected to decline further in 1995. Tightened financial policies slowed price increases in the second half of 1994, but underlying monthly inflation remained very high. The pace of structural reform has been slow but started gathering momentum around late 1994, particularly with the liberalization of bread and energy prices.

Financial stabilization was largely successful in Moldova and in the Kyrgyz Republic in 1994, allowing a sharp decrease in nominal interest rates coupled with a stable or appreciating nominal exchange rate. While output continued to decline sharply, it is expected to begin to recover in 1995. In Moldova, the fiscal situation remained difficult owing to the severe contraction in real output and a sharp increase in ex-

---

[23]See Ernesto Hernández-Catá, "Russia and the IMF: The Political Economy of Macro-Stabilization," *Problems of Post-Communism*, Vol. 41 (May/June 1995), pp. 20–27.

Box 8. The Output Collapse in Russia

According to the State Statistics Committee (Goskomstat), by 1994 real GDP had shrunk by almost half from its 1989 pre-transition peak. This decline far exceeded any contraction experienced during the previous seventy years in Russia and was much larger than the 31 percent drop in U.S. output during the Great Depression of 1929–33.[1]

While production indeed collapsed in many sectors of the Russian economy, the official figures probably exaggerate the magnitude of the plunge in aggregate output. The statistical authorities themselves recognize that, as in other transition economies, the tools at their disposal fail to capture a significant component of economic activity, particularly in the service sector and among new enterprises.[2] Corroborating evidence includes the relative resilience of household consumption and electricity use compared to officially measured GDP, and various discrepancies between financial and production indicators.[3]

Official real GDP data in Russia are derived only from the production side. By re-estimating real GDP from the demand side, based partly on new estimates of retail sales that include sales through informal channels, it is possible to capture some of the activities that are missed on the production side. These estimates suggest that real GDP declined by at most one third between 1989 and 1994 (see chart). Because these estimates are based on conservative assumptions, the actual cumulative decline could be significantly smaller.

Notwithstanding uncertainties about the precise magnitude of the output loss, a number of factors suggest that average household living standards have been less seriously affected. First, investment declined much more than consumption, partly as a reflection of the prior overaccumulation of capital. Second, many consumer goods that are no longer produced were not desired by consumers. Third, price liberalization reduced searching and

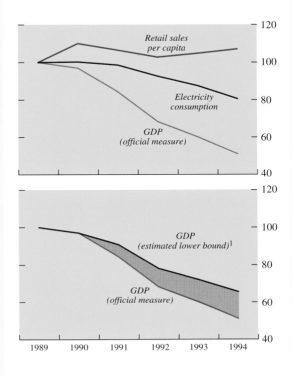

Russia: Indicators of Real Economic Activity
(1989 = 100)

Sources: Goskomstat of the Russian Federation; and IMF staff estimates.
[1]No re-estimate for 1990.

---

[1]Cumulative output declines of the same order of magnitude were reported by the statistical authorities in Ukraine and Kazakhstan. Much of the following discussion also applies to these countries.

[2]This has been pointed out by the Chairman of Goskomstat, Yurii Yurkov, in "The Statistical Mirror of the Market," *Ekonomika i Zhizn*, No. 35 (August 1994). Efforts are reportedly under way at Goskomstat to re-evaluate estimates of real GDP.

[3]For details, see Evgeny Gavrilenkov and Vincent Koen, "How Large Was the Output Decline in Russia? Alternative Estimates and Welfare Implications," IMF Working Paper 94/154 (December 1994). Electricity use per unit of output may have increased because of declines in the relative price of electricity.

queuing costs, and improved the variety and quality of available goods and services. Lastly, the demise of central planning and the gradual hardening of budget constraints on enterprises cut down on waste and other forms of inefficient resource use.

At the same time, it is important to recognize that living standards and the welfare of some segments of the population have undoubtedly suffered more than suggested by indicators of per capita output and consumption insofar as income inequality and uncertainty about employment prospects have increased during the transition.

penditures to ameliorate the effects of weather-related disasters in the third quarter. After several months of hyperinflation, bold adjustment programs were adopted by Armenia in mid-1994 and by Georgia in the autumn of 1994. Given their weak fiscal and external positions, economic reconstruction will continue to require substantial external financial assistance. In Azerbaijan, the monetization of a fiscal deficit on the order of 13 percent of GDP triggered hyperinflation, with monthly price increases exceeding

50 percent by late 1994. Financial conditions were tightened at the beginning of 1995, however, and in February the bread price subsidy was removed and energy prices were brought closer to international levels.

Except for Uzbekistan, where real GDP fell by only 2½ percent, large output declines were recorded in the central Asian countries of the former Soviet Union in 1994. In Uzbekistan, significant price liberalization measures were taken in 1994, and inflation slowed in the second half of the year as a result of stricter monetary policy. Turkmenistan effectively suffered a large negative terms of trade shock in 1994, owing to arrears on its energy exports. Some progress on exchange rate unification was achieved in Turkmenistan and Uzbekistan. In Tajikistan, most prices were freed in December 1994 and preparations for the launch of a new currency are under way.

As macroeconomic stabilization is achieved and activity turns around in the more advanced transition economies, the question arises of what is a sustainable medium-term path for inflation and output growth. Any projections in this regard are highly tentative, not least owing to the tremendous statistical uncertainty surrounding indicators of performance to date. With this caveat, sound financial policies coupled with continuing structural reforms should allow further disinflation and enable output in most transition economies to expand at a rate of 5 percent a year or more over the medium term, not least because of the considerable scope for productivity gains. Open markets will continue to be important, as exports will need to contribute substantially to overall growth in most transition economies. Growth could be even higher in those countries of central and eastern Europe where a high degree of confidence in prudent financial policies and market-oriented institutions may help to mobilize domestic saving and attract foreign investment. Conversely, medium-term growth prospects may be lower in those countries of central Asia where starting conditions are more difficult. In all cases, delays with structural reform, imprudent financial management, or protectionist measures by trading partners could result in a slower expansion.

External Viability and Capital Flows

In the early stages of the transition, capital flight, debt servicing, and the limited availability of foreign loans resulted in net outflows of capital from the former centrally planned countries.[24] In central and eastern Europe, these outflows were reversed in 1992 reflecting external assistance from official creditors,

including in the form of debt relief, and rising inflows of foreign direct investment. In Russia and the other transition countries where the transformation process is less advanced, net capital flows were in all likelihood still negative in 1994, and in all but a few cases the scale of foreign direct investment remained small. Overall, the magnitude of capital flows to transition economies has been smaller than generally expected early in the transition.[25] Total inflows amounted to $15 billion in 1993 and preliminary estimates suggest a decline to about $10 billion for 1994.

Assistance in the form of lending from the international financial institutions and debt restructuring, however, has been substantial since the onset of the transition.[26] Since the last *World Economic Outlook*, Poland has completed the restructuring of its commercial bank debt, nearly halving Poland's contractual liabilities to banks and considerably easing the debt-service burden.[27] Negotiations between Russia and London and Paris Club creditors have continued.[28]

In many transition countries, private capital inflows were initially dwarfed by capital flight. Despite the maintenance of restrictions on capital flows, the opening up of the economy enabled residents to diversify their financial portfolios away from often low-yielding or excessively risky domestic assets. Persistent macroeconomic instability created strong incentives for households and enterprises to seek safer investment opportunities. At the same time, potential foreign investors facing sizable output declines, high inflation, inappropriate exchange rate and trade policies, and other obstacles frequently have postponed investment decisions. Foreign bank loans to domestic financial intermediaries were considered risky given the lack of reliable balance sheet information, the weakness of most bank asset portfolios, and limited prudential supervision. Barriers to the entry of foreign banks in Russia and several other countries created difficulties in establishing local subsidiaries. Portfolio investment opportunities were also limited by the thinness of domestic bond and stock markets, and by the absence or weakness of capital market infrastructures. Finally, for reasons discussed below, foreign direct investment projects were slow to materialize.

---

[24]See Guillermo A. Calvo, Ratna Sahay, and Carlos A. Végh, "Capital Flows in Central and Eastern Europe: Evidence and Policy Options," IMF Working Paper (forthcoming, 1995).

[25]For an overview of estimates from various studies see Steven Symansky and Leonardo Bartolini, "Financing the Transition of Previously Centrally Planned Economies: Macroeconomic Effects on Western Europe," IMF Working Paper 94/157 (December 1994), Table 1.

[26]See the May 1994 *World Economic Outlook*, pp. 75–79.

[27]Poland also recently normalized relations with countries of the former Soviet Union through a "zero option" agreement with Russia.

[28]On a bilateral basis, Russia in March 1995 agreed to restructure Ukraine's arrears outstanding at the end of 1994 and principal falling due in 1995, amounting in total to over $2½ billion. Furthermore, Turkmenistan agreed to spread the payment of $714 million in unpaid gas bills by Ukraine over seven years.

Table 11. Countries in Transition: Indicators of External Viability, 1994

(In percent of GDP, unless otherwise noted)

	Fiscal Balance	Current Account[1]	Gross Stock of Reserves[1,2]	External Debt[1]	Debt Service[1,3]
Central and eastern Europe					
Albania	−13	−13	3	58	10
Belarus	−3	−8	—	21	9
Bulgaria	−8	−2	2	161	8
Croatia	2	2	2	21	11
Czech Republic	1	−1	4	28	14
Estonia	—	−6	3	7	—
Hungary	−6	−10	7	46	53[4]
Latvia	−4	−3	5	−3	5
Lithuania	−4	−4	3	8	2
Macedonia, former Yugoslav Republic of	−2	−10	1	32	15
Moldova	−8	−9	3	9	2
Poland	−3	−1	3	43	12
Romania	−3	−1	2	19	7
Slovak Republic	−2	5	2	31	9
Slovenia	1	3	4	26	5
Ukraine	−9	−6	1	18	7
Russia	**−10**	**—**	**1**	**32**	**5**
Transcaucasus and central Asia					
Armenia	—	−54	1	—	—
Azerbaijan	−13	−17	...	21	—
Georgia	−18	−40	—	...	—
Kazakhstan	−7	−9	4	24	7
Kyrgyz Republic	−8	−20	3	42	6
Mongolia	−5	1	3	65	14
Tajikistan	−29	−12	—	—	11
Turkmenistan	−1	21	7	17	2
Uzbekistan	−3	−9	5	27	17

[1]Generally excluding transactions or assets and liabilities among the Baltic countries, Russia, and the other countries of the former Soviet Union.

[2]In months of imports of goods and services.

[3]As a percent of exports of goods and nonfactor services, and on a cash basis.

[4]Excluding debt prepayments; including prepayment of amortization, the debt-service ratio is 63 percent.

As stabilization took hold, capital inflows rose substantially in some countries, both through repatriation of domestic funds and through new foreign financing. In the Czech Republic, the Slovak Republic, and the Baltic states, where most fundamental indicators of creditworthiness inspired confidence (Table 11), large net inflows reduced or eliminated the need for exceptional balance of payments financing and exerted strong upward pressures on exchange rates.[29] Even in Russia, capital inflows increased significantly around mid-1994 as the likelihood of stabilization seemed to improve, and as the cash privatization process got under way. This upsurge proved short-lived, however, as the stance of financial policies visibly loosened during the autumn of 1994, confidence receded, and the ruble again came under heavy downward pressure.

In Hungary, foreign capital has long played a much more important role than in other transition economies. Hungary has an impeccable debt-servicing record and a high level of international reserves, but market concerns about external viability have increased during the past year, reflecting the combination of large current account and fiscal deficits, relatively large debt and debt-service ratios, and policy uncertainties. Under these circumstances, a bold and comprehensive fiscal adjustment effort is urgently required to increase national saving and reduce the dependency on capital inflows. Even if fully implemented, the aforementioned March 1995 policy package is unlikely to prevent a further buildup in net external indebtedness in 1995; further fiscal reforms are called for.

In those countries where stabilization has not yet been achieved and private nonresidents are not yet significant asset holders, the risk is not so much that of a withdrawal of foreign capital, but rather that a confidence crisis could trigger a resumption or acceleration of capital flight, and postpone fresh capital in-

---

[29]It should be borne in mind, however, that the low debt and debt-service ratios appearing in Table 11 for some countries of the former Soviet Union reflect the transfer to Russia of U.S.S.R. debt, and arrears on debt-service payments.

flows. In a few countries, such as Georgia, net external debt has already reached disquieting levels even though private capital inflows have thus far been negligible. The best way to reduce the risk of such a confidence crisis is through sustained implementation of macroeconomic stabilization policies and structural reforms to establish the institutions of a market economy.

Foreign Direct Investment and Macroeconomic Performance

Access to foreign direct investment marks a turning point for the economies in transition, which were virtually closed off to foreign investors under central planning.[30] With reforms came the realization that foreign capital was needed to revitalize obsolete methods of production. It was expected that foreign direct investment would play a critical role, sparking and sustaining economic growth. Although foreign direct investment has increased, flows remain modest compared with earlier predictions, mainly due to the deterring effects of continuing macroeconomic instability and insufficient institutional reforms.[31]

The economies in transition stand to reap considerable benefits from foreign direct investment, although long-term economic growth primarily requires sustained financial adjustment and efforts to mobilize domestic financial resources. Domestic financial markets lack depth, however, and are plagued by adverse selection and moral hazard problems, and loans are often allocated on the basis of criteria other than creditworthiness. In such a context, foreign direct investment in the form of joint ventures, acquisitions, and new businesses—greenfields—offers access to capital that might otherwise be unavailable. Joint ventures, in particular, have facilitated the privatization process in some countries with foreign companies taking shares in formerly state-owned enterprises. In addition to the inflow of capital, foreign direct investment has beneficial effects that are particularly important during the initial stage of the transition process. These include access to modern technology, worker training, managerial know-how and accounting practices, as well as access to foreign markets. Over time, these influences will improve the productive potential of the economy.[32]

There are strong incentives for foreign firms to invest in transition countries.[33] With a population of over 420 million, these countries offer enormous potential as a consumer goods market, and firms investing early are in a better position to establish a market presence. The backwardness of infrastructure, especially in areas such as telecommunications, provides vast investment opportunities, as does participation in the tapping of natural resources, such as oil in Romania, Russia, Azerbaijan, and Kazakhstan, and natural gas in Turkmenistan. Transition countries also offer considerably lower labor costs, even after adjusting for lower productivity. An additional incentive is that using eastern Europe as a base for production meets EU criteria for content requirements, thereby providing preferential access into the EU.[34]

Foreign direct investment in all transition countries increased from about $200 million in 1989 to about $6 billion in 1993 and then fell somewhat in 1994.[35] The flows have so far been predominantly to the countries of central and eastern Europe, mainly reflecting the earlier start in the transition process. For example, in 1992–94, Hungary, the Czech Republic, and Poland accounted for more that half of the total dollar value of foreign investment (Chart 19). Data on the number of announced investment projects indicate a similar pattern (Chart 20). The Baltic countries, and especially Estonia, have attracted foreign direct investment inflows that are very large compared to the size of those economies (Box 9).[36]

In Russia and the Transcaucasian and central Asian countries, foreign direct investment has so far been very small, increasing from about $800 million in

---

[30]Subsequent references to foreign investment relate to foreign direct investment, as opposed to portfolio investment, which except for Hungary and the Czech Republic remains trivial in most transition countries compared with the emerging equity markets of Asia and Latin America. Foreign direct investment involves the ownership by a foreign entity of at least 10 percent of the ordinary shares or voting power (or the equivalent) of a domestic enterprise. See IMF, *Balance of Payments Manual* (Washington: 5th ed., 1993), p. 86.

[31]On factors influencing foreign direct investment in general, see Edward M. Graham, "Foreign Direct Investment in the World Economy," IMF Working Paper (forthcoming, 1995).

[32]For example, in Estonia, recent evidence suggests that inflows of foreign direct investment have supported productivity growth in the tradable goods sector. See Saavalainen, "Stabilization in the Baltic Countries."

[33]For a survey of incentives for firms to invest abroad, and in particular in the transition countries, see Bruce Kogut, "Direct Investment and Corporate Governance in Transition Economies," paper prepared for a Joint Conference of the World Bank and the Central European University Privatization Project held in Washington, December 15–16, 1994.

[34]Provided that 60 percent of the value be added in eastern Europe. In some sectors, however, access to the EU market remains restricted.

[35]Data on foreign direct investment are generally unreliable and should be interpreted with caution. The balance of payments statistics compiled by the IMF represent the most accurate and comparable source across countries, but they encompass cash inflows only, excluding flows in kind (such as the transfer of technology) and reinvested profits. For a detailed discussion of data problems, see Klaus E. Meyer, "Direct Foreign Investment in Central and Eastern Europe: Understanding the Statistical Evidence," CIS—Middle Europe Centre, London Business School, Discussion Paper Series 12 (June 1994).

[36]Although the overall flows to the transition countries are small compared with foreign direct investment in the developing countries, on a per capita basis, direct investment flows to many countries in central and eastern Europe during 1992–94 exceeded flows to Asia ($10), and for the Czech Republic, Estonia, Hungary, and Slovenia, the flows were larger than those to Latin America ($31).

1992 to about 1½ billion in 1994.[37] Russia and Kazakhstan have attracted well over three fourths of the total flows to these countries in value terms and about 90 percent in terms of the number of announced projects. While much of this investment has been from industrial countries, Russia has been a significant investor in the Baltic States and the other countries of the former Soviet Union. For example, Russia accounted for one fourth of foreign direct investments in Estonia in 1994. In some cases, it has been envisaged that the clearing of large arrears to Russia, notably on energy deliveries, may involve Russian direct investments in the form of debt-equity swaps.

More than half of the announced foreign direct investment projects during 1990–93 in the transition countries originated from the United States, Germany, or Austria (Chart 21). Almost half of these were joint ventures as opposed to greenfields or acquisitions. However, while many joint ventures undoubtedly represent the initial stage of legitimate foreign investment projects, some may simply be facades for illegal activities, and others may substitute for domestically financed investment—such as when offshore flight capital returns in the guise of foreign direct investment. Most of the announced projects in 1990–93 were in the manufacturing sector, particularly in electronics and transport equipment (Chart 22). In services, the largest number of announced projects was in banking and financial services.

Policy Issues Related to Foreign Direct Investment

Several factors have prevented foreign direct investment from reaching the levels anticipated only a few years ago. In many countries, macroeconomic instability, ambiguities with respect to future policies and economic reform, and weak governance have created an uncertain investment environment. The lack of a transparent and stable legal structure in most countries has been a serious impediment to foreign direct investment—not least because of the implied high transaction costs—despite steady progress to improve commercial legislation affecting foreign investors.[38] Many countries, for example, have eliminated requirements that foreign investors find domestic partners,

Chart 19. Selected Countries in Transition: Foreign Direct Investment, 1992–94[1]
(In millions of U.S. dollars, and percent of total)

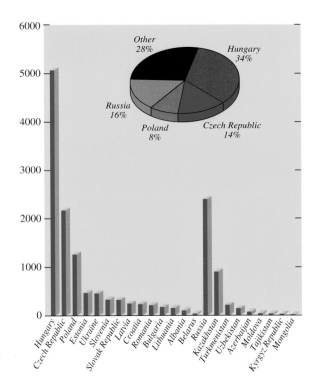

Sources: National authorities; and IMF staff estimates.
[1]Based on balance of payments definition.

---

[37]In contrast, in 1992–93, Russia received a total of $38 billion in official financial assistance. See the May 1994 *World Economic Outlook*, p. 78.

[38]Laws regulating foreign investment vary considerably across countries: the Baltic countries, the Czech and Slovak Republics, and Hungary have the most advanced legal system in terms of commercial law and property rights; Bulgaria, Romania, and Russia have made advances on particular issues but are still in need of serious reform; and Albania, Belarus, Kazakhstan, and Ukraine have only a rudimentary legal framework.

Chart 20. Countries in Transition:
Foreign Investment Projects by Host Country, 1990–93[1]
(Number of announced projects, and in percent of total)

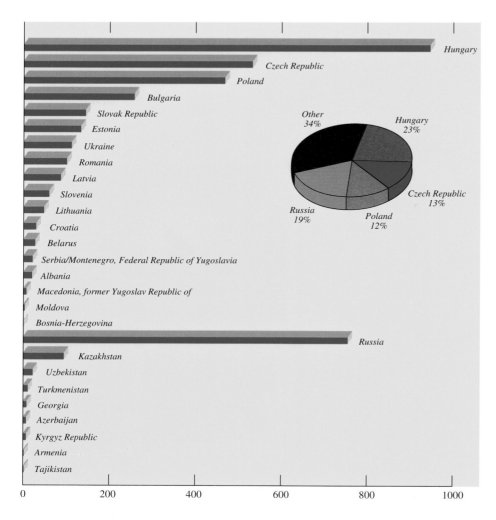

Source: Dixon & Co., *East European Investment Magazine* data base.
[1]Projects are dated when they are announced rather than when concluded, with any failed projects excluded.
Total includes projects in east Germany, except those originating in west Germany.

thus allowing wholly foreign-owned subsidiaries; adopted legislation that provides compensation for investors in case an industry is renationalized; allowed repatriation of profits; and established tax laws that clearly lay out corporate tax obligations and incentives. Further improvements are still needed, notably with respect to enforcement of legal contracts.[39]

[39]For example, since 1987, Russia promulgated about 100 laws, resolutions, and Presidential decrees formulating and strengthening the legislative framework to attract foreign capital. However, foreign investment in Russia remains modest partly due to implementation failures.

Inadequate accounting procedures and insufficient marketing and strategic planning capabilities, together with other weak business practices, have also discouraged foreign investors and made them reluctant to take on enterprise restructuring. Finally, privatization programs have often given preferential treatment to the employees of state-owned enterprises over foreign investors, reflecting the fear that domestic companies would be purchased for undervalued prices, and that jobs would be eliminated and wages cut.

To offset some of these impediments, many countries have offered generous tax breaks and other financial incentives to attract foreign direct investment,

Box 9. Foreign Direct Investment in Estonia

Foreign direct investment has contributed significantly to a vigorous recovery of output in Estonia.[1] By the end of 1994, the total stock of foreign investment was about $471 million, and the number of fully or partially foreign-owned companies grew to over 7,700 (*see chart*).[2] Finland has accounted for the largest number of these foreign-owned companies, followed by Russia and Sweden.[3] The bulk of these investments was concentrated in manufacturing (36 percent) and trade (32 percent), but foreign capital was also channeled into transport and communications (15 percent), banks (6 percent), and real estate and business services (5 percent).

Several factors underpin Estonia's relative success in attracting foreign investment compared with the other Baltic countries. Bold economic reform, currency stabilization, and a liberal trade regime created an appealing business environment. The large-scale and rapid privatization that began in mid-1993 has actively encouraged foreign investor participation, with public tender auctions making no material distinction between foreign and domestic investors. Estonia's foreign investment legislation, which is relatively more advanced than that of many other transition economies, has been transparent and generally liberal. No restrictions on capital flows or repatriation of profits exist. A foreign investment license is required only for investments in certain sectors such as mining, energy, railways, and telecommunications. In the past, various tax incentives have also attracted foreign capital. These tax incentives, which were recently eliminated, included a three-year tax holiday and a 50 percent tax reduction for the subsequent five years for investments of more than $1 million that provided at least 50 percent of a firm's capital, and a two-year tax holiday and a 50 percent tax reduction for the subsequent two years when foreign share ownership exceeded $50,000 and provided 30 percent of the capital.

---

[1]See Seija Lainela and Pekka Sutela, *The Baltic Economies in Transition* (Helsinki: Bank of Finland, 1994); and Kari Liuhto, "Foreign Investment in Estonia Since 1987—Statistical Approach," Turku School of Economics and Business Administration, Business Research and Development Center and Institute for East-West Trade, Series C Discussion 9/94 (Turku, Finland, 1994).

[2]About one third of this total value was in the form of loans and reinvested earnings. Although foreign-owned companies account for about 10 percent of all companies in Estonia, preliminary data suggest that about 20–30 percent of companies with foreign participation are not in operation.

[3]Based on the total value of foreign capital, however, Sweden has accounted for 28 percent followed by Finland (22 percent) and Russia (12 percent).

Estonia: Fully or Partially Owned Foreign Companies

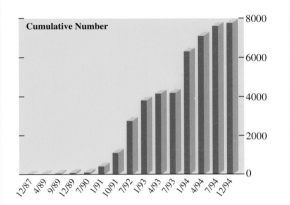

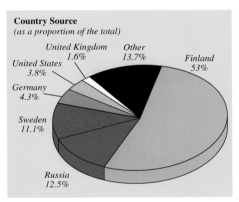

Sources: Estonian Investment Agency; and Liuhto, "Foreign Investment in Estonia."

Sweden and Finland's geographic proximity and cultural kinship with Estonia have also facilitated foreign investment from those two countries. With monthly wages in Estonia averaging about 10 percent of levels in Finland and Sweden, subcontracting labor-intensive work to Estonian subsidiaries has become an attractive alternative to outsourcing production in other low-cost countries.

---

including reduced corporate tax rates, tax holidays, and sector-specific tax exemptions. Some countries, such as Albania, Bulgaria, and Russia, have also used reductions in, or exemptions from, various customs

duties, which may be particularly important if no credit is given for value-added taxes (VAT) paid on capital goods or if VAT refunds are slow. Experience has generally shown, however, that tax incentives are

Chart 21. Countries in Transition: Foreign Investment Projects, 1990–93[1]

(As a share of total number of announced projects)

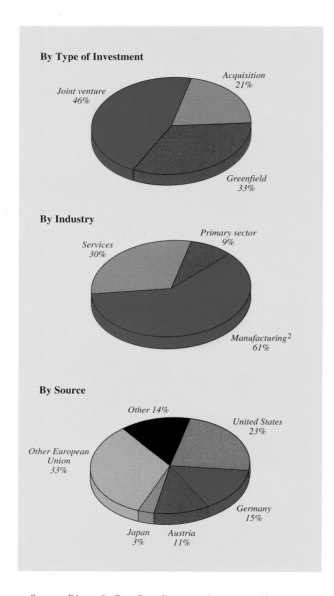

By Type of Investment

Joint venture 46%

Acquisition 21%

Greenfield 33%

By Industry

Services 30%

Primary sector 9%

Manufacturing[2] 61%

By Source

Other 14%

United States 23%

Other European Union 33%

Germany 15%

Japan 3%

Austria 11%

Source: Dixon & Co., *East European Investment Magazine* data base.

[1]See footnote of Chart 20.

[2]Includes food distribution.

not an effective way to attract foreign direct investment.[40] Although lower tax rates may improve short-term profitability, the principal beneficiaries are likely to be enterprises that are already profitable, and hence need no incentives. In the long run, there is no conclusive evidence that tax incentives boost foreign direct investment. And because tax breaks erode revenue collections, many countries that have had a widespread revenue collapse during the transition have had to eliminate these incentives.[41] Furthermore, tinkering with the tax system creates loopholes and legislative confusion, requires additional tax administration efforts, and encourages nonproductive rent-seeking behavior. As demonstrated by the Czech Republic, where such investment incentives have been avoided, foreign direct investment flows respond positively and substantially to a favorable overall economic climate.

Provided that heightened macroeconomic uncertainty does not disrupt current investment flows and cause foreign companies to abandon or postpone projects, foreign direct investment in the transition countries is likely to expand. Substantial inflows of foreign direct investment, however, are likely to raise a number of new policy issues for the recipient economies. First, in central and eastern Europe, foreign direct investment has often been concentrated in large dominant companies in oligopolistic industries, such as food processing, telecommunications, and automobiles, where investment returns are likely to be high.[42] Antitrust policies need to be strengthened to increase competition and ensure that market entry is possible. Second, foreign direct investment is often accompanied by rising imports and a deteriorating current account as investors import unavailable capital equipment. These trade deficits need not be a cause for concern because they are a reflection of capacity-increasing productive investment, in contrast to deficits associated primarily with consumer goods imports. Finally, rising foreign direct investment has both a temporary and a permanent effect on the real exchange rate.[43] Flows of foreign direct investment stimulate demand for nontraded inputs, such as labor and materials, and bid up their relative prices. Until the flows recede and relative input prices revert to their previous levels, there is a temporary real exchange rate appreciation. Such upward pressure on the real exchange rate should not be a cause for concern. Countries with considerable unemployment are less

[40]See Jack M. Mintz and Thomas Tsiopoulos, "Corporate Income Taxation and Foreign Direct Investment in Central and Eastern Europe," Foreign Investment Advisory Service Occasional Paper No. 4 (World Bank, 1992).

[41]See Chapter V in the October 1994 *World Economic Outlook*.

[42]See Kogut, "Direct Investment and Corporate Governance."

[43]See Calvo, Sahay, and Végh, "Capital Flows in Central and Eastern Europe."

Chart 22. Countries in Transition:
Foreign Investment Projects by Target Industry, 1990–93[1]
(Number of announced projects)

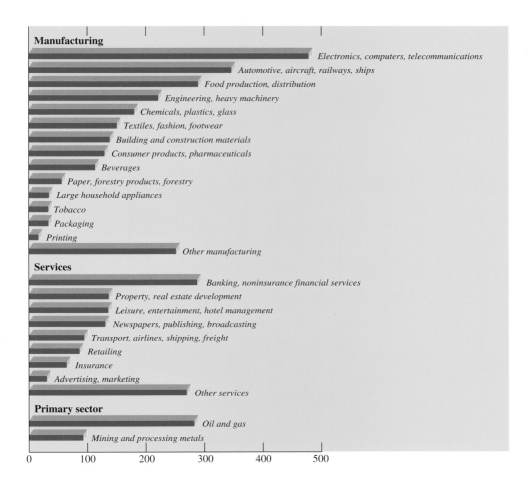

Manufacturing

- Electronics, computers, telecommunications
- Automotive, aircraft, railways, ships
- Food production, distribution
- Engineering, heavy machinery
- Chemicals, plastics, glass
- Textiles, fashion, footwear
- Building and construction materials
- Consumer products, pharmaceuticals
- Beverages
- Paper, forestry products, forestry
- Large household appliances
- Tobacco
- Packaging
- Printing
- Other manufacturing

Services

- Banking, noninsurance financial services
- Property, real estate development
- Leisure, entertainment, hotel management
- Newspapers, publishing, broadcasting
- Transport, airlines, shipping, freight
- Retailing
- Insurance
- Advertising, marketing
- Other services

Primary sector

- Oil and gas
- Mining and processing metals

Source: Dixon & Co., *East European Investment Magazine* data base.
[1]See footnote of Chart 20.

likely to experience these relative price shifts, whereas those with low unemployment, such as the Czech Republic, are more susceptible. At the same time, increases in foreign direct investment add to the domestic capital stock thus improving the marginal productivity of labor, which implies a permanent real appreciation. Attempting to prevent such real exchange rate movements would slow the adjustment process by interfering with and distorting relative prices.

* * *

Many transition economies have made significant progress toward the objectives and policy require-

ments set out in the Interim Committee's October 1994 Madrid Declaration. Stabilization and reform efforts have been sustained in virtually all of the countries that started early on the road to a market economy. In the others, the costs of delaying the introduction of financial discipline and bold systemic changes have become increasingly apparent in terms of hyperinflation and continued output declines. These countries are now beginning to implement belated, but serious, adjustment measures. Even in the few countries that continue to hesitate to undertake decisive market-oriented reforms, partial progress is being made in areas such as price and exchange rate liberalization.

Notwithstanding the progress to date, continued financial prudence and substantial further institution building will be required in the years ahead, even in the most advanced countries in transition. In most countries, there has been insufficient progress in the areas of enterprise privatization and restructuring and in financial sector reform. The social safety nets necessary to cushion the effects of such changes are often still far from adequate, thus contributing to the postponement of critical reforms. The contribution to growth of spontaneous capital inflows, particularly in the form of foreign direct investment, will be commensurate with the soundness of the macroeconomic fundamentals, the extent of structural transformation, and the success in strengthening and mobilizing domestic saving, which remain the key to economic recovery and the realization of potentially high medium-term growth prospects.

V

Saving in a Growing World Economy

Saving is the process by which an economy sets aside part of its output and uses it to generate income in the future. Individuals, corporations, and governments save. Households set aside money for home ownership and for retirement, businesses store up earnings to construct new factories, and governments build up assets in public pension systems and infrastructure. Aggregate savings provide the ultimate constraint on global investment spending, and therefore play a critical macroeconomic role as well. Since investment spending provides a key link to productivity and real income growth, there must be an adequate supply of saving for the world economy to advance at an acceptable pace.

With today's large potential investment demands, especially in emerging market economies in the developing world and among the countries in transition from central planning, the question naturally arises whether the supply of saving will be adequate to finance worthwhile projects around the world. The question is made sharper because of growing pressures on savings. Since the early 1980s, government absorption of private sector saving has increased sharply, and the retirement-age populations of some industrial countries are starting to increase rapidly. Meanwhile world real interest rates in the mid-1990s are already high by historical standards. What are the trends in world saving patterns and how important is saving for economic growth? What are the main determinants of saving and why do saving rates vary across countries and over time? To what extent can international capital flows allow countries to borrow savings from abroad? To what extent is a "saving shortage" already putting upward pressure on world interest rates? And what policies might be used to encourage more saving? These issues are the focus of this chapter.

Saving is an enormously complex issue and many aspects of the process are still not well understood. There are disagreements even about the basic definition of saving, and there are myriad data problems.[44] Most definitions, for example, view saving as a resid-

ual concept—as income less consumption, or in an international context, as investment demand minus net capital inflows. As a result, measures of saving can vary greatly because of small differences in the measurement of other difficult-to-measure concepts. Further, many assumptions that are necessary to test key hypotheses about saving, such as assumptions that financial markets offer flexible opportunities for borrowing and saving, or that world capital markets are well integrated, may simply not be justified. In short, it is not surprising that analyses of the saving process do not produce the clean, conclusive results that policymakers might like.[45]

Trends in Saving Patterns

Long-run historical data on saving patterns suggest that before the 1920s most industrial countries, including Australia, Canada, France, Japan, and the United Kingdom, had very low gross national saving rates—in the range of 10 to 15 percent of GDP.[46] The exception was the United States, which as early as the 1870s had a saving rate of almost 20 percent. While the U.S. saving rate stayed remarkably constant over most of the twentieth century until the 1980s, virtually all other industrial countries and fast-growing developing countries have seen their saving rates move up to the 20 percent range. A few, such as Japan, China, and some of the newly industrializing Asian economies have had rates that exceeded 30 percent.

The world saving rate climbed steadily over the 1960s, driven partly by rapid increases in Japan's saving rate. The saving rate registered twin peaks during the oil price spikes in the 1970s, and has fallen no-

---

[44]For the Fund's standard definition of saving, see Commission of the European Communities, IMF, OECD, UN, and World Bank, *System of National Accounts 1993* (Brussels/Luxembourg, New York, Paris, and Washington, 1993), p. 206.

[45]For the analysis of trends in global saving, an important issue is the choice of weights for aggregation. Japan, for example, has a high saving rate and a much higher weight of world GDP using current exchange rates than it does using purchasing-power-parity (PPP) exchange rates. Some high-saving developing countries, on the other hand—especially China—have a much larger weight in world GDP using PPP weights. In this chapter, the convention is to use PPP weights, which more accurately reflect the real resources behind the saving concept. However, current exchange rates are relevant for actual financial flows among countries.

[46]See Angus Maddison, "A Long-Run Perspective on Saving," *Scandinavian Journal of Economics*, Vol. 94, No. 2 (1992), pp. 181–96.

Chart 23. World Saving Rate[1]
(In percent of GDP; PPP basis)

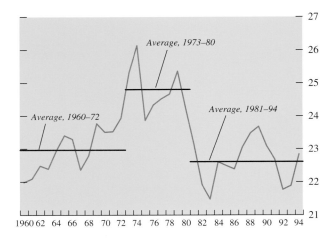

Average, 1973–80

Average, 1960–72

Average, 1981–94

[1]Data before 1970 represent less-than-complete country coverage.

Chart 24. Major Industrial Countries: Gross National Saving Rates[1]
(In percent of GDP; PPP basis)

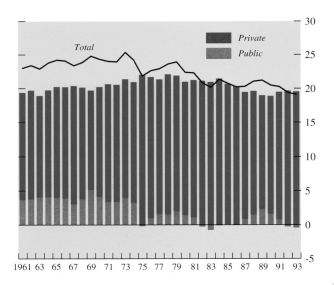

Total

Private
Public

[1]Data prior to 1963 exclude France.

ticeably since 1980 (Chart 23). Statistical tests find evidence of structural breaks in the level and trend of the world saving rate after 1972 and again after 1980, so it is convenient to look at saving behavior over three time periods: the pre-oil shock years, 1960–72; the period of adjustment to the oil shocks, 1973–80; and the post-oil shock period, 1981 to the present. Using this breakdown, the world saving rate averaged 23 percent in the first period, increased to 25 percent in the oil-shock period, and then declined to 22½ percent in the most recent period. Over 1992 and 1993, the most recent years for which there are historical data, the world saving rate averaged just 21¾ percent—down over 2 percentage points from the late 1960s and 1970s.

What sectors were responsible for this decline in the saving rate in the 1980s? Breaking down the national saving data for the major industrial countries—which account for roughly half of world saving—into private and public saving reveals that *virtually all of the decline took place in public sector saving* (Chart 24). For these countries, the private saving rate averaged 20 percent in both the 1960–72 and 1981–93 periods.[47] But the public saving rate fell from 4 percent of GDP in the 1960–72 period, to just ½ of 1 percent in the 1981–93 era. Declines in the public saving rate occurred in every major industrial country except Japan.

In contrast to the industrial countries, the average national saving rate in developing countries has shown a sharp upward trend—from about 19 percent of GDP in 1970 to 27 percent today (Chart 25). Much of the boost has been due to increases in Asian countries. The saving rate for developing Asian economies rose by over 10 percentage points, from 21 percent in 1969 to over 31 percent in 1993, mainly because of increases in private saving rates. Some developing countries that have been successful in sustaining high growth rates have even seen their saving rates double over the past twenty years or so, including Chile, Korea, Malaysia, and Thailand. In contrast, there was a decline in the saving rate in Africa, largely attributable to a falling public saving rate. The aggregate saving rate in developing Western Hemisphere countries rose during the 1970s, but has been declining since 1989, mainly because of decreases in private saving rates. Among the factors responsible for the fall in the saving rate in these countries were the surge in capital flows and financial liberalization, which resulted in increased access to domestic and foreign borrowing.

Saving trends in many eastern European countries in transition are hard to analyze because of data limitations. Saving rates in these countries were high before transition, largely because limited consumption

---

[47]Private sector saving rates actually have been falling in several of these countries, especially the United States and Canada, but the increasing GDP weight of high-saving Japan tends to camouflage this in the aggregate for the major industrial countries.

opportunities led to so-called forced saving. Private saving rates have probably been declining during the early phase of transition. Household saving rates have fallen because of negative income shocks, and business sector savings have almost certainly diminished, although data limitations make quantification difficult.[48] Most of these countries have also experienced significant government dissaving—on the order of 5 to 15 percent of GDP a year. There is little doubt that aggregate saving rates in these countries are much lower than they were before transition.

Chart 26 shows the relationship between per capita income levels and the gross national saving rate for the period 1989–93. These data suggest that national saving rates tend to increase sharply as per capita income increases, and that saving rates level off or even decline somewhat in high-income economies. Very low saving rates are most often observed in low per capita income countries, in part because subsistence limits the ability to save. The tendency of saving rates in middle-income countries to rise substantially is noticed particularly among newly industrializing Asian economies. And the leveling off of saving rates (or even declines), are most noticeable in such high per capita income countries as Canada, the United Kingdom, and the United States.

When thinking about the overall supply of saving to meet world investment demands, it is both the actual quantity of saving and the ability for it to move across international borders that matters. Predictably, the largest suppliers of gross saving are also the largest economies (Chart 27). Japan and the newly industrializing Asian economies supply proportionally more saving than the size of their GDPs would suggest, while the United States supplies less. The fact that the industrial countries supply about half of total world saving clearly understates their role, since most of the developing countries and the transition countries are still less than fully integrated into world financial markets. It is still the industrial countries that dominate world capital markets, an issue that will be taken up below.

Important Questions About Saving

Does Saving Cause Growth or Does Growth Cause Saving? One of the most striking regularities in cross-country data is the relationship between the rate of saving and the growth of output. High-saving countries generally grow faster than do low-saving countries (Chart 28). Fourteen of the world's 20 fastest growing economies over the past ten years had a saving rate over 25 percent, and none had a saving rate

Chart 25. Saving Rates
(In percent of GDP; PPP basis)

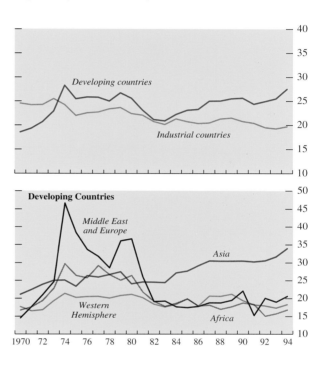

---

[48]There are also some forces working to increase saving rates, including a move to private pensions, which encourages individuals to save more for their retirements.

Chart 26. Gross National Saving Rates and Per Capita Income Levels[1]

(Average, 1989–93)

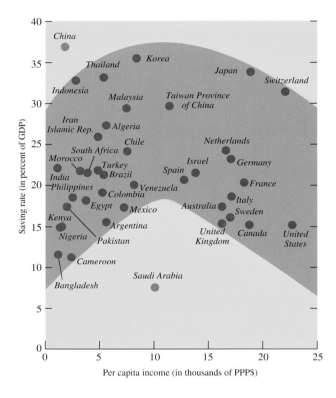

under 18 percent. Meanwhile 8 of the world's slowest-growing 20 economies over the same period had a saving rate below 10 percent, and 14 were below 15 percent.[49] But the linkage from saving to economic growth is not ironclad. Some countries have had very high saving rates and comparatively low economic growth—Switzerland, for example—while others have experienced healthy economic growth despite a relatively low saving rate, at least for a period of time. Chile, for example, has enjoyed over 6 percent average annual real GDP growth over the past ten years, while its saving rate has averaged just 18 percent.

Understanding the direction of causation that underlies the relationship between saving and growth is difficult—indeed, there is good reason to believe that there are positive effects running in both directions. The positive effect of saving on growth is the more straightforward: higher saving raises the growth rate of output by increasing capital accumulation.[50] The traditional policy recommendation flowing from this view is that in order to increase the pace of economic growth, countries need to think first about boosting their saving in order to spur capital formation.

Empirical evidence suggests that income growth also has a positive effect on saving. Visual examination of data from the high-saving, high-growth countries of east Asia, for example, suggests that these countries experienced high growth *before* their saving rates rose. In the 1950s, 1960s, and early 1970s, for example, increases in saving rates in Japan and Korea lagged a few years behind increases in GDP growth rates (Chart 29). And the slowdown in Japanese growth in the late 1960s was followed by a decline in the saving rate. Recent research, including statistical causality tests, increasingly points in the direction of a link from growth to saving.[51] The experience of the industrial countries, where saving rates fell in the presence of slow output and productivity growth following 1973, is also consistent with this view.

While the latest research on the causality between growth and saving may not be totally conclusive, the data suggest that there may be a virtuous circle between growth and saving. Increases in growth raise the saving rate, which in turn feeds back to increase growth. This has potentially broad ramifications. It might suggest that an acceleration of growth in developing countries is possible even in the absence of an

[49]These calculations exclude war-torn countries and countries of the former Soviet Union and eastern Europe, for which the quality of the saving rate data may be unreliable.

[50]This is the interpretation of the data presented in N. Gregory Mankiw, David Romer, and David N. Weil, "A Contribution to the Empirics of Economic Growth," *Quarterly Journal of Economics*, Vol. 107 (May 1992), pp. 407–37.

[51]See, for example, the Granger causality tests conducted by Chris Carroll and David N. Weil, "Saving and Growth: A Reinterpretation," *Carnegie-Rochester Conference Series on Public Policy*, Vol. 40 (June 1994), pp. 133–92.

initial jump in saving, if say, the boost came from technology transfer.[52] It would also suggest that much of the saving that fast-growing developing countries will need in the future to fund their investment needs will probably be self-generated.

What Is the Right Amount of World Saving? Is It Possible to Save Too Much? According to some, the world economy saves and invests too little, and more saving would always be better. The world economy today *would* benefit from higher saving and investment rates, but it *is* theoretically possible for the world to save too much. The question of optimal saving belongs in the domain of welfare economics and growth theory, where the answer depends to a large extent upon subjective judgments, such as the weights one would give to the interests of different households, generations, or countries. Theoretical growth models have been used to identify "golden rules"—saving and investment rates that would lead to optimal economic growth under hypothetical conditions. In one formulation, additional increases in the saving rate increase welfare as long as the rate of return (determined by the supply of saving) exceeds the rate of population growth. In another variation, a higher saving rate improves welfare as long as the dividend flow from investment projects is positive. Both of these conditions easily hold for the world economy today, suggesting that too much saving is hardly a problem.

While oversaving is theoretically possible in a closed economy and might lower domestic welfare, excess saving by one country may be invested in other countries in a world of open capital markets. The other countries would benefit from lower interest rates and more capital formation, and hence would enjoy higher economic growth. However, such a situation would also be characterized by trade imbalances that could fuel perceptions of unfair trading practices and lead to political frictions and financial market pressures. In practice, there may therefore be limits on the extent to which a country can accumulate assets abroad.[53]

Why Do Some Countries Save So Much? Will They Continue to Do So? Chart 30 shows the world's highest- and lowest-saving economies in each decade since 1960.[54] At the top of the list are Japan, Korea, Taiwan Province of China, and China. The extremely high saving rates of a set of east Asian economies is re-

---

[52]There is an extensive economic growth literature that assesses the impacts of factors such as macroeconomic stability, technology transfer, trade policy, and education. See also Box 6.

[53]Small countries may be relatively unconstrained in their ability to accumulate assets abroad.

[54]Prior to economic transformation, eastern European economies, the Baltic countries, Russia, and other countries of the former Soviet Union were high-saving countries owing to forced savings. Because of data comparability issues, however, they are not included in these comparisons.

Chart 27. Share of World Output and Saving, 1993
(In percent; PPP basis)

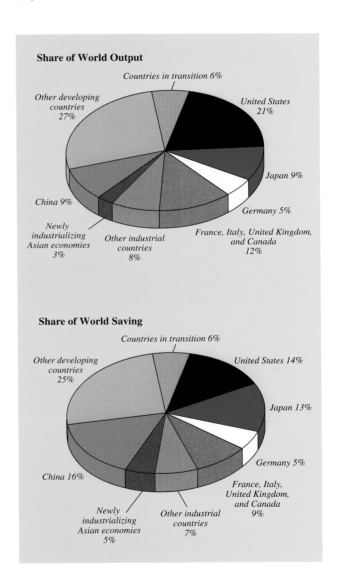

Share of World Output

Countries in transition 6%
Other developing countries 27%
United States 21%
Japan 9%
Germany 5%
France, Italy, United Kingdom, and Canada 12%
Other industrial countries 8%
Newly industrializing Asian economies 3%
China 9%

Share of World Saving

Countries in transition 6%
Other developing countries 25%
United States 14%
Japan 13%
Germany 5%
France, Italy, United Kingdom, and Canada 9%
Other industrial countries 7%
Newly industrializing Asian economies 5%
China 16%

Chart 28. Saving Rate and Per Capita Real GDP Growth[1]

(Average, 1973–93)

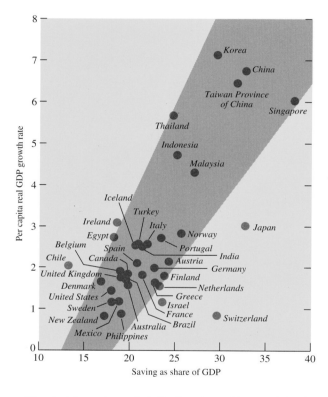

[1]The shaded area is merely indicative of a positive correlation between the saving rate and the real per capita GDP growth.

markable: Japan's saving rate averaged 34 percent in 1990–93, Korea's 35 percent, China's 37 percent, and Taiwan Province of China's 29 percent. In the absence of these "supersavers," the world saving rate would be significantly lower. For example, if Japan's saving rate in 1993 had fallen to the 16 percent average rate of the other major industrial countries, the world saving rate would have been 1½ percentage points lower. Among the lowest-saving countries are Zaïre, Côte d'Ivoire, and Cameroon. Perhaps the most interesting case is Korea, which was one of the world's lowest-saving countries in the early 1960s, and one of the highest-saving countries in the 1980s and 1990s.

The importance of these high-saving countries raises the questions of why this phenomenon is observed, and whether it can be expected to continue. Numerous causes have been suggested for high saving. In several east Asian countries, government policy has favored saving, either through public saving, mandatory private saving, restrictions on consumer access to credit, or the provision of widely accessible savings vehicles. Many observers have suggested that cultural factors are at work, and while that may be part of the explanation, it is not the complete story. For example, there is little evidence of high saving in east Asia before World War II, while in the late nineteenth century the United States stood out as a relatively high-saving country.[55]

No fully convincing case can be made for any one explanation for high saving, but a natural suspect is high growth, as described earlier. If fast growth does promote saving, then future saving may be expected to fall, at least in one high-saving country, Japan. Japanese growth over the period 1970–93 averaged 4¼ percent a year. While a return to high growth in Japan cannot be ruled out, it seems unlikely since the process of catching up has been largely completed. In addition, the population in Japan is starting to age more rapidly, and this will also work to reduce the Japanese saving rate. Overall it seems very likely that the Japanese saving rate will show steady erosion over the coming years. On the other hand, there does not appear to be any strong reason why China's saving rate will not remain high for some time, especially if growth remains high.

Key Factors Affecting Saving

To better understand the likely future supply of world saving, the key factors that influence saving behavior should be examined. There have been two fun-

---

[55]Maddison does find evidence of a high saving rate in Taiwan Province of China early in the twentieth century. See Maddison, "A Long-Run Perspective on Saving."

damentally different theoretical views about the prime motivation for saving. In one view, saving is seen as resulting from a choice between present and future consumption.[56] Individuals compare their rate of time preference to the interest rate, and smooth their consumption over time to maximize their utility. The interest rate is the key mechanism by which saving and investment are equilibrated. The other view sees a close link between current income and consumption, with the residual being saving. In this view, saving and investment are equilibrated mainly by movements in income, with the interest rate having a smaller effect. A hybrid view attempts to reconcile consumption smoothing with the income determination of consumption, by seeing a concept of permanent income as driving the consumption process.

The extensive literature on the determinants of saving is still open on many key questions, including whether there is substantial intertemporal smoothing of consumption, as held by the first view, or whether consumption (and hence saving) is mainly determined by current income patterns, as held by the second view. The thorny question of causality between income growth and the saving rate, as discussed earlier, also remains indeterminate. And the impact of changes in the real interest rate on the saving rate is theoretically and empirically ambiguous: there is both a positive substitution effect and a possibly negative income effect (if, for example, a rising interest rate causes a drop in the required contributions to a defined benefit pension plan), and empirical studies usually find little effect. Public pensions also might affect private saving, because they might substitute for private pension contributions, but again the empirical evidence is mixed.

The literature has reached tentative conclusions on other saving issues. Empirical research has tended to reject the notion that swings in government fiscal position are fully offset or matched by private savers (so-called Ricardian equivalence) for both industrial and developing countries.[57] The typical result is a roughly one-half offset, although some researchers find a larger offset among countries with particularly high rates of government dissaving. The literature generally finds a negative impact of financial liberalization on saving behavior in industrial countries, although the effect should be transitory. New outlets for financial saving may become available and encourage saving, but the loosening of constraints on borrowing is usually viewed as the dominant factor at least in the

Chart 29. Japan and Korea: Growth and Saving Rates[1]

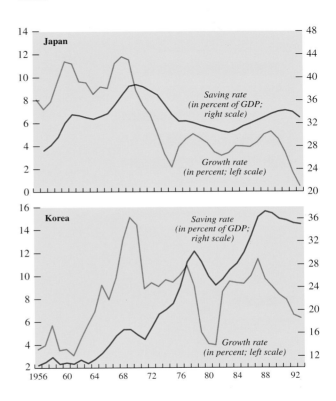

[1]Three-year centered moving average.

[56]See Irving Fisher, *The Theory of Interest* (New York: Macmillan, 1930).

[57]See Douglas Bernheim, "Ricardian Equivalence: An Evaluation of Theory and Evidence," in *NBER Macroeconomics Annual 1987*, ed. by Stanley Fischer (Cambridge, Massachusetts: MIT Press, 1987), and Vittorio Corbo and Klaus Schmidt-Hebbel, "Public Policies and Saving in Developing Countries," *Journal of Development Economics*, Vol. 36 (July 1991), pp. 89–115.

Chart 30. Highest- and Lowest-Saving Economies[1]

(In percent of GDP, averages over ten-year intervals)

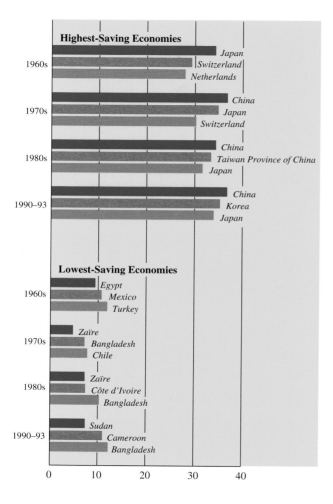

[1]Excluding economies in transition and major oil exporting countries.

short run.[58] The literature also finds generally ambiguous effects of taxation on saving behavior. This is because taxes and saving subsidies work through their effects on the real after-tax interest rate, and as mentioned above, the saving rate shows little sensitivity to changes in the real interest rate.

Age-specific effects on saving are generally found to be significant. The life-cycle model, where saving is seen as providing for retirement, predicts that the saving rate should decline as the retired proportion of the population increases. This result is often extended to those below labor-force age as well, with the general result that a higher share of dependents implies a lower saving rate. Finally, a temporary improvement in the terms of trade is considered to increase the saving rate, because it suggests a boost in transitory income. This effect can be huge if the swing in the terms of trade is large. For example, the oil shocks of the 1970s represented a massive shift in the terms of trade in favor of oil exporters and led to sharp though temporary increases in the world saving rate. The funds that flooded into OPEC (Organization of Petroleum Exporting Countries) coffers simply could not be spent as rapidly as they mounted.[59]

For developing countries, there are some further determinants of saving. Outlets for financial saving are more limited because capital market imperfections are more widespread, financial markets are less developed, a lack of confidence in the banking system may exist, and interest rates tend to be heavily regulated. As a result, and because of liquidity constraints and subsistence considerations, the effect of the interest rate on saving tends to be weaker. This effect may also vary with income and wealth, with countries closer to subsistence levels less able to substitute intertemporally (Box 10).

In many developing countries, foreign saving can be a determinant of total saving because foreign borrowing is rationed. Although foreign saving can promote growth by increasing the total saving available for investment, it may partially replace national saving by raising domestic consumption. There is some empirical evidence of a negative relationship between domestic saving and foreign saving in certain developing regions.[60] Some studies suggest that capital flows to major Latin American countries on average have *lowered* national saving rates, whereas flows to high-

---

[58]See Tamim Bayoumi, "Financial Deregulation and Household Saving," *Economic Journal*, Vol. 103 (November 1993), pp. 1432–43.

[59]A large decline in the price of oil may also tend to raise the world saving rate temporarily as the gainers may take longer to adjust their spending patterns than the losers, particularly if the latter are financially constrained.

[60]See Alberto Giovannini, "Saving and the Real Interest Rate in LDCs," *Journal of Development Economics*, Vol. 18 (August 1985), pp. 197–217.

Box 10. Saving and Real Interest Rates in Developing Countries

There is little consensus on the size or significance of the response of saving to changes in real interest rates in developing countries. This may reflect data problems, the lack of sophistication and depth in domestic financial markets, or regulations that limit the scope for market-determined interest rates in many low-income developing countries. Most important, perhaps, is that interest rates may have little or no impact simply because household saving may be essentially zero in countries that are at or near subsistence income levels.

Recent studies have attempted to estimate the interest rate sensitivity of household saving in developing countries using macroeconomic data. This sensitivity depends on how easily households can substitute their consumption over time—technically, the *intertemporal elasticity of substitution* in consumption. In contrast to other studies, the approach adopted does not require the interest sensitivity of saving to be equal across countries with different per capita incomes, which is consistent with subsistence considerations, and allows relative prices of imports and home goods to enter into households' saving decisions.[1] A temporary reduction in import prices may reduce saving since the price of imports is a component of the consumer price index, whose changes over time (like the change in interest rates) affect incentives to consume today or to save in order to consume more in the future.

The results suggest that the household saving rate in upper middle-income developing countries is likely to in-crease significantly as interest rates move up, and the response is unlikely to be very different from what would typically be observed in industrial countries. However, the interest elasticity of saving varies considerably with the level of wealth in the way predicted by the subsistence model: in low-income countries, the interest elasticity of private saving is close to zero, but it rises markedly in low middle-income countries, and increases further in upper middle- and high-income countries. Financial liberalization—and the resulting increases in interest rates—may have a number of positive effects, including increasing the efficiency of investment and strengthening economic growth, but the direct impact of such policies on household saving behavior is likely to be relatively small in low-income countries. Increasing national saving in such countries may require an alternative strategy. The experience of a number of high-performing east Asian economies highlights the role of prudent fiscal policies, low inflation, and macroeconomic stability as important means of increasing national saving.[2] In addition, trade liberalization and other structural reforms strengthen price signals, help financial resources flow more efficiently, stimulate the growth of productivity and output, and hence promote saving.

[1]See Jonathan D. Ostry and Carmen M. Reinhart, "Private Saving and Terms of Trade Shocks," *Staff Papers* (IMF), Vol. 39 (September 1992), pp. 495–517; and Masao Ogaki, Jonathan D. Ostry, and Carmen M. Reinhart, "Saving Behavior in Low- and Middle-Income Developing Countries," IMF Working Paper 95/3 (January 1995).

[2]See World Bank, *The East Asian Miracle: Economic Growth and Public Policy*, Policy Research Report (New York: Oxford University Press for the World Bank, 1993). Compulsory saving programs may also have been effective in boosting saving in some Asian countries. Other factors that may have contributed to high saving rates in the Asian countries included effective prudential supervision of banks, which enhanced confidence in the financial system, and regulation of interest rate spreads, which may have lowered the costs of financial intermediation.

growth Asian countries have arguably added to national saving and increased overall investment.[61] Another important source of external saving in poorer developing countries is foreign aid. Empirical evidence on the impact of foreign aid on saving is mixed, although it tends to be negative. Recent studies suggest that about 40 percent of foreign aid on average goes into consumption, reflecting the fact that in most cases foreign aid goes to countries where per capita income is low and subsistence considerations dominate saving decisions.[62]

A background study carried out by the staff for this chapter has tested how these kinds of factors might in-fluence the private saving rate.[63] The study performed both time-series and cross-section regressions using panel data for 21 industrial countries and 64 developing countries over the period 1971–93. The analysis found that most standard economic variables are correctly signed and generally significant. Higher output growth, higher real interest rates, and improved terms of trade tended to increase the private saving rate, whereas increases in government surplus, greater wealth, higher per capita income relative to the United States (a proxy for catch-up effects in growth), and a higher fraction of young and old all suggested a lower private saving rate. Generally speaking, the study found less support for standard saving theories among lower-income developing countries, perhaps because of less reliable data.

[61]See Chapter IV of the October 1994 *World Economic Outlook* and Chapter III of the present issue.

[62]See Victor Levy, "Aid and Growth in Sub-Saharan Africa: The Recent Experience," *European Economic Review*, Vol. 32 (November 1988), pp. 1777–95, and *Adjustment in Africa: Reform, Results, and the Road Ahead*, World Bank Policy Research Report (New York: Oxford University Press for the World Bank, 1994).

[63]Paul Masson, Tamim Bayoumi, and Hossein Samiei, "Saving Behavior in Industrial and Developing Countries," in *Staff Studies for the World Economic Outlook* (Washington: IMF, forthcoming 1995).

Box 11. Pension Reform in Developing Countries

Pension systems differ in the way they finance and provide pensions, in whether they fix benefits or contributions, and in whether they are run by the state or by the private sector. In most countries, pension systems are state run and offer benefits that are determined by law rather than by lifetime contributions. These unfunded, defined benefit systems operate on a pay-as-you-go basis that transfers resources from the contributors to the beneficiaries.

Although unfunded public pension systems may have advantages over privately run, fully funded systems in terms of the extent of coverage, the protection of the retirees, and equity considerations, there are well-known problems with these systems. The lack of a direct relationship between benefits and contributions can seriously strain government budgets; wage taxes may distort labor markets and encourage tax evasion; and the aging of populations, especially in industrial countries, is increasingly making these systems unsustainable in the long run.

Several developing countries, in particular in Latin America, have increasingly moved toward fully funded pension schemes, while some east Asian countries have used such schemes for a number of years.[1] Chile, where the traditional pay-as-you-go system had developed a host of problems by the late 1970s, has adopted the most far-reaching reforms. Pension reform began in 1981 when the fiscal surplus was sufficiently large to finance the transition to a fully funded system, and after the retirement age was increased to 65. A privatized savings plan was introduced whereby workers were required to place 10 percent of their earnings in any one of a number of highly regulated intermediaries; at retirement, they could choose between a sequence of phased withdrawals or an annuity. There are indications that the increase in the retirement age and the fiscal consolidation that accompanied the reforms contributed importantly to

the subsequent surge in private saving and to a strengthening of potential and actual growth.[2]

Moreover, Chile's capital markets have been deepened by creation of a market for indexed annuities, by the steady flow of contributions into investment funds, and by significant improvements in the functioning of capital markets. The reforms have also insulated the pension system against the possible budgetary risks of a state-run defined benefit systems. Administrative costs—roughly 30 percent of mandatory saving—are high relative to a single compulsory system, however, partly because of the costs of competitive attempts to attract customers. Moreover, in contrast to a defined benefit system, uncertainties regarding the length of working life, the duration of retirement, and the return on invested contributions make pension benefits somewhat unpredictable.

Pension reform is also being discussed or implemented elsewhere in Latin America. In Colombia, the 1993 pension reform overcame many of the flaws of the previous system by reducing net benefits paid to future pensioners and by gradually phasing in a dual pay-as-you-go, fully funded system.[3] In Brazil, one proposal based on the Chilean experience would raise the retirement age to 65 and substitute a fully funded system based on individual accounts for the current pay-as-you-go system; another proposal would combine defined benefit and defined contribution schemes in order to protect retirees and reduce the fiscal cost by preserving a partial pay-as-you-go system. In Argentina, the minimum retirement age was raised to 65, phased in over a number of years, and a privately capitalized system was introduced in July 1994. The privately administered pension funds, which presently cover some 6.3 million enrollees, co-exist with the pay-as-you go system, pre-

[1]See Patricio Arrau and Klaus Schmidt-Hebbel, "Pension Systems and Reforms: Country Experiences and Research Issues," *Revista de Analisis Economico*, Vol. 9 (June 1994), pp. 3–20.

[2]See Peter Diamond, "Privatization of Social Security: Lessons from Chile," *Revista de Analisis Economico*, Vol. 9 (June 1994), pp. 21–33; and references in *The Chilean Economy: Policy Lessons and Challenges*, ed., by Barry Bosworth, Rudiger Dornbusch, and Raul Laban (Washington: Brookings Institution, 1994).

[3]See Klaus Schmidt-Hebbel, "Colombia's Pension Reform: Fiscal and Macroeconomic Implications," Policy Research Department (Washington: The World Bank, October 1994).

Among the staff study's main conclusions are that changes in government fiscal position seem to lead to only a partial offset in private saving. A simple average of both industrial and developing country results suggest a value of about three fifths—considerably below the unity implied by full Ricardian equivalence and in line with other estimates in the literature. Another conclusion is that demographic effects are significant and have generally worked to increase saving rates over the past twenty-five years. A third finding is that there does appear to be a positive association between GDP growth and the saving rate, and in addition, there is

some evidence that the saving rate may flatten out or even decline at high per capita income levels. The study also finds that changes in the terms of trade have a strong positive effect on saving. For developing countries, foreign saving reduces private saving, but increases total saving available for investment. Finally, the study concludes that a 100–basis-point increase in the real interest rate causes the saving rate to increase by a bare 0.2 percent of GDP in industrial countries.

With respect to changes in public saving, three factors can be distinguished: business cycle effects in the short run, political will to contain the accumulation of

dominantly for older contributors who preferred to remain in the existing system.

Several east Asian countries have used variations of the defined contribution system, in part as a tool of development policy.[4] The pension systems in Malaysia and Singapore rely primarily on provident-fund, fully funded, defined contribution schemes, where compulsory contributions are maintained in a central fund with separate accounts for individual contributors. Upon retirement, benefits consist of accumulated contributions plus interest and take the form of a lump-sum payment. Compulsory coverage is generally restricted to wage earners in the formal sector, and those with low wages or with short employment records receive limited coverage. One of the virtues of provident-fund systems is that they may generate higher saving. While it is possible that voluntary private saving may be reduced as compulsory saving increases, the experience of Malaysia and Singapore, where national saving rates typically exceed 30 percent, suggests that provident funds may have contributed to high overall national saving rates.

The experience of developing countries that have reformed their pension systems indicates that a combination of mandatory fully funded schemes with supplementary defined benefit arrangements relieves pressures on budgets while providing protection for retirees. The mandatory, fully funded pillar of the system may lead to higher saving by making people more aware of the need to save for the future, and through forced saving. It is also likely to deepen capital markets through private sector participation in the investment of pension funds. To the extent that reforms lead to higher saving, they are likely to have a positive effect on growth. The increased capital market deepening that results from the reforms is also likely to contribute to higher output growth, which in turn would generate higher saving.[5]

---

[4]See Frederick Ribe, "Funded Social Security Systems: A Review of Issues in Four East Asian Countries," *Revista de Analisis Economico*, Vol. 9 (June 1994), pp. 169–82.

[5]The experience of reforms in relatively high-income developing countries may not be applicable to low-income countries because of the less-developed institutional and financial environment.

public debt in the medium term, and structural government obligations in the long run. Business cycle effects will not be discussed because of the medium- to long-run focus of this study. Over the medium term, however—say five to ten years—it seems that reasonably major shifts in public saving are possible if political will is strong. Over the longer term, the most important government obligation by far is public pension liabilities.[64] As of 1990, it was estimated that the present value of net pension liabilities for the major industrial countries on average exceeded 130 percent of their GDP.[65] With aging populations, a financing crunch seems unavoidable, and only a few choices are available. Countries might increase contribution rates, which would tend to increase directly the public saving rate. They could reduce pension benefits over time, which would probably cause the private saving rate to increase as workers sought to provide some private offset for the reduced benefits. They could try to shift responsibilities back to the private sector (Box 11). Or countries could raise the retirement age—another way to reduce benefits—which would cut the dependency ratio, lead to fewer aggregate retirement years, and likely give an upward boost to the private saving rate.[66] The overall outcome is hard to predict, but as countries begin to address their pension difficulties, it seems likely that both public and private saving rates will have to increase.

Future Supply of Saving

Overall the prospects for world saving over the next fifteen or twenty years are not necessarily grim, especially if rapid growth in high-saving countries can be sustained. The key will be what happens to public saving. Private saving rates, as mentioned, have remained roughly flat over the past three decades, and will probably not experience any sharp upward or downward movement over the next couple of decades. The world public saving rate fell sharply after 1980, however, and was the dominant cause of the overall decline in the world saving rate over the period 1981–93. Even a modest swing in the world's public saving position over the next couple of decades will probably dominate other movements.

Perhaps surprisingly, world population trends are not likely to have a major overall effect on the world private saving rate over the next twenty years. There will be gradual further declines in the aggregate private saving rate in industrial countries because of steady increases in their dependency ratios.[67] On av-

---

[64]This issue was discussed in the October 1993 *World Economic Outlook*, pp. 56–62.

[65]This estimate is by Paul Van den Noord and Richard Herd, "Pension Liabilities in the Seven Major Economies," OECD Working Paper 142 (Paris, December 1993).

[66]Having to pay for fewer retirement years by itself would tend to reduce the private saving rate, but the more dominant force is probably the higher income, which would tend to cause the private saving rate to increase.

[67]Some have argued that with the post-World War II baby boom cohort now moving into the 45–60 year age bracket, which arguably has a high saving rate, industrial country saving rates may soon be boosted. While this is possible, it would appear risky to make such an assumption. Aggregating across many industrial countries greatly reduces the peaking effect of the baby boom—the Japanese boom, for example, was much later than the one in the United States. Also most studies find that other forces often dominate demographic effects.

erage, the dependency ratio in industrial countries will increase from about 66 percent in 1995—about its trough level—to roughly 70 percent by 2015, which should tend to reduce the industrial country saving rate by less than 1 percentage point (Chart 31).[68] The effect on Japan will be much more noticeable: its dependency ratio will increase by roughly 20 percentage points, which should cause the Japanese saving rate to decline by roughly 3 percentage points—say from 33 percent to 30 percent if other things remain equal.[69]

But this drop in the private saving rate in the industrial countries is likely to be offset by steadily falling dependency ratios in developing countries.[70] After peaking at more than 120 percent in 1970, the average dependency ratio in developing countries has been dropping steadily, and should continue to drop over at least the next twenty years according to United Nations demographic projections. Between 1995 and 2015, for example, the dependency ratio will drop from about 90 percent to about 70 percent, which could raise the developing country private saving rate by about 3 percentage points. Given that developing countries represent approximately one third of world GDP on a PPP basis, this increase should roughly offset any private saving decline in the industrial countries. Moreover, the developing country share of world GDP is likely to increase substantially over the next twenty years, and that in itself should also boost the world saving rate.

The impact on the saving rate of increases or decreases in real interest rates is likely to be fairly small. The effect of economic growth—as captured through the stages of economic development effect—is hard to quantify. While the private saving rates in maturing economies may decline somewhat, new groups of countries should achieve economic takeoff and experience sharp increases in their saving rates. It is difficult to predict which countries will grow fastest, but it certainly is not inconceivable that fast growth and saving surges in countries like Brazil, China, India, or Indonesia could offset or even dominate saving declines in countries like Japan or France.

The key factor that will influence the future supply of world saving is the fiscal position of governments, which remains a big unknown. Suppose, on the one hand, that governments cut their deficits and increased their public saving rates to one half of the major indus-

Chart 31. Dependency Rates[1]

(Youth and elderly as percent of working age population)

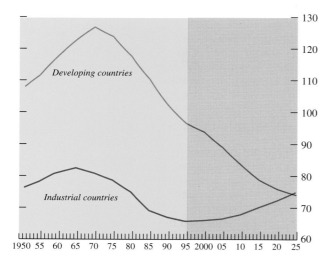

[1]The blue shaded area indicates the United Nations population projections.

---

[68]Other studies, including previous Fund research, have found larger effects on the saving rate.

[69]This estimate for Japan uses the staff study's combined panel results for all countries.

[70]The increase in the dependency ratio for industrial countries mainly reflects an increase in the elderly population, whereas the drop for the developing countries reflects a reduction in the share of children. These developments have very different implications for future investment needs for education and health care. In addition, there is uncertainty about whether higher saving from reduced youth dependency rates will in fact more than offset the fall in saving from higher elderly dependency rates.

trial country rate in the 1960–72 period—to 2 percent. That would represent an increase in the public saving rate of about 1½ percentage points of GDP (compared with the 1981–93 average saving rate of ½ of 1 percent of GDP), and with roughly a one-half private sector saving offset, would suggest an increase in the world saving rate of about ¾ of a 1 percentage point. Or suppose that governments increased their public saving rates all the way to the 1960–72 average rate of 4 percent of GDP. That would represent an upward shift of government saving of 3½ percentage points, which after the private saving offset would give an upward boost of roughly 1¾ percentage points to the world saving rate.

On balance, the future supply of world saving depends upon two critical variables: the pace of economic growth among developing countries and the amount of public dissaving among industrial countries. If some large developing countries grow rapidly and experience high saving rates, and if the industrial countries return to their public saving rates of the 1960–72 era, the world saving rate could easily increase by 2 to 4 percentage points—despite steady declines in private saving rates in Japan and other industrial countries. This might be called the optimistic saving scenario. On the other hand, a pessimistic saving scenario might develop: in the face of stagnant economic growth in key developing countries and even larger budget deficits in industrial countries, the world saving rate could decline by an additional 2 or 3 percentage points over the next fifteen to twenty years.

Limits on Borrowing the Saving of Others

It has been argued that the amount of saving supplied and demanded by developing countries and countries in transition may be a key force that will influence world real interest rates. If countries with high demands for saving enter the world capital market, the world real interest rate will rise, while the interest rate will fall if countries with potential surplus saving enter the market. Recent attention has focused on the possibility that eastern Europe, the former Soviet Union, and developing countries with newly liberalized capital markets will absorb large amounts of world saving over the coming decades.

In assessing the importance of these new capital demands, a key question is the potential volume of such saving flows. Generally speaking, the net flow of saving to a given country will be a function of the gap between domestic savings and domestic investment demand at the world interest rate, the country's size, and the openness of its capital market to international flows (Box 12). This openness, in turn, will depend on institutional characteristics, such as legal restrictions on profit repatriation or foreign ownership, and on the premium over world interest rates demanded by foreign investors.

Massive net flows of saving from one country to another remain the exception rather than the rule even after substantial financial liberalization. Feldstein and Horioka, for example, found in 1980 that national rates of saving and investment were highly correlated—a fact that has been interpreted as evidence that changes in domestic savings translate mostly into corresponding changes in domestic investment, and not into capital flows.[71] More recent research has found that the correlation between national saving and investment has been slowly falling over time.[72] Work done at the Fund suggests that part of the reason for the high correlation between domestic saving and investment ratios is that some governments attempt to target the current account and adjust fiscal policy accordingly.[73] An additional reason is that financial markets may be unwilling to finance large current account deficits on a sustained basis. (A corollary is that investment demands in most successful developing countries will almost always be funded largely by domestic saving; given the apparent link between economic growth and saving described earlier, this may be natural to expect and not necessarily worrisome.)

Historical experience may suggest an upper bound on the potential magnitude and sustainability of net capital inflows, and their possible effects on world interest rates.[74] Measured relative to GDP, Korea was perhaps the most extreme case of a net capital importer in the postwar period. Over the 27 years from 1953–80, Korea's net capital inflows averaged 9 percent of GDP a year. Although the eventual outcome for Korea has been quite favorable, sustained capital inflows of this magnitude did lead to a severe balance of payments problem in the late 1970s, which required an adjustment effort supported by the Fund. Mexico's net capital inflow averaged almost 7 percent of GDP over the period from 1991–94 and, as illustrated by recent events, also appears to have been in the danger zone. On the other hand, net capital inflows into Canada averaged 7 percent of GDP a year over the 43-year period

[71]See Martin Feldstein and Charles Horioka, "Domestic Saving and International Capital Flows," *Economic Journal*, Vol. 90 (June 1980), pp. 314–29.

[72]See, for example, Michael Mussa and Morris Goldstein, "The Integration of World Capital Markets," in *Changing Capital Markets: Implications for Monetary Policy*, a symposium sponsored by the Federal Reserve Bank of Kansas City, 1993. See also Martin Feldstein and Philippe Bacchetta, "National Saving and International Investment," and Jeffrey Frankel, "Quantifying International Capital Mobility in the 1980s," both in *National Saving and Economic Performance*, ed. by Douglas Bernheim and John B. Shoven (Chicago: University of Chicago Press, 1991).

[73]See Bayoumi, "Financial Deregulation and Household Saving"; and Michael Artis and Tamim Bayoumi, "Saving, Investment, Financial Integration, and the Balance of Payments," in *Staff Studies for the World Economic Outlook* (IMF, September 1990), pp. 19–35.

[74]The historical data in this section come from Maddison, "A Long-Run Perspective on Saving."

Box 12. Cross-Border Capital Flows and Capital Market Integration

Capital market *integration* is best thought of as the cross-border integration of markets for tradable financial securities, and to a lesser degree, as the integration of markets for physical capital (direct investment) and bank loans and deposits. Capital market integration means *accessibility* to foreign financial markets, where accessibility is measured by the direct and indirect costs associated with transacting in a foreign financial market relative to the costs of a similar transaction in the domestic market. Capital market *efficiency* has a number of meanings, many of which are viewed as synonymous with capital market integration, but the efficiency of financial markets is only part of the integration process. Capital flows provide a measure of the desire to invest capital abroad but are only indirect barometers of accessibility, efficiency, and thus of capital market integration.

The scale and growth of securities transactions between residents and nonresidents provide a good measure of accessibility to foreign capital markets. As a rough indicator, close to 50 percent of equity transactions for firms located in the European Union takes place outside the home country, and one out of every seven trades worldwide involves a foreigner as a counterpart.[1] In addition, cross-border financial transactions in most industrial countries expanded from less than 10 percent of GDP in 1980 to well in excess of 100 percent of GDP in 1992 (*see table*). Issuers of securities have increasingly turned to international securities markets. The outstanding amount of international bond issues rose from $574 billion in 1985 to $2 trillion in June 1994. Over the same period, international bank loans tripled to $4 trillion.[2]

Secondary market turnover of fixed income securities through the international securities clearers, Euroclear and Cedel, has also accelerated in recent years. Turnover of $4 trillion in 1987 had increased to $21 trillion by 1993, an average annual growth of 31 percent.[3] Turnover of equities in domestic markets by, or on the behalf of, foreign-based investors rose from $73 billion in 1979 to $1½ trillion in 1990.[4] In comparison, turnover of equities and bonds on the New York Stock Exchange fell from $1.87 trillion in 1987 to $1.76 trillion in 1992, an average annual decrease of 1.4 percent.

Trading in the global foreign exchange (forex) market has accelerated in tandem with international securities

Cross-Border Securities Transactions
(As a percent of GDP)

	1980	1992
United States	9.3	109.4
Japan	7.0	69.9
Germany	7.5	91.2
France	8.0	122.0
Italy	1.1	118.4
United Kingdom	266.0	1015.8
Canada	9.6	113.1

Sources: Bisignano, "Internationalization of Financial Markets"; and IMF staff estimates.

transactions. Most estimates put current turnover at around $1 trillion a day in the global forex spot market, a 25-fold increase since 1980.[5] The current level of activity in foreign exchange markets is much too large to be accounted for by the growth in world trade in goods and services. Rather, it reflects the tremendous increase in world trade in financial assets. Use of exchange-traded and over-the-counter derivative instruments also points to the integration of capital markets. The outstanding amount of currency swaps grew by five and a half times between 1988 and 1994, reaching over $1 trillion. The notional amounts outstanding of currency forwards, futures, and options displayed similar growth, reaching over $10 trillion in 1994.[6]

A driving force behind the growth in cross-border financial market activity has been the institutionalization of savings. The most important nonbank financial participants in the forex market are institutional investors. Total assets of the 300 largest U.S. institutional investors rose from 30 percent of U.S. GDP in 1975 ($535 billion) to more than 110 percent of GDP in 1993 ($7¼ trillion).[7] Similar growth of total assets under management has occurred in other industrial countries. The importance of the institutionalization of savings for capital market integration is that it underpinned a shift toward international diversification of portfolios. This factor may be at least as important in the capital market integration process as financial deregulation, technological developments, and other "supply-side" factors. Cross-border equity holdings in the United States, Europe, and Japan increased from $800 billion in 1986 to $1¼ trillion in 1991, while total cross-border ownership of debt and equity holdings is estimated at $2½ trillion in 1991. Foreign ownership of government debt securities also points to the integration of capital markets (*see table opposite*).

[1]See Morris Goldstein and Michael Mussa, "The Integration of World Capital Markets," IMF Working Paper 93/95 (December 1993).

[2]See Joseph Bisignano, "The Internationalization of Financial Markets: Measurement, Benefits and Unexpected Interdependence," *Cahiers Economiques et Monétaires*, Banque de France, Vol. 43 (1994), pp. 9–71; and Bank for International Settlements, *International Banking and Financial Market Developments* (Basle, various issues).

[3]See Eurostat, "Ecu Statistics," *Monetary and Financial Statistics* (Luxembourg: Statistical Office of the European Communities, April 1994).

[4]See Philip Turner, "Capital Flows in the 1980s: A Survey of Major Trends," BIS Economic Papers No. 30 (Basle: Bank for International Settlements, April 1991).

[5]See Morris Goldstein and others, *International Capital Markets: Part I. Exchange Rate Management and International Capital Flows*, World Economic and Financial Surveys (IMF, April 1993).

[6]Bank for International Settlements (Basle).

[7]The figures on institutional investor behavior are taken from *Institutional Investor* (July 1994) and the sources cited in previous footnotes.

Government Debt Held by Foreign Investors

(As a percent of outstanding amount)

	1979	1992
United States	18.5	20.4
Japan	2.3	5.6
Germany	5.0	25.9
France	0.0	31.8
Italy	1.2	6.1
United Kingdom[1]	11.4	12.5
Canada	15.0	27.7

Sources: Bisignano, "Internationalization of Financial Markets"; and IMF staff estimates.

[1]1985 and 1991, respectively.

Cross-border positions as a percent of portfolio assets differ markedly by country. For example, mutual funds in Germany and the United Kingdom had foreign asset holdings that were well over 30 percent of managed assets in 1991, whereas U.S. mutual funds' foreign securities holdings were under 7 percent of managed assets. These cross-country differences in foreign security holdings may reflect the infancy of the capital market integration process. However, despite the relatively small fractions of foreign assets in institutional investors' portfolios for some countries, the magnitude of the underlying assets translates into potentially large international portfolio holdings—the 100 largest institutional investors in Europe and in the United States had about $1 trillion of foreign investments in tradable securities in 1991. Based on recent trends, their holdings of foreign securities as a percent of gross assets may well double between 1991 and 1996. In addition, institutional investors have diversified significantly into emerging markets during the 1990s.

There are a variety of formal approaches to measuring the trend and level of the capital market integration process. One approach is simply to identify barriers to capital flows, including regulatory barriers such as capital controls and limits on foreign ownership, and also less tangible barriers such as language, information, and relevant cultural differences. But because barriers can often be avoided to varying degrees, a key problem with this approach is that it does not provide a measure of capital market integration that is easily quantifiable.

A second approach is to examine the extent to which returns on similar assets that are traded in different markets have been equalized, presumably by capital flows. Most of these "law-of-one-price" tests study the equality of nominal or real interest rates on short-term government bonds across countries. Tests for equality of nominal interest rates when currency risk is hedged in the forward market—covered interest parity—suggest that there has been a convergence of (covered) interest rates in the 1980s, especially for countries that have removed capital controls. Industrial countries are further along in the integration process than developing countries, based on departures from covered interest parity, although many developing countries exhibit a high degree of capital mobility as well.

A third approach is to compare actual investment portfolios with the highly internationally diversified portfolios that standard finance theory predicts in an integrated global capital market. The increase in cross-border transactions and holdings of foreign securities does suggest a trend toward integrated capital markets. The interesting question, however, is, How far have portfolios moved toward an "optimally diversified portfolio?" The answer, it turns out, is not very far.

Empirical studies indicate that investors in major industrial countries still have a strong "home-asset preference," implying limited international diversification. U.S. investors, for example, hold about 94 percent of their equity holdings in the form of U.S. securities; in Japan, the United Kingdom, and Germany, the percentages exceed 85 percent; and the 300 largest pension funds in the world had only about 7 percent of their assets in foreign securities in 1991. In addition, domestic ownership on the five largest stock exchanges is very high: 92 percent in the United States, 96 percent in Japan, 79 percent in Germany, 89 percent in France, and 92 percent in the United Kingdom.[8] Many reasons have been put forward to explain this home-asset preference—transactions costs, externally imposed prudential limits on foreign assets, uncertainties about expected returns, and unfamiliarity with foreign markets and tax laws—but the fact remains that the capital market integration process has a way to go.

Another approach to draw inferences from these co-movements about capital mobility and financial market integration is to study co-movements of certain variables either within a country (e.g., savings and investment) or across countries (e.g., consumption and stock indices). Although the hypothesis of high capital mobility is typically rejected, all of these tests rely on a number of strong assumptions that may color conclusions about capital market integration.

Despite the clearly impressive trends in the capital market integration process, we are a long way from a world capital market. One reason for this is that, as Morris Goldstein and Michael Mussa put it: "Nearly fifty years after Bretton Woods, less than one fifth of the IMF's 178 member countries and territories voluntarily refrain from either restricting payments or using separate exchange rates for some or all capital account transactions." Even for the industrial countries with few barriers to cross-border investment, the scale of international diversification is limited. Except for the wholesale markets for heavily traded, highly liquid, largely default-free financial assets, international integration of asset markets for the broader categories of world saving and wealth appears to be limited.

---

[8]See Kenneth R. French and James M. Poterba, "Investor Diversification and International Equity Markets," NBER Working Paper No. 3609 (Cambridge, Massachusetts: National Bureau of Economic Research, January 1991).

from 1870 to 1913, and Australia has habitually recorded net capital inflows of between 1½ and 4 percent of GDP over most of the past century. These data suggest that in terms of broad orders of magnitude, a net capital inflow in the range of 4 to 6 percent of GDP may be sustainable under the right circumstances.[75] Even so, those circumstances are rarely present. A key factor that influences the sustainability of large net inflows is the degree to which the external resources add to overall investment and are invested profitably. Experience also shows that the form of the capital flow—foreign direct investment, portfolio investment, or bank lending—might make some difference.

Of course, the other factor that determines the size of net capital flows is the supply of saving by capital exporters. Before World War I, the big net capital exporter was the United Kingdom. Over the 1870–1913 period, its net investment abroad averaged 4½ percent of GDP a year. In recent decades, Japan and Germany have been large saving exporters. But the biggest sustained net capital outflow in history as a percentage of GDP was arguably from Taiwan Province of China in the 1980s, which averaged 9½ percent of GDP. Today the net supply of capital from industrial countries that is available for developing countries is constrained because most capital goes to other industrial countries. Chart 32 shows which countries supplied net capital to the world (defined as average current surplus) over the five-year period from 1989–93, and which countries were the largest users of those resources. These data suggest that Japan was by far the world's dominant supplier of net capital to the world over this period, and that the United States was the dominant net user. Indeed, the magnitude of the bilateral capital flow from Japan to the United States—about $80 billion a year—represented about a third of the total world net flows of capital over this period.[76] Other heavy users of world capital have been the United Kingdom, Canada, Mexico, Spain, Italy, and Australia. The chief reason for such heavy capital flows to these and other industrial countries has been large government budget deficits. Over the 1989–93 period, net capital flows to developing countries averaged close to $100 billion a year—only about 1 percent of developing country GDP and only about 18 percent of the aggregate in-dustrial country budget deficits over these same years.[77]

With the discipline of financial markets limiting the effective demand for capital by developing countries, and with the large absorption of industrial country saving by other industrial countries limiting the supply, net capital flows to developing countries are likely to remain relatively modest. As a result, capital flows to developing countries should have only small effects on world interest rates. Much more important will be the future budget paths in the larger industrial countries. Although capital flows to developing countries increased substantially over the 1991–93 period and hit $161 billion in 1993, the flow slowed to $134 billion in 1994 and will slow even further in 1995. The surge likely was related to the sharp and prolonged industrial country recessions over this period.[78] With sharply reduced industrial country investment demands and historically low interest rates, returns in developing countries looked very good and attracted saving from industrial countries. But with the industrial countries now showing good forward momentum again and the uptick in interest rates in the United States and some other industrial countries, flows to traditional industrial country markets have been picking up, and flows to developing countries have started to decline.[79] This phenomenon is reducing capital flows to emerging market stock and bond markets.

In any case, it is far from obvious that developing countries need large amounts of foreign capital to develop successfully. While the benefits from large inflows of foreign direct investment can be substantial, it is important to note that the investment projects that attract foreign direct investment often tend to be financed to a large extent by complementary financing raised in the host country.[80] In contrast, history suggests that even if large portfolio or debt-raising capital flows were available, as they were in the wake of the oil price increases of 1974 and 1979, for example, they probably would not be sustainable. Besides, the large capital inflows may increasingly substitute for national saving and might also cause the stock of foreign debt to increase relative to GDP.

Admittedly, the special capital requirements of the countries in transition may justify a relatively large-scale use of foreign saving. However, if the conditions and incentives are not in place to encourage national

---

[75]There is some reason to think that abundant natural resources, whose value is well-known to foreign investors, may make larger net capital inflows more sustainable. Large energy and mineral reserves may have been important in making the capital flows into Australia and Canada sustainable, for example. This factor might also become important for Russia and other resource-rich countries of the former Soviet Union.

[76]This is interesting given that Japan was only a small supplier of net savings to the world over most of the past century—becoming a big player only since about 1980—and that the United States has been a *supplier* of net savings over almost the entire twentieth century until the late 1970s.

[77]Of course, some developing economies were net exporters of capital over this period, especially Taiwan Province of China, Hong Kong, and China.

[78]Portfolio diversification forces were also at play, but were probably of secondary importance.

[79]See Chapter III for a more detailed discussion of the outlook for capital flows to developing countries, and the risks and consequences of a significant slowdown.

[80]See Graham, "Foreign Direct Investment in the World Economy."

saving and investment, then economic performance will remain unsatisfactory, and that will bring into question the ability of these countries to service their foreign debt. As mentioned, when capital inflows exceed a range of 4 to 6 percent of GDP, even highly successful developing countries, such as Korea, have sometimes had trouble making principal and interest payments on their foreign debts. On the other hand, once the proper institutions, financial market instruments, and incentives to save have been established, domestic saving is likely to increase on its own because of the dynamics of the growth process, and should go a long way toward meeting domestic investment needs. In short, if developing and transition countries maintain a good overall policy mix, foreign saving can provide a boost to capital formation and can help to promote economic growth, but most investment spending is likely to be self-financed.

Global Real Interest Rate as an Indicator of Saving Adequacy

Economic theory and national accounting conventions require that saving has to equal investment, and one of the equilibrating mechanisms that brings this equality about is the interest rate. A high real interest rate suggests that investment demands are putting pressure on saving. A low real interest rate suggests an adequate supply of saving relative to investment demands. With current real interest rates high by the standards of the past one-third century, many feel there is at least prima facie evidence of a saving adequacy problem (Chart 33).

Rather than using a spectrum of national interest rates to analyze trends, the increased integration of the world's capital markets suggests using a single global interest rate. Such a global interest rate is of course synthetic—there is no world interest rate to be observed because each country issues its own bonds in its own currency. Instead, a global interest rate can be thought of as the underlying dominant factor that ties together the various observed national interest rates and implicitly equilibrates supply and demand in all markets simultaneously.[81] There are several ways of constructing such a global interest rate. The proxy for the global interest rate used below is a simple weighted average of interest rates for eight countries that were deemed to have effectively open capital markets over the period 1960–93. A short-term (three-month) real interest rate was constructed using ex post inflation, and a long-term (usually ten-

Chart 32. Largest Suppliers and Users of Net Capital Flows, 1989–93
(Current exchange rates; as shares of total net capital flows)

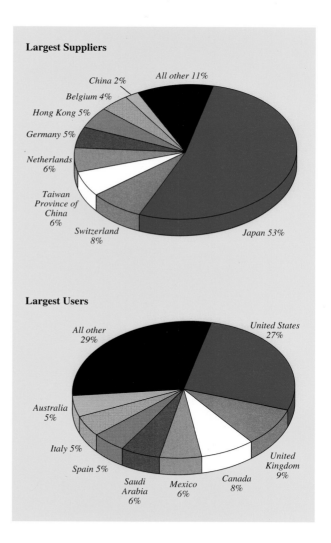

---

[81]This global interest rate is not like the return on a risk-free asset, to which various risk premiums would be added. Rather it is a weighted-average interest rate, with some country interest rates above it and some below it. National interest rates will always differ to the extent that there are differences in factors such as political risk, foreign exchange risk, and taxation policies.

year) real government bond rate was constructed using a long-memory measure of inflation expectations.

Both short- and long-term global real interest rates were markedly higher in the 1980s and 1990s than in the 1960s and 1970s. In keeping with the breaks in saving trends noted earlier, three distinct regimes appear during this 35-year period: (1) a regime of low and fairly stable real interest rates between 1960 and 1972, (2) an oil-shock-adjustment regime between 1973 and 1980, and (3) a regime of high real interest rates from 1981 to the present. The global long-term real interest rate averaged about 3 percent in the first regime, about ½ of 1 percent during the second regime, and about 4¾ percent in the third regime. The global long-term real interest rate declined somewhat over the early 1990s, probably reflecting industrial country recessions. The rate seems to have returned to the range of 4 to 5 percent since 1994 and shows no statistical evidence of a regime shift since 1981. The global short-term real interest rate averaged about 1¼ percent during the 1960–72 regime, fell to about negative 1¼ percent during the turbulence of the oil-shock regime, but increased dramatically to average 4 percent in the 1981–93 period. Real short-term interest rates have diverged considerably across countries since the beginning of this decade, with some countries pursuing more expansionary monetary policies than others. Nevertheless, the global short-term real interest rate has been between 2 and 3 percent since 1991.

While the oil-shock period presents an analytical challenge because of the possibility that markets persistently underestimated inflation, a more relevant comparison is between the 1960–72 and 1981–93 periods. The evidence suggests that the global short-term real interest rate has been about 250 basis points higher in the latter period, and that the long-term real interest rate has been about 175 basis points higher. How can this increase in short- and long-term global real interest rates be explained? One obvious answer, that there was an exogenous upward shift in world investment demand, cannot be completely ruled out but seems unlikely. The ratio of ex post world investment to world GDP was lower in the 1981–93 period than it was in the 1960–72 period (see Chart 23). Instead, it appears that the high degree of public dissaving over the 1980s and 1990s has been a key factor. To quantify this and other effects, the staff constructed a simple model of the global short-term real interest rate that looks at three categories of determinants: economic environment factors, government budget policy, and monetary policy.[82]

Among the economic environment factors are a change in the world rate of return on productive capacity (perhaps due to a technological shift or some other innovation), financial market liberalization, and

Chart 33. Global Short-Term and Long-Term Real Interest Rates
(In percent)

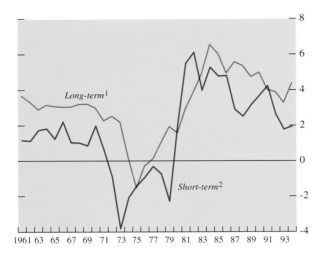

1961 63 65 67 69 71 73 75 77 79 81 83 85 87 89 91 93

[1]GDP-weighted average of ten-year (or nearest maturity) government bond rates for the United States, Japan, Germany, the United Kingdom, Canada, Belgium, the Netherlands, and Switzerland minus long memory inflation estimate.

[2]GDP-weighted average of three-month treasury bill note for same countries minus actual inflation.

---

[82]See Thomas Helbling and Robert Wescott, "Determinants of the Global Real Interest Rate," IMF Working Paper (forthcoming, 1995).

the removal or relaxation of capital controls (both internal and external). Increases in the world economy's rate of return, measured via an aggregate stock market return measure, would tend to increase the world real interest rate. In the simplest terms, if stock markets start offering higher returns to investors, bond issuers will have to raise interest rates to attract funds.[83] Financial liberalization, as discussed earlier, might also tend to increase the world real interest rate, although this relationship is complex and there would be economic forces working in both directions. A newfound availability to borrow, whether within countries or across countries, would tend to reduce the incentive to save, and as saving fell, the interest rate would rise. Financial liberalization also might transform some agents with notional demand for saving into effective demanders, leading to higher interest rates.[84] These two factors, rate of return and financial liberalization, are probably interrelated. The move toward more liberal world capital markets may have contributed to an upward movement in the world rate of return, because making capital freer to flow to projects with the highest returns—wherever they exist—rather than keeping it captive in inefficient uses, should boost returns.

A rise in government budget deficits and increased levels of government debt are generally associated with higher real interest rates. There is an active literature about the complex relationship between government budget deficits and the response of private savers. As described earlier, however, the empirical evidence suggests that there is less than a one-for-one increase in private saving when governments dissave, so overall, national saving and world saving decline when governments run higher budget deficits. Over shorter time periods, deficits could be expected to help explain movements in real interest rates, whereas the debt-to-GDP ratio may be thought of as a long-run factor.

The relationship between money supply and real interest rates is not straightforward. To the extent that monetary authorities expand the money supply faster than expected, they could encourage higher long-term real interest rates by increasing perceived risk premiums beyond the normal "expected inflation" premium, which would be a component of the nominal interest rate, but not the real interest rate. On the other hand, over shorter time periods, it is possible to envision a negative relationship between money supply and a real short-term interest rate, if, say, a countercyclical role for monetary policy is allowed.

Empirical estimates of the effects of these factors on the global real interest rate are not wholly conclu-

sive, and the results are not always robust with respect to specification. Some researchers find large effects of budget deficits or government debt on interest rates, while others find effectively no effects.[85] Studies that find relatively small interest rate movements often concentrate on U.S. (or other single-country) data, and probably understate deficit effects because capital moves to the United States so freely. The scale of international capital movements today clearly requires that analysis of the relationship between budget deficits and government debt and interest rates be done in an international context.

Econometric results based on a model that looks at the issue in a global context suggest that shifts in government debt can explain the bulk of the increase in real interest rates from the 1960–72 period to the 1981–93 period. Gross government debt averaged 45 percent of world GDP in the 1960–72 period, over 55 percent over 1981–93, and ended 1994 at over 70 percent. This shift seems to explain roughly 200 of the 250-basis-point increase in the real short-term interest rate between the two periods, or about 145 of the 175-basis-point increase in the real long-term interest rate. On average, each percentage point increase in the ratio of world government debt to GDP adds about 14 basis points to the global long-term real interest rate. Alternative specifications using the ratio of world government fiscal surplus to GDP found that each percentage point increase in government dissaving caused the short-term real interest rate to increase by 50 to 75 basis points. The increase in the rate of return on productive capacity is also statistically significant in explaining a share of the movement of the global real interest rates. The rate of return increased from $3\frac{1}{2}$ percent a year in 1960–72 to $7\frac{1}{4}$ percent a year in the 1981–93 period, and this change explains about 20 basis points of increase in both short- and long-term real interest rates.

For purely illustrative purposes, it is of interest to explore what the optimistic and pessimistic saving scenarios sketched out earlier would suggest for global real interest rates over the next fifteen to twenty years. Using the implied relationship between saving rates and real interest rates developed in this section, global real interest rates could well decline by 100 to 200 basis points if the supply of world saving increased as described in the optimistic scenario. On the other hand, if the pessimistic scenario came to pass, the global real interest rate could easily increase by

---

[83]Although the modeling framework used here takes this increase as exogenous, there may have been some interaction with the real interest rate, through, say, portfolio rebalancing effects.

[84]Of course, to the extent that financial liberalization offered new vehicles for financial saving, it could increase the supply of saving and tend to lower interest rates.

[85]Robert Ford and Douglas Laxton "World Public Debt and Real Interest Rates," IMF Working Paper 95/30 (March 1995) find that measures of world government debt have been an important part of the explanation for why real interest rates have increased in countries with liberalized capital markets. On the other hand, Paul Evans in "Do Budget Deficits Raise Nominal Interest Rates? Evidence from Six Industrial Countries," in *Journal of Monetary Economics*, Vol. 20 (September 1987), pp. 281–300, finds essentially no effect.

Box 13. Effects of Increased Government Debt: Illustrative Calculations

Net public debt in the industrial countries has increased from 20 percent of GDP in 1979 to 42 percent in 1994 (*see chart*). Gross debt has increased from 40 percent of GDP to 71 percent of GDP over the same period. Many analyses examining the implications of higher public debt have focused on a particular country and implicitly assume that the effects on the equilibrium world real interest rate will be insignificant. Although such an assumption may be appropriate when a country is small, the fact that so many countries together have run persistent government deficits suggests that the combined effects of the debt buildup on world real interest rates may have been large.

The long-term effects on real interest rates will depend on the extent to which consumers view government debt as wealth.[1] If consumers are connected to all future generations and can borrow against their future income streams, changes in government debt will not crowd out private consumption and investment because consumers change their saving behavior today to prepare for tax liabilities in future. This invariance proposition is referred to as Ricardian equivalence, although David Ricardo himself did not believe that the economic consequences

of deficits were unimportant. Indeed, Ricardo was concerned that if government expenditures were financed by issuing government debt, the private sector would underestimate their future tax liabilities and in such circumstances there would be an incentive to overconsume available resources.[2] In an economy with scarce resources, an incentive to overconsume would result in higher real interest rates and a lower capital stock. Because a lower capital stock diminishes the level of output and, hence, the real income that the world economy can generate, an increase in government debt also reduces the sustainable level of consumption in the future.

The effects of government debt can be illustrated using an extended version of Blanchard's model.[3] The model has been used extensively to study fiscal policy issues,

---

[1]See Robert Barro, "Are Government Bonds Net Wealth?" *Journal of Political Economy*, Vol. 82 (November–December 1974), pp. 1095–117.

[2]See Piero Sraffa, *The Works and Correspondence of David Ricardo*, Vol. 4, ed. by Piero Sraffa and M.H. Dobb (Cambridge: Cambridge University Press, 1951). For a discussion of why Ricardian equivalence does not hold, see Willem Buiter, "Death, Birth, Productivity Growth and Debt Neutrality," *Economic Journal*, Vol. 98 (June 1988), pp. 279–93.

[3]See Olivier Blanchard, "Debt, Deficits and Finite Horizons," *Journal of Political Economy*, Vol. 93 (April 1985), pp. 223–47. The extensions are discussed in Hamid Faruqee, Douglas Laxton, and Steven Symansky, "Government Debt, Life-Cycle Income, and Liquidity Constraints: Beyond Approximate Ricardian Evidence" (mimeograph, IMF, 1995).

Estimates of Long-Run Effects of a Change in Government Debt from an Initial Steady State Debt-to-GDP Ratio of 40 Percent

	Debt-to-GDP Ratio						
	0	10	20	30	40	50	60
Output (in percent)	8.39	6.21	4.08	2.01	—	−1.94	−3.81
Consumption (in percent)	4.30	3.27	2.21	1.11	—	−1.12	−2.24
Capital stock (in percent)	25.87	18.78	12.10	5.85	—	−5.44	−10.50
Real interest rate (basis points)	−203	−154	−104	−53	—	54	109

---

another 100 or 150 basis points. These measures obviously should be treated with caution given the uncertainties about the precise magnitude of effect of government saving on interest rates. However, the crucial point is that government fiscal positions unquestionably do matter for the level of real interest rates, and that the effects of significant changes in fiscal policy probably are important.

World Economic Performance Under Different Saving Scenarios

The long-term implications of increasing government debt or of a fundamental change in saving behavior are worth considering. As just described, the buildup

of government debt over the last twenty-five years has important consequences for real interest rates. But it also has implications for the world capital stock and welfare over the long term, since a lower capital stock will result in a decline in the sustainable level of consumption. In order to illustrate the effects of government debt, the staff has examined saving issues with an extended version of Blanchard's model. This model has been used extensively to study fiscal policy issues because it captures intertemporal aspects and gives rise to well-defined long-run properties. Consequently, this model provides a useful framework to examine the long-run effects of government debt.

One scenario for the world economy suggests that a continued rise in government debt in the industrial

Industrial Countries: Net Public Debt
(In percent of GDP; PPP terms)

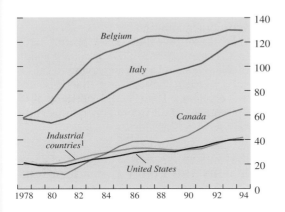

Source: OECD, *Economic Outlook* data base.
[1]Excludes Australia, Austria, Greece, Ireland, New Zealand, Portugal, and Switzerland.

because it captures essential intertemporal aspects and has well-defined long-run properties. In order to develop some illustrative quantitative estimates of the effects of governmentdebt, the basic model has been extended in two ways. First, it is assumed that a significant proportion of the population, 40 percent, consume out of their current disposable income. This is consistent with time series evidence that attempts to measure the "excess sensitivity" of consumption to innovations in disposable income. The second extension is to incorporate more realistic income profiles, which initially rise with age and then decline as workers reach retirement, into the basic model. In line with the available evidence, it is also as-

sumed that consumption is fairly insensitive to changes in the real interest rate.

To establish a benchmark, a long-run equilibrium solution for the real interest rate was computed assuming that the current net public debt ratio of about 40 percent of GDP in the industrial countries would stabilize at this level. Several scenarios with higher and lower levels of government debt were considered to illustrate the potential long-run effects of government debt. At one extreme, the implications of eliminating all government debt in the OECD countries, and at the other extreme, the implications of allowing the government debt ratio to continue to drift up by an additional 20 percentage points, were examined. The latter would be similar to repeating the experience of the past two decades. The table reports illustrative estimates for real interest rates, output, consumption, and the capital stock for these two extreme cases and for intermediate cases.

These illustrative estimates suggest that eliminating all government debt in the industrial countries would reduce real interest rates by 200 basis points in the long run. The calculations imply that the buildup in government debt since the late 1970s has caused an increase in real interest rates of about 100 basis points. The effects of government debt on the cost of capital permanently lower both the capital stock and the sustainable level of consumption. In equilibrium, the higher real interest rate on financial assets is supported by a higher marginal product of capital owing to the lower capital stock. These simulations ignore other important channels that may result in even larger effects on the capital stock and real interest rates. For example, the model simulations assume that interest payments on the higher level of government debt can be financed with nondistortionary labor taxes. If the higher interest burden is financed through distortionary capital taxes or reduced infrastructure expenditures, there may be additional adverse effects on thecapital stock and real interest rates. Some recent econometric evidence suggests that the permanent effects of the debt buildup may be even larger than what is suggested by these simulations, although the empirical evidence is far from conclusive.

countries, equal to the increase over the last twenty-five years, would result in a permanent increase in the world real interest rate of at least 100 basis points (Box 13). This increase would lead to a permanent 12 percent reduction in the capital stock, which in turn would reduce the sustainable level of consumption by 2 percent—a reduction that the model sees as persisting forever. This would be a substantial reduction in world welfare—equivalent, say, to the total loss of a year's output for each generation.

Another scenario considers the effects of a hypothetical reduction in world private saving. Since Japan, which accounts for about 15 percent of world saving, is widely viewed as the world's supersaver, this scenario assumes that the private saving rate in Japan gradually

falls by 10 percentage points.[86] To put this shock in perspective, it would be similar to an assumption that the world saving rate fell by 1 percentage point. In the short and medium term, the shock would lead to an increase in aggregate demand in Japan (Chart 34). Higher consumption in Japan would cause real GDP to rise above a baseline level for about fifteen years. This higher level of output would not be sustainable, however, because a lower saving rate would cause an increase in world real

---

[86]MULTIMOD, the Fund's multicountry econometric model, was used for this scenario; see Paul R. Masson, Steven A. Symansky, and Guy Meredith, *MULTIMOD Mark II: A Revised and Extended Model*, IMF Occasional Paper 71 (July 1990).

Chart 34. The Effects of a Lower Saving Rate in Japan: A Simulation Exercise

(Deviations from baseline)

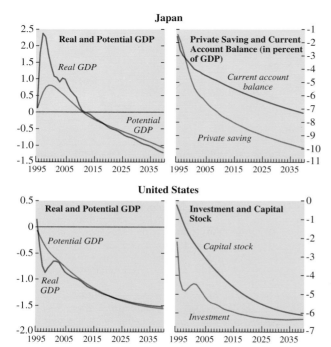

interest rates and a reduction in the capital stock. Results are reported for a single representative country, the United States, but the impacts on the other industrial economies would be very similar. The shock would increase the world real interest rate by about 75 basis points in the long run. An increase in real interest rates of this magnitude would induce a permanent reduction in the capital stock of 6 percent and a permanent reduction in real GDP of about 1 percent in the United States and in most other countries.

Both of these potential developments, a sharply higher government debt-to-GDP ratio and a significant downward movement in private saving in one or more industrial countries, show the importance of saving for the world economy. Both would substantially cut the consumption path of all future generations and mean a sharp long-term welfare loss.

Conclusions and Policy Considerations

There is some evidence of a world saving adequacy problem. No single indicator alone proves this conclusion, but a variety of evidence points in this direction, including relatively high global real interest rates, relatively low world saving and investment rates, relatively high rates of return on productive capacity, and relatively low world real income growth, compared with pre-1973 experience. The period between 1960 and 1972 is arguably a relevant reference period—GDP growth was strong, the ratio of investment to GDP was high, productivity performance was excellent, and real income gains were healthy. Compared with that period, global real interest rates today are noticeably higher and the ratio of world investment to GDP is lower. Real returns on productive capacity, as measured by the world's stock markets, were nearly twice as high in the 1981–93 period as they were in the 1960–72 period, suggesting more relative scarcity of capital. And productivity and real income growth have been noticeably lower over the 1981–93 period than they were in the 1960–72 period—at least in part because of the lower investment rate. The declining trend in the world saving rate draws much of the blame.

A dramatic decline in the public saving rate since about 1980 seems to be the root cause of the saving slowdown. Private saving has remained roughly steady—in the 20 percent range—over most of the past three decades. Public saving in the industrial countries by contrast has fallen sharply since the 1960s—averaging 4 percent in the 1960–72 period, but only ½ of 1 percent on average over the years from 1981 to 1993. Meanwhile gross public debt increased from 45 percent in the 1960–72 period, to 55 percent on average during the years between 1981 and 1993, and to over 70 percent by 1993. Econometric analysis suggests that this increase in government debt has been a key factor contributing to the rise in global real interest rates since the 1960s. The economic cost is substantial. An illustrative staff scenario suggests that the cost of this pattern of lower saving, higher interest rate, and lower investment is a permanent loss of roughly 2 percent of world consumption.

Where are saving and interest rates heading on present trends? Demographic swings—toward higher dependency ratios in the industrial countries, and toward lower dependency ratios in the developing countries—will probably roughly cancel each other out in terms of their impact on the world private saving rate over the next fifteen to twenty years. But two issues will be key. First is the rate of economic growth in developing countries, especially large countries such as China, India, and Brazil, and the extent to which they generate large quantities of saving. And second is the degree to which government dissaving in industrial countries is reversed. Global real interest rates could decline noticeably if developing country saving picked up strongly and if public saving rates in industrial countries returned to their levels of the 1960s and early 1970s. On the other hand, global real interest rates could easily increase further if negative outcomes occur instead.

Firm and committed policy actions are necessary to reverse current pressures on saving. The 1960s started out with a high ratio of world government debt to GDP. But as the decade progressed and as governments enjoyed strong economic growth, they used the opportunity to run fiscal surpluses, cut the ratio of government debt to GDP sharply, and saw the world saving rate increase steadily. That is because government budget deficits *do* matter for overall national and world saving. While there is some tendency for private savers to adjust their saving upward in the face of increased government dissaving, the offset is only partial. Although the causality runs both ways, it probably was no coincidence that the strong fiscal positions in the 1960s were associated with relatively affordable investment funds, a high ratio of investment to GDP, and good macroeconomic performance. With the industrial world now poised for solid growth again, there appear to be opportunities for a replay if governments choose to take advantage of them. There are growing dangers of not acting. With increasingly integrated world capital markets, the global real interest rate rises for everyone when individual governments run budget deficits—that is, the burden gets shared. This suggests the need for a cooperative effort to alleviate the problem—countries should set good examples for others to follow.

Who must act? World capital flows and financial conditions are largely determined by the industrial countries and the trend toward public dissaving is also heavily an industrial country problem. These are the countries where fiscal consolidation can help boost world saving the most. The case of the United States is noteworthy—after four consecutive years of healthy GDP growth, the federal budget deficit remains near 3 percent of GDP. Most other industrial countries are roughly in the same league as the United States in terms of fiscal deterioration compared with the 1960s or 1970s.[87]

Developing countries cannot be complacent. Many have enjoyed large inflows of capital over the past few years as the industrial countries posted poor economic growth. This has buffered developing countries from the growing world saving squeeze. But with the industrial countries now on track for more healthy economic growth, their investment demands are picking up again, reducing the availability of funds to developing countries. Increasing pressure on saving will reveal policy imbalances and structural economic weaknesses everywhere, and each country must put its own house in order. From some perspectives, for example, Mexico's current situation is not just a simple crisis of confidence. Mexico has had a very low saving rate, and arguably, an unsustainable dependence on foreign saving.

The scope for microeconomic policies to encourage private saving, especially in industrial countries, appears to be more limited. Cross-country data suggest a natural evolution of the private saving rate, which increases sharply in the high-growth phase, levels off as an economy matures, and may decline somewhat as populations age. This means that as some countries mature and see their saving decline, other new industrial countries will be created, and should help to boost the world supply of saving. Some of the emerging countries may become net suppliers of saving to the world. Because private saving has such a strong internal dynamic, government policy can probably make mainly indirect contributions through structural reforms that promote economic growth. With private saving behavior only mildly sensitive to changes in the real interest rate, for example, the scope for tax policy to have a major impact on saving rates would seem to be limited. Of course, tax policy changes that would improve allocative efficiency should always be considered. In developing countries in particular, there is evidence that tax changes and structural reforms may be important in promoting allocative efficiency. Overall it seems clear, however, that fiscal responsibility is likely to offer most governments the biggest potential payoff for total saving.

---

[87]Japan, Norway, and Finland are among the few industrial countries that have been successful in maintaining high rates of public saving in order to accumulate assets for pensions. Norway is the only industrial country that currently has a net positive asset position. However, Japan and Finland have been particularly affected by recent recessions and will need to resume fiscal consolidation.

Annex I

Factors Behind the Financial Crisis in Mexico

On December 20, 1994, in the face of heavy losses of international reserves, the Mexican authorities widened the exchange rate intervention band that had been in place since late 1991. Two days later, as capital flight from Mexico persisted, the exchange rate was allowed to float and the value of the peso plummeted. This annex describes the economic developments that preceded the Mexican financial crisis and discusses three complementary views that have been advanced to help explain how and why the crisis erupted.

Developments During 1988–93

From 1988 to 1993, Mexico followed a strategy of economic adjustment and reform that strengthened the process of fiscal consolidation and structural transformation initiated after the onset of the 1982 debt crisis. The strategy aimed at restoring macroeconomic stability, attaining external viability, reducing the role of the public sector in the economy, and laying the foundations for private sector led growth. The key elements of the strategy were the maintenance of tight financial policies, a major external debt restructuring, and a comprehensive program of structural reforms including, notably, privatization and trade liberalization.

The main objective of the December 1987 stabilization program was to reduce inflation—which was running at an annual rate of 160 percent. This program marked the start of a new phase in Mexico's adjustment strategy. The program centered around a further tightening of fiscal and monetary policies, a fixed exchange rate, a temporary freezing of public sector prices and wages, and further liberalization of the trade and financial sectors. A key element of the program was an explicit agreement on policies between labor, business, and the government—the *Pacto*—which provided the framework for revising and updating the main guidelines for economic policy. The Pacto, renewed periodically, remained in effect over the period 1988–94.

The exchange rate was the main nominal anchor of the system throughout the period, with incomes poli-

cies playing an important supportive role. The Mexican peso was fixed to the U.S. dollar from March to December 1988 and allowed to depreciate during the following three years at a preannounced rate. In November 1991, the authorities added some more flexibility to exchange rate management by creating a publicly announced intervention band. As the floor of the band was kept constant while the ceiling depreciated at a predetermined rate, the band widened gradually from less than $1\frac{1}{2}$ percent at the end of 1991 to about 9 percent at the end of 1993.

Fiscal policy was tightened through a combination of revenue-enhancing and expenditure-restraining measures. The major tax reform of 1987 was supplemented by measures aimed at broadening the tax base, reducing marginal tax rates, and increasing tax compliance; public sector prices were maintained at competitive levels; the pace of privatization of large public enterprises was accelerated; and strict control was exercised over noninterest expenditures. A crucial element in the process of fiscal consolidation was the lowering of interest payments as a result of the successful rescheduling of official external debt and the completion of an innovative debt-reduction agreement with foreign commercial banks in 1989–90. This agreement was the first implemented under the Brady initiative and was financed in part with resources from the IMF, the World Bank, and Japan.

The main goals of monetary policy throughout the period were to bring down inflation and stabilize the value of the peso. The other objectives of the authorities were to foster financial deepening and facilitate the private sector's access to bank credit. To meet its primary goals, the monetary authorities intervened in the foreign exchange market and adopted a policy of partial sterilization of capital flows—using a variety of government-issued instruments—aimed at keeping growth in the monetary base broadly in line with the growth of nominal income consistent with the inflation target. To address the secondary goals, the authorities undertook a rapid liberalization of the financial system in 1988–89: interest rates were freed, credit controls and lending restrictions were removed, and reserve requirements and compulsory liquidity ratios were abolished. A further push to the liberalization process occurred from mid-1990 to mid-1992, when Mexico's 18 commercial banks, which had been nationalized in 1982, were sold back to the private sector.

This annex was prepared by Miguel A. Savastano, Jorge Roldós, and Julio Santaella.

In addition to the privatization of large public enterprises and commercial banks and the liberalization of the financial system, Mexico embarked on an ambitious trade reform comprising further unilateral cuts in import tariffs and the negotiation of free trade agreements with several Western Hemisphere countries, including the NAFTA with the United States and Canada. Restrictions on foreign investment and foreign ownership were eased, and a number of key sectors, such as agriculture, mining, telecommunications, and transportation, were deregulated. Overall, these reforms signaled a strong commitment by the authorities to deepen Mexico's transformation into a market-based economy.

The December 1987 program and those that followed produced encouraging results. Real GDP growth recovered from an average of ½ of 1 percent a year over the period 1985–88 to 3½ percent in the period 1989–92; inflation fell from 160 percent in 1987 to 12 percent in 1992 and reached single-digit levels in 1993 for the first time in over two decades; real interest rates turned positive; the overall economic balance and the operational balance of the public sector improved by about 13 and 6 percentage points of GDP, respectively, between 1988 and 1992; and the total public external debt dropped relative to GDP from 50 percent in 1988 to 22 percent in 1992 (Table 12).

The successful restructuring of the external debt paved the way for a resumption of access to international financial markets. Private capital inflows surged to an average of over 6 percent of GDP in the period 1990–93. About one fifth of the inflows were in the form of foreign direct investment, while the rest—some $60 billion over the four-year period—consisted of foreign portfolio investment in the domestic capital market, direct foreign borrowing by private sector firms and financial entities, and repatriation of flight capital. The inflows resulted in a marked strengthening of Mexico's international reserves position: by the end of 1993, the Bank of Mexico's gross international reserves stood at $25½ billion, up from $6½ billion at the end of 1989.

The sharp drop in inflation, in conjunction with the increased access to domestic and foreign credit and the demands for resource reallocation brought about by the structural reforms, contributed to a rise in private sector spending. Private consumption and investment recovered strongly—albeit from relatively low levels—from 1988 to 1992, while private saving fell by 10 percentage points of GDP. Total imports (measured in U.S. dollars) grew at an average annual rate of 24 percent during 1989–92, outpacing the increase of non-oil exports—14 percent on average—over the same period. The combination of these forces led to a gradual widening of the current account deficit from 2½ percent of GDP in the period 1988–89 to 6¾ percent of GDP in 1992. These factors, together with the maintenance of the exchange rate anchor policy, led to

a real effective appreciation of the peso of over 60 percent from the end of 1987 to the end of 1992. A good part of the appreciation took place under the fixed exchange rate system adopted in the initial stages of the stabilization program, but the real appreciation of the peso continued under the preannounced crawling peg and after the introduction of the band system in November 1991.

The behavior of money and credit aggregates reflected the process of reintermediation in the domestic financial system and, more generally, the improved outlook for Mexico over the period. The combined effects of financial sector reform, lower inflation, fiscal adjustment, and less-than-full sterilization of capital flows led to a sharp rise in financial deepening and eased the private sector's access to credit. From 1989 to 1992, broad money (M4) increased at an average annual rate of 40 percent in nominal terms (14 percent in real terms), whereas nominal narrow money (M1) rose at a yearly average rate of 60 percent (30 percent in real terms). During the same period, net credit to the private sector from the financial system expanded at an average annual rate of 66 percent in nominal terms, largely offsetting the decline in credit to the public sector allowed by the much-improved fiscal position.

A number of developments in 1993 contrasted with some of the broad underlying trends observed in the period 1988–92. Specifically, output growth slowed to ½ of 1 percent, private consumption and investment fell in real terms, import growth flattened out, the primary and operational surpluses of the public sector declined by about 1½ percentage points of GDP, and the deterioration in the external current account was arrested. The main factors contributing to these developments appear to have been the ongoing restructuring of firms in the manufacturing sector, a tightening of credit conditions by the monetary authorities, a credit squeeze resulting from the deterioration in the quality of banks' loan portfolios, and uncertainty about the approval of NAFTA, which was only cleared up in November. In the event, the exchange rate regime turned out to be resilient enough to withstand the pressures that arose in the financial and foreign exchange markets—especially around the start of the fourth quarter—and by year-end the peso had fallen back into the bottom half of the intervention band, and private capital inflows had resumed.

Developments in 1994

Macroeconomic policy in 1994 was expected to continue in the same general vein as in previous years. The preannounced ceiling of the exchange rate band was allowed to depreciate at an annual rate of about 4 percent, which implied that the intervention band would widen to 14 percent by the end of December, while inflation was expected to remain in single digits.

Table 12. Mexico: Selected Economic Indicators

	1987	1988	1989	1990	1991	1992	1993	1994
Real sector								
Real GDP growth (percent change)	1.7	1.2	3.5	4.5	3.6	2.8	0.6	3.5
				In percent of GDP				
National saving	21.6	18.2	18.5	18.7	17.6	16.0	14.1	13.7
Private[1]	14.3	18.8	16.1	12.1	10.0	8.7	8.9	9.1
Public[1]	7.3	−0.7	2.4	6.6	7.6	7.3	5.2	4.6
Gross domestic investment	19.3	20.4	21.4	21.9	22.4	22.8	20.6	21.6
External current account balance	2.2	−2.3	−2.9	−3.2	−4.8	−6.8	−6.4	−8.0
Prices, exchange rates and interest rates								
Consumer price inflation (end-period)	159.2	51.7	19.7	29.9	18.8	11.9	8.3	7.1
Nominal exchange rate (pesos per U.S. dollar, end-period)	2.199	2.257	2.637	2.939	3.075	3.118	3.106	4.990
Real effective exchange rate index (end-period)[2]	56.3	73.1	73.3	77.4	85.9	93.3	99.3	90.6
Interest rates on 28-day Cetes (annual rates; end-period)	122.0	52.3	40.6	26.0	16.7	16.9	11.8	30.0
				In percent of GDP				
Public sector								
Primary balance	5.0	6.0	7.9	7.8	5.5	5.4	3.9	2.6
Operational balance	2.0	−3.0	−1.1	1.2	2.8	3.3	1.5	0.4
Overall economic balance	−15.0	−11.6	−5.2	−3.6	0.4	1.5	0.7	—
Public sector debt								
Foreign debt (excluding IMF)	61.5	49.7	40.5	31.7	26.1	22.2	23.0	24.2
Domestic debt	16.5	18.7	23.9	23.5	19.7	12.9	12.0	13.2
			Twelve-month rates of growth, end of period					
Monetary sector								
Currency in circulation	139.2	79.8	36.7	36.7	31.7	17.3	13.7	22.2
Narrow money (M1)	129.8	58.1	40.7	62.6	119.8	17.3	17.7	5.7
Broad money (M4)	161.2	58.9	50.8	46.4	30.9	19.9	25.0	17.1
Net domestic assets of the financial system	112.8	39.3	32.9	22.6	31.6	20.8	15.5	32.0
Net credit to public sector	113.4	28.6	15.9	3.9	−1.6	−31.7	−46.2	25.3
Net credit to private sector	154.6	79.8	77.9	63.2	53.3	57.1	26.4	31.9
Net domestic credit of commercial banks	141.4	42.9	56.6	49.4	48.6	20.9	24.3	. . .
Net domestic credit of development banks	157.6	4.3	7.7	−10.1	18.8	23.4	47.4	42.2
				In billions of U.S. dollars				
External sector								
Current account balance	2.9	−3.8	−6.1	−7.5	−14.9	−24.8	−23.4	−29.5
Capital account balance	3.8	−2.9	5.1	10.9	22.5	26.7	30.5	11.6
Public sector, net	3.6	1.2	−0.7	−0.2	3.0	1.5	7.5	2.5
Private sector, net	0.2	−4.1	5.8	11.1	19.5	25.2	23.0	9.1
Foreign direct investment	1.8	1.7	2.7	2.6	4.8	4.4	4.9	7.9
Overall balance of payments	6.7	−6.8	−1.1	3.4	7.6	1.9	7.1	−17.9
Gross international reserves (end-period)	8.0	6.0	6.5	10.1	17.9	19.4	25.4	6.3
			Twelve-month rates of growth, end of period					
Total exports value[3]	38.8	2.8	12.9	17.6	1.7	4.4	9.9	13.6
Non-oil exports value[3]	23.7	18.7	11.1	12.9	12.1	5.3	17.0	17.0
Total imports value[3]	16.4	52.4	25.5	22.9	22.1	26.2	1.5	20.3

Sources: Ministry of Finance; Bank of Mexico; and IMF staff estimates.

[1]Adjusted for the inflation component of interest payments on the public sector debt denominated in domestic currency.

[2]1980 = 100; increase means appreciation.

[3]Expressed in U.S. dollars.

In the face of the output slowdown that had taken place in 1993 and the impending elections, the authorities envisaged some relaxation of the fiscal position, essentially involving tax cuts and increases in social spending, while preserving overall economic balance in the public sector. With the approval of NAFTA in November 1993, foreign investment was expected to grow strongly and bring an added impetus to exports and output growth.

In the event, economic activity did experience a significant recovery in 1994, amidst a series of episodes of financial turbulence that ended in the December balance of payments crisis. Real GDP growth increased during the year, reaching 4 percent by the sec-

Table 13. Mexico: Quarterly Economic Indicators

	1993				1994			
	Q1	Q2	Q3	Q4	Q1	Q2	Q3	Q4
Output and inflation								
Real GDP growth	2.4	0.3	−0.8	−0.1	0.5	3.8	4.5	4.0
Consumer price inflation (end-period)	10.4	9.9	9.5	8.0	7.1	6.9	6.7	7.1
In percent of GDP								
Public sector								
Primary balance	5.0	5.0	3.9	0.7	3.6	3.9	2.7	0.4
Overall economic balance	2.2	2.4	0.1	−1.7	0.5	1.4	−0.1	−1.9
Twelve-month rates of growth, end of month								
Monetary sector								
Liabilities to the private sector	21.0	26.3	21.8	18.5	20.1	17.5	24.4	27.4
Net domestic credit of the banking system	21.0	25.1	22.7	15.5	19.8	29.1	29.7	32.0
To the public sector	−31.0	−32.3	−26.8	−46.2	−30.8	−0.8	11.8	25.3
To the private sector	45.9	38.5	33.2	26.4	27.7	28.2	27.3	31.9
Net credit from commercial banks	45.5	36.2	32.0	24.3	25.4	26.0	26.2	29.6
Net credit from development banks	38.6	37.5	33.6	47.4	49.5	48.2	36.5	51.6
In billions of U.S. dollars								
External sector								
Current account balance	−5.7	−5.7	−6.7	−5.3	−6.9	−7.4	−7.8	−7.4
Capital account balance	8.1	7.6	7.0	7.9	7.9	−1.8	7.9	−2.5
Public sector, net	1.0	0.5	−0.5	6.4	2.6	−0.9	1.1	−0.3
Private sector, net[1]	7.1	7.1	7.5	1.5	5.3	−1.0	6.8	−2.2
Foreign direct investment	1.5	1.3	1.0	1.2	1.9	1.6	2.4	2.1
Overall balance of payments	2.4	1.9	0.4	2.5	1.0	−9.2	0.1	−9.9
Gross international reserves (end-period)	21.8	23.5	23.6	25.6	26.3	16.9	16.8	6.7

Sources: Ministry of Finance; Bank of Mexico, and IMF staff estimates.

[1]Includes errors and omissions.

ond half and 3½ percent for 1994 as a whole; inflation continued its declining trend, averaging about 7 percent, the lowest rate in decades; and manufacturing exports continued growing at an annual rate of 17 percent, accounting for more than 80 percent of total exports (Table 13). However, the improved economic outlook that followed the approval of NAFTA coupled with a strong expansion of credit throughout the year led to a resumption in the growth of private spending and imports, and as a result the external current account deficit increased to 8 percent of GDP.

The series of episodes of financial turbulence experienced by the Mexican economy during 1994 had as their proximate cause both external economic and domestic political shocks. On the external front, the strong growth momentum in the United States and the general pickup in other industrial countries increased the demand for investment funds worldwide. At the same time, financial conditions began to tighten in those industrial countries that were the most advanced in the expansion, especially the United States. Both of these factors prompted international investors to reassess the share of their portfolios invested in emerging markets, including in Mexico. On the domestic front, the sequence of disturbances included the uprising in Chiapas in January, the assassinations of presidential candidate Colosio in March and of the secre-

tary general of the ruling party in September, and a second Chiapas uprising in December. All these events contributed to an environment of considerable political and economic uncertainty.

The large capital inflows that followed the passage of NAFTA fell abruptly following the assassination of presidential candidate Colosio on March 23. International reserves, which stood at $28¼ billion before the assassination, dropped by $11 billion during April; the exchange rate hit the ceiling of the band; and interest rates on short-term, peso-denominated paper (Cetes) doubled to 18 percent (Charts 35 and 36).

The monetary authorities' decision to let interest rates rise, along with the approval of a $6¾ billion short-term credit line from the NAFTA partners to defend the Mexican peso, helped to ease the immediate pressures in financial markets. From the end of April to early November, the stock of international reserves remained fairly stable—at about $16–17 billion— while the exchange rate traded close to the ceiling of the band and interest rates started to decline. At the same time, a sizable amount of Cetes was replaced by Tesobonos, short-term instruments indexed to the U.S. dollar but repayable in pesos. In effect, around $13 billion of private sector holdings of Cetes were swapped for Tesobonos from March to October.

Throughout this period, fiscal policy was broadly consistent with the target of overall economic balance in the nonfinancial public sector. However, credit from the Bank of Mexico to the financial system and from commercial and development banks to the private sector expanded rapidly; net credit expansion from trust funds and development banks reached 4½ percent of GDP in 1994, 2 percentage points higher than in the previous year.

The results of the presidential election in August, together with the renewal of the Pacto in September, seemed to take the pressure off the financial markets. However, as the new administration was about to take office, a new burst of political instability, coupled with increased rumors about possible changes in exchange rate policy, sparked a flight from the Mexican peso and led to a loss of reserves of about $3½ billion. In contrast to the response to the March–April episode, interest rates on 28-day Cetes were maintained at the 13–14 percent range until the second week of December. On December 1, President Zedillo was sworn into office, and days later, tensions in Chiapas resumed. By December 20, international reserves had fallen to $10½ billion and the Mexican authorities attempted in vain to widen the exchange rate intervention band by lifting its ceiling by 15 percent. Two days later, after an additional loss of reserves of $4 billion, the peso was allowed to float. The decision to abandon the commitment to a managed exchange rate regime despite repeated pronouncements to the contrary had strongly adverse effects on financial market expectations. At least in part, this change in market sentiment appears to explain the size and speed of the financial upheaval and sharp peso depreciation of early 1995, as markets questioned Mexico's ability to service its short-term debt. On January 31, 1995, with a peso worth 40 percent less than in mid-December, the international community announced a financial rescue package in support of Mexico.

Factors Behind the Crisis

As the crisis in Mexico unfolded and its wide-ranging consequences became increasingly apparent, a debate on the factors that contributed to its occurrence emerged. Analytically, the various factors advanced as causes of the crisis can be grouped into three broad and complementary views. The first considers Mexico as having been hit by a set of adverse shocks, which turned out to be more severe and persistent than appeared at the time and served to undermine the authorities' economic strategy. The second argues that the size of Mexico's current account deficits in recent years was not sustainable and needed to be addressed by major changes in the stance of macroeconomic policy, including a realignment of the nominal exchange rate. Finally, the third

Chart 35. Mexico: Nominal Exchange Rate
(New Mexican pesos per U.S. dollar; daily quotations)

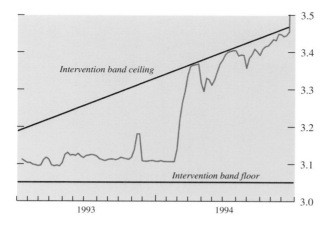

Sources: Bank of Mexico; and Bloomberg Financial Markets.

view claims that, while the overall direction of macroeconomic policy was sound, the Mexican authorities allowed inconsistencies in macroeconomic policy to arise during 1994, which ultimately eroded the confidence of domestic and foreign investors in the authorities' commitment to maintain a coherent medium-term economic strategy.

It is useful to consider briefly the merits and drawbacks of these three views. Since they are not necessarily competing explanations of the crisis, the discussion simply lays out their main elements. Furthermore, in all likelihood, future and more comprehensive analyses of this episode will find that many, if not all, of the factors emphasized by these views played a role in the crisis.

The "Adverse Shocks" View

Mexico was indeed subject to a large number of adverse domestic political and external economic shocks during 1994. It has been argued that it was very difficult, if not plainly impossible, for the authorities to gauge the size or anticipate the recurrent nature of these shocks. Moreover, the relative calm in foreign exchange and financial markets from May to November—signaled by the stable level of international reserves and the falling interest rates on Cetes and Tesobonos—and the absence of inflationary pressures may have suggested to the Mexican authorities that their reaction to the March events sufficed to restore foreign investors' confidence in the exchange rate regime. Under these conditions, it may well have appeared reasonable to continue with the policy of sterilizing the monetary impact of international reserve losses to offset the effects of what were perceived as temporary political shocks, which would be resolved quickly once the elections took place and the new administration was in office.

The main problem with this view is that there were certain developments in the economy that suggested that at least some of the shocks were not transitory. Specifically, the persistent rise in foreign interest rates would be expected to provide a higher floor for rates on both peso- and dollar-indexed paper. This development, combined with the ongoing substitution from Cetes to Tesobonos and the drop in stock market prices from mid-September on, should have raised questions about the assumed stability of the demand for domestic money and the likely continuation of the process of financial deepening, and, thus, led to a tightening of monetary conditions.

The "Unsustainable External Position" View

This view can be summarized as follows. Typically, an exchange-rate-based stabilization under capital mobility leads to a fall in the real interest rate and an expansion in aggregate demand that cause protracted

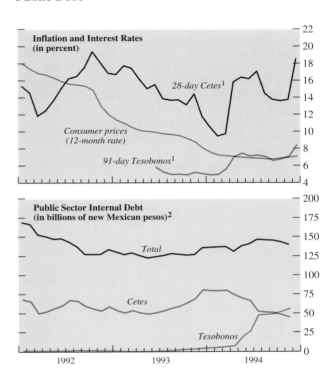

Chart 36. Mexico: Inflation, Interest Rates, and Public Debt

Source: Bank of Mexico.
[1]Monthly average of weekly auctions.
[2]End-of-period holdings at market value. Excludes monetary regulation deposits.

current account deficits and a real exchange rate appreciation. The appreciation reflects not only a different speed of adjustment of traded and nontraded goods prices, but also, and more important, the effects on aggregate spending of the implied increase in private sector wealth. The removal of credit constraints resulting from financial liberalization and other structural reforms tend to amplify these trends. Even though they are driven by private sector behavior, rather than an inadequate fiscal position, the current account deficit and the real appreciation can eventually become unsustainable. Therefore, at some point a real exchange rate depreciation is needed to restore the initial level of competitiveness and current account equilibrium. In the case of Mexico, supporters of this view point to the size of the current account deficit—over 7 percent of GDP in 1992–94 and 8 percent of GDP projected in the budget for 1995—the substantial decline in the rates of national and private saving since 1988, and the large real appreciation of the peso, as clear signs of the unsustainability of the external position and of the need for a nominal exchange rate realignment.

It can be argued, however, that large current account deficits and real exchange rate appreciation are, at least to some extent, the equilibrium response to the process of stabilization and structural reforms. This response will involve a slow growth of real income, owing to adjustment costs associated with investment and the sectoral reallocation of resources, while consumption of domestic and foreign goods is boosted by the expected rise in permanent income and wealth. Under this framework, the ensuing external deficit would subside over time, as improvements in productivity lead to gradual increases in competitiveness and exports, with no need for a devaluation. In the case of Mexico, this somewhat optimistic interpretation receives some support from the behavior of investment and exports. Investment rose gradually but steadily up to 1992; the trend was interrupted in 1993, owing in part to uncertainties about NAFTA and tighter credit policies, but resumed strongly in 1994—as evidenced, in particular, by a sharp increase in foreign direct investment. Similarly, manufacturing exports grew at a fairly rapid pace during 1988–94, while the peso was appreciating in real terms, owing in part to the increases in total factor productivity resulting from the rapid trade liberalization and wide-ranging deregulation of previous years.

The "Policy Slippages" View

This view would argue that the large number of adverse shocks that hit Mexico in 1994, added to the potential vulnerability stemming from weakness in the external accounts, called for a much tighter monetary policy than the one followed, and probably also for an early widening of the intervention band, so as to reassure the markets that the authorities were fully committed to sustaining the exchange rate regime. The behavior of interest rates, the management of government short-term debt, and the expansion of credit from the financial system during the year appear to provide support to this view. The policy of partial sterilization of reserve losses followed by the monetary authorities required placing part of the burden of adjustment on interest rates. However, except for the rise that followed the Colosio incident, interest rates in Mexico in 1994 do not appear to have conformed to this requirement. Indeed, the gradual decline of the interest rate differential between Mexican government securities (Cetes and Tesobonos) and U.S. dollar instruments from May to November suggests that the authorities were attempting to accelerate the convergence of domestic interest rates to international levels. Moreover, the authorities seem to have been reluctant to raise interest rates as the crisis resumed in November and December: interest rates on Cetes fluctuated around the 13–14 percent range until the second week of December, although, since the end of October, international reserves had been falling at about $1 billion a week. The vulnerability of the financial system seems to have been compounded by the decision to accommodate a dollar-indexation of short-term debt—which reduced interest payments in the short run but raised de facto the cost of an eventual funding crisis—and to leave unchecked the substantial expansion of credit from commercial and development banks in the run-up to, and immediate aftermath of, the presidential elections.

At least two arguments can be made against the policy slippages view. First, as noted before, it was very difficult to gauge the size and nature of the shocks, even as they started to emerge. Second, it is not clear at the outset what a tightened monetary policy stance would have involved in terms of output and employment losses, or whether it would have sufficed to avert the crisis. Regarding the latter, evidence from similar episodes elsewhere suggests that a substantial hike in interest rates late in the day probably would have been insufficient to preclude the crisis, although it is arguable that such actions may have helped to convince financial markets that Mexico remained committed to a consistent medium-term economic strategy. Thus, it would seem that a much earlier tightening of credit supported by a more restrictive fiscal stance might have been needed to stave off the pressures on the exchange rate regime. In principle, however, the effects of the credit tightening on output and on the solvency of the banking system may not have been qualitatively different from those that seem to have arisen in the aftermath of the December crisis.

* * *

The various factors behind the crisis that have been discussed in this annex probably all played a role.

Domestic and external shocks undoubtedly contributed to a reassessment of Mexico's economic and financial situation by domestic and foreign investors. The accommodating stance of monetary policy during 1994 led to a strong expansion of liquidity that was incompatible with the exchange rate regime. In this situation, markets became increasingly concerned about the sustainability of the large current account deficit. In retrospect, such concerns do appear to have been warranted in the light of the fact that the large capital inflows since 1990 had a much larger impact on consumption than on investment, resulting in a sharp decline in the national saving rate.

The program that has now been adopted by the Mexican authorities, with strong support from multilateral and bilateral creditors, will need to tackle the root causes of the crisis. The chief objectives of the program are to restore confidence and reduce the dependence on foreign saving through a strong stabilization effort. In addition, the program will need to sustain the substantial progress made by Mexico in recent years in the areas of structural reform and the liberalization of trade and capital flows. The immediate adjustment efforts will undoubtedly involve weaker economic activity for some time. However, the successful implementation of the stabilization program will help to restore investors' confidence and put Mexico back on a higher medium-term growth path. Mexico's increased openness and membership in NAFTA underscore the country's considerable economic potential, as illustrated by its relatively strong economic performance from 1989 to 1992.

Annex II

Adjustment in Sub-Saharan Africa

Economic performance in sub-Saharan Africa during the past decade and a half has been unsatisfactory. Real per capita incomes continued to decline, thus widening the gap in living standards relative to other developing countries.[1] The poor aggregate performance, however, masks the important progress made by an increasing number of African countries, particularly since the mid-1980s, in lowering internal and external imbalances and addressing structural rigidities. The countries that effectively implemented broadly appropriate macroeconomic policies and structural reforms during this period, for the most part under programs supported by the IMF, have performed much better than the nonadjusting countries. Average real per capita incomes in the group of adjusting countries have risen since the mid-1980s. The continuation of these efforts and the adoption of growth-oriented adjustment programs by the CFA franc countries in support of the exchange rate adjustment of January 1994, in the context of an improved external environment, have strengthened the medium-term growth prospects for sub-Saharan Africa. The main challenge remains the effective implementation of appropriate reform policies, entailing in particular a strengthening of government revenue mobilization and the encouragement of private sector development; the latter requires, inter alia, improved economic incentives and governance, the reduction of dissavings of public enterprises, the restructuring of financial institutions in distress, and the alleviation of other structural and institutional impediments to growth.

Overview, 1980–94

In contrast to the strong gains recorded by other developing countries, particularly in Asia, sub-Saharan Africa experienced further losses in per capita real GDP of almost 1 percent a year during 1980–85; these

---

This annex was prepared by Michael T. Hadjimichael and Dhaneshwar Ghura.

[1]The coverage of sub-Saharan Africa in this annex is somewhat narrower than in the rest of the *World Economic Outlook*, in that it is limited to 39 countries in the IMF's African Department (excluding South Africa and, because of data limitations, Angola, Eritrea, Liberia, and Namibia); it also excludes Djibouti, Mauritania, Somalia, and Sudan, which are in the Middle Eastern Department.

losses continued during 1986–94, but at a somewhat lower rate of ½ of 1 percent (Table 14). The declining trend in per capita real incomes coincided with widening domestic and external imbalances, mounting external debt burdens and debt-servicing difficulties, and a worsening in the plight of economically and socially vulnerable groups. A number of factors, both exogenous and policy related, have contributed to the disappointing overall economic performance.

The external environment has been generally unfavorable, with sharp declines in world commodity prices and substantial losses in the terms of trade of sub-Saharan African countries (Table 15). The deterioration in the terms of trade has been particularly pronounced since 1985. While the decline in commodity prices has also affected other developing countries, the impact on sub-Saharan African countries has been far more serious, as the structure of their economies makes them especially vulnerable to terms of trade losses. The export earnings of virtually all African countries are heavily concentrated on one or two commodities while, for some countries, government revenue relies heavily on export taxes.

For many countries, the adverse effects of the terms of trade losses have been compounded by unfavorable weather in some years. Recurring severe droughts in the Sahel, the Horn of Africa, and other parts of western and southern Africa have taken their toll on food production and export crops. In view of the large share of GDP typically accounted for by agriculture and the high proportion of the population living in rural areas, unfavorable weather tends to have a pronounced effect on output growth and the plight of the rural population.

Virtually all sub-Saharan African countries are confronted with deep-rooted developmental constraints—rapid population growth, low human capital development, inadequate economic and social infrastructure, and structural rigidities—which are both a cause and consequence of poor economic performance. These factors constitute major impediments to the development of the private sector and the supply response of the economy.

Moreover, political factors have severely worsened and, in some cases, devastated the economic environment. Ethnic conflicts, political instability, adverse security conditions, or protracted civil wars have held back economic performance in a number

Table 14. Sub-Saharan Africa: Growth, Inflation, and Fiscal Performance

	Average		1986	1993	Estimates 1994	Projections 1995	Projections 1996
	1980–85	1986–94	1986	1993	1994	1995	1996
	Annual percent change						
Real GDP growth							
Sub-Saharan Africa	2.3	2.5	3.7	1.5	0.6	5.0	5.3
Strong adjusters	1.5	4.0	4.0	4.0	3.8	5.2	5.4
Slow adjusters	2.7	1.7	3.5	—	-1.4	5.0	5.2
CFA franc countries	4.9	0.2	3.7	-1.5	1.7	4.9	5.2
Real per capita GDP growth							
Sub-Saharan Africa	-0.9	-0.5	0.6	-1.5	-2.4	1.9	2.2
Strong adjusters	-1.6	0.9	1.0	1.0	0.8	2.2	2.4
Slow adjusters	-0.6	-1.3	0.4	-3.0	-4.3	1.8	2.0
CFA franc countries	1.6	-2.7	0.6	-4.4	-1.3	1.8	2.2
Consumer price inflation							
Sub-Saharan Africa	22.4	246.6	17.2	144.5	1428.3	39.7	11.7
Excluding Zaïre	20.0	24.4	14.1	32.9	36.4	29.9	11.9
Strong adjusters	26.6	24.4	25.4	21.4	25.4	14.2	7.1
Slow adjusters	20.3	379.5	13.0	217.2	2281.0	55.3	14.6
Excluding Zaïre	16.2	24.5	7.2	40.3	43.8	40.5	15.1
CFA franc countries	10.2	4.5	3.4	-0.9	30.4	12.1	3.9
	In percent of GDP						
Overall fiscal balance[1]							
Sub-Saharan Africa	-6.0	-8.7	-6.6	-11.4	-8.9	-7.0	-5.8
Strong adjusters	-6.3	-6.2	-7.2	-7.5	-6.7	-5.2	-4.5
Slow adjusters	-5.9	-10.0	-6.2	-13.3	-10.0	-7.8	-6.6
CFA franc countries	-6.4	-9.2	-5.8	-10.3	-9.4	-6.5	-4.5
Primary fiscal balance[1]							
Sub-Saharan Africa	-3.6	-3.3	-2.7	-5.4	-2.8	-1.7	0.2
Strong adjusters	-4.3	-2.7	-4.1	-3.7	-2.2	-1.1	-0.7
Slow adjusters	-3.2	-3.6	-2.1	-6.3	-3.2	-2.0	0.9
CFA franc countries	-3.1	-4.4	-2.4	-4.6	-3.0	-0.7	0.8
Total government revenue[1]							
Sub-Saharan Africa	15.2	17.9	18.0	16.4	16.7	17.2	19.9
Strong adjusters	11.7	21.8	19.2	22.3	23.9	23.5	23.9
Slow adjusters	17.0	15.8	17.5	13.5	12.6	14.0	17.2
CFA franc countries	22.5	18.3	23.5	16.1	15.9	16.7	17.5
Total government expenditure							
Sub-Saharan Africa	21.2	26.5	24.6	27.8	25.5	24.1	25.7
Strong adjusters	18.0	28.0	26.3	29.7	30.6	28.7	28.3
Slow adjusters	22.9	25.8	23.7	26.8	22.6	21.8	23.8
CFA franc countries	28.8	27.5	29.3	26.4	25.2	23.3	22.0

[1]Excluding grants.

of countries—Angola, Burundi, Ethiopia, Liberia, Mozambique, Nigeria, Rwanda, Sierra Leone, Togo, and Zaïre—for at least part of the period since 1980. In addition, concerns about governance have been compounded by the legacy of repressive regimes in several African countries and the associated lack of effective systems of political checks and balances, as well as by bloated and inefficient public administrations, ineffective judicial systems, and complex administrative and institutional frameworks.

Inappropriate economic policies still being pursued by several African countries, including three of the largest countries in terms of real GDP and population, Cameroon, Nigeria, and Zaïre, have also contributed to the weak aggregate economic performance. The overall performance, however, disguises the considerable diversity in institutional arrangements and economic policies pursued by individual countries. Despite the existing formidable constraints, the countries that have effectively implemented structural adjustment programs have significantly improved their economic fundamentals, permitting an increase of real GDP growth and gains in real per capita incomes in many cases. The reform efforts of many African countries have been supported by the IMF, mainly in the context of the enhanced structural adjustment facility. The number of sub-Saharan African countries implementing broadly appropriate policies has risen

Table 15. Sub-Saharan Africa: External Sector Performance

	Average				Estimates	Projections	
	1980–85	1986–94	1986	1993	1994	1995	1996
External current account[1]			*In percent of GDP*				
Sub-Saharan Africa	−5.3	−6.6	−7.7	−7.0	−6.3	−5.2	−5.8
Strong adjusters	−5.4	−7.1	−5.0	−8.3	−7.4	−7.0	−5.5
Slow adjusters	−5.3	−6.4	−8.9	−6.3	−5.6	−4.3	−5.9
CFA franc countries	−8.6	−8.3	−10.6	−7.4	−5.5	−4.5	−3.8
External debt			*In percent of exports*				
Sub-Saharan Africa	196.1	350.7	321.3	388.8	392.0	354.9	334.5
Strong adjusters	257.3	338.9	306.4	388.2	360.5	342.5	323.8
Slow adjusters	177.2	356.0	327.9	389.1	409.8	361.3	340.1
CFA franc countries	187.6	320.6	227.7	395.6	377.0	329.0	297.5
Nominal effective exchange rate			*1985 = 100*				
Sub-Saharan Africa	191.1	53.3	77.5	49.5	35.1	...	...
Strong adjusters	276.8	56.2	80.1	46.9	35.2	...	...
Slow adjusters	148.9	51.7	76.2	51.0	35.1	...	...
CFA franc countries	99.1	131.8	108.1	173.6	96.4	...	...
Real effective exchange rate							
Sub-Saharan Africa	105.6	57.2	82.1	46.8	42.4	...	...
Strong adjusters	125.4	64.2	87.9	53.1	49.5	...	...
Slow adjusters	96.0	53.3	79.1	43.1	38.2	...	...
CFA franc countries	105.0	99.2	108.8	94.8	59.6	...	...
Terms of trade							
Sub-Saharan Africa	98.4	72.6	83.0	65.4	66.3	67.0	67.0
Strong adjusters	98.4	89.8	103.1	79.8	86.3	86.2	85.1
Slow adjusters	98.2	63.0	72.6	56.9	54.2	55.2	55.8
CFA franc countries	96.2	68.4	86.9	58.8	59.7	64.5	64.8

[1]Excluding grants.

markedly since the late 1980s, reaching about two thirds of the total by 1994, which augurs well for Africa's performance in the period ahead. Progress in removing structural and institutional rigidities and in strengthening the supply response of the private sector, while positive, has been uneven across countries and has fallen short of initial expectations. In particular, only modest progress has been made in reforming the public enterprise and financial sectors and the legal and administrative frameworks, owing in part to the weak management and implementation capacity of the public sector and the severity of the initial macroeconomic imbalances.

Overall, notwithstanding the progress achieved so far, saving and investment rates in sub-Saharan Africa, particularly of the private sector, remain significantly lower than in other developing countries, and too low to support satisfactory sustainable growth (Table 16).[2] Moreover, human capital development and adminis-

trative inefficiencies have also substantially impeded the efficiency of capital and the growth in total factor productivity, which in some sub-Saharan African countries has been negative. Low productivity has contributed to the lack of convergence to the performance of other developing countries.[3]

---

[3]An important prediction of neoclassical growth models is that the output levels of countries with similar technologies should converge. Other things being equal, the assumption of diminishing marginal returns to capital implies that developing countries with low capital-labor ratios should have higher returns to capital and should be expected to attract investment from advanced countries and thus grow faster. Empirical studies, however, have found support only for conditional convergence, after allowing for differences in technology, human capital development, and other determinants of steady-state growth. For more details, see Chapter IV of the May 1994 *World Economic Outlook* and Box 11 of the October 1994 *World Economic Outlook*; Mohsin S. Khan and Manmohan S. Kumar, "Public and Private Investment and the Convergence of Per Capita Incomes in Developing Countries," IMF Working Paper 93/51 (June 1993); and Malcolm Knight, Norman Loayza, and Delano Villanueva, "Testing the Neoclassical Theory of Economic Growth: A Panel Data Approach," *Staff Papers* (IMF), Vol. 40 (September 1993), pp. 512–41.

---

[2]It is estimated that an investment-GDP ratio of about 25 percent would be needed to sustain real GDP growth in sub-Saharan Africa of about 6 percent.

Table 16. Sub-Saharan Africa: Saving and Investment

(In percent of GDP)

	Average		1986	1993	Estimates 1994	Projections	
	1980–85	1986–94	1986	1993	1994	1995	1996
Gross investment							
Sub-Saharan Africa	16.5	17.7	17.9	16.0	19.9	22.3	22.0
Strong adjusters	11.3	19.9	14.9	20.1	23.0	24.2	24.3
Slow adjusters	19.2	16.6	19.3	13.8	18.1	21.3	20.4
CFA franc countries	23.0	17.0	21.3	14.4	16.3	18.1	18.8
Government investment							
Sub-Saharan Africa	8.2	6.7	7.5	6.7	6.9	7.9	7.5
Strong adjusters	4.5	7.1	6.2	7.4	8.2	7.7	7.8
Slow adjusters	10.2	6.5	8.2	6.3	6.1	8.1	7.4
CFA franc countries	10.4	5.9	8.8	4.3	5.4	5.5	5.7
Private investment[1]							
Sub-Saharan Africa	8.2	11.0	10.4	9.3	13.0	14.3	14.5
Strong adjusters	6.8	12.8	8.7	12.7	14.7	16.5	16.6
Slow adjusters	9.0	10.0	11.2	7.5	12.2	13.2	13.0
CFA franc countries	12.6	11.1	12.5	10.1	11.0	12.6	13.1
Gross national savings[2]							
Sub-Saharan Africa	11.6	11.1	10.2	9.0	13.6	17.1	16.2
Strong adjusters	5.8	12.8	9.9	11.7	15.5	17.2	18.7
Slow adjusters	14.7	10.2	10.4	7.6	12.5	17.1	14.5
CFA franc countries	15.1	8.7	10.7	7.0	10.8	13.7	15.0
Government savings[2]							
Sub-Saharan Africa	2.2	–1.9	1.0	–4.7	–12.0	1.0	1.8
Strong adjusters	–1.8	0.9	–1.0	—	1.5	2.5	3.3
Slow adjusters	4.3	–3.4	1.9	–7.0	–3.9	0.3	0.8
CFA franc countries	4.0	–3.3	3.0	–6.0	–4.0	–1.0	1.2
Private savings[1]							
Sub-Saharan Africa	9.4	13.0	9.3	13.7	15.5	16.1	14.4
Strong adjusters	7.7	12.0	10.9	11.8	14.0	14.7	15.4
Slow adjusters	10.3	13.6	8.5	14.6	16.4	16.8	13.7
CFA franc countries	11.0	12.0	7.7	13.0	14.8	14.7	13.8

[1]The private sector includes public enterprises.
[2]Excluding grants.

Adjustment, 1986–94

The considerable diversity in the performance of individual countries or country groups during 1986–94 reflected mainly differences in policy response to the worsening external environment (Chart 37). The countries that have implemented broadly appropriate policies (the strong adjusters)—cushioning the impact of large cumulative losses in their terms of trade by improving their external competitiveness and implementing a range of structural reforms—have done much better than others. The strong adjusters achieved higher rates of savings and investment, and lower inflation, as well as positive growth in per capita real GDP (Chart 38).[4] This experience contrasts markedly with the performance of the more slowly adjusting

countries, which followed generally inappropriate policies during this period, although terms of trade losses for this group of countries were much larger during 1986–94 than for the strong adjusters.[5] Looked at from the point of view of institutional arrangements, the economic performance of the CFA franc

---

[4]This group of countries is defined to comprise 14 countries that effectively implemented broadly appropriate policies under IMF-supported programs for at least three years during 1986–93 (namely, Benin, Burundi, The Gambia, Ghana, Kenya, Lesotho,

Malawi, Mali, Mozambique, Niger, Senegal, Tanzania, Togo, and Uganda); a few of these countries did not sustain a satisfactory performance throughout this period. In addition, the strong adjusters include a group of 5 countries characterized during this period by relatively low internal and external imbalances (Botswana, Mauritius, Seychelles, Swaziland, and Zimbabwe).

[5]For a comprehensive assessment of the recent economic performance of sub-Saharan Africa, see Michael T. Hadjimichael, Dhaneshwar Ghura, Martin Mühleisen, Roger Nord, and Murat Uçer, *Sub-Saharan Africa: Growth, Savings, and Investment, 1986–93*, IMF Occasional Paper No. 118 (January 1995). The empirical analysis of the paper, based on cross-sectional data for 1986–92, suggests that, after population growth and unfavorable weather, inappropriate macroeconomic policies were the second most important factor contributing to the poor per capita growth performance of sub-Saharan African countries.

Chart 37. Sub-Saharan Africa: Terms of Trade and Real Effective Exchange Rates[1]

(1985 = 100)

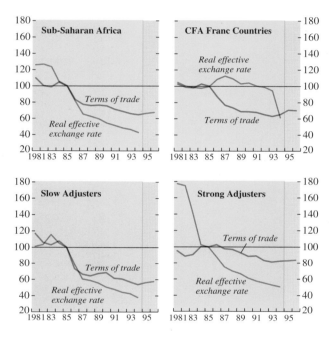

[1]Blue shaded areas indicate IMF staff projections.

countries was also very poor in relation to that of the non-CFA franc countries. Given their adherence to a fixed nominal exchange rate peg, the CFA franc countries relied until January 1994 entirely on internal adjustment measures to address their intensifying adjustment needs in the face of a protracted decline in their terms of trade.

Real GDP growth for sub-Saharan African countries as a group averaged 2½ percent a year during 1986–94, well short of average population growth; as a consequence, per capita real GDP declined further, by ½ of 1 percent a year. Aggregate inflation has been high because of hyperinflation in Zaïre, where annual inflation rose to 23,900 percent in 1994. Excluding Zaïre, consumer price inflation in sub-Saharan Africa remained within a range of 14–36 percent, without any clear trend, and averaged 24 percent a year during 1986–94. The variability of inflation largely reflected changes in the stance of monetary policy and the impact of adverse weather on food prices,[6] as well as the impact of nominal exchange rate adjustments in countries with flexible exchange rate arrangements and inadequately restrictive monetary conditions.

In broad terms, however, financial policies in sub-Saharan African countries as a group fell short of bringing inflation under control and reducing external imbalances. Although some countries and country groups have made varying degrees of progress toward macroeconomic stability, the attainment of this objective has eluded most sub-Saharan African countries. The stance of fiscal policy, as measured by changes in the primary government budget balance (excluding grants) as a ratio to GDP, fluctuated from year to year. With increasing interest payments on public debt, the overall budget deficit (excluding grants) widened markedly, to about 9 percent of GDP by 1994, a level still significantly higher than that required to stabilize the ratio of public debt to GDP. The growth in (broad) money supply also fluctuated from year to year, reflecting in part a sizable variability in the velocity of circulation. While some progress was made by several countries to establish positive real interest rates, they remain negative for sub-Saharan Africa as a group.

External sector developments since 1986 have been characterized by large current account deficits (excluding official transfers) as a ratio to GDP and a steep expansion in the external public debt in relation to both GDP and export earnings, thus underscoring the unsustainable nature of the external imbalances. In annual average terms, the external performance worsened substantially during 1986–94 relative to the first half of the 1980s. Movements in the current account balance reflected developments in the external environment, the stance of domestic financial policies, and

---

[6]Food items comprise the bulk of the goods included in the consumer price indices of virtually all sub-Saharan African countries.

the impact of exogenous supply-side developments induced mainly by changes in the weather. In the early 1990s, the external environment of sub-Saharan African countries worsened sharply as a result of a marked weakening in economic activity in industrial countries, which constitute the main destination of the primary commodity exports of African countries, and a collapse of economic activity in the countries in transition. These events exacerbated the long-term downward trend in real commodity prices and resulted in large cumulative losses in the terms of trade of African countries, amounting to about 34 percent between 1985 and 1994 for sub-Saharan Africa as a whole. There were, however, some notable differences in the magnitude of terms of trade changes among countries or country groups; a small number of countries actually had significant gains in their terms of trade.

The widening external financing requirements of sub-Saharan African countries were covered mainly by increasing inflows of foreign assistance in the form of grants and concessional long-term loans and by debt reschedulings by Paris Club and other creditors. Several countries also accumulated external debt-service payments arrears. Inflows of foreign direct investment remained very modest and were exceeded by short-term private capital outflows.[7] Despite sizable debt forgiveness provided by several official creditors, the external public debt burden of sub-Saharan African countries as a group increased markedly during 1986–94. The debt-to-GDP ratio rose from an annual average of 33 percent during 1980–85 to an estimated 98 percent by 1994, a level substantially higher than that of other developing countries. Moreover, with the stagnation of export earnings and major nominal exchange rate adjustments since 1990, the ratio of debt to exports increased sharply to about 390 percent by 1994, almost twice its level during 1980–85.

A clearer indication of the progress made by sub-Saharan African countries in reducing their domestic and external imbalances on a durable basis and attaining a viable balance of payments position is provided by the evolution of aggregate and sectoral savings and investment ratios.[8] Developments in savings and investment balances reflect not only the stance of financial policies but, more important, the impact of structural and institutional factors, particularly on the evolution of private saving and investment. In virtually all of sub-Saharan Africa, private sector activity

Chart 38. Sub-Saharan Africa: Real GDP and Per Capita Income[1]

(Annual percent change)

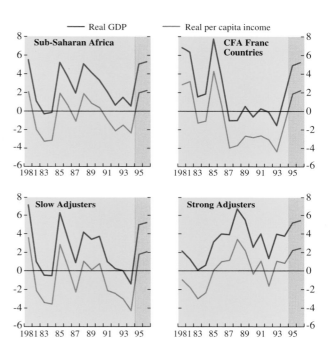

[1]Blue shaded areas indicate IMF staff projections.

---

[7]Total inflows of foreign direct investment of developing countries are estimated at about $134 billion during 1991–93, with the bulk (about 78 percent) flowing into Asian and Latin American countries and only about $2 billion (1½ percent) going to sub-Saharan Africa.

[8]Estimates of aggregate and sectoral savings and investment balances in sub-Saharan Africa are subject to major data deficiencies and thus should be interpreted with caution.

has been strongly impeded by a broad range of structural, legal, administrative, and other institutional constraints. These impediments, combined with inappropriate domestic policies and the impact of external shocks, contributed to the emergence of major imbalances and declines in real incomes prior to 1986.

In recent years, as an integral part of their adjustment programs, many countries have implemented a number of structural reforms aimed at alleviating these impediments and stimulating the development of the private sector. These measures have included the lifting of controls on retail and producer prices and on marketing arrangements for agricultural products; the liberalization of exchange and trade systems; the lifting of interest rate controls, the introduction of government financial instruments, the restructuring of commercial banks, and other monetary policy and financial sector reforms; the broadening of the tax base and other tax reforms to strengthen economic incentives and promote equity; the restructuring and privatization of public enterprises; the implementation of civil service and other administrative reforms to improve efficiency and enhance the economic management capacity of the public sector; and the introduction of legal and institutional reforms. The range and effectiveness of the various reform measures have varied significantly from country to country.

For sub-Saharan Africa as a whole, private saving rose markedly between 1986 and 1994, facilitating both a modest increase in private investment and a strong improvement in the private sector net financial balance. This improvement offset a widening in the government net financial deficit, caused by a decline in government saving that was only in part compensated by a decline in government investment, and allowed a modest narrowing of the external current account deficit.

Strong Adjusters

While a rather heterogeneous set of countries, the strong adjusters generally pursued fairly comprehensive programs of macroeconomic adjustment and structural reforms during 1986–94. What differentiates the performance of these countries from that of the slow adjusters is the significantly greater progress toward establishing macroeconomic stability and effectively implementing a broad range of structural reforms. For the most part, they have also managed to sustain the gains from these reforms. An improvement in their external competitiveness was a crucial beneficial effect of these policies. The decline in their real effective exchange rates came about through nominal exchange rate adjustments, domestic cost containment, or both, which markedly exceeded the cumulative losses in their terms of trade during 1986–94. The resulting strengthening of economic incentives and

the alleviation of structural and institutional impediments to growth have strengthened the supply response of these countries. The lifting of interest rate controls and the other far-reaching financial sector reforms introduced by several strong adjusters, such as Ghana and Kenya, have improved the flexibility of macroeconomic policies and the capacity of these countries to more adequately respond to domestic and external shocks.

The broadening of the tax bases and the tax reforms implemented by the strong adjusters facilitated a steep increase in government revenue and expenditure, while allowing also for a narrowing of fiscal imbalances, in sharp contrast to the experience of the other sub-Saharan African countries. Government savings and investment rose relative to GDP between 1986 and 1994, as well as relative to the first half of the 1980s, fostering private sector development. Private investment increased twice as fast as private savings. The counterpart to this was a modest widening of the external current account deficit. However, the larger current account imbalances were covered fully by larger inflows of official grants, reflecting the increasing support provided by bilateral and multilateral donors to the reform efforts of the strong adjusters.

As a consequence, despite the impact of the severe drought in southern Africa in the early 1990s, real GDP growth of the strong adjusters accelerated from 1½ percent a year during the first half of the 1980s to an annual average rate of 4 percent during 1986–94, a rate substantially higher than that of sub-Saharan Africa as a whole. The decline in per capita real GDP of 1½ percent a year during 1980–85 was reversed, with gains of 1 percent a year during 1986–94.

Slow Adjusters

Until 1993, the slowly adjusting countries were characterized by too modest progress toward macroeconomic stability, as well as by more timid efforts in implementing structural reforms. The policy effort was weak compared with other sub-Saharan African countries and disappointing relative to the seriousness of the distortions in these economies. The overall and the primary budget deficits of the slowly adjusting countries more than doubled in relation to GDP between 1986 and 1993 because of declining government revenue and increasing government expenditure. With the adoption of corrective measures in 1994 by several of these countries, fiscal imbalances narrowed sharply, but on average fiscal deficits during 1986–94 remained significantly larger than in the first half of the 1980s. For the 1986–94 period as a whole, government saving declined sharply, inducing both a significant reduction in government investment and a widening of the government net financial deficit. Private saving almost doubled relative to GDP during the period; private investment declined markedly during 1986–93 but is estimated to have recovered in 1994. Overall, and reflecting financing constraints, the slow adjusters recorded a narrowing of their external current account deficit. Until 1993, however, this was the result of a sharper reduction in aggregate investment than in total saving, indicative of the poor investment climate and generally weak economic incentives in this group of countries.

As a consequence, real GDP growth of the slow adjusters decelerated and turned negative by 1994. The annual average declines in per capita real GDP steepened from ½ of 1 percent during 1980–85 to over 1 percent during 1986–94. Average inflation also rose steeply, even after excluding the impact of hyperinflation in Zaïre.

CFA Franc Countries

The CFA franc countries, some of which are included in the group of slowly adjusting countries, were the only country group in sub-Saharan Africa to record positive gains in real per capita incomes during the first half of the 1980s. Nonetheless, their broadly inadequate policy responses to the worsening in their terms of trade after 1985 resulted in stagnation in real GDP and accelerating losses in real per capita incomes during the period to 1993. The fixed value of the CFA franc vis-à-vis the French franc and the sharp reduction in inflation in France resulted in exceptionally low inflation in the CFA franc countries during 1986–93, amounting on average to a mere 1½ percent a year. However, the strong value of the French franc and real effective depreciations of the currencies of the main trading partners contributed to an appreciation of the CFA franc in nominal effective terms. This appreciation, notwithstanding the excellent inflation performance, limited the gains in the CFA franc countries' external competitiveness during 1986–93 to only 5 percent—a too modest improvement, given the cumulative decline in their terms of trade of 41 percent.

As a result of the real appreciation and the decline in export prices, export earnings declined, disposable incomes fell, and the government revenue base narrowed sharply. In the face of declining government saving, government investment was cut. This did not, however, prevent a large widening of fiscal imbalances and the emergence of domestic and external government payments arrears, undermining the financial health of commercial banks. The inappropriate mix of fiscal and monetary policies gave rise to increasing real interest rates. Combined with the structural and institutional rigidities, the inappropriate stance of policies stifled private sector activity and contributed to a decline in private investment. Total investment and, to a lesser extent, aggregate saving declined relative to GDP during 1986–93, which reduced the external current account deficit somewhat.

The attempt to contain the external imbalances of the CFA franc countries largely through internal adjustment policies was clearly deflationary and unsustainable, as evidenced by the marked losses in real per capita incomes and the difficulties experienced in implementing cuts in public expenditures and wages. The internal adjustment measures that several CFA franc countries implemented, while necessary, were not sufficient to adequately address the impact of the worsening terms of trade. In response to this realization, CFA franc countries devalued by 50 percent (Comoros, by 33 percent) the external value of their currency in early January 1994 and have since begun to implement comprehensive, growth-oriented adjustment strategies.[9]

The first results from the implementation of the stepped-up reform efforts since early 1994 are broadly encouraging. The removal of most of the distortions in the structure of relative prices, including agricultural producer prices, combined with a recovery in world commodity prices, strengthened economic incentives and boosted output growth despite a sharp reduction in real domestic demand. Real GDP is estimated to have increased 1½ percent in 1994 after a decline of the same magnitude in 1993. The inflationary impact of the devaluation was contained through a marked moderation of wage increases in both the government and private sectors. After an initial large adjustment in consumer prices in the first quarter of 1994, price increases slowed sharply, containing average inflation for the year as a whole to about 30 percent.

Difficulties arose, however, in effectively implementing tax and other structural reforms, particularly among the six countries that are members of the Central African Economic and Monetary Community. Government revenues did not pick up, owing largely to difficulties in implementing customs reforms, a weakening in tax administration, and a modest expansion in taxable imports. Nonetheless, cuts in government consumption have helped to raise government saving and reduce fiscal deficits. The private sector is estimated to have responded to the new policy environment by raising saving and, to a lesser extent, investment. Overall, the external current account deficit declined, contributing to a significant improvement in the gross official reserve position of the CFA franc countries as a group. This improvement reflected also the resumption of external assistance, including sizable debt relief by Paris Club and other creditors, as well as a reversal of private capital flight.

---

[9]For a review of the adjustment experience in the CFA franc countries and an outline of the objectives and policies of the new adjustment programs, see Mamoudou Touré and Jean A.P. Clement in *IMF Survey*, Special Supplement on African Franc Zone (March 21, 1994), and Box 8 in the May 1994 *World Economic Outlook*.

Challenges for the Period Ahead

While the overall economic performance of sub-Saharan Africa in recent years has been less than satisfactory, a number of positive developments have taken place that augur well for an improved performance in the period ahead.

Virtually all African countries have come to accept that a reversal of existing imbalances and the establishment of a foundation for sustainable growth require the maintenance of macroeconomic stability and the removal of structural rigidities to strengthen and realize growth potential. This requires increased reliance on market-based instruments of policy, improved transparency and governance, and the establishment of a supportive environment for the development of the private sector, the main engine of growth. Consequently, an increasing number of sub-Saharan African countries have embarked on growth-oriented adjustment programs, with support from the IMF and the World Bank as well as from bilateral and multilateral donors. The increasing "ownership" of these programs by individual countries has been a crucial factor behind their successful implementation. Owing primarily to a number of political, social, and security difficulties, the remaining countries have not yet mustered the domestic political consensus and commitment needed to adopt comprehensive adjustment programs.

While much remains to be done to achieve macroeconomic stability and remove structural and institutional impediments to growth, virtually all sub-Saharan African countries, including the slow adjusters, have already removed the bulk of the distortions in relative prices. With the recent exchange rate parity adjustment by the CFA franc countries, existing exchange rates in sub-Saharan African countries are considered to have been brought close to their equilibrium levels, a major achievement in comparison with the sizable misalignments of the early 1980s. In addition, far-reaching reforms have been introduced in the exchange and trade systems of all sub-Saharan African countries. Several countries have by now fully liberalized their payments and transfers for current international transactions. Moreover, while the external imbalances remain large, several African countries—including most of the strong adjusters and, more recently, several CFA franc countries—have strengthened their gross official reserve positions, thus providing a much-needed cushion against potential future shocks.

Nonetheless, a number of key policy challenges remain, which need to be addressed with determination in the period ahead.

- First, adjustment efforts need to be consolidated or intensified in countries that have already embarked on comprehensive adjustment programs, while appropriate adjustment programs need to be adopted by the remaining sub-Saharan African countries as a matter of urgency. The adoption and effective implementation of reform programs by Cameroon, Nigeria, and Zaïre, the three largest African countries, would play a crucial role in improving the economic performance of sub-Saharan Africa as a whole.

- Second, fiscal imbalances are still unduly large. The progress made so far in lowering or containing these imbalances is often fragile or precarious. Deficit reduction has relied often on government expenditure restraint, because government revenues have declined in recent years in relation to GDP in several sub-Saharan African countries. Accordingly, intensified efforts are needed to strengthen government revenue mobilization and government saving, so as to finance the needed expansion in the economic and social infrastructure while allowing a further reduction in fiscal imbalances. Budgeting and control procedures for government expenditure should also be strengthened through public expenditure reviews to eliminate unproductive expenditure and increase efficiency. In many countries, there is a need to press ahead with the restructuring of public spending, through reform of the civil service and the scaling down of budgetary transfers and subsidies.

- Third, an acceleration of per capita real GDP growth will require a significant further increase in saving and investment by both the government and the private sector, as well as improvements in the efficiency of capital and labor and gains in total factor productivity. Stronger efforts to boost domestic and foreign private investment will be critically important. To this end, the restructuring of public enterprises, and structural and institutional reforms in general, would need to be intensified.

- Finally, stepped-up efforts are also needed to enhance the economic management and monitoring capacity of the public sector and to improve governance more generally. Political liberalization efforts in recent years in several sub-Saharan African countries—including the lifting of restrictions on the formation of political parties and on freedom of the press, as well as the holding of multiparty parliamentary and presidential elections—constitute a major step toward strengthening governance. The increased public debate, and improved accountability and transparency in the application of economic decisions, likely to result from this process should enhance governance and help foster political consensus on the need for economic reforms.

Against the background of a significant improvement in the external environment, the short-term outlook for sub-Saharan Africa is better than it has been in decades. Real GDP growth is expected to average a robust 5 percent a year during 1995–96, allowing gains in real per capita incomes of 2 percent a year. At the same time, average inflation is projected to slow to 12 percent by 1996, and the external current account deficit is expected to narrow. The improved growth prospects largely reflect the expected pursuit of appropriate reform efforts by most of the sub-Saharan African countries. The pickup in world demand has already raised world commodity prices, including the prices of the agricultural, mineral, and other primary commodities exported by African countries. However, the overall gains in the terms of trade are expected to be very modest, except for the CFA franc countries.

Over the medium term, prospects for exports will be favorably influenced by the completion of the Uruguay Round and the associated liberalization of trade in agricultural products and improved access to industrial country markets.[10] The reduction in protection by industrial countries will support the outward-oriented trade policies pursued by sub-Saharan African countries and help stimulate output growth. The economic liberalization and restructuring efforts

being undertaken in South Africa will facilitate closer integration of that country into the regional and world economy, thus giving a potential additional boost to trade and productivity for the region. Overall, these factors should help sustain medium-term growth in sub-Saharan Africa at a level substantially higher than the poor performance of the past couple of decades.

It should be recognized, however, that the above projections, while potentially well within reach, are subject to sizable downside risks. First, they are crucially dependent on effective implementation of the adjustment programs adopted by individual countries, including the countries that have so far been slow to embark on sufficiently ambitious reform programs. The risk of slippages or deviations from the announced programs is particularly high for some of the largest African countries, given their weak record of policy implementation. The prospects for reduced inflation, for example, hinge critically on a successful implementation of the anti-inflation program adopted by the new government in Zaïre. Second, the projected real GDP growth assumes normal weather. Finally, the attainment of external objectives is conditional on the timely provision of adequate foreign financial and technical assistance. Given their heavy external debt-servicing burden, sub-Saharan African countries will continue to rely in the foreseeable future on concessional assistance from bilateral and multilateral donors, as well as on additional debt relief from Paris Club and other creditors. In this context, the recent decision by Paris Club creditors to increase the level of concessionality of their debt relief would contribute to meeting the still large exceptional financing needs of sub-Saharan African countries.

---

[10]Some African countries that are net food importers have expressed concern that the higher food prices likely to result from this liberalization might adversely affect their external position; however, it is likely that this would be alleviated over time by the positive response of food production and productivity to the higher food prices.

Annex III

Structural Fiscal Balances in Smaller Industrial Countries

Faced with large fiscal deficits and, in many instances, heavy and growing public debt burdens, most industrial countries are engaged in medium-term efforts at fiscal consolidation. Volatile short-term macroeconomic conditions, however, often make it difficult to assess the need for consolidation, as they introduce temporary changes in deficits that obscure the permanent or structural stance of fiscal policies. For these reasons, previous issues of the *World Economic Outlook* have made extensive use of staff estimates of structural fiscal balances for the major industrial economies. The current issue extends the use of this indicator, which abstracts from cyclical variations, to a number of smaller industrial countries. While data problems in some countries require that the results be interpreted with caution, the figures are useful indicators of underlying fiscal developments.

Estimates of the structural fiscal balance result from a decomposition of fiscal revenues, expenditures, and balances into structural and cyclical elements.[1] By construction, the structural component of each aggregate is the estimated level that would obtain in a given year if output were at its potential level. The cyclical component of each is the difference between the actual and structural levels. To do these calculations, it is necessary to have estimates of potential GDP, the percentage deviation or "gap" of actual output with respect to potential, and estimates of the responsiveness of revenues and expenditures to these cyclical output gaps. Estimates of the responsiveness of revenues are based primarily on estimates of the cyclical elasticities of national revenue systems. The responsiveness of expenditures reflects the responsiveness of unemployment insurance to cyclical variations of unemployment around the level estimated to be consistent with nonaccelerating inflation.

A useful means of approximating the staff's estimates of the responses of fiscal aggregates to changes in the output gap is through cyclical response coefficients. These coefficients show the likely sensitivities of the ratios of aggregate revenues and expenditures to GDP with respect to a 1 percentage point increase in the output gap. The coefficients allow the cyclical element of each fiscal aggregate to be computed as the product of the output gap and the corresponding cyclical response coefficient in each year. The structural component of each fiscal aggregate is then derived by subtracting the estimated cyclical element from the observed level.

Conceptually, potential GDP is the level of output that would be predicted by an aggregate production function if multifactor productivity and labor force participation were at their noncyclical trend levels and if the unemployment rate were equal to the nonaccelerating inflation rate of unemployment (NAIRU). For a number of countries, the estimates of potential output are based on estimated production functions embodying these considerations. In other cases, the estimates are based on statistical estimates of trend output. In some countries, such as Finland, Ireland, New Zealand, and Norway, the staff has adjusted the estimates to account for the influences of divergent sectoral developments, structural changes, volatile labor markets, and other shocks; in these cases, the results must be regarded as highly tentative and should be interpreted with particular care.[2] For the group of smaller industrial countries considered here, the estimates suggest that the annual growth of potential output has been about 2½ percent during the 1980s and the early 1990s (Table 17). This overall behavior masks considerable variation among countries. In the first half of the 1990s, potential output growth was estimated to be the most rapid in Ireland, owing to rapid growth of the capital stock and, to a lesser extent, increases in the labor force, and in Australia, reflecting productivity improvements from structural reforms. In the middle years of the decade, estimated potential growth in New Zealand accelerates strongly as a result of structural reforms in that country.

This annex was prepared by Frederick Ribe.

[1]For a detailed description of the methodology used to estimate structural balances, as well as alternative approaches, see Annex I of the October 1993 *World Economic Outlook*. Projections of actual fiscal balances are prepared by IMF staff.

[2]Estimates for Finland, where real GDP dropped by 12 percent in 1990–93, must take into account the sharply diverging developments in the export-oriented manufacturing sector compared with the weak domestically oriented sectors. In Norway, the differential behavior of mainland and offshore production must be taken into consideration. In New Zealand, extensive recent programs of deregulation and structural reform have significantly affected the efficiency of capital allocation and with it both the level and trend of total-factor productivity. Finally, estimates of the labor force and of unemployment in Ireland are heavily affected by the cyclical variability of net rates of emigration.

Table 17. Selected Smaller Industrial Countries: Potential Output

(Average annual percent change)

	1971–79	1980–89	1990–95
Australia	3.7	3.2	3.2
Austria	3.6	2.1	2.8
Belgium	3.2	2.2	2.1
Denmark	2.5	2.0	2.3
Finland	. . .	3.0	1.3
Ireland	4.1	3.5	5.0
Netherlands	3.3	2.1	2.4
New Zealand[1]	2.3	1.8	1.6
Norway[2]	3.4	2.1	1.5
Spain	3.8	2.5	2.9
Sweden	2.9	2.1	1.3
Average of above countries	3.4	2.4	2.5

Source: IMF staff estimates.

[1]Potential output growth is estimated to average 2.9 percent during 1993–95.

[2]Mainland Norway; excludes oil sector.

Estimates of the responsiveness of revenues and expenditures to cyclical output gaps reflect both observed ratios of these aggregates to GDP and the estimated elasticities of revenues and expenditures with respect to cyclical fluctuations in GDP.[3] Revenues are particularly sensitive to the cycle in countries whose revenue structures depend heavily on cyclically elastic taxes, such as corporate or progressive personal income taxes. The cyclical responsiveness of expenditures depends on the level of unemployment benefits and on the response of unemployment to cyclical fluctuations in output. The staff has used OECD estimates of revenue elasticities and its own estimates of the responsiveness of unemployment rates to cyclical variations in output in different countries.[4]

The separate coefficient estimates for revenues and expenditures are combined to generate a response coefficient for the fiscal balance. For example, a response coefficient of 1 indicates that a 1 percentage point increase in the output gap leads to a cyclical deterioration of 1 percentage point in the ratio of the fiscal balance to GDP. Using this, it is possible to infer how much the actual balance changes as a result of movements in the output gap. The coefficient estimates show wide variation in the cyclical sensitivity of the ratios of revenues and expenditures to GDP across countries (Table 18). Particularly on the revenue side, the variation among countries far exceeds that among the major industrial countries, largely because of the high cyclical sensitivity for countries such as Sweden, the Netherlands, and Norway. The strong cyclical responsiveness in these countries reflects the high ratios of revenue to GDP (about 60 percent in all three countries) and revenue systems that are very elastic with respect to cyclical changes in the economy. While the ratio of expenditures to GDP is much less sensitive to the cycle in all countries, there is significant cyclical responsiveness in some, especially Belgium, Denmark, and Sweden. This sensitivity largely reflects high current levels of unemployment and unemployment benefits.

The estimates of structural budget balances suggest that in a number of countries significant fiscal consolidation efforts will be necessary to reduce the large structural deficits expected in 1995–96 (Table 19). These estimates should be interpreted as broadly indicative of the structural component of budget balances rather than precise estimates because of the margin of uncertainty that attaches to estimates of potential output and to tax and expenditure elasticities with respect to national income, particularly during periods of structural change. Moreover, it is important to note that changes in structural budget balances are not necessarily attributable to policy changes, but may also reflect the built-in momentum of existing expenditure programs.

[3]Viewed in relation to revenues, the relationship between the elasticity, E, and the cyclical response parameter, C, is approximated by $C \approx R \cdot E$, where R is the revenue-GDP ratio. The cyclical response coefficient for expenditures is derived similarly. Owing to collection lags for corporate income taxes and lags in the response of unemployment to changes in the GDP gap, the cyclical components of revenues and expenditures in a given year are based on current and lagged response coefficients. For simplicity, however, current and lagged effects have been consolidated in the estimates presented here.

[4]See Claude Giorno, Pete Richardson, Debbie Roseveare, and Paul van den Noord, "Estimating Potential Output, Output Gaps and Structural Budget Balances," OECD Economics Department Working Paper No. 152 (forthcoming, 1995). IMF staff estimates were used for the New Zealand revenue elasticity. In the case of New Zealand, extensive fiscal reforms in recent years may have altered the cyclical responsiveness of revenues and expenditures compared with the 1980s.

Table 18. Selected Smaller Industrial Countries: Cyclical Responsiveness of General Government Budget[1]

	Revenues	Expenditures	Balance
Australia	0.34	−0.10	0.43
Austria	0.45	−0.13	0.58
Belgium	0.52	−0.24	0.75
Denmark	0.49	−0.19	0.68
Finland	0.50	−0.08	0.58
Ireland	0.51	−0.09	0.60
Netherlands	0.65	−0.14	0.79
Norway	0.70	−0.08	0.78
New Zealand	0.40	−0.10	0.50
Spain	0.45	−0.16	0.61
Sweden	0.76	−0.21	0.98

Source: IMF staff estimates.

[1]Percentage point change in the ratio of fiscal aggregate to GDP for a 1 percentage point change in the output gap. Figures consolidate current and lagged effects.

Table 19. Selected Smaller Industrial Countries: General Government Structural Balances, Actual Balances, and Output Gaps[1]

	1987	1988	1989	1990	1991	1992	1993	1994	1995–96
Australia									
Structural balance	−0.9	0.4	0.4	−0.2	−1.6	−2.7	−1.7	−1.4	−1.1
Output gap	1.4	2.3	3.6	1.7	−2.7	−3.8	−3.3	−1.9	−0.5
Actual balance	−0.7	1.0	1.6	0.5	−2.6	−4.6	−3.6	−2.7	−1.6
Austria									
Structural balance	−3.1	−2.8	−4.0	−3.6	−3.5	−2.5	−3.3	−3.5	−4.2
Output gap	−1.8	−0.3	1.2	2.0	1.3	—	−2.2	−1.7	−0.7
Actual balance	−4.3	−3.0	−2.8	−2.2	−2.4	−2.0	−4.1	−4.0	−4.1
Belgium									
Structural balance	−4.9	−6.0	−6.7	−6.8	−7.9	−7.7	−5.1	−3.9	−3.8
Output gap	−3.1	−0.6	0.6	1.6	1.6	1.3	−2.3	−2.0	−0.7
Actual balance	−7.4	−6.6	−6.2	−5.4	−6.5	−6.7	−6.6	−5.4	−4.3
Denmark									
Structural balance	1.1	−0.2	−0.5	−1.3	−1.3	−0.4	−0.8	−2.4	−1.8
Output gap	1.7	1.0	−0.3	−0.7	−1.4	−3.3	−5.3	−2.0	−0.3
Actual balance	2.4	0.6	−0.5	−1.5	−2.1	−2.6	−4.4	−4.3	−2.0
Finland									
Structural balance	0.7	2.6	3.3	2.4	—	−1.2	−1.2	—	−1.9
Output gap	0.8	3.0	6.2	5.4	−2.5	−6.6	−9.0	−7.6	−4.2
Actual balance	1.1	4.1	6.3	5.4	−1.5	−5.9	−7.8	−5.5	−4.8
Ireland									
Structural balance	−6.7	−0.2	−2.0	−3.4	−2.7	−2.8	−2.4	−2.5	−2.6
Output gap	−4.3	−4.2	−1.5	0.8	−0.6	—	−0.5	−0.1	—
Actual balance	−9.8	−3.3	−2.6	−2.5	−2.9	−2.9	−2.7	−2.5	−2.5
Netherlands									
Structural balance	−4.8	−3.5	−5.1	−6.7	−4.5	−4.7	−2.5	−2.6	−2.9
Output gap	−1.6	−1.5	0.6	2.2	2.0	0.8	−1.3	−1.1	−0.2
Actual balance	−5.9	−4.6	−4.7	−5.1	−2.9	−3.9	−3.3	−3.5	−3.1
New Zealand									
Structural balance[2]	−2.5	−1.6	−0.7	−1.1	−0.8	−0.3	0.1	1.2	2.5
Output gap	−0.7	0.2	−1.0	−1.7	−4.1	−5.3	−3.2	−1.2	0.4
Actual balance[2]	−2.4	−1.6	−1.3	−2.4	−3.4	−3.6	−1.9	0.3	2.5
Norway									
Structural balance	3.8	3.6	4.9	6.2	1.9	−0.4	−2.3	−1.9	−1.8
Excluding oil revenues	3.8	3.8	1.8	0.4	−4.6	−6.6	−7.8	−6.7	−9.2
Output gap	4.9	1.7	−1.8	−1.9	−3.7	−3.0	−2.6	−0.9	0.3
Actual balance	7.3	5.3	4.0	4.6	−0.9	−3.2	−4.7	−3.1	−1.5
Spain									
Structural balance	−3.0	−4.0	−4.2	−5.1	−5.6	−3.6	−4.2	−3.0	−2.9
Output gap	0.3	1.8	2.2	1.3	0.3	−1.7	−4.6	−5.0	−4.0
Actual balance	−3.1	−3.3	−2.8	−3.9	−5.0	−4.5	−7.5	−6.7	−5.9
Sweden									
Structural balance	0.5	−0.1	1.9	0.9	−1.9	−5.4	−8.1	−7.5	−6.2
Output gap	5.1	4.6	4.2	2.7	—	−2.2	−4.7	−3.7	−2.5
Actual balance	4.2	3.5	5.4	4.2	−1.1	−7.4	−13.3	−11.4	−8.4
Smaller industrial countries[3]									
Structural balance	−2.2	−2.0	−2.2	−3.0	−3.7	−3.6	−3.3	−2.8	−2.8
Output gap	0.3	1.1	1.9	1.6	−0.3	−1.6	−3.5	−2.9	−1.6
Actual balance	−2.1	−1.5	−1.2	−2.0	−3.7	−4.8	−6.1	−5.2	−4.3

[1]The structural budget balance is the budgetary position that would be observed if the level of actual output coincided with potential output. Changes in the structural budget balance consequently include effects of temporary fiscal measures, the impact of fluctuations in interest rates and debt-service costs, and other noncyclical fluctuations in the budget balance. The computations of structural budget balances are based on staff estimates of potential GDP and revenue and expenditure elasticities (see the text). Structural balances are expressed as a percent of potential output, and the output gap is defined as actual output minus potential output, as a percent of potential output.

[2]Excludes privatization receipts.

[3]Averages for countries listed above.

While most smaller industrial countries have experienced significant fiscal deficits during the first half of the 1990s, the structural component of these imbalances has varied considerably.[5] Recent deficits in Australia, Denmark, Finland, and New Zealand are estimated to have been largely cyclical. In Finland, the deterioration in the structural balance between 1994 and 1995–96 is caused mainly by the direct fiscal impact of accession to the European Union. By contrast, while recent economic recoveries have brought about some reductions in overall deficits, a significant structural component has remained in several European countries. This is particularly true in Austria, Belgium, and Sweden; and, to a lesser extent, in Ireland, the Netherlands, and Spain. In some of these countries, the scope for further cyclical improvements in the deficit appears to have been largely exhausted. In Norway, the relatively small structural deficit reflects substantial oil revenues, amounting to roughly 6 percent of mainland GDP in recent years, that have been used to finance mainland fiscal expenditure.

---

[5]IMF staff estimates for the major industrial countries are presented in Chapter II (Table 4).

Statistical Appendix

Assumptions

The statistical tables in this appendix have been compiled on the basis of information available on April 10, 1995. The estimates and projections for 1995 and 1996, as well as those for the 1997–2000 medium-term scenario, are based on a number of assumptions and working hypotheses.

- For the industrial countries, real effective exchange rates are assumed to remain constant at their average level during March 1–24, 1995, except for the bilateral exchange rates among the ERM currencies, which are assumed to remain constant in nominal terms. For 1995 and 1996, these assumptions imply average U.S. dollar/SDR conversion rates of 1.522 and 1.535, respectively.
- "Established" policies of national authorities will be maintained.
- The price of oil will average $16.90 a barrel in 1995 and 1996. In the medium term, the oil price is assumed to remain unchanged in real terms.
- Interest rates, as represented by the London interbank offered rate (LIBOR) on six-month U.S. dollar deposits, will average 6¾ percent in 1995 and 7 percent in 1996; the three-month certificate of deposit rate in Japan will average 1¾ percent in 1995 and 2¾ percent in 1996; and the three-month interbank deposit rate in Germany will average 5¼ percent in 1995 and 6 percent in 1996.

Data and Conventions

Data and projections for more than 180 countries form the statistical basis for the *World Economic Outlook* (the World Economic Outlook data base). The data are maintained jointly by the IMF's Research Department and area departments, with the latter regularly preparing country projections based on consistent global assumptions, such as those summarized above.

Although national statistical agencies are the ultimate providers of historical data and definitions, international organizations are also involved in statistical issues, with the aim of harmonizing differences among national statistical systems, of setting international standards with respect to definitions, and of pro-

viding conceptual frameworks for measurement and presentation of economic statistics. As regards the World Economic Outlook data base, updates and revisions by both national source agencies and international organizations are used.

Over the past several years, two developments of major importance for improving the standards of economic statistics and analysis have been the comprehensive work to revise the United Nations' standardized *System of National Accounts* (*SNA*) and the IMF's *Balance of Payments Manual (BPM)*. Work on both projects was completed in late 1993, and the *System of National Accounts 1993* as well as the fifth edition of the *Balance of Payments Manual* have been issued.[1] The IMF was actively involved in both projects, particularly the new *Balance of Payments Manual*, which is central to the IMF's interest in countries' external positions. Key changes introduced with the new *Manual* were summarized in the May 1994 *World Economic Outlook* (Box 13).

Beginning with this *World Economic Outlook*, a process of adapting country balance of payments data to the definitions of the new *Balance of Payments Manual* has begun. However, full concordance with the *BPM* is ultimately dependent on national statistical compilers providing revised country data, and hence the *World Economic Outlook* estimates are now only partly adapted to the *BPM*. In accordance with *BPM*, trade in goods and services exclude net factor income. Hence, in Statistical Appendix Tables A36, A38, A42, and A43, ratios to goods and services will tend to be higher than in previous *World Economic Outlook*s. Also beginning with this *World Economic Outlook*, estimates for foreign trade in goods and for trade prices are drawn as far as possible from national accounts data. For countries lacking national accounts data on exports and imports of goods, balance of payments data on trade values are used; trade unit values are used to generate foreign trade in constant prices.

Composite data for country groups in the *World Economic Outlook* are either sums or weighted averages of data for individual countries. Arithmetic

---

[1]Commission of the European Communities, IMF, OECD, UN, and World Bank, *System of National Accounts 1993* (Brussels/Luxembourg, New York, Paris, and Washington, 1993); and IMF, *Balance of Payments Manual* (Washington: 5th ed., 1993).

weighted averages are used for all data except inflation and money growth for nonindustrial country groups, for which geometric averages are used. The following conventions apply.

- Country group composites for interest rates, exchange rates, and the growth of monetary aggregates are weighted by GDP converted to U.S. dollars at market exchange rates (averaged over the preceding three years) as a share of world or group GDP.
- Composites for other data relating to the domestic economy, whether growth rates or ratios, are weighted by GDP valued at purchasing power parities (PPPs) as a share of total world or group GDP.[2]
- Composite unemployment rates and employment growth are weighted by labor force as a share of group labor force.
- For data relating to the external economy, composites are sums of individual country data after conversion to U.S. dollars, for balance of payments at the average exchange rates in the years indicated, and for debt denominated in other currencies than U.S. dollars, at end of period exchange rates. Composites of foreign trade prices, however, are arithmetic averages of percentage changes for individual countries weighted by the U.S. dollar value of exports or imports as a share of total world or group exports or imports (in the preceding year). Group composites of trade volumes are derived as sums of trade values deflated by corresponding group composites of prices.

For central and eastern European countries in existence before 1991, external transactions in nonconvertible currencies (through 1990) are converted to U.S. dollars at the implicit U.S. dollar/ruble conversion rates obtained from each country's national currency exchange rate for the U.S. dollar and for the ruble. Trade *among* the Baltic states, Russia, and other countries of the former Soviet Union is not yet included in the data for these countries' external transactions because of insufficient information.

Unless otherwise indicated, multiyear averages of growth rates are expressed as compound annual rates of change.

---

[2]See the May 1993 *World Economic Outlook*, Annex IV, pp. 116–19; and Anne-Marie Gulde and Marianne Schulze-Ghattas, "Purchasing Power Parity Based Weights for the *World Economic Outlook*," in *Staff Studies for the World Economic Outlook* (Washington: IMF, December 1993), pp. 106–23.

Classification of Countries

Summary of the Country Classification

The country classification in the *World Economic Outlook* divides the world into three major groups:

Table A. Industrial Countries: Classification by Standard *World Economic Outlook* Groups, and Their Shares in Aggregate GDP and Exports of Goods and Services, 1994[1]

	Number of Countries Included in Group	Percentage of			
		Total GDP of		Total exports of goods and services of	
		Industrial countries	World	Industrial countries	World
Industrial countries	**23**	**100.0**	**54.6**	**100.0**	**70.8**
United States		38.8	21.2	18.7	13.2
Japan		15.4	8.4	11.9	8.4
Germany		9.2	5.0	12.9	9.1
France		6.6	3.6	9.3	6.6
Italy		6.2	3.4	7.5	5.3
United Kingdom		6.1	3.3	7.1	5.0
Canada		3.4	1.9	4.9	3.5
Other industrial countries	16	14.3	7.8	27.7	19.6
Industrial country groups					
Seven major industrial countries	7	85.7	46.8	72.3	51.2
European Union	15	38.6	21.1	57.5	40.7
Industrial countries except the United States, Japan, and Germany	20	36.6	20.0	56.5	40.0
Industrial countries except the United States, the European Union and Japan	6	9.5	5.2	17.0	12.1
Major European industrial countries	4	28.0	15.3	36.8	26.1

[1]The GDP shares are based on the purchasing power parity (PPP) valuation of country GDPs.

Table B. Developing Countries and Countries in Transition: Classification by Standard *World Economic Outlook* Groups and Their Shares in Aggregate GDP, Exports of Goods and Services, and Total Debt Outstanding, 1994[1]

		Percentage of				
		Total GDP of		Total exports of goods and services of		Total debt of
	Number of Countries Included in Group	Developing countries	World	Developing countries	World	Developing countries
Developing countries	**132**	**100.0**	**40.1**	**100.0**	**25.9**	**100.0**
By region						
Africa	50	8.2	3.3	6.8	1.8	15.1
Asia	30	57.6	23.1	63.0	16.3	33.9
Middle East and Europe	18	12.0	4.8	15.2	4.0	18.7
Western Hemisphere	34	22.2	8.9	15.0	3.9	32.3
Sub-Saharan Africa	45	3.3	1.3	2.3	0.6	8.5
Four newly industrializing Asian economies	4	7.7	3.1	36.7	9.5	5.2
By predominant export						
Fuel	19	21.3	8.5	19.7	5.1	28.7
Nonfuel exports	113	78.7	31.6	80.3	20.8	71.3
Manufactures	11	55.7	22.3	59.8	15.5	35.2
Primary products	54	9.8	3.9	7.1	1.9	18.4
Agricultural products	40	7.6	3.0	5.2	1.3	12.8
Minerals	14	2.2	0.9	2.0	0.5	5.6
Services, income, and private transfers	35	5.9	2.4	3.7	1.0	8.0
Diversified export base	13	7.4	3.0	9.5	2.5	9.7
By financial criteria						
Net creditor countries	8	7.8	3.1	16.6	4.3	3.9
Net debtor countries	124	92.2	37.0	83.4	21.6	96.1
Market borrowers	22	54.7	22.0	61.2	15.9	47.7
Diversified borrowers	33	25.6	10.3	15.6	4.1	30.1
Official borrowers	69	11.9	4.8	6.6	1.7	18.4
Countries with recent debt-servicing difficulties	72	31.0	12.4	22.0	5.7	54.5
Countries without debt-servicing difficulties	52	61.2	24.6	61.4	15.9	41.6
Other groups						
Small low-income economies	45	7.3	2.9	2.9	0.7	10.2
Least developed countries	46	4.1	1.7	1.5	0.4	8.1
Fifteen heavily indebted countries	15	24.6	9.9	16.9	4.4	36.7
Countries in transition	**28**	...	**5.3**	...	**3.2**	...
Central and eastern Europe	18	...	2.7	...	1.6	...
Excluding Belarus and Ukraine	16	...	2.0	...	1.5	...
Russia	1	...	2.1	...	1.4	...
Transcaucasus and central Asia	9	...	0.5	...	0.2	...

[1]The GDP shares are based on the purchasing power parity (PPP) valuation of country GDPs.

industrial countries, developing countries, and countries in transition.[3] Rather than being based on strict criteria, economic or otherwise, this classification has

[3]As used here, the term "country" does not in all cases refer to a territorial entity that is a state as understood by international law and practice. It also covers some territorial entities that are not states, but for which economic policies are formulated, and statistical data are maintained, on a separate and independent basis.

evolved over time and is intended only to facilitate the analysis and provide a reasonably meaningful organization of data. Each of the three main country groups is further divided into a number of subgroups. Tables A and B provide an overview by these standard groups in the *World Economic Outlook*, showing the number of countries in each group and the average 1994 shares of groups in aggregate PPP-valued GDP, total exports of goods and services, and total debt outstanding.

The general features and the compositions of groups in the *World Economic Outlook* classification are as follows.[4]

The group of *industrial countries* (23 countries) comprises

Australia	Greece	Norway
Austria	Iceland	Portugal
Belgium	Ireland	Spain
Canada	Italy	Sweden
Denmark	Japan	Switzerland
Finland	Luxembourg	United Kingdom
France	Netherlands	United States
Germany	New Zealand	

The seven largest countries in this group in terms of GDP—the United States, Japan, Germany, France, Italy, the United Kingdom, and Canada—are collectively referred to as the *major industrial countries*.

The current members of the *European Union* (15 countries) are also distinguished as a subgroup.[5] They are

Austria	Germany	Netherlands
Belgium	Greece	Portugal
Denmark	Ireland	Spain
Finland	Italy	Sweden
France	Luxembourg	United Kingdom

In 1991 and subsequent years, data for *Germany* refer to west Germany *and* the new eastern Länder (that is, the former German Democratic Republic). Before 1991, economic data are not available on a unified basis or in a consistent manner. In general, data on national accounts and domestic economic and financial activity through 1990 cover west Germany only, whereas data for the central government, foreign trade, and balance of payments apply to west Germany through June 1990 and to unified Germany thereafter.

The group of *developing countries* (132 countries) includes all countries that are not classified as industrial countries or as countries in transition, together with a few dependent territories for which adequate statistics are available.

The *regional breakdowns* of developing countries in the *World Economic Outlook* conform to the IMF's *International Financial Statistics (IFS)* classification, with one important exception. Because all of the developing countries in Europe except Cyprus, Malta, and Turkey are included in the group of countries in transition, the *World Economic Outlook* classification places these three countries in a combined Middle East and Europe region. It should also be noted that in both classifications, Egypt and the Libyan Arab Jamahiriya are included in this region, not in Africa. Two additional regional groupings are included in the *World Economic Outlook* because of their analytical significance. These are sub-Saharan Africa[6] and four newly industrializing Asian economies.[7]

The developing countries are also grouped according to *analytical criteria*: predominant export, financial criteria, and other groups. The export criteria are based on countries' export composition in 1984–86, whereas the financial criteria reflect net creditor and debtor positions as of 1987, sources of borrowing as of the end of 1989, and experience with debt servicing during 1986–90.

The first analytical criterion, by *predominant export*, distinguishes among five groups: fuel (Standard International Trade Classification—SITC 3); manufactures (SITC 5 to 8, less diamonds and gemstones); nonfuel primary products (SITC 0, 1, 2, 4, and diamonds and gemstones); services, factor income, and private transfers; and diversified export base. A further distinction is made among the exporters of nonfuel primary products on the basis of whether countries' exports of primary commodities consist primarily of agricultural commodities (SITC 0, 1, 2 except 27, 28, and 4) or minerals (SITC 27 and 28, and diamonds and gemstones).

The *financial criteria* first distinguish between net creditor and net debtor countries. Countries in the latter, much larger group are then differentiated on the basis of two additional financial criteria: by predominant type of creditor and by experience with debt servicing.

The country groups shown under *other groups* constitute the small low-income economies, the least developed countries, and 15 heavily indebted countries.

The group of *countries in transition* (28 countries) comprises central and eastern European countries, Russia, non-European states of the former Soviet Union, and Mongolia. A common characteristic of these countries is the transitional state of their economies from a centrally administered system to one based on market principles. The group of countries in transition comprises

Albania	Hungary	Russia
Armenia	Kazakhstan	Slovak Republic
Azerbaijan	Kyrgyz Republic	Slovenia
Belarus	Latvia	Tajikistan
Bosnia and	Lithuania	Turkmenistan
Herzegovina	Macedonia, former	Ukraine
Bulgaria	Moldova	Uzbekistan
Croatia	Mongolia	Yugoslavia, Fed. Rep. of
Czech Republic	Poland	(Serbia/Montenegro)
Estonia	Romania	
Georgia		

---

[4]A number of countries are presently not included in the groups featured below, either because they are not IMF members, and their economies therefore are not monitored by the IMF, or because data bases have not yet been compiled. Cuba and the Democratic People's Republic of Korea are examples of countries that are not IMF members, whereas San Marino, among the industrial countries, and Eritrea, among the developing countries, are examples of economies for which data bases have not been completed.

[5]Composite data shown in the tables under the heading "European Union" cover the current 15 members of the European Union for all years, even though the membership has changed over time.

[6]Excluding Nigeria and South Africa.

[7]Hong Kong, Korea, Singapore, and Taiwan Province of China.

The countries in transition are classified in three subgroups: *central and eastern Europe*, *Russia*, and *Transcaucasus and central Asia*. The Transcaucasian and central Asian countries include Kazakhstan for purposes of the *World Economic Outlook*. The countries in central and eastern Europe (18 countries) are

Albania	Estonia	Romania
Belarus	Hungary	Slovak Republic
Bosnia and	Latvia	Slovenia
Herzegovina	Lithuania	Ukraine
Bulgaria	Macedonia, former	Yugoslavia, Fed. Rep. of
Croatia	Moldova	(Serbia/Montenegro)
Czech Republic	Poland	

The countries in the Transcaucasian and central Asian group (9 countries) are

Armenia	Kazakhstan	Tajikistan
Azerbaijan	Kyrgyz Republic	Turkmenistan
Georgia	Mongolia	Uzbekistan

Detailed Description of the Developing Country Classification by Analytical Group

Countries Classified by Predominant Export

Fuel exporters (19 countries) are countries whose average ratio of fuel exports to total exports in 1984-86 exceeded 50 percent. The group comprises

Angola	Iran, Islamic Rep. of	Qatar
Algeria	Iraq	Saudi Arabia
Cameroon	Kuwait	Trinidad and Tobago
Congo	Libya	United Arab Emirates
Ecuador	Mexico	Venezuela
Gabon	Nigeria	
Indonesia	Oman	

Nonfuel exporters (113 countries) are countries with total exports of goods and services including a substantial share of (a) manufactures, (b) primary products, or (c) services and private transfers. However, those countries whose export structure is so diversified that they do not fall clearly into any one of these three groups are assigned to a fourth group, (d) diversified export base.

(a) Economies whose exports of manufactures accounted for over 50 percent of their total exports on average in 1984–86 are included in the group of *exporters of manufactures* (11 countries). This group includes

Brazil	Israel	Thailand
China	Korea	Tunisia
Hong Kong	Singapore	Turkey
India	Taiwan Province of China	

(b) The group of *exporters of primary products* (54 countries) consists of those countries whose exports of agricultural and mineral primary products (SITC 0, 1, 2, 4, and diamonds and gemstones) accounted for at least half of their total exports on average in 1984–86. These countries are

Afghanistan, Islamic	Ghana	Papua New Guinea
State of	Guatemala	Paraguay
Argentina	Guinea	Peru
Bhutan	Guinea-Bissau	Rwanda
Bolivia	Guyana	Sao Tome and Principe
Botswana	Honduras	Solomon Islands
Burundi	Kenya	Somalia
Central African Rep.	Lao People's	Sri Lanka
Chad	Dem. Rep.	St. Vincent and the
Chile	Liberia	Grenadines
Colombia	Madagascar	Sudan
Comoros	Malawi	Suriname
Costa Rica	Mali	Swaziland
Côte d'Ivoire	Mauritania	Togo
Djibouti	Mauritius	Uganda
Dominica	Myanmar	Uruguay
El Salvador	Namibia	Viet Nam
Equatorial Guinea	Nicaragua	Zaïre
Gambia, The	Niger	Zambia

Among exporters of primary products, a further distinction is made between exporters of agricultural products and minerals. The group of *mineral exporters* (14 countries) comprises

Bolivia	Liberia	Suriname
Botswana	Mauritania	Togo
Chile	Namibia	Zaïre
Guinea	Niger	Zambia
Guyana	Peru	

All other exporters of primary products are classified as *agricultural exporters* (40 countries).

(c) The *exporters of services and recipients of factor income and private transfers* (35 countries) are defined as those countries whose average income from services, factor income, and private transfers accounted for more than half of total average export earnings in 1984–86. This group comprises

Antigua and	Grenada	Nepal
Barbuda	Jamaica	Netherlands Antilles
Aruba	Jordan	Pakistan
Bahamas, The	Kiribati	Panama
Barbados	Lebanon	Seychelles
Burkina Faso	Lesotho	St. Kitts and Nevis
Cambodia	Maldives	St. Lucia
Cape Verde	Malta	Tanzania
Cyprus	Marshall Islands	Tonga
Dominican Rep.	Micronesia,	Vanuatu
Egypt	Federated States of	Western Samoa
Ethiopia	Mozambique, Rep. of	Yemen, Rep. of
Fiji		

(d) *Countries with a diversified export base* (13 countries) are those whose export earnings in 1984–86 were not dominated by any one of the categories mentioned under (a) through (c) above. This group comprises

Bahrain	Malaysia	South Africa
Bangladesh	Morocco	Syrian Arab Rep.
Belize	Philippines	Zimbabwe
Benin	Senegal	
Haiti	Sierra Leone	

Countries Classified by Financial Criteria

Net creditor countries (8 countries) are defined as developing countries that were net external creditors in 1987 or that experienced substantial cumulated current account surpluses between 1967–68 (the beginning of most balance of payments series in the World Economic Outlook data base) and 1987. The net creditor group consists of the following economies:

Iran, Islamic Rep. of	Oman	Taiwan Province of China
Kuwait	Qatar	United Arab Emirates
Libya	Saudi Arabia	

Net debtor countries (124 countries) are disaggregated according to two criteria: (a) predominant type of creditor and (b) experience with debt servicing.

(a) Within the classification by *predominant type of creditor* (sources of borrowing), three subgroups are identified: market borrowers, official borrowers, and diversified borrowers.

Market borrowers (22 countries) are defined as net debtor countries with more than two thirds of their total liabilities outstanding at the end of 1989 owed to commercial creditors. This group comprises

Algeria	Israel	Singapore
Antigua and Barbuda	Kiribati	Suriname
Argentina	Korea	Thailand
Bahamas, The	Malaysia	Trinidad and Tobago
Brazil	Mexico	Uruguay
Chile	Panama	Venezuela
China	Papua New Guinea	
Hong Kong	Peru	

Official borrowers (69 countries) are defined as net debtor countries with more than two thirds of their total liabilities outstanding at the end of 1989 owed to official creditors. This group comprises

Afghanistan, Islamic State of	Gambia, The	Netherlands Antilles
Aruba	Ghana	Nicaragua
Bangladesh	Grenada	Niger
Belize	Guinea	Nigeria
Bhutan	Guinea-Bissau	Pakistan
Bolivia	Guyana	Rwanda
Botswana	Haiti	Sao Tome and Principe
Burkina Faso	Honduras	Somalia
Burundi	Jamaica	St. Kitts and Nevis
Cambodia	Lao People's	St. Lucia
Cameroon	Dem. Rep.	St. Vincent and the
Cape Verde	Lesotho	Grenadines
Central African	Madagascar	Sudan
Rep.	Malawi	Swaziland
Chad	Maldives	Tanzania
Comoros	Mali	Togo
Djibouti	Malta	Tonga
Dominica	Mauritania	Tunisia
Dominican Rep.	Mauritius	Uganda
Egypt	Morocco	Viet Nam
El Salvador	Mozambique,	Western Samoa
Equatorial Guinea	Rep. of	Yemen, Rep. of
Ethiopia	Myanmar	Zaïre
Gabon	Namibia	Zambia
	Nepal	

Diversified borrowers (33 countries) consist of those net debtor developing countries that are classified neither as market nor as official borrowers.

(b) Within the classification by *experience with debt servicing*, a further distinction is made. *Countries with recent debt-servicing difficulties* (72 countries) are defined as those countries that incurred external payments arrears or entered into official or commercial bank debt-rescheduling agreements during 1986–90. Information on these developments is taken from relevant issues of the IMF's *Annual Report on Exchange Arrangements and Exchange Restrictions.*

All other net debtor countries are classified as *countries without debt-servicing difficulties* (52 countries).

Other Groups

The group of *small low-income economies* (45 countries) include those IMF members—excluding China and India—whose GDP per capita, as estimated by the World Bank, did not exceed the equivalent of $425 in 1986. This group comprises

Afghanistan, Islamic State of	Guinea-Bissau	Pakistan
Bangladesh	Guyana[8]	Rwanda
Benin	Haiti	Sao Tome and
Bhutan	Kenya	Principe
Burkina Faso	Lao People's	Senegal
Burundi	Dem. Rep.	Sierra Leone
Cambodia	Lesotho	Somalia
Central African Rep.	Madagascar	Sri Lanka
Chad	Malawi	Sudan
Comoros	Maldives	Tanzania
Equatorial Guinea	Mali	Togo
Ethiopia	Mauritania	Uganda
Gambia, The	Mozambique, Rep. of	Vanuatu
Ghana	Myanmar	Viet Nam
Guinea	Nepal	Zaïre
	Niger	Zambia

The countries currently classified by the United Nations as the *least developed countries* (46 countries) are[9]

Afghanistan, Islamic State of	Guinea	Rwanda
Bangladesh	Guinea-Bissau	Sao Tome and
Benin	Haiti	Principe
Bhutan	Kiribati	Sierra Leone
Botswana	Lao People's	Solomon Islands
Burkina Faso	Dem. Rep.	Somalia
Burundi	Lesotho	Sudan
Cambodia	Liberia	Tanzania
Cape Verde	Madagascar	Togo
Central African Rep.	Malawi	Uganda
Chad	Maldives	Vanuatu
Comoros	Mali	Western Samoa
Djibouti	Mauritania	Yemen, Rep. of
Equatorial Guinea	Mozambique, Rep. of	Zaïre
Ethiopia	Myanmar	Zambia
Gambia, The	Nepal	
	Niger	

---

[8]Although Guyana's estimated GDP per person slightly exceeded the threshold of $425 in 1986, it dropped considerably in 1987; therefore Guyana is included in this group.

[9]The United Nations classification also covers Tuvalu, which is not included in the *World Economic Outlook* classification.

117

The group of *15 heavily indebted countries*[10] (the Baker Plan countries) includes those countries associated with the "Program for Sustained Growth" proposed by the Governor for the United States at the 1985 IMF–World Bank Annual Meetings in Seoul. This group comprises

[10]The former Socialist Federal Republic of Yugoslavia and, after its dissolution, the successor states—Bosnia and Herzegovina, Croatia, the former Yugoslav Republic of Macedonia, Slovenia, and the Federal Republic of Yugoslavia (Serbia/Montenegro)—are included in this group of developing countries even though they are now classified as countries in transition.

Argentina	Côte d'Ivoire	Peru
Bolivia	Ecuador	Philippines
Brazil	Mexico	Uruguay
Chile	Morocco	Venezuela
Colombia	Nigeria	Yugoslavia, former

List of Tables

	Page

Output

A1. Summary of World Output — 121
A2. Industrial Countries: Real GDP and Total Domestic Demand — 122
A3. Industrial Countries: Components of Real GDP — 123
A4. Industrial Countries: Employment, Unemployment, and Real Per Capita GDP — 125
A5. Developing Countries: Real GDP — 127
A6. Developing Countries—By Country: Real GDP — 128
A7. Countries in Transition: Real GDP — 131

Inflation

A8. Summary of Inflation — 132
A9. Industrial Countries: GDP Deflators and Consumer Prices — 133
A10. Industrial Countries: Hourly Earnings, Productivity, and Unit Labor Costs in Manufacturing — 134
A11. Developing Countries: Consumer Prices — 135
A12. Developing Countries—By Country: Consumer Prices — 136
A13. Countries in Transition: Consumer Prices — 139

Financial Policies

A14. Summary Financial Indicators — 140
A15. Industrial Countries: General and Central Government Fiscal Balances and Balances Excluding Social Security Transactions — 141
A16. Industrial Countries: General Government Structural Balances and Fiscal Impulses — 143
A17. Industrial Countries: Monetary Aggregates — 144
A18. Industrial Countries: Interest Rates — 145
A19. Industrial Countries: Exchange Rates — 146
A20. Developing Countries: Central Government Fiscal Balances — 147
A21. Developing Countries: Broad Money Aggregates — 148

Foreign Trade

A22. Summary of World Trade Volumes and Prices — 149
A23. Industrial Countries: Export Volumes, Import Volumes, and Terms of Trade — 150
A24. Developing Countries—By Region: Total Trade in Goods — 151
A25. Developing Countries—By Predominant Export: Total Trade in Goods — 153
A26. Developing Countries: Nonfuel Commodity Prices — 155

Current Account Transactions

A27. Summary of Payments Balances on Current Account — 156
A28. Industrial Countries: Balance of Payments on Current Account — 157
A29. Developing Countries: Current Account Transactions — 158
A30. Developing Countries: Payments Balances on Current Account — 159
A31. Developing Countries—By Region: Current Account Transactions — 161
A32. Developing Countries—By Analytical Criteria: Current Account Transactions — 163

	Page

External Financing

A33. Summary of External Financing — 167
A34. Developing Countries—By Region: External Financing — 169
A35. Developing Countries—By Analytical Criteria: External Financing — 171
A36. Developing Countries: Reserves — 175
A37. Net Credit and Loans from IMF — 177

External Debt and Debt Service

A38. Summary of External Debt and Debt Service — 178
A39. Developing Countries—By Region: External Debt, by Maturity and
    Type of Creditor — 180
A40. Developing Countries—By Analytical Criteria: External Debt, by Maturity
    and Type of Creditor — 181
A41. Developing Countries: Ratio of External Debt to GDP — 184
A42. Developing Countries: Debt-Service Ratios — 185
A43. IMF Charges and Repurchases to the IMF — 187

Flow of Funds

A44. Summary of Sources and Uses of World Saving — 188

Medium-Term Baseline Scenario

A45. Summary of Medium-Term Baseline Scenario — 192
A46. Developing Countries—Medium-Term Baseline Scenario:
    Selected Economic Indicators — 193

Table A1. Summary of World Output[1]

(Annual percent change)

	Average 1977–86	1987	1988	1989	1990	1991	1992	1993	1994	1995	1996
World	**3.4**	**4.0**	**4.6**	**3.4**	**2.4**	**1.3**	**2.0**	**2.5**	**3.7**	**3.8**	**4.2**
Industrial countries	**2.7**	**3.2**	**4.4**	**3.3**	**2.4**	**0.8**	**1.5**	**1.2**	**3.0**	**3.0**	**2.7**
United States	2.7	3.1	3.9	2.5	1.2	–0.6	2.3	3.1	4.1	3.2	1.9
European Union[2]	2.1	2.9	4.2	3.5	3.0	1.1	1.0	–0.4	2.8	3.2	3.1
Japan	4.0	4.1	6.2	4.7	4.8	4.3	1.1	–0.2	0.6	1.8	3.5
Other industrial countries	2.7	3.4	3.9	3.1	1.0	–1.1	0.6	1.4	3.9	3.8	3.0
Developing countries	**4.6**	**5.7**	**5.2**	**3.9**	**3.9**	**4.9**	**5.9**	**6.1**	**6.3**	**5.6**	**6.1**
By region											
Africa	2.1	1.6	3.6	3.4	2.0	1.9	0.8	0.7	2.7	3.7	5.3
Asia	6.9	8.1	9.1	6.0	5.6	6.4	8.2	8.7	8.6	7.6	7.3
Middle East and Europe	2.5	5.0	–0.8	0.5	4.8	3.1	5.5	3.7	0.7	2.9	4.7
Western Hemisphere	3.2	3.3	1.1	1.6	0.6	3.5	2.7	3.2	4.6	2.3	3.7
By analytical criteria											
Fuel exporters	2.6	2.1	1.0	3.1	4.7	4.5	4.6	2.3	2.9	2.5	5.1
Nonfuel exporters	5.3	6.9	6.4	4.2	3.7	5.0	6.3	7.2	7.2	6.4	6.4
Net creditor countries	1.9	1.3	–0.8	1.9	6.9	6.8	6.3	3.6	3.0	4.0	5.5
Net debtor countries	4.8	6.1	5.7	4.1	3.7	4.7	5.9	6.4	6.5	5.8	6.2
Market borrowers	5.5	6.9	6.2	3.7	3.3	6.3	7.5	8.2	8.4	6.2	6.5
Official borrowers	4.0	4.0	3.7	3.6	3.6	3.7	2.7	2.4	3.6	4.3	5.3
Countries with recent debt-servicing difficulties	3.0	3.8	1.8	2.0	0.5	2.5	2.2	2.7	4.1	2.6	4.1
Countries without debt-servicing difficulties	6.4	7.8	8.2	5.4	5.6	6.0	8.0	8.3	7.8	7.3	7.2
Countries in transition	**3.3**	**2.6**	**4.0**	**2.0**	**–3.9**	**–11.6**	**–15.3**	**–9.2**	**–9.4**	**–3.8**	**3.5**
Central and eastern Europe	...	...	...	...	...	–11.1	–11.4	–6.2	–3.8	0.4	3.5
Excluding Belarus and Ukraine	...	...	...	...	...	–11.9	–9.4	–2.0	2.7	3.6	4.3
Russia	...	...	...	...	...	–13.0	–19.0	–12.0	–15.0	–9.0	4.5
Transcaucasus and central Asia	...	...	...	...	...	–7.7	–17.6	–11.9	–14.9	–5.7	—
Memorandum											
Median growth rate											
Industrial countries	2.6	3.1	4.1	3.6	2.1	1.3	1.2	–0.1	2.8	3.2	3.0
Developing countries	3.7	3.6	3.5	3.5	3.2	2.9	3.7	3.2	3.5	4.5	4.8
Countries in transition	3.6	2.8	5.3	3.0	–2.3	–11.8	–15.5	–9.7	–1.3	1.6	4.0
Output per capita											
Industrial countries	2.0	2.6	3.7	2.5	1.6	—	0.8	0.6	2.4	2.4	2.0
Developing countries	2.1	3.4	4.7	0.6	2.2	3.1	3.6	4.3	4.3	3.6	4.1
Countries in transition	2.6	1.9	3.4	1.5	–4.5	–11.8	–15.6	–9.4	–9.5	–4.0	3.3

[1] Real GDP. For most countries included in the group "countries in transition," total output is measured by real net material product (NMP) or by NMP-based estimates of GDP.

[2] In this table and the tables that follow the European Union includes the 15 current members. See "Classification of Countries" in the introduction to this Statistical Appendix.

Table A2. Industrial Countries: Real GDP and Total Domestic Demand
(Annual percent change)

	Average 1977–86	1987	1988	1989	1990	1991	1992	1993	1994	1995	1996	Fourth Quarter[1] 1994	1995	1996
Real GDP														
Industrial countries	**2.7**	**3.2**	**4.4**	**3.3**	**2.4**	**0.8**	**1.5**	**1.2**	**3.0**	**3.0**	**2.7**	...	...	...
Major industrial countries	2.8	3.2	4.5	3.2	2.4	0.8	1.6	1.4	3.1	3.0	2.6	3.5	2.8	2.5
United States	2.7	3.1	3.9	2.5	1.2	-0.6	2.3	3.1	4.1	3.2	1.9	4.1	2.3	1.9
Japan	4.0	4.1	6.2	4.7	4.8	4.3	1.1	-0.2	0.6	1.8	3.5	0.9	3.3	3.6
Germany	...	...	...	...	...	2.8	2.2	-1.1	2.9	3.2	3.3	3.9	3.3	3.1
West Germany	1.9	1.5	3.7	3.6	5.7	5.0	1.8	-1.7	2.3	2.6	2.8	3.3	2.5	2.7
France	2.2	2.3	4.4	4.3	2.5	0.8	1.2	-1.0	2.5	3.2	3.0	3.6	3.3	2.8
Italy	2.7	3.1	4.1	2.9	2.1	1.2	0.7	-0.7	2.5	3.0	3.0	3.6	3.1	3.1
United Kingdom[2]	2.1	4.8	5.0	2.2	0.4	-2.0	-0.5	2.2	3.8	3.2	2.8	3.9	3.1	2.7
Canada	3.1	4.2	5.0	2.4	-0.2	-1.8	0.6	2.2	4.5	4.3	2.6	5.6	3.2	2.5
Other industrial countries	2.1	3.2	3.8	4.0	2.7	1.0	1.0	0.2	2.8	3.3	3.1	...	...	...
Spain	1.7	5.7	5.2	4.7	3.6	2.2	0.8	-1.0	1.9	3.0	3.0	...	...	...
Netherlands	1.6	1.2	2.6	4.7	4.1	2.3	1.3	0.4	2.4	3.0	2.7	...	...	...
Belgium	1.2	2.0	4.9	3.5	3.2	2.3	1.9	-1.7	2.3	3.0	2.9	...	...	...
Sweden	1.7	3.1	2.3	2.4	1.4	-1.1	-1.9	-2.1	2.2	2.4	2.6	...	...	...
Austria	2.0	1.7	4.1	3.8	4.2	3.0	1.8	-0.1	2.8	3.0	2.8	...	...	...
Denmark	2.3	0.3	1.2	0.6	1.4	1.0	1.3	1.4	4.6	3.6	2.5	...	...	...
Finland	3.2	4.1	4.9	5.7	—	-7.1	-3.6	-1.6	3.9	5.2	4.8	...	...	...
Greece[3]	2.4	-0.5	4.5	3.5	-1.0	3.2	0.8	-0.5	1.5	1.8	2.3	...	...	...
Portugal	2.8	5.1	5.4	5.4	4.2	2.2	1.5	-1.0	1.0	3.5	4.5	...	...	...
Ireland	3.2	4.6	4.3	7.4	8.6	2.9	5.0	4.0	5.2	6.2	4.9	...	...	...
Luxembourg	3.1	4.2	6.4	7.8	4.6	2.7	2.8	2.8	2.8	3.0	3.3	...	...	...
Switzerland	2.0	2.0	2.9	3.9	2.3	—	-0.3	-0.9	2.0	2.3	3.2	...	...	...
Norway	3.8	2.0	-0.5	0.6	1.7	1.6	3.4	2.3	5.5	3.6	1.7	...	...	...
Iceland	4.8	8.6	-0.1	0.3	1.1	1.3	-3.3	0.9	2.0	2.1	1.5	...	...	...
Australia	2.9	4.7	4.1	4.5	1.3	-1.3	2.1	3.7	4.7	4.4	3.8	...	...	...
New Zealand	1.6	-1.7	3.0	-0.5	-0.1	-2.1	-0.2	4.1	4.8	4.4	3.3	...	...	...
Memorandum														
European Union	2.1	2.9	4.2	3.5	3.0	1.1	1.0	-0.4	2.8	3.2	3.1	...	...	...
Real total domestic demand														
Industrial countries	**2.6**	**3.6**	**4.5**	**3.4**	**2.2**	**0.5**	**1.5**	**1.0**	**3.2**	**2.9**	**2.7**	...	...	...
Major industrial countries	2.7	3.5	4.5	3.1	2.1	0.5	1.6	1.4	3.3	2.8	2.6	3.6	2.7	2.6
United States	3.0	2.7	3.0	1.8	0.8	-1.3	2.6	3.9	4.7	2.9	1.6	4.5	1.9	1.6
Japan	3.5	5.1	7.6	5.8	5.0	2.9	0.3	—	1.0	2.8	4.5	1.0	4.5	4.3
Germany	...	...	...	...	...	6.1	3.0	-1.2	2.6	3.0	3.3	...	...	...
West Germany	1.6	2.4	3.6	2.9	5.2	4.9	1.3	-2.2	1.7	2.3	3.0	2.9	2.4	3.1
France	2.0	3.3	4.6	3.9	2.8	0.6	0.2	-1.8	2.9	3.0	3.0	4.4	3.1	2.9
Italy	2.4	4.2	4.4	2.8	2.5	1.9	0.8	-5.0	2.3	2.6	3.0	4.2	2.4	3.1
United Kingdom	2.0	5.3	7.9	2.9	-0.6	-3.1	0.3	2.2	3.0	2.6	2.7	3.0	2.2	2.8
Canada	2.9	5.3	5.5	4.3	-0.5	-1.0	0.3	1.8	2.9	3.0	2.5	2.5	3.3	2.1
Other industrial countries	1.7	3.8	4.3	5.1	2.6	0.6	0.6	-1.2	2.5	3.3	3.2	...	...	...
Memorandum														
European Union	1.8	3.9	4.9	3.8	3.0	1.7	1.1	-1.6	2.4	2.9	3.0	...	...	...

[1] From fourth quarter of preceding year.
[2] Average of expenditure, income, and output estimates of GDP at market prices.
[3] Based on revised national accounts for 1988 onward.

Table A3. Industrial Countries: Components of Real GDP

(Annual percent change)

	Average 1977–86	1987	1988	1989	1990	1991	1992	1993	1994	1995	1996
Private consumer expenditure											
Industrial countries	**2.8**	**3.5**	**4.0**	**2.9**	**2.5**	**1.1**	**2.0**	**1.5**	**2.6**	**2.7**	**2.8**
Major industrial countries	2.9	3.5	4.2	2.8	2.4	0.9	2.1	1.8	2.7	2.7	2.8
United States	3.0	2.8	3.6	1.9	1.5	−0.4	2.8	3.3	3.5	2.9	1.8
Japan	3.6	4.2	5.2	4.3	3.9	2.2	1.7	1.0	2.2	2.7	4.7
Germany	. . .	. . .	. . .	. . .	. . .	5.4	3.0	0.5	1.3	1.6	3.0
West Germany	1.9	3.4	2.7	2.8	5.4	5.7	2.2	0.2	0.8	1.2	2.8
France	2.4	2.9	3.3	3.0	2.7	1.4	1.3	0.6	1.6	2.6	2.6
Italy	3.2	4.2	4.2	3.5	2.5	2.7	1.4	−2.1	2.0	3.2	3.6
United Kingdom	2.7	5.3	7.5	3.2	0.6	−2.2	—	2.7	2.6	2.3	2.5
Canada	2.9	4.4	4.5	3.4	1.0	−1.5	1.3	1.6	3.1	3.2	2.9
Other industrial countries	1.8	3.4	3.2	3.7	2.7	2.1	1.7	−0.4	2.1	2.6	2.8
Memorandum											
European Union	2.3	3.9	4.1	3.3	3.0	2.3	1.6	—	1.7	2.4	2.9
Public consumption											
Industrial countries	**2.6**	**2.4**	**1.7**	**1.7**	**2.6**	**1.7**	**1.1**	**0.1**	**0.6**	**0.6**	**0.9**
Major industrial countries	2.6	2.3	1.6	1.5	2.5	1.5	1.0	—	0.5	0.6	0.8
United States	2.6	3.0	0.6	2.0	3.1	1.2	−0.7	−0.8	−0.7	0.3	0.7
Japan	3.5	0.4	2.2	2.0	1.9	1.6	2.7	1.7	2.8	2.6	2.8
Germany	. . .	. . .	. . .	. . .	. . .	0.1	4.5	−1.2	1.2	1.0	1.0
West Germany	1.9	1.5	2.1	−1.6	2.2	0.3	4.0	−1.2	1.1	1.0	1.0
France	2.7	2.8	3.4	0.5	2.1	2.6	3.0	0.5	1.6	1.0	0.5
Italy	2.8	3.4	2.8	0.8	1.2	1.6	1.0	0.8	0.2	−2.3	−0.1
United Kingdom	1.0	1.0	0.7	1.4	2.5	2.6	—	1.0	1.6	0.8	0.4
Canada	2.2	1.7	4.1	4.0	3.2	2.8	1.2	0.5	−2.1	−1.2	−3.2
Other industrial countries	2.9	3.3	2.5	3.4	3.1	2.9	1.6	0.8	1.7	0.5	1.3
Memorandum											
European Union	2.3	2.6	2.3	1.1	2.2	2.0	2.2	0.3	1.3	0.3	0.8
Gross fixed capital formation											
Industrial countries	**2.7**	**3.9**	**7.4**	**4.6**	**1.8**	**−2.4**	**1.5**	**2.0**	**5.8**	**5.7**	**4.1**
Major industrial countries	2.9	3.6	7.2	4.0	1.8	−2.4	2.1	3.1	6.2	5.6	3.8
United States	3.9	−0.5	4.2	0.1	−1.7	−7.6	5.5	11.3	12.3	7.3	2.5
Japan	3.2	9.6	11.9	9.3	8.8	3.7	−1.1	−1.8	−2.3	2.3	4.6
Germany	. . .	. . .	. . .	. . .	. . .	9.6	4.2	−4.5	4.3	6.1	4.2
West Germany	1.1	1.8	4.4	6.3	8.5	5.8	0.3	−8.3	1.2	3.9	3.6
France	0.4	4.8	9.6	7.9	2.8	−0.7	−2.5	−5.0	1.5	5.7	6.2
Italy	1.3	5.0	6.9	4.3	3.8	0.6	−2.0	−11.1	—	3.1	3.1
United Kingdom	1.4	10.2	14.0	6.0	−3.5	−9.5	−1.2	0.3	3.2	4.3	5.8
Canada	3.9	10.8	10.3	6.1	−3.5	−2.2	−2.8	−0.2	6.0	5.9	6.6
Other industrial countries	1.0	5.6	8.7	8.8	1.8	−2.6	−2.4	−4.4	3.2	6.6	5.6
Memorandum											
European Union	0.9	5.5	8.7	7.2	3.8	0.4	−0.7	−5.6	2.1	5.3	5.0

Table A3 *(concluded)*

	Average 1977–86	1987	1988	1989	1990	1991	1992	1993	1994	1995	1996
Final domestic demand											
Industrial countries	**2.7**	**3.5**	**4.4**	**3.2**	**2.5**	**0.6**	**1.6**	**1.1**	**2.6**	**2.9**	**2.7**
Major industrial countries	2.8	3.4	4.4	3.0	2.5	0.6	1.7	1.4	2.7	2.8	2.6
United States	3.1	2.3	3.1	1.7	1.3	–1.2	2.5	3.7	4.1	3.2	1.8
Japan	3.5	5.4	7.0	5.7	5.3	2.6	0.8	0.1	0.8	2.6	4.5
Germany	...	...	...	...	...	5.2	3.6	–1.0	2.0	2.5	2.9
West Germany	1.8	2.7	3.0	2.6	5.4	4.7	2.1	–2.0	1.0	1.7	2.6
France	2.0	3.3	4.6	3.6	2.6	1.1	0.8	–0.6	1.6	2.9	2.9
Italy	2.7	4.2	4.5	3.3	2.6	2.1	0.6	–3.5	1.3	2.3	2.9
United Kingdom	2.1	5.2	7.2	3.4	0.2	–2.6	–0.2	1.9	2.5	2.4	2.7
Canada	2.9	5.1	5.6	4.1	0.4	–0.8	0.4	1.0	2.7	2.9	2.5
Other industrial countries	1.7	3.8	4.2	4.8	2.5	1.2	0.8	–1.1	2.3	3.1	3.1
Memorandum											
European Union	1.9	3.9	4.6	3.7	3.0	1.8	1.2	–1.2	1.7	2.6	2.9
Stock building[1]											
Industrial countries	**–0.1**	**0.1**	**0.1**	**0.2**	**–0.3**	**–0.1**	**–0.1**	**–0.1**	**0.6**	**—**	**—**
Major industrial countries	–0.1	0.1	0.1	0.1	–0.4	—	–0.1	–0.1	0.6	—	—
United States	—	0.4	–0.1	0.2	–0.5	–0.1	0.1	0.3	0.6	–0.3	–0.2
Japan	—	–0.3	0.6	0.2	–0.3	0.3	–0.5	–0.2	0.2	0.2	0.1
Germany	...	...	...	...	...	0.9	–0.6	–0.2	0.7	0.5	0.4
West Germany	–0.1	–0.2	0.6	0.3	–0.1	0.2	–0.8	–0.2	0.7	0.5	0.4
France	—	0.1	—	0.4	0.2	–0.6	–0.6	–1.2	1.3	0.1	0.1
Italy	–0.3	—	—	–0.4	—	–0.1	0.3	–1.6	1.0	0.3	0.1
United Kingdom	—	0.1	0.7	–0.4	–0.8	–0.5	0.5	0.3	0.5	0.2	—
Canada	—	0.1	–0.1	0.2	–1.0	–0.2	–0.1	0.8	0.2	0.1	–0.1
Other industrial countries	—	—	0.1	0.3	0.2	–0.6	–0.1	–0.1	0.2	0.2	0.1
Memorandum											
European Union	–0.1	—	0.3	0.1	–0.1	–0.1	–0.1	–0.5	0.7	0.3	0.1
Foreign balance[1]											
Industrial countries	**—**	**–0.4**	**–0.2**	**–0.1**	**0.2**	**0.3**	**—**	**0.2**	**–0.2**	**0.1**	**—**
Major industrial countries	–0.1	–0.3	–0.1	0.1	0.2	0.2	—	—	–0.3	0.1	—
United States	–0.4	0.3	0.9	0.6	0.4	0.7	–0.3	–0.8	–0.7	0.3	0.3
Japan	0.5	–0.9	–1.2	–1.1	–0.2	1.3	0.8	–0.2	–0.4	–1.0	–1.0
Germany	...	...	...	...	...	–3.1	–0.8	—	0.2	0.1	—
West Germany	0.3	–0.8	0.3	0.9	0.8	0.4	0.6	0.4	0.7	0.5	—
France	0.1	–1.1	–0.3	0.3	–0.3	0.2	1.0	0.9	–0.3	0.2	—
Italy	—	–1.1	–0.5	—	–0.5	–0.8	–0.1	4.6	0.2	0.5	—
United Kingdom	–0.1	–0.5	–2.9	–0.8	1.0	1.3	–0.9	—	0.6	0.6	0.1
Canada	0.2	–0.9	–1.2	–1.6	0.6	–0.7	0.4	0.3	1.4	1.2	0.1
Other industrial countries	0.3	–0.7	–0.6	–1.3	0.2	0.5	0.3	1.3	0.4	—	—
Memorandum											
European Union	0.2	–0.9	–0.7	–0.3	0.1	–0.6	–0.1	1.3	0.4	0.3	—

[1]Changes expressed as percent of GDP in the preceding period.

Table A4. Industrial Countries: Employment, Unemployment, and Real Per Capita GDP

(In percent)

	Average[1] 1977–86	1987	1988	1989	1990	1991	1992	1993	1994	1995	1996
Unemployment rate											
Industrial countries	**6.7**	**7.3**	**6.8**	**6.2**	**6.0**	**6.8**	**7.7**	**8.1**	**8.1**	**7.6**	**7.4**
Major industrial countries	6.4	6.8	6.2	5.7	5.6	6.4	7.2	7.3	7.2	6.7	6.6
United States[2]	7.5	6.2	5.5	5.3	5.5	6.7	7.4	6.8	6.1	5.5	5.7
Japan	2.4	2.8	2.5	2.3	2.1	2.1	2.2	2.5	2.9	2.9	2.8
Germany	. . .	. . .	. . .	. . .	. . .	6.6	7.7	8.8	9.6	9.1	8.6
West Germany	5.8	7.9	7.8	6.8	6.2	5.5	5.8	7.3	8.3	8.1	7.7
France	7.6	10.5	10.0	9.4	8.9	9.4	10.3	11.6	12.6	12.1	11.4
Italy[3]	8.3	10.5	10.7	10.5	9.4	8.8	10.7	10.2	11.3	11.3	10.6
United Kingdom	7.8	10.0	8.0	6.3	5.8	8.1	9.7	10.3	9.3	8.3	8.1
Canada	9.3	8.8	7.8	7.5	8.1	10.4	11.3	11.2	10.4	9.2	9.0
Other industrial countries	8.0	9.8	9.5	8.4	8.2	8.9	10.2	12.2	12.6	12.1	11.6
Spain	14.5	20.5	19.5	17.3	16.3	16.3	18.4	22.7	24.2	24.0	23.5
Netherlands	6.6	8.4	8.4	7.7	7.0	6.6	6.7	7.7	8.8	8.8	8.5
Belgium	9.8	11.5	10.1	8.5	7.6	7.5	8.2	9.4	10.1	9.8	9.3
Sweden	2.6	1.9	1.6	1.4	1.5	2.9	5.3	8.2	7.9	7.3	6.9
Austria	3.3	5.6	5.3	3.0	3.3	3.7	3.8	4.3	4.1	4.0	4.0
Denmark	8.3	7.8	8.6	9.3	9.6	10.5	11.3	12.2	12.1	10.3	10.0
Finland	5.5	4.7	4.5	3.5	3.5	7.6	13.1	17.9	18.5	16.5	14.0
Greece	6.5	7.4	7.7	7.5	7.0	7.7	8.7	9.8	10.0	10.3	10.2
Portugal	8.1	7.1	7.0	5.0	4.7	4.1	4.1	5.5	6.8	5.8	5.7
Ireland	11.6	16.7	16.1	14.7	13.4	14.7	15.5	15.7	14.8	13.8	13.5
Luxembourg	1.2	1.7	1.5	1.4	1.3	1.4	1.6	2.1	2.8	3.0	2.6
Switzerland	0.6	0.7	0.6	0.5	0.5	1.1	2.6	4.6	4.8	4.3	3.4
Norway	2.3	2.1	3.2	4.9	5.2	5.5	5.9	6.0	5.5	5.0	4.5
Iceland	0.6	0.4	0.6	1.7	1.8	1.5	3.1	4.4	4.8	4.6	4.9
Australia	7.3	8.1	7.2	6.2	6.9	9.6	10.8	10.9	9.9	8.9	8.3
New Zealand	4.3	4.4	6.8	7.3	9.2	10.8	10.4	9.4	8.2	7.2	6.8
Memorandum											
European Union	7.8	10.2	9.6	8.5	7.9	8.5	9.8	11.0	11.6	11.1	10.6
Growth in employment											
Industrial countries	**1.0**	**1.7**	**1.9**	**1.9**	**1.2**	**–0.5**	**–0.3**	**–0.2**	**1.1**	**1.3**	**1.1**
Major industrial countries	1.2	1.7	2.0	1.8	1.1	–0.5	–0.1	0.1	1.2	1.3	1.0
United States	2.1	2.6	2.3	2.0	0.5	–0.9	0.6	1.5	3.1	2.0	1.0
Japan	1.1	1.0	1.7	1.9	2.0	1.9	1.1	0.2	0.1	0.2	0.7
Germany	. . .	. . .	. . .	. . .	. . .	–2.2	–1.6	–1.8	–0.9	0.8	0.8
West Germany	0.4	0.7	0.8	1.5	3.0	2.5	0.9	–1.6	–1.3	0.4	0.6
France	—	0.4	0.9	1.5	1.1	0.2	–0.7	–1.1	0.7	1.6	1.5
Italy	0.5	–0.3	0.6	–0.1	1.3	0.8	–0.9	–2.8	–1.7	—	1.0
United Kingdom	–0.1	2.3	4.2	2.7	0.4	–3.1	–2.5	–1.0	0.5	1.4	0.9
Canada	2.1	2.7	3.2	2.1	0.6	–1.9	–0.6	1.4	2.1	3.0	2.0
Other industrial countries	0.3	1.6	1.7	2.2	1.7	–0.4	–1.3	–1.7	0.5	1.6	1.6
Memorandum											
European Union	0.1	1.1	1.7	1.7	1.6	–0.9	–1.5	–1.9	–0.2	1.1	1.2

Table A4 *(concluded)*

	Average[1] 1977–86	1987	1988	1989	1990	1991	1992	1993	1994	1995	1996
Growth in real per capita GDP											
Industrial countries	**2.0**	**2.6**	**3.7**	**2.5**	**1.6**	**—**	**0.8**	**0.6**	**2.4**	**2.4**	**2.0**
Major industrial countries	2.1	2.6	3.8	2.4	1.5	—	0.9	0.7	2.4	2.3	1.9
United States	1.7	2.2	3.0	1.6	0.2	–1.7	1.2	2.0	3.0	2.2	0.9
Japan	3.2	3.6	5.8	4.3	4.5	3.9	0.8	–0.5	0.3	1.5	3.2
Germany	. . .	. . .	. . .	. . .	. . .	2.0	1.4	–1.8	2.6	2.6	2.7
West Germany	2.0	1.5	3.1	2.6	3.8	3.7	0.5	–2.7	1.9	1.9	2.1
France	1.7	1.8	4.0	3.8	2.0	0.4	0.8	–1.4	2.1	2.8	2.6
Italy	2.5	3.0	3.9	2.8	2.0	0.9	1.1	0.7	2.4	2.9	3.0
United Kingdom	2.0	4.5	4.8	1.9	0.1	–2.6	–0.8	2.0	3.5	3.0	2.6
Canada	2.0	2.9	3.6	0.7	–1.7	–3.0	–0.5	1.1	3.2	3.2	1.5
Other industrial countries	1.6	2.7	3.5	3.4	2.1	0.3	0.4	–0.5	2.2	2.7	2.6
Memorandum											
European Union	1.9	2.7	3.9	3.1	2.3	0.6	0.7	–0.5	2.5	2.8	2.7

[1]Compound annual rate of change for employment and per capita GDP; arithmetic average for unemployment rate.
[2]The projections for unemployment have been adjusted to reflect the new survey techniques adopted by the U.S. Bureau of Labor Statistics in January 1994.
[3]New series starting in 1993, reflecting revisions in the labor force surveys and the definition of unemployment to bring data in line with those of other industrial countries.

Table A5. Developing Countries: Real GDP

(Annual percent change)

	Average 1977–86	1987	1988	1989	1990	1991	1992	1993	1994	1995	1996
Developing countries	**4.6**	**5.7**	**5.2**	**3.9**	**3.9**	**4.9**	**5.9**	**6.1**	**6.3**	**5.6**	**6.1**
By region											
Africa	2.1	1.6	3.6	3.4	2.0	1.9	0.8	0.7	2.7	3.7	5.3
Asia	6.9	8.1	9.1	6.0	5.6	6.4	8.2	8.7	8.6	7.6	7.3
Middle East and Europe	2.5	5.0	–0.8	0.5	4.8	3.1	5.5	3.7	0.7	2.9	4.7
Western Hemisphere	3.2	3.3	1.1	1.6	0.6	3.5	2.7	3.2	4.6	2.3	3.7
Sub-Saharan Africa	2.8	3.2	2.5	2.2	1.3	1.6	1.0	1.6	2.3	5.2	5.4
Four newly industrializing Asian economies	8.1	11.9	9.5	6.3	7.1	7.8	5.7	6.0	7.2	6.8	6.6
By predominant export											
Fuel	2.6	2.1	1.0	3.1	4.7	4.5	4.6	2.3	2.9	2.5	5.1
Nonfuel exports	5.3	6.9	6.4	4.2	3.7	5.0	6.3	7.2	7.2	6.4	6.4
Manufactures	6.3	8.2	8.0	5.2	4.1	5.4	7.5	8.7	8.1	7.2	6.8
Primary products	2.5	3.8	1.2	0.7	1.9	4.1	4.9	4.8	5.1	5.0	4.7
Agricultural products	2.4	3.0	1.3	0.8	2.5	4.1	5.4	4.8	4.8	5.0	4.7
Minerals	2.5	6.1	0.7	0.5	0.3	4.0	3.5	4.5	6.2	4.9	4.9
Services, income, and private transfers	5.1	7.1	2.9	2.2	2.9	4.9	3.4	2.7	3.5	4.2	5.1
Diversified export base	4.3	2.8	6.8	3.8	4.1	3.4	2.3	3.4	5.8	4.5	6.0
By financial criteria											
Net creditor countries	1.9	1.3	–0.8	1.9	6.9	6.8	6.3	3.6	3.0	4.0	5.5
Net debtor countries	4.8	6.1	5.7	4.1	3.7	4.7	5.9	6.4	6.5	5.8	6.2
Market borrowers	5.5	6.9	6.2	3.7	3.3	6.3	7.5	8.2	8.4	6.2	6.5
Diversified borrowers	4.1	5.7	5.6	5.0	4.5	2.2	4.2	4.5	4.0	5.5	5.8
Official borrowers	4.0	4.0	3.7	3.6	3.6	3.7	2.7	2.4	3.6	4.3	5.3
Countries with recent debt-servicing difficulties	3.0	3.8	1.8	2.0	0.5	2.5	2.2	2.7	4.1	2.6	4.1
Countries without debt-servicing difficulties	6.4	7.8	8.2	5.4	5.6	6.0	8.0	8.3	7.8	7.3	7.2
Other groups											
Small low-income economies	4.9	3.8	3.3	3.5	3.8	4.4	3.6	3.1	3.9	5.9	5.6
Least developed countries	4.6	2.7	2.5	2.9	2.6	2.2	3.1	3.3	3.7	5.9	4.9
Fifteen heavily indebted countries	3.0	2.8	1.9	2.0	0.7	2.7	1.3	2.5	4.5	2.3	4.0
Memorandum											
Real per capita GDP											
Developing countries	2.1	3.4	4.7	0.6	2.2	3.1	3.6	4.3	4.3	3.6	4.1
By region											
Africa	–0.8	–1.3	0.9	0.6	–0.6	–0.8	–1.9	–1.8	–0.3	1.6	2.2
Asia	4.9	6.2	10.5	1.8	4.0	4.7	6.5	7.1	7.0	5.9	5.7
Middle East and Europe	–1.1	1.2	–3.6	–1.2	3.3	1.9	–0.3	1.7	–2.1	0.4	1.0
Western Hemisphere	0.9	1.3	–0.7	–0.8	–1.4	1.5	0.7	1.3	2.6	–0.3	1.9

Table A6. Developing Countries—By Country: Real GDP[1]

(Annual percent change)

	Average 1977–86	1987	1988	1989	1990	1991	1992	1993	1994
Africa	**2.1**	**1.6**	**3.6**	**3.4**	**2.0**	**1.9**	**0.8**	**0.7**	**2.7**
Algeria	2.5	−0.7	−1.9	4.9	−0.6	0.2	1.6	−2.2	−0.2
Angola	...	9.4	−8.4	4.4	−5.3	−1.6	1.3	−23.8	2.7
Benin	3.9	−1.5	2.1	−2.5	3.1	4.7	4.1	3.2	3.4
Botswana	10.8	12.2	14.1	9.2	7.3	7.6	2.3	0.4	2.8
Burkina Faso	3.6	−1.4	6.6	0.9	−1.5	10.0	2.5	−0.8	1.2
Burundi	3.6	5.5	5.0	1.3	3.5	5.0	2.7	−5.7	−11.9
Cameroon	8.0	0.5	−12.9	−3.5	−4.5	−6.7	−4.8	−2.2	−3.8
Cape Verde	4.6	7.6	7.6	6.9	2.4	1.0	2.9	4.3	4.5
Central African Republic	2.0	−2.9	1.9	2.3	1.0	−1.6	−2.4	−3.0	5.8
Chad	0.9	−1.8	13.8	5.8	−2.3	13.2	8.1	−12.0	4.1
Comoros	4.5	1.6	2.7	−3.2	2.5	2.1	1.6	1.3	0.8
Congo	7.1	0.2	1.8	2.6	1.0	—	1.5	2.6	−1.5
Côte d'Ivoire	2.9	−1.6	−2.0	−1.1	−2.1	−0.8	—	−0.8	1.7
Djibouti	0.4	0.5	1.2	−0.9	−0.6	1.3	2.4	−2.3	−3.3
Equatorial Guinea	1.5	4.4	2.7	−1.2	3.3	−1.1	13.0	7.1	2.5
Ethiopia	1.6	9.9	2.4	1.2	−2.2	−1.0	−3.2	−12.3	1.3
Gabon	−4.5	−15.4	3.5	7.0	4.0	6.7	−3.4	3.7	0.3
Gambia, The	3.5	2.8	1.7	4.3	5.7	2.2	4.4	2.1	—
Ghana	1.1	4.8	5.6	5.1	3.3	5.3	3.9	5.0	3.8
Guinea	1.8	3.3	6.3	4.0	4.3	2.4	3.0	4.7	4.0
Guinea-Bissau	6.5	5.6	6.9	4.5	3.2	3.0	2.8	2.7	6.3
Kenya	5.1	5.9	6.0	4.5	4.3	2.3	0.3	0.1	3.0
Lesotho	−0.7	5.1	12.9	11.9	4.6	1.7	2.6	5.6	16.7
Liberia	0.5	1.3	3.1	−10.8	0.3	2.9	1.9	2.2	2.2
Madagascar	2.5	1.2	3.4	4.1	3.1	−6.3	1.1	1.9	3.3
Malawi	2.9	1.6	3.2	1.3	5.7	8.7	−7.3	9.4	−7.9
Mali	1.6	1.2	−0.2	11.8	0.4	−2.5	7.8	−0.8	2.4
Mauritania	4.2	2.9	3.1	2.2	−1.8	2.6	1.7	4.9	4.2
Mauritius	3.1	10.8	8.7	5.7	4.7	6.3	4.7	6.7	4.7
Morocco	4.2	−2.7	10.4	2.5	3.9	6.8	−4.4	−1.1	11.8
Mozambique, Rep. of	−1.4	14.7	8.2	6.5	1.0	4.9	−0.8	19.3	5.4
Namibia	...	3.1	7.0	0.7	1.0	5.7	6.4	−2.2	3.8
Niger	2.1	−3.6	6.9	0.9	−1.3	2.5	−6.5	1.4	4.0
Nigeria	−1.2	−0.7	9.9	7.2	8.2	4.8	3.5	1.6	0.6
Rwanda	3.8	−0.3	3.8	1.0	0.4	0.3	0.4	−10.9	...
Sao Tome and Principe	0.5	−1.5	2.0	3.1	−2.2	1.5	1.5	1.3	1.5
Senegal	2.0	4.0	5.1	−1.4	4.5	0.7	2.9	−2.0	2.0
Seychelles	3.5	4.9	5.3	10.3	7.5	2.7	6.9	5.8	−1.1
Sierra Leone	0.3	4.0	2.5	2.4	−0.1	0.7	−0.8	1.5	3.5
Somalia	2.9	4.1	−5.0	2.4	−0.2	...	...	...	...
South Africa	2.0	2.1	4.2	2.4	−0.3	−1.0	−2.2	1.1	2.3
Sudan	1.0	1.3	1.4	1.5	—	6.1	8.6	7.6	5.5
Swaziland	3.8	16.9	10.0	3.5	8.8	3.8	3.8	4.1	3.5
Tanzania	1.8	6.1	4.2	3.0	3.5	3.8	4.5	5.1	5.0
Togo	1.8	0.5	6.2	3.9	0.1	−0.9	−3.7	−13.5	10.7
Tunisia	4.5	6.7	0.1	3.7	5.9	3.9	8.0	2.1	4.4
Uganda	0.8	7.5	6.1	6.0	5.4	3.6	8.6	5.1	7.0
Zaïre	1.0	2.7	0.5	−1.4	−2.3	−7.2	−11.2	−16.6	−11.0
Zambia	0.3	2.8	1.9	1.0	−0.5	−0.2	−5.2	9.2	1.4
Zimbabwe	2.5	−0.5	7.3	4.5	2.2	4.3	−6.2	2.1	4.5

Table A6 (continued)

	Average 1977–86	1987	1988	1989	1990	1991	1992	1993	1994
Asia	**6.9**	**8.1**	**9.1**	**6.0**	**5.6**	**6.4**	**8.2**	**8.7**	**8.6**
Afghanistan, Islamic State of	0.5	–10.3	–8.3	–7.1	–2.6	0.8	1.0	–3.1	–3.0
Bangladesh	9.4	4.3	3.5	5.0	5.1	4.1	4.8	4.9	5.0
Bhutan	6.9	17.8	1.0	4.7	6.6	3.5	3.7	5.2	5.0
Cambodia	. . .	. . .	9.9	3.5	1.2	7.6	7.0	3.9	5.2
China	9.0	10.9	11.3	4.3	3.8	8.2	13.1	13.7	12.0
Fiji	2.1	–5.9	3.5	13.4	5.6	–0.2	4.4	2.7	3.3
Hong Kong	8.3	13.0	8.0	2.6	3.4	5.1	6.0	5.8	5.7
India	4.8	4.8	8.7	7.4	5.5	1.8	3.8	3.8	4.9
Indonesia	5.6	4.9	5.8	7.5	7.2	6.9	6.5	6.5	7.0
Kiribati	–5.8	0.3	10.2	–2.2	–2.9	2.8	3.1	2.9	3.5
Korea	7.8	11.5	11.3	6.4	9.5	9.1	5.1	5.5	8.3
Lao P.D. Republic	4.9	–1.0	–2.1	9.9	6.7	4.0	7.0	6.1	8.4
Malaysia	5.8	5.4	8.9	9.2	9.7	8.7	7.8	8.3	8.5
Maldives	8.4	8.9	8.7	9.3	16.2	7.6	6.3	6.2	5.7
Marshall Islands	. . .	15.4	5.1	–1.7	3.2	0.1	0.1	2.5	2.0
Micronesia, Fed. States of	. . .	9.6	12.4	–1.7	–2.7	4.3	–1.2	5.2	–0.4
Myanmar	4.9	–3.3	–9.5	–0.4	3.0	0.2	6.8	6.7	6.3
Nepal	3.2	3.9	7.2	3.9	8.0	4.6	2.1	4.8	5.1
Pakistan	6.3	6.4	4.8	4.7	5.6	8.2	4.8	2.5	4.1
Papua New Guinea	1.5	2.8	2.9	–1.4	–3.0	9.5	11.8	16.6	1.2
Philippines	2.0	4.3	6.8	6.2	2.7	–0.2	0.3	2.1	4.5
Singapore	6.8	9.5	11.1	9.2	8.8	6.7	6.0	9.9	7.0
Solomon Islands	2.5	8.4	1.3	4.3	1.0	1.7	10.5	0.5	3.7
Sri Lanka	5.2	1.5	2.7	2.3	6.2	4.6	4.3	6.9	5.4
Taiwan Province of China	8.4	12.3	7.3	7.6	4.9	7.2	6.5	6.1	6.2
Thailand	6.2	9.5	13.3	12.2	11.6	8.4	7.9	8.2	8.5
Vanuatu	3.5	0.4	0.6	4.5	5.2	6.5	0.6	1.7	3.7
Viet Nam	5.6	2.5	5.1	7.8	4.9	6.0	8.6	8.1	8.7
Western Samoa	2.3	0.5	0.3	1.9	–9.4	–1.9	–1.3	5.3	–5.5
Middle East and Europe	**2.5**	**5.0**	**–0.8**	**0.5**	**4.8**	**3.1**	**5.5**	**3.7**	**0.7**
Bahrain	4.8	–1.2	10.9	1.2	1.3	4.6	7.7	5.6	5.1
Cyprus	7.0	7.0	8.7	8.0	7.3	1.2	10.3	1.3	4.0
Egypt	6.2	8.7	3.5	2.7	2.3	1.2	0.4	1.5	1.3
Iran, Islamic Republic of	–0.8	–2.2	–9.7	–7.7	11.7	11.4	5.7	1.8	1.9
Iraq	1.1	28.3	–10.2	12.0	–26.0	–61.3	—	—	1.0
Israel	3.0	6.1	3.1	1.3	5.8	6.2	6.6	3.5	6.8
Jordan	7.2	2.9	–1.9	–13.4	1.0	1.8	16.1	5.8	5.7
Kuwait	–2.2	8.1	–10.0	25.0	–30.2	–47.6	94.6	33.6	7.8
Lebanon	11.7	16.7	–28.2	–42.2	–13.4	38.2	4.5	7.0	7.0
Libya	–2.6	–23.6	–10.2	7.2	7.0	2.9	–2.9	–4.7	–3.0
Malta	4.3	4.1	8.4	8.2	6.3	6.2	4.7	4.5	4.3
Oman	7.7	–3.7	6.1	3.3	7.5	9.2	6.8	7.0	5.0
Qatar	–0.8	0.9	4.7	5.3	2.1	–0.8	5.6	1.5	–0.1
Saudi Arabia	3.2	–1.4	6.6	0.5	9.3	9.9	2.2	0.5	0.3
Syrian Arab Republic	3.1	1.9	13.3	–9.0	7.6	7.1	10.5	3.9	5.5
Turkey	3.9	9.6	1.9	0.6	9.3	0.8	6.1	7.5	–5.6
United Arab Emirates	–1.2	5.5	–2.6	13.3	17.5	0.2	2.8	–1.5	1.1
Yemen Arab Republic, former	7.9	4.4	6.7	3.4	1.7	. . .	. . .	. . .	. . .
Yemen, former P.D. Republic of	0.8	1.4	1.0	2.5	3.0	. . .	. . .	. . .	. . .
Yemen, Republic of	. . .	. . .	. . .	. . .	. . .	–4.2	4.2	5.9	6.0

Table A6 (concluded)

	Average 1977–86	1987	1988	1989	1990	1991	1992	1993	1994
Western Hemisphere	**3.2**	**3.3**	**1.1**	**1.6**	**0.6**	**3.5**	**2.7**	**3.2**	**4.6**
Antigua and Barbuda	6.9	9.0	7.7	6.3	3.4	4.3	1.7	2.6	2.9
Argentina	0.5	2.6	−1.9	−6.2	0.1	8.9	8.7	6.0	7.1
Aruba	...	15.9	16.7	9.1	11.7	3.8	3.8	3.8	3.8
Bahamas, The	5.0	3.7	2.3	2.3	1.2	−3.1	0.1	2.0	2.3
Barbados	2.8	3.8	3.1	3.7	−3.3	−5.2	−5.3	1.3	2.4
Belize	3.9	12.6	9.6	12.9	8.0	4.7	4.9	4.2	2.3
Bolivia	−0.4	2.6	3.0	3.6	4.4	4.6	2.8	4.1	4.2
Brazil	3.8	3.6	0.3	3.3	−4.4	1.1	−0.9	4.3	5.7
Chile	3.7	6.6	7.3	9.9	3.3	7.3	11.0	6.3	4.2
Colombia	3.9	5.4	4.1	3.4	4.3	2.0	3.8	5.3	5.3
Costa Rica	3.0	4.8	3.4	5.6	3.6	2.2	7.3	6.0	3.5
Dominica	3.7	6.8	7.4	−1.1	6.3	2.3	2.8	1.8	1.0
Dominican Republic	2.9	7.9	1.6	4.1	−5.0	−0.9	7.8	3.0	5.0
Ecuador	3.7	−5.9	10.4	0.3	3.0	4.9	3.5	1.7	3.2
El Salvador	−0.8	2.7	1.6	1.0	3.4	3.5	5.0	5.3	5.8
Grenada	4.5	7.7	6.8	5.0	6.8	2.4	−1.0	1.0	0.8
Guatemala	1.5	3.5	4.0	3.9	3.1	3.7	4.8	4.0	5.0
Guyana	−2.6	0.9	−2.6	−3.3	−5.3	6.0	7.8	8.3	6.0
Haiti	1.5	0.6	−1.5	−1.5	−3.0	−4.0	−10.8	−4.0	2.0
Honduras	3.5	6.1	4.5	4.3	0.1	3.3	5.6	6.0	−1.5
Jamaica	1.6	7.7	−4.0	4.7	4.1	0.8	1.8	2.0	3.0
Mexico	3.8	1.9	1.2	3.3	4.4	3.6	2.8	0.6	3.5
Netherlands Antilles	1.4	0.2	2.6	3.1	0.6	5.8	5.2	−1.8	3.0
Nicaragua	−2.4	−0.7	−12.5	−1.7	−0.1	−0.2	0.5	−1.0	2.0
Panama	4.7	2.4	−15.6	−0.4	4.6	9.6	8.6	5.9	5.0
Paraguay	5.7	4.3	6.4	5.8	3.1	2.5	1.8	3.7	3.5
Peru	1.9	8.3	−8.2	−11.8	−4.2	2.8	−2.3	6.5	12.9
St. Kitts and Nevis	4.8	7.4	9.8	6.7	3.0	3.9	3.0	4.5	3.2
St. Lucia	6.6	1.9	12.2	9.1	4.1	2.3	7.1	3.1	2.8
St. Vincent and the Grenadines	5.9	6.3	8.9	6.5	5.4	3.1	4.9	1.4	1.6
Suriname	0.2	−7.3	8.5	4.0	0.1	2.9	4.3	−3.0	−0.8
Trinidad and Tobago	−0.9	−4.7	−4.0	−0.9	1.5	2.7	−1.7	−1.7	4.0
Uruguay	1.3	7.9	—	1.3	0.9	2.9	7.4	1.7	2.1
Venezuela	1.0	3.6	5.8	−8.6	6.5	9.7	6.1	−0.4	−3.3

[1]For many countries, figures for recent years are IMF staff estimates. Data for some countries are for fiscal years.

Table A7. Countries in Transition: Real GDP[1]

(Annual percent change)

	Average 1977–86	1987	1988	1989	1990	1991	1992	1993	1994
Central and eastern Europe	...	...	...	...	...	**−11.1**	**−11.4**	**−6.2**	**−3.8**
Albania	1.6	−0.8	−1.4	9.8	−10.0	−27.7	−9.7	11.0	7.4
Belarus	...	...	...	...	...	−1.2	−9.6	−9.5	−21.7
Bulgaria	5.7	5.7	2.4	−0.5	−9.1	−11.7	−5.7	−4.2	—
Croatia	...	...	...	...	...	...	...	−3.2	1.8
Czech Republic	...	...	...	...	...	...	...	−0.9	2.6
Czechoslovakia, former	2.7	2.1	2.5	4.5	−0.4	−15.9	−8.5	...	...
Estonia	...	...	...	...	...	−7.9	−21.6	−6.6	6.0
Hungary	2.5	4.1	−0.1	0.7	−3.5	−11.9	−4.3	−2.3	2.6
Latvia	...	...	...	...	...	−11.1	−35.2	−14.8	2.0
Lithuania	...	...	...	...	...	−13.1	−56.6	−16.5	1.5
Macedonia, former Yugoslav Rep. of	...	...	...	...	...	...	...	−15.5	−7.2
Moldova	...	...	...	...	...	−18.1	−20.6	−8.7	−22.1
Poland	1.4	2.0	4.1	0.2	−11.6	−7.0	2.6	3.8	6.0
Romania	4.0	0.8	−0.5	−5.8	−5.6	−12.9	−10.1	1.3	3.4
Slovak Republic	...	...	...	...	...	...	...	−4.1	5.3
Slovenia	...	...	...	...	...	...	...	1.3	5.0
Ukraine	...	...	...	...	...	−11.9	−17.0	−17.1	−23.0
Yugoslavia, former	3.1	−1.0	−2.0	0.8	−7.5	−17.0	−34.0	...	...
Russia	...	...	...	...	...	**−13.0**	**−19.0**	**−12.0**	**−15.0**
Transcaucasus and central Asia	...	...	...	...	...	**−7.7**	**−17.6**	**−11.9**	**−14.9**
Armenia	...	...	...	...	...	−11.8	−52.4	−14.8	—
Azerbaijan	...	...	...	...	...	−0.7	−22.1	−23.3	−21.9
Georgia	...	...	...	...	...	−20.6	−42.7	−39.2	−10.0
Kazakhstan	...	...	...	...	...	−13.0	−14.0	−12.0	−25.0
Kyrgyz Republic	...	...	...	...	...	−5.0	−19.1	−16.0	−26.5
Mongolia	6.9	3.5	8.5	4.2	−2.0	−9.9	−7.6	−1.2	2.5
Tajikistan	...	...	...	...	...	−8.7	−30.0	−27.6	−16.3
Turkmenistan	...	...	...	...	...	−4.7	−5.3	−10.0	−19.5
Uzbekistan	...	...	...	...	...	−0.9	−11.1	−2.4	−2.6

[1]Data for many countries refer to real net material product (NMP) or are estimates based on NMP. For many countries, figures for recent years are IMF staff estimates. The figures should be interpreted only as indicative of broad orders of magnitude because reliable, comparable data are not generally available. In particular, the growth of output of new private enterprises or of the informal economy is not fully reflected in the recent figures.

Table A8. Summary of Inflation
(In percent)

	Average 1977–86	1987	1988	1989	1990	1991	1992	1993	1994	1995	1996
GDP deflators											
Industrial countries	**7.1**	**3.2**	**3.7**	**4.4**	**4.4**	**4.2**	**3.2**	**2.5**	**1.9**	**2.3**	**2.7**
United States	6.4	3.1	3.9	4.6	4.3	3.8	2.8	2.2	2.1	2.5	3.1
European Union	9.1	4.0	4.3	4.9	5.3	5.6	4.5	3.7	2.6	3.0	2.8
Japan	3.1	—	0.4	1.8	2.2	2.0	1.5	0.9	0.2	0.3	1.1
Other industrial countries	7.2	5.3	5.4	5.7	4.6	3.4	1.7	1.8	1.6	2.4	2.6
Consumer prices											
Industrial countries	**7.3**	**3.1**	**3.4**	**4.4**	**5.0**	**4.5**	**3.3**	**3.0**	**2.4**	**2.6**	**2.7**
United States	6.8	3.7	4.1	4.8	5.4	4.2	3.0	3.0	2.6	3.1	3.5
European Union	8.9	3.2	3.5	4.7	5.4	5.3	4.5	3.8	3.1	3.1	2.8
Japan	3.8	0.1	0.7	2.3	2.8	3.3	1.7	1.3	0.7	0.3	0.7
Other industrial countries	7.6	5.3	4.8	5.2	5.9	5.0	2.1	2.5	1.3	2.7	2.4
Developing countries	**26.1**	**33.6**	**52.5**	**59.4**	**61.7**	**33.4**	**35.9**	**43.0**	**48.0**	**17.5**	**8.9**
By region											
Africa	15.7	14.7	17.5	19.6	16.3	24.7	29.7	26.8	33.6	21.4	10.0
Asia	7.5	7.0	11.5	11.1	6.6	7.7	7.1	9.4	13.5	9.9	6.6
Middle East and Europe	20.4	23.0	27.1	22.2	22.0	25.8	25.4	24.5	32.3	22.5	10.9
Western Hemisphere	69.3	122.2	243.9	337.4	440.8	128.8	152.6	212.3	225.8	36.1	14.2
By analytical criteria											
Fuel exporters	20.3	37.5	36.6	18.5	16.7	17.9	17.1	16.2	17.9	22.5	11.9
Nonfuel exporters	28.6	32.4	57.7	74.1	78.2	38.4	42.0	51.6	57.4	16.3	8.1
Market borrowers	39.6	53.8	94.2	113.4	118.8	47.2	54.6	70.9	77.1	20.2	8.9
Official borrowers	16.9	17.7	22.5	23.5	21.2	25.9	22.0	20.6	23.1	15.7	8.5
Countries with recent debt-servicing difficulties	49.4	84.2	149.7	194.6	240.9	91.7	106.2	140.1	150.2	30.6	12.6
Countries without debt-servicing difficulties	11.3	9.6	14.8	13.7	9.5	10.9	10.9	12.5	17.4	12.6	7.7
Countries in transition	**6.4**	**9.4**	**13.6**	**37.1**	**44.1**	**94.8**	**722.3**	**675.1**	**295.2**	**126.9**	**18.9**
Central and eastern Europe	...	...	...	...	...	96.5	368.4	458.8	203.2	109.9	21.2
Excluding Belarus and Ukraine	...	...	...	...	...	100.0	183.2	139.2	87.1	60.4	20.8
Russia	...	...	...	...	...	92.7	1,353.0	896.0	302.0	143.0	12.3
Transcaucasus and central Asia	...	...	...	...	...	95.7	915.0	1,241.2	1,337.6	163.4	34.0
Memorandum											
Median inflation rate											
Industrial countries	7.9	4.1	4.6	4.8	5.4	4.2	3.1	3.0	2.4	2.5	2.5
Developing countries	10.6	7.5	8.2	9.2	9.7	11.7	9.8	9.0	10.1	8.0	5.0
Countries in transition	1.0	1.3	0.6	2.0	5.6	96.5	883.6	685.5	207.7	60.4	18.3

Table A9. Industrial Countries: GDP Deflators and Consumer Prices
(*Annual percent change*)

	Average 1977–86	1987	1988	1989	1990	1991	1992	1993	1994	1995	1996	Fourth Quarter[1] 1994	1995	1996
GDP deflators														
Industrial countries	**7.1**	**3.2**	**3.7**	**4.4**	**4.4**	**4.2**	**3.2**	**2.5**	**1.9**	**2.3**	**2.7**	...	...	...
Major industrial countries	6.7	2.9	3.4	4.1	4.1	4.0	3.0	2.3	1.7	2.1	2.6	1.6	2.6	2.5
United States	6.4	3.1	3.9	4.6	4.3	3.8	2.8	2.2	2.1	2.5	3.1	2.3	3.0	3.2
Japan	3.1	—	0.4	1.8	2.2	2.0	1.5	0.9	0.2	0.3	1.1	–0.7	1.2	1.1
Germany	...	...	...	...	...	4.9	5.5	3.9	2.2	2.0	2.1	...	...	...
West Germany	3.6	1.8	1.6	2.4	3.2	3.9	4.4	3.2	2.0	1.9	2.0	1.8	2.1	2.1
France	9.2	3.0	2.8	3.0	3.1	3.1	2.3	2.4	1.4	1.9	2.0	1.7	2.0	2.0
Italy	14.4	6.0	6.6	6.2	7.6	7.7	4.5	4.4	3.5	4.8	4.0	3.7	5.3	3.3
United Kingdom	9.6	5.0	6.0	7.1	6.4	6.5	4.3	3.4	2.0	2.7	2.9	1.9	2.9	2.7
Canada	6.5	4.7	4.6	4.8	3.1	2.7	1.4	1.1	0.6	1.5	1.9	0.3	2.0	1.9
Other industrial countries	9.5	5.1	5.4	6.1	6.0	5.3	4.2	3.5	3.1	3.4	3.1	...	...	...
Spain	14.2	5.8	5.7	7.0	7.4	7.0	6.5	4.5	4.5	4.2	3.5	...	...	...
Netherlands	3.8	–0.5	1.2	1.2	2.3	2.7	2.5	1.6	1.4	3.1	2.1	...	...	...
Belgium	5.3	2.3	1.8	4.8	3.1	2.7	3.4	4.4	2.2	2.5	2.5	...	...	...
Sweden	8.8	4.8	6.5	8.0	8.8	7.6	1.4	2.9	2.5	3.4	3.3	...	...	...
Austria	4.9	2.4	1.7	2.9	3.3	4.0	4.2	3.6	3.0	2.7	2.9	...	...	...
Denmark	7.8	4.7	3.4	4.2	2.7	2.5	2.0	1.8	1.3	2.5	2.5	...	...	...
Finland	8.3	4.7	7.0	6.1	5.8	2.5	0.7	2.4	2.5	2.0	2.8	...	...	...
Greece	18.1	14.3	15.5	12.7	20.5	18.4	14.2	13.6	11.0	9.0	7.1	...	...	...
Portugal	21.7	11.3	11.3	11.8	14.5	14.0	13.0	6.5	6.0	5.0	4.5	...	...	...
Ireland	11.9	2.2	3.1	4.4	–1.7	1.1	1.3	3.6	3.2	2.3	1.7	...	...	...
Luxembourg	6.0	–3.1	1.0	0.2	1.3	3.8	3.8	0.6	3.2	2.1	2.3	...	...	...
Switzerland	3.5	2.6	2.4	4.2	5.7	5.5	2.6	2.1	1.8	1.4	1.6	...	...	...
Norway	7.5	7.1	4.5	5.9	4.5	2.5	–1.0	2.1	–0.3	2.5	3.0	...	...	...
Iceland	32.4	20.2	23.4	20.4	14.3	7.3	3.3	1.0	2.4	1.4	2.2	...	...	...
Australia	8.5	7.4	8.4	7.4	4.6	2.0	1.5	1.2	2.1	3.7	3.8	...	...	...
New Zealand	14.9	14.1	7.7	8.0	4.2	2.7	3.8	2.2	2.5	3.0	1.5	...	...	...
Memorandum														
European Union	9.1	4.0	4.3	4.9	5.3	5.6	4.5	3.7	2.6	3.0	2.8	...	...	...
Consumer prices														
Industrial countries	**7.3**	**3.1**	**3.4**	**4.4**	**5.0**	**4.5**	**3.3**	**3.0**	**2.4**	**2.6**	**2.7**	...	...	...
Major industrial countries	7.0	2.8	3.2	4.3	4.8	4.4	3.2	2.8	2.2	2.5	2.7	2.2	2.6	2.7
United States	6.8	3.7	4.1	4.8	5.4	4.2	3.0	3.0	2.6	3.1	3.5	2.6	3.3	3.6
Japan	3.8	0.1	0.7	2.3	2.8	3.3	1.7	1.3	0.7	0.3	0.7	0.9	0.1	1.0
Germany	...	...	...	...	...	4.6	4.9	4.7	3.1	2.0	2.0	...	...	...
West Germany	3.5	0.2	1.3	2.8	2.7	3.5	4.0	4.1	3.0	2.0	2.0	2.8	1.7	2.0
France	9.3	3.3	2.7	3.5	3.4	3.2	2.4	2.1	1.7	2.0	2.0	1.4	2.2	2.2
Italy	14.2	4.7	5.0	6.3	6.5	6.3	5.3	4.4	4.0	5.2	4.2	4.0	5.8	3.3
United Kingdom[2]	9.2	4.1	4.6	5.9	8.1	6.8	4.7	3.0	2.4	2.9	2.8	2.2	3.1	2.7
Canada	7.5	4.4	4.0	5.0	4.8	5.6	1.5	1.8	0.2	2.0	1.9	—	2.3	1.7
Other industrial countries	9.1	4.9	4.7	5.6	6.4	5.4	4.2	3.7	3.2	3.4	3.0	...	...	...
Memorandum														
European Union	8.9	3.2	3.5	4.7	5.4	5.3	4.5	3.8	3.1	3.1	2.8	...	...	...

[1]From fourth quarter of preceding year.
[2]Retail price index excluding mortgage interest.

Table A10. Industrial Countries: Hourly Earnings, Productivity, and Unit Labor Costs in Manufacturing

(Annual percent change)

	Average 1977–86	1987	1988	1989	1990	1991	1992	1993	1994	1995	1996
Hourly earnings											
Industrial countries	**8.6**	**3.8**	**4.7**	**5.5**	**6.3**	**6.5**	**5.1**	**3.8**	**3.0**	**2.9**	**3.8**
Major industrial countries	8.1	3.4	4.4	5.4	6.0	6.3	4.9	3.7	2.8	2.7	3.8
United States	7.1	2.2	4.0	3.9	5.2	5.5	4.1	3.3	2.9	2.6	3.3
Japan	4.9	1.0	3.2	6.7	6.5	5.9	4.6	2.6	2.7	1.3	4.1
West Germany	5.9	5.2	3.9	4.2	5.7	7.3	7.1	6.1	1.6	4.4	4.2
France	11.6	4.6	3.9	4.8	4.8	5.3	4.6	3.3	2.5	2.7	3.5
Italy	16.1	7.6	7.5	9.7	8.6	9.4	7.0	4.5	3.1	3.6	4.9
United Kingdom	11.8	7.4	7.9	9.0	9.6	9.3	6.4	5.3	4.4	4.4	4.8
Canada	7.6	3.4	3.9	5.3	5.2	4.7	3.5	2.1	1.6	1.3	2.8
Other industrial countries	11.3	6.5	6.1	6.2	7.9	7.6	6.1	4.4	4.3	4.2	4.1
Memorandum											
European Union	11.1	6.2	5.8	6.6	7.4	7.8	6.6	5.0	3.2	4.0	4.3
Productivity											
Industrial countries	**2.9**	**4.8**	**4.2**	**2.3**	**1.9**	**2.2**	**1.9**	**2.7**	**4.4**	**2.4**	**2.6**
Major industrial countries	2.7	5.3	4.3	2.3	2.1	2.2	1.8	2.5	4.7	2.4	2.7
United States	1.7	6.4	2.4	0.6	1.7	2.4	2.0	3.2	4.9	2.3	2.2
Japan	3.3	4.1	7.4	4.5	2.8	1.5	–3.7	–1.6	3.4	2.1	4.2
West Germany	2.9	1.9	4.2	3.4	3.5	2.9	1.3	2.4	8.2	3.2	2.5
France	5.6	7.8	8.8	4.2	0.4	3.0	8.4	5.6	2.0	1.2	1.8
Italy	3.6	5.0	5.6	2.8	1.5	1.8	3.8	3.1	4.7	3.0	2.5
United Kingdom	2.9	4.9	5.1	4.4	2.2	2.2	4.4	4.7	4.5	3.6	3.9
Canada	2.0	2.5	0.5	0.5	3.4	1.1	3.7	3.4	2.8	2.4	1.7
Other industrial countries	4.2	1.9	3.8	2.2	1.0	1.7	2.5	3.4	3.1	1.9	1.8
Memorandum											
European Union	4.0	4.0	5.3	3.4	1.7	2.3	3.8	3.8	4.8	2.6	2.4
Unit labor costs											
Industrial countries	**5.6**	**–0.9**	**0.5**	**3.2**	**4.3**	**4.2**	**3.3**	**1.1**	**–1.4**	**0.6**	**1.2**
Major industrial countries	5.3	–1.8	0.2	3.0	3.9	4.0	3.2	1.1	–1.8	0.3	1.0
United States	5.3	–3.9	1.6	3.3	3.4	3.0	2.1	0.1	–2.0	0.3	1.0
Japan	1.5	–3.0	–3.9	2.0	3.5	4.3	8.6	4.3	–0.7	–0.8	—
West Germany	2.9	3.3	–0.2	0.8	2.1	4.2	5.7	3.6	–6.1	1.2	1.7
France	5.6	–3.0	–4.6	0.6	4.4	2.3	–3.5	–2.2	0.5	1.4	1.7
Italy	12.2	2.4	1.8	6.7	6.9	7.5	3.1	1.4	–1.6	0.6	2.3
United Kingdom	8.6	2.5	2.7	4.4	7.3	7.0	1.9	0.6	–0.1	0.8	0.9
Canada	5.5	0.8	3.4	4.8	1.8	3.6	–0.3	–1.2	–1.2	–1.0	1.1
Other industrial countries	6.9	4.5	2.3	3.9	6.9	5.8	3.6	1.0	1.2	2.2	2.2
Memorandum											
European Union	6.9	2.2	0.5	3.2	5.6	5.4	2.8	1.1	–1.4	1.4	1.8

Table A11. Developing Countries: Consumer Prices

(Annual percent change)

	Average 1977–86	1987	1988	1989	1990	1991	1992	1993	1994	1995	1996
Developing countries	**26.1**	**33.6**	**52.5**	**59.4**	**61.7**	**33.4**	**35.9**	**43.0**	**48.0**	**17.5**	**8.9**
By region											
Africa	15.7	14.7	17.5	19.6	16.3	24.7	29.7	26.8	33.6	21.4	10.0
Asia	7.5	7.0	11.5	11.1	6.6	7.7	7.1	9.4	13.5	9.9	6.6
Middle East and Europe	20.4	23.0	27.1	22.2	22.0	25.8	25.4	24.5	32.3	22.5	10.9
Western Hemisphere	69.3	122.2	243.9	337.4	440.8	128.8	152.6	212.3	225.8	36.1	14.2
Sub-Saharan Africa	20.4	22.5	24.2	22.8	23.2	39.0	39.9	35.1	50.8	20.2	8.4
Four newly industrializing Asian economies	8.4	2.5	5.0	5.8	7.0	7.5	5.9	4.6	5.7	5.1	4.9
By predominant export											
Fuel	20.3	37.5	36.6	18.5	16.7	17.9	17.1	16.2	17.9	22.5	11.9
Nonfuel exports	28.6	32.4	57.7	74.1	78.2	38.4	42.0	51.6	57.4	16.3	8.1
Manufactures	27.5	34.3	63.3	77.4	82.2	39.2	53.2	70.1	78.7	18.8	8.3
Primary products	57.2	51.3	111.6	190.8	201.5	76.3	32.5	25.6	24.2	13.4	9.4
Agricultural products	58.4	49.7	84.8	175.3	165.7	62.6	24.5	20.7	17.8	12.7	9.3
Minerals	53.3	56.2	226.8	247.3	358.5	131.2	64.1	44.0	48.9	15.8	9.6
Services, income, and private transfers	12.0	16.5	13.7	15.6	16.5	18.0	15.8	12.9	12.8	9.8	7.1
Diversified export base	11.9	10.6	9.7	8.8	10.0	11.1	8.4	6.6	7.9	6.8	6.3
By financial criteria											
Net creditor countries	9.8	9.6	10.0	7.5	5.3	10.5	10.0	9.6	13.6	9.2	4.2
Net debtor countries	27.9	36.0	56.7	64.6	67.7	35.7	38.5	46.3	51.4	18.2	9.3
Market borrowers	39.6	53.8	94.2	113.4	118.8	47.2	54.6	70.9	77.1	20.2	8.9
Diversified borrowers	15.1	15.7	17.9	15.2	18.2	19.7	18.1	16.4	19.2	15.1	10.5
Official borrowers	16.9	17.7	22.5	23.5	21.2	25.9	22.0	20.6	23.1	15.7	8.5
Countries with recent debt-servicing difficulties	49.4	84.2	149.7	194.6	240.9	91.7	106.2	140.1	150.2	30.6	12.6
Countries without debt-servicing difficulties	11.3	9.6	14.8	13.7	9.5	10.9	10.9	12.5	17.4	12.6	7.7
Other groups											
Small low-income economies	15.8	17.5	18.7	18.9	21.1	27.4	24.1	21.3	25.8	12.9	7.0
Least developed countries	16.9	22.0	23.9	25.8	26.8	40.8	37.1	29.5	37.5	16.1	9.6
Fifteen heavily indebted countries	62.0	109.2	209.3	315.4	369.0	112.0	159.1	209.9	214.9	42.4	15.5
Memorandum											
Median											
Developing countries	10.6	7.5	8.2	9.2	9.7	11.7	9.8	9.0	10.1	8.0	5.0
By region											
Africa	11.2	7.0	7.6	9.4	8.9	9.5	9.7	9.5	23.9	9.4	5.0
Asia	8.2	6.9	8.4	7.2	8.6	9.6	8.8	7.0	8.0	6.5	5.0
Middle East and Europe	9.0	5.0	5.8	6.9	9.5	10.4	8.9	7.9	6.8	6.5	3.9
Western Hemisphere	12.5	14.6	12.1	14.3	21.8	22.7	12.1	10.7	7.7	5.0	5.0

Table A12. Developing Countries—By Country: Consumer Prices[1]

(Annual percent change)

	Average 1977–86	1987	1988	1989	1990	1991	1992	1993	1994
Africa	**15.7**	**14.7**	**17.5**	**19.6**	**16.3**	**24.7**	**29.7**	**26.8**	**33.6**
Algeria	11.0	5.9	5.9	9.2	16.7	25.9	31.7	20.5	29.0
Angola	. . .	. . .	. . .	. . .	. . .	80.1	299.0	1,379.0	950.0
Benin	8.9	3.2	4.3	0.5	1.1	2.1	5.9	0.5	38.6
Botswana	11.9	9.8	8.4	10.0	11.5	11.6	13.8	15.1	12.5
Burkina Faso	8.3	–2.9	4.2	–0.3	–0.8	2.5	–2.0	0.6	24.7
Burundi	10.0	7.1	4.5	11.7	7.0	9.0	4.5	9.7	12.8
Cameroon	11.0	2.8	1.7	1.6	1.5	–0.6	1.9	–3.7	12.7
Cape Verde	14.2	4.0	3.7	6.9	6.6	7.0	5.2	4.4	4.6
Central African Republic	10.7	0.8	–4.0	0.7	–0.2	–2.8	–0.8	–2.9	24.6
Chad	6.7	–2.7	14.9	–4.9	0.5	4.0	–3.8	–7.0	41.3
Comoros	7.4	4.0	1.1	5.7	1.6	1.7	–1.4	1.9	25.0
Congo	9.8	1.2	4.0	4.1	2.0	0.1	2.1	0.7	40.3
Côte d'Ivoire	11.0	7.0	6.9	1.0	–0.7	1.6	4.2	2.1	25.8
Djibouti	8.9	4.2	6.4	3.0	7.8	6.8	5.0	5.8	1.7
Equatorial Guinea	18.1	–9.0	–3.4	5.2	2.7	–0.9	0.9	1.6	40.6
Ethiopia	9.5	–9.5	2.2	9.6	5.2	20.9	21.0	10.0	1.5
Gabon	10.0	–1.0	–9.8	6.6	6.0	1.9	1.5	2.2	35.2
Gambia, The	13.0	46.2	12.4	10.8	10.2	9.1	12.0	5.9	4.0
Ghana	58.2	39.8	31.4	25.2	37.2	18.0	10.1	25.0	24.8
Guinea	25.6	36.7	27.4	28.3	19.4	19.6	16.6	7.1	4.1
Guinea-Bissau	30.2	86.8	60.3	80.8	33.0	57.6	69.6	48.1	15.2
Kenya	12.4	5.1	8.3	9.9	15.7	19.6	27.3	46.0	28.8
Lesotho	14.4	11.6	14.9	14.4	15.8	14.0	18.8	12.0	9.5
Liberia	5.9	5.0	9.7	25.3	10.0	10.0	10.0	10.0	10.0
Madagascar	15.7	15.5	26.3	9.0	11.8	8.5	15.3	13.2	18.0
Malawi	12.0	26.8	28.0	7.5	14.0	8.3	36.1	18.4	37.2
Mali	11.4	–15.0	8.5	–0.2	1.6	1.5	–4.2	0.9	32.0
Mauritania	4.4	8.2	6.3	9.0	6.4	5.6	10.1	9.3	4.1
Mauritius	12.3	0.7	1.5	16.0	10.7	12.8	2.9	8.9	9.4
Morocco	9.8	2.7	2.4	3.1	7.0	8.0	5.7	5.2	5.0
Mozambique, Rep. of	13.3	163.3	50.1	42.0	49.2	33.2	45.1	42.4	63.1
Namibia	. . .	12.6	12.9	15.1	12.0	11.9	17.7	8.6	8.0
Niger	8.7	–6.6	0.6	–0.8	–2.0	–1.9	–1.7	–0.4	35.6
Nigeria	15.8	10.2	34.5	50.5	7.4	13.0	44.6	57.2	57.5
Rwanda	8.0	4.1	3.0	1.0	4.2	19.6	9.5	12.5	64.0
Sao Tome and Principe	5.7	23.8	41.2	44.8	40.5	36.1	27.4	21.8	37.7
Senegal	9.8	–4.1	–1.8	0.4	0.3	–1.8	—	–0.7	32.0
Seychelles	7.2	2.6	1.8	1.6	3.9	2.0	3.2	1.3	1.0
Sierra Leone	36.9	178.7	32.7	62.8	111.0	102.7	65.5	17.6	18.4
Somalia	35.5	28.1	82.0	111.0	216.8	. . .	. . .	. . .	. . .
South Africa	13.9	16.2	12.7	14.7	14.4	15.3	13.9	9.7	9.0
Sudan	27.9	21.5	62.9	65.3	65.2	123.5	117.6	111.0	101.0
Swaziland	15.4	13.2	12.2	12.9	13.5	13.0	9.0	8.0	8.0
Tanzania	24.7	29.9	31.2	25.8	19.7	22.3	22.1	23.5	25.1
Togo	8.0	0.1	0.2	–1.2	1.0	0.4	3.7	–3.6	41.4
Tunisia	8.3	8.2	7.2	7.7	6.5	8.2	5.8	4.0	4.7
Uganda	79.6	256.0	180.1	61.5	33.1	63.0	–0.6	16.1	7.5
Zaïre	52.5	89.8	82.8	104.3	81.3	2,153.8	4,130.0	1,893.0	23,913.0
Zambia	22.2	47.0	54.0	128.3	109.6	93.4	191.3	187.3	53.0
Zimbabwe	12.5	11.9	7.1	11.6	15.5	23.9	42.7	25.4	23.2

Table A12 (continued)

	Average 1977–86	1987	1988	1989	1990	1991	1992	1993	1994
Asia	**7.5**	**7.0**	**11.5**	**11.1**	**6.6**	**7.7**	**7.1**	**9.4**	**13.5**
Afghanistan, Islamic State of	10.9	18.2	29.2	89.8	157.8	166.0	58.2	34.0	20.0
Bangladesh	12.6	9.5	9.6	8.7	9.1	6.9	3.2	1.6	2.9
Bhutan	5.9	11.1	7.9	6.4	6.7	6.7	11.4	9.0	8.0
Cambodia	...	...	...	90.5	152.3	87.9	176.8	31.0	26.0
China	3.4	7.3	18.5	17.8	2.1	2.9	5.4	13.0	21.7
Fiji	7.1	5.7	11.9	6.1	8.1	6.5	4.9	5.2	1.5
Hong Kong	8.6	5.5	7.5	10.1	9.7	11.6	9.3	8.5	8.0
India	8.4	9.0	8.9	6.5	9.9	13.0	10.7	7.9	10.1
Indonesia	11.3	9.3	8.1	6.4	8.1	9.4	7.6	9.7	8.5
Kiribati	7.4	6.5	3.1	5.3	3.8	5.7	4.0	6.5	4.0
Korea	10.8	3.0	7.1	5.7	8.6	9.3	6.2	4.8	6.3
Lao P.D. Republic	55.9	6.1	14.8	59.7	35.7	13.4	9.8	6.3	6.8
Malaysia	4.4	0.8	2.5	2.8	3.1	4.4	4.7	3.6	4.1
Maldives	10.5	11.7	6.5	7.2	3.6	14.7	16.8	20.2	14.2
Marshall Islands	...	–0.6	2.6	2.2	0.7	4.0	10.3	5.0	2.8
Micronesia, Fed. States of	...	–3.1	3.7	4.5	3.5	4.0	5.0	6.0	5.0
Myanmar	3.3	23.3	17.3	27.5	17.6	32.3	21.9	31.7	22.2
Nepal	10.3	13.3	11.0	8.1	9.7	9.8	20.8	8.0	7.0
Pakistan	7.6	4.9	3.3	7.2	9.7	11.0	9.2	10.5	12.8
Papua New Guinea	6.6	3.1	5.7	4.7	7.5	7.0	4.3	5.0	2.8
Philippines	15.3	3.8	9.1	10.6	12.7	18.7	8.9	7.6	9.1
Singapore	3.5	0.5	1.5	2.4	3.4	3.5	2.3	2.4	4.0
Solomon Islands	10.3	11.5	16.8	14.9	8.6	15.2	10.7	9.2	13.7
Sri Lanka	11.4	7.7	14.0	11.6	21.5	12.2	11.4	11.7	8.4
Taiwan Province of China	6.1	0.5	1.3	4.4	4.1	3.6	4.5	2.9	4.1
Thailand	7.1	2.5	3.9	5.5	6.0	5.7	4.1	3.3	5.0
Vanuatu	7.2	14.7	8.4	7.5	5.0	6.5	4.1	4.4	5.0
Viet Nam	62.8	316.7	394.0	35.0	67.0	68.1	17.5	5.2	14.4
Western Samoa	14.0	4.6	8.5	6.5	15.2	–1.3	8.5	1.7	18.0
Middle East and Europe	**20.4**	**23.0**	**27.1**	**22.2**	**22.0**	**25.8**	**25.4**	**24.5**	**32.3**
Bahrain	5.5	–1.7	0.2	1.2	1.3	0.8	—	2.0	2.0
Cyprus	7.2	2.8	3.4	3.8	4.5	5.0	6.5	4.9	4.7
Egypt	15.0	18.8	18.0	19.3	16.7	19.8	13.6	12.0	8.1
Iran, Islamic Republic of	17.1	27.7	28.9	17.4	9.0	20.7	24.4	22.9	35.0
Iraq	16.0	18.0	15.0	15.0	50.0	50.0	50.0	75.0	60.0
Israel	121.1	19.9	16.3	20.2	17.2	19.0	11.9	10.9	12.3
Jordan	7.3	–0.2	6.7	25.6	16.2	8.2	4.0	3.3	3.6
Kuwait	4.7	0.6	1.5	3.3	1.8	16.9	–16.0	0.5	0.5
Lebanon	30.5	487.2	155.0	72.7	68.8	51.5	120.0	29.1	10.6
Libya	10.9	4.4	3.1	1.3	8.6	11.7	15.0	20.0	30.0
Malta	5.4	0.4	1.0	0.9	3.0	2.6	1.6	4.1	5.4
Oman	3.2	2.5	1.6	1.3	10.0	4.6	1.0	0.9	0.5
Qatar	6.3	4.5	4.6	3.3	3.0	4.4	3.0	3.1	3.0
Saudi Arabia	2.7	–1.6	0.9	1.0	2.1	4.6	–0.4	0.8	0.8
Syrian Arab Republic	13.8	59.5	34.6	10.0	11.1	9.0	11.0	13.2	15.0
Turkey	45.9	38.8	73.7	63.3	60.3	66.0	70.1	66.1	106.3
United Arab Emirates	8.2	5.5	5.0	3.3	0.6	5.5	6.8	4.7	4.6
Yemen Arab Republic, former	14.5	20.7	13.9	19.4	14.0	...	...	...	...
Yemen, former P.D. Republic of	6.3	2.5	0.5	—	2.1	...	...	...	...
Yemen, Republic of	...	...	...	...	...	44.9	50.6	62.3	75.0

Table A12 *(concluded)*

	Average 1977–86	1987	1988	1989	1990	1991	1992	1993	1994
Western Hemisphere	**69.3**	**122.2**	**243.9**	**337.4**	**440.8**	**128.8**	**152.6**	**212.3**	**225.8**
Antigua and Barbuda	10.8	3.6	6.8	3.7	7.0	5.7	3.0	3.0	4.5
Argentina	216.7	131.3	343.0	3,080.5	2,314.7	171.7	24.9	10.6	4.1
Aruba	. . .	3.6	3.1	4.0	5.8	5.6	3.9	5.2	5.2
Bahamas, The	6.5	6.0	4.1	5.4	4.6	7.3	5.7	2.7	3.2
Barbados	8.8	3.6	4.7	6.3	3.0	6.3	6.0	1.1	2.4
Belize	4.1	2.0	3.2	2.1	3.0	5.6	2.8	1.8	2.0
Bolivia	227.9	14.6	16.0	15.2	17.1	21.4	12.1	8.5	7.7
Brazil	109.4	224.8	684.6	1,319.9	2,738.8	413.7	991.1	2,103.3	2,407.3
Chile	31.3	19.9	14.7	17.0	26.0	21.8	15.4	12.7	11.4
Colombia	23.6	23.3	28.1	25.9	29.1	30.5	27.0	22.4	22.6
Costa Rica	21.6	16.8	20.8	16.5	19.0	28.7	21.8	9.8	10.0
Dominica	9.6	4.7	2.2	6.8	1.9	6.2	5.3	1.3	7.0
Dominican Republic	13.2	15.9	44.4	45.4	59.4	53.9	4.6	4.8	4.6
Ecuador	20.2	29.5	58.2	75.7	48.4	48.8	54.6	45.0	25.5
El Salvador	15.8	25.3	19.9	17.6	24.0	14.4	11.2	18.5	10.8
Grenada	11.8	–4.4	4.0	5.6	2.7	2.7	3.8	2.3	3.2
Guatemala	12.1	12.3	10.8	11.4	41.2	33.2	10.1	13.5	10.0
Guyana	16.0	28.7	39.9	89.7	63.6	101.5	28.2	11.3	14.0
Haiti	8.1	–5.1	2.9	10.9	20.6	19.8	25.2	30.7	21.2
Honduras	8.2	2.8	6.6	6.2	19.0	25.4	12.1	10.7	22.4
Jamaica	20.7	11.2	8.2	14.3	21.9	51.0	77.3	22.1	30.0
Mexico	46.4	131.8	114.2	20.0	26.7	22.7	15.5	9.8	7.0
Netherlands Antilles	6.3	3.8	2.6	3.8	3.7	3.9	1.5	1.9	3.5
Nicaragua	69.0	911.9	14,315.8	4,709.3	7,484.9	2,945.0	23.7	20.4	7.2
Panama	4.3	1.0	0.2	–0.2	0.8	1.3	1.8	0.5	2.0
Paraguay	17.9	21.8	23.0	26.0	38.2	24.9	15.5	18.3	10.0
Peru	78.0	114.5	1,722.3	2,775.3	7,649.7	409.2	73.2	48.6	23.7
St. Kitts and Nevis	9.3	0.9	0.2	5.1	4.2	4.2	2.9	1.8	2.6
St. Lucia	7.1	7.0	0.8	4.4	3.8	6.1	5.7	0.8	1.8
St. Vincent and the Grenadines	8.9	2.9	0.3	2.7	7.3	6.0	3.7	4.3	0.5
Suriname	10.0	53.4	7.3	0.8	21.8	26.0	43.7	143.4	357.0
Trinidad and Tobago	12.4	13.4	12.1	9.3	9.5	2.3	8.5	13.5	5.9
Uruguay	53.5	63.6	62.2	80.4	112.5	102.0	68.5	54.1	42.1
Venezuela	11.5	28.1	29.4	84.5	40.7	34.2	31.4	38.1	60.8

[1]For many countries, figures for recent years are IMF staff estimates. Data for some countries are for fiscal years.

Table A13. Countries in Transition: Consumer Prices[1]

(Annual percent change)

	Average 1977–86	1987	1988	1989	1990	1991	1992	1993	1994
Central and eastern Europe	...	...	...	...	...	**96.5**	**368.4**	**458.8**	**203.2**
Albania	—	—	—	—	—	36.0	225.2	85.0	22.6
Belarus	...	...	...	...	...	83.5	969.0	1,188.0	2,220.0
Bulgaria	1.4	2.7	2.5	6.4	23.9	333.5	82.0	72.8	96.0
Croatia	...	...	...	...	...	...	...	1,516.0	97.5
Czech Republic	...	...	...	...	...	...	...	20.8	10.0
Czechoslovakia, former	1.9	0.1	0.2	1.4	10.8	59.0	11.0	...	...
Estonia	...	...	...	...	...	210.6	1,069.0	89.0	47.8
Hungary	6.5	8.6	15.7	16.9	29.0	34.2	23.0	22.5	18.8
Latvia	...	...	...	...	...	124.4	951.2	109.0	35.6
Lithuania	...	...	...	...	...	224.7	1,020.5	410.4	72.2
Macedonia, former Yugoslav Rep. of	...	...	...	...	...	...	...	247.6	55.0
Moldova	...	...	...	...	...	162.0	1,276.0	837.0	111.1
Poland	20.4	25.2	60.2	251.1	585.8	70.3	43.0	35.3	32.2
Romania	2.9	1.1	2.6	0.9	4.7	161.1	210.3	256.0	137.0
Slovak Republic	...	...	...	...	...	...	...	23.1	13.4
Slovenia	...	...	...	...	...	...	...	32.0	20.0
Ukraine	...	...	...	...	...	91.2	1,209.7	4,734.9	891.2
Yugoslavia, former	39.0	120.8	194.1	1,239.9	583.1	117.4	6,146.6	...	...
Russia	...	...	...	...	...	**92.7**	**1,353.0**	**896.0**	**302.0**
Transcaucasus and central Asia	...	...	...	...	...	**95.7**	**915.0**	**1,241.2**	**1,337.6**
Armenia	...	...	...	...	...	100.3	824.5	3,731.8	5,267.8
Azerbaijan	...	...	...	...	...	105.6	912.6	1,129.7	1,664.4
Georgia	...	...	...	...	...	78.5	913.0	3,421.5	21,068.1
Kazakhstan	...	...	...	...	...	91.0	1,381.0	1,662.3	1,879.9
Kyrgyz Republic	...	...	...	...	...	85.0	854.6	1,208.7	278.4
Mongolia	0.2	—	—	—	—	20.2	202.6	268.4	87.6
Tajikistan	...	...	...	...	...	111.6	1,156.7	2,194.9	315.6
Turkmenistan	...	...	...	...	...	102.5	492.9	3,102.4	2,397.0
Uzbekistan	...	...	...	...	...	105.0	645.0	534.0	723.0

[1] For some countries, figures for recent years are IMF staff estimates. The figures should be interpreted only as indicative of broad orders of magnitude because reliable, comparable data are not generally available.

Table A14. Summary Financial Indicators

(In percent)

	1987	1988	1989	1990	1991	1992	1993	1994	1995	1996
Industrial countries										
Central government fiscal balance[1]										
Industrial countries	-3.2	-2.6	-2.3	-2.7	-3.1	-4.2	-4.4	-3.7	-3.3	-3.1
United States	-3.3	-2.8	-2.3	-2.9	-3.5	-4.7	-3.8	-2.4	-2.3	-2.4
European Union	-3.8	-3.3	-2.9	-3.5	-3.9	-4.8	-5.9	-5.2	-4.2	-3.6
Japan	-2.2	-1.3	-1.2	-0.5	-0.2	-1.6	-2.6	-4.0	-4.2	-4.2
Other industrial countries	-1.2	-0.7	-0.4	-1.0	-2.9	-4.2	-5.6	-4.3	-3.5	-2.3
General government fiscal balance[1]										
Industrial countries	-2.5	-1.8	-1.2	-2.0	-2.8	-3.8	-4.4	-3.8	-3.4	-3.0
United States	-2.5	-2.0	-1.5	-2.5	-3.2	-4.3	-3.4	-2.0	-1.9	-2.1
European Union	-3.8	-3.2	-2.4	-3.6	-4.4	-5.1	-6.4	-5.8	-4.8	-4.0
Japan	0.5	1.5	2.5	2.9	3.0	1.5	-1.4	-3.0	-3.4	-3.0
Other industrial countries	-0.8	—	0.3	-0.5	-3.6	-5.3	-6.1	-4.8	-4.2	-3.0
Growth of broad money										
Industrial countries	7.5	8.2	8.8	7.8	4.1	3.0	3.7	3.4	...	...
United States	4.3	5.3	4.8	4.0	2.9	1.9	1.4	3.0	...	...
European Union	9.4	9.7	10.5	11.8	6.4	5.6	6.2	4.0	...	...
Japan	10.8	10.2	12.0	7.4	2.3	-0.2	2.2	2.2	...	...
Other industrial countries	9.8	10.9	10.8	7.1	3.8	2.7	3.8	5.1	...	...
Short-term interest rates[2]										
United States	5.8	6.7	8.1	7.5	5.4	3.4	3.0	4.2	6.2	6.6
Japan	3.9	4.0	4.7	6.9	7.0	4.1	2.7	1.9	1.7	2.7
Germany	4.0	4.3	7.1	8.4	9.2	9.5	7.2	5.3	5.2	5.9
LIBOR	7.3	8.1	9.3	8.4	6.1	3.9	3.4	5.1	6.8	7.0
Developing countries										
Central government fiscal balance[1]										
Weighted average	-6.0	-5.4	-4.5	-3.3	-3.3	-2.8	-3.0	-2.7	-1.9	-1.6
Median	-5.4	-5.8	-4.9	-4.4	-4.4	-4.2	-4.9	-4.3	-3.3	-2.8
Growth of broad money										
Weighted average	46.5	67.7	81.5	77.5	59.2	66.6	70.8	56.1	19.0	16.5
Median	16.2	18.4	16.5	17.4	17.7	15.3	14.0	15.0	11.9	11.6
Countries in transition										
Central government fiscal balance[1,3]	-2.0	-2.0	-2.3	-4.0	-9.1	-11.9	-7.0	-7.6	-4.6	...
Growth of broad money	18.4	22.9	34.8	21.6	122.9	627.8	403.9	195.6	...	...

[1] In percent of GDP.

[2] For the United States, three-month treasury bills; for Japan, three-month certificates of deposit; for Germany, three-month interbank deposits; for LIBOR, London interbank offered rate on six-month U.S. dollar deposits.

[3] Because of country differences in definition and coverage, the estimates for this group of countries should be interpreted only as indicative of broad orders of magnitude.

Table A15. Industrial Countries: General and Central Government Fiscal Balances and Balances Excluding Social Security Transactions[1]

(In percent of GDP)

	1987	1988	1989	1990	1991	1992	1993	1994	1995	1996
General government fiscal balance										
Industrial countries	**−2.5**	**−1.8**	**−1.2**	**−2.0**	**−2.8**	**−3.8**	**−4.4**	**−3.8**	**−3.4**	**−3.0**
Major industrial countries	−2.5	−1.8	−1.1	−2.0	−2.6	−3.6	−4.1	−3.5	−3.2	−2.9
United States	−2.5	−2.0	−1.5	−2.5	−3.2	−4.3	−3.4	−2.0	−1.9	−2.1
Japan	0.5	1.5	2.5	2.9	3.0	1.5	−1.4	−3.0	−3.4	−3.0
Germany[2]	−1.9	−2.1	0.1	−1.9	−3.2	−2.6	−3.3	−2.5	−2.2	−1.8
France[3]	−1.9	−1.6	−1.3	−1.6	−2.2	−3.9	−5.8	−5.8	−4.7	−3.7
Italy[4]	−11.0	−10.7	−9.9	−10.9	−10.2	−9.5	−9.5	−9.2	−8.5	−7.9
United Kingdom[5]	−1.4	1.0	0.9	−1.2	−2.6	−6.1	−7.8	−6.9	−4.0	−2.4
Canada	−3.8	−2.5	−2.9	−4.1	−6.6	−7.1	−7.1	−5.3	−4.4	−3.5
Other industrial countries	−2.4	−1.8	−1.5	−2.2	−3.7	−4.6	−6.1	−5.3	−4.6	−3.9
Spain	−3.1	−3.3	−2.8	−3.9	−5.0	−4.5	−7.5	−6.7	−5.9	−5.8
Netherlands	−5.9	−4.6	−4.7	−5.1	−2.9	−3.9	−3.3	−3.5	−3.2	−3.0
Belgium	−7.4	−6.6	−6.2	−5.4	−6.5	−6.7	−6.6	−5.4	−4.4	−4.2
Sweden	4.2	3.5	5.4	4.2	−1.1	−7.4	−13.3	−11.4	−10.1	−6.8
Austria	−4.3	−3.0	−2.8	−2.2	−2.4	−2.0	−4.1	−4.0	−4.5	−3.7
Denmark	2.4	0.6	−0.5	−1.5	−2.1	−2.6	−4.4	−4.3	−2.5	−1.6
Finland	1.1	4.1	6.3	5.4	−1.5	−5.9	−7.8	−5.5	−5.5	−4.1
Greece	−11.8	−12.9	−16.2	−15.6	−12.9	−11.4	−13.3	−12.9	−11.5	−10.0
Portugal	−6.8	−4.2	−3.7	−6.5	−6.5	−3.5	−7.3	−6.5	−6.0	−5.5
Ireland	−9.8	−3.3	−2.6	−2.5	−2.9	−2.9	−2.7	−2.5	−2.5	−2.5
Luxembourg	1.0	1.8	5.2	5.7	−0.5	−0.9	−0.5	0.5	1.0	1.0
Switzerland	1.2	1.0	0.8	—	−2.1	−3.4	−4.3	−4.5	−3.9	−3.3
Norway	7.3	5.3	4.0	4.6	−0.9	−3.2	−4.7	−3.1	−2.1	−1.0
Iceland	−0.9	−2.1	−4.6	−3.5	−3.4	−3.6	−4.5	−4.0	−4.0	−4.0
Australia	−0.7	1.0	1.6	0.5	−2.6	−4.6	−3.6	−2.7	−2.0	−1.1
New Zealand	1.8	2.4	3.3	2.9	−0.1	−3.6	−1.9	0.3	0.8	1.6
Memorandum										
European Union	−3.8	−3.2	−2.4	−3.6	−4.4	−5.1	−6.4	−5.8	−4.8	−4.0
Fiscal balance excluding social security transactions										
United States	−4.3	−4.2	−3.8	−4.7	−5.2	−5.9	−5.0	−4.2	−4.1	−4.2
Japan	−2.3	−1.6	−0.7	−0.6	−0.7	−2.3	−5.2	−6.9	−7.1	−6.7
Germany	−2.2	−2.2	−0.6	−2.6	−3.9	−2.5	−3.6	−2.7	−2.3	−2.0
France	−2.1	−1.9	−1.5	−1.6	−1.9	−3.2	−4.5	−4.7	−3.8	−3.1
Italy	−6.6	−5.8	−4.9	−5.3	−5.1	−4.0	−4.5	−4.6	−4.7	−4.4
Canada	−2.0	−0.7	−1.0	−2.3	−4.6	−4.8	−4.6	−2.7	−2.1	−1.3

Table A15 *(concluded)*

	1987	1988	1989	1990	1991	1992	1993	1994	1995	1996
Central government fiscal balance										
Industrial countries	**–3.2**	**–2.6**	**–2.3**	**–2.7**	**–3.1**	**–4.2**	**–4.4**	**–3.7**	**–3.3**	**–3.1**
Major industrial countries	–3.3	–2.7	–2.3	–2.7	–3.1	–4.2	–4.2	–3.6	–3.2	–3.0
United States[6]	–3.3	–2.8	–2.3	–2.9	–3.5	–4.7	–3.8	–2.4	–2.3	–2.4
Japan[7]	–2.2	–1.3	–1.2	–0.5	–0.2	–1.6	–2.6	–4.0	–4.2	–4.2
Germany[8,9]	–1.4	–1.7	–0.9	–1.8	–1.9	–1.3	–2.1	–1.5	–1.5	–1.6
France[9]	–1.9	–1.7	–1.4	–1.6	–1.7	–3.0	–4.4	–4.6	–3.7	–3.0
Italy[10]	–11.2	–11.0	–10.7	–10.1	–10.3	–10.4	–9.9	–9.4	–7.8	–7.2
United Kingdom	–1.1	1.1	1.2	–1.1	–2.3	–6.9	–7.9	–6.7	–3.9	–2.4
Canada	–3.8	–3.2	–3.3	–3.9	–4.6	–4.2	–4.6	–3.4	–2.9	–1.9
Other industrial countries	–2.6	–2.1	–1.8	–2.2	–3.2	–4.0	–5.7	–4.7	–4.1	–3.3
Memorandum										
European Union	–3.8	–3.3	–2.9	–3.5	–3.9	–4.8	–5.9	–5.2	–4.2	–3.6

[1] On a national income accounts basis except as indicated in footnotes.
[2] Data through 1990 apply to west Germany only.
[3] Adjusted for valuation changes of the foreign exchange stabilization fund.
[4] Includes imputed interest due on tax refund liabilities not replaced by government bonds.
[5] Excludes asset sales.
[6] Data are on a budget basis.
[7] Data are on a national income basis and exclude social security transactions.
[8] Data through June 1990 apply to west Germany only.
[9] Data are on an administrative basis and exclude social security transactions.

[10] Data refer to the state sector and cover the transactions of the state budget as well as those of several autonomous entities operating at the same level; data do not include the gross transactions of social security institutions, only their deficits. Includes imputed interest due on tax refund liabilities not replaced by government bonds.

Table A16. Industrial Countries: General Government Structural Balances and Fiscal Impulses[1]

(In percent of GDP)

	1987	1988	1989	1990	1991	1992	1993	1994	1995	1996
Structural balance[2]										
Major industrial countries	**-2.6**	**-2.7**	**-2.3**	**-3.0**	**-2.8**	**-3.1**	**-2.9**	**-2.4**	**-2.4**	**-2.3**
United States	-3.0	-3.0	-2.6	-3.2	-2.9	-3.7	-3.0	-2.1	-2.4	-2.4
Japan	0.6	0.9	1.8	2.1	2.2	1.7	0.1	-0.7	-0.8	-0.9
Germany[3]	-1.2	-2.0	-0.4	-3.5	-5.3	-3.6	-2.0	-1.0	-1.0	-1.0
France	-0.8	-1.6	-2.1	-2.4	-2.1	-3.1	-3.3	-3.4	-2.9	-2.4
Italy	-11.3	-11.6	-11.4	-12.3	-11.2	-9.6	-8.1	-8.0	-7.7	-7.4
United Kingdom	-1.3	-0.8	-2.0	-3.6	-2.7	-3.7	-4.4	-4.1	-2.2	-1.2
Canada	-4.9	-4.5	-4.8	-4.7	-4.8	-4.3	-4.3	-3.6	-3.8	-2.9
Other industrial countries[4]	-2.2	-2.0	-2.2	-3.0	-3.7	-3.6	-3.3	-2.8	-2.9	-2.6
Memorandum										
European Union[5]	-3.3	-3.6	-3.6	-5.0	-5.1	-4.7	-4.1	-3.6	-3.2	-2.9
Fiscal impulse[6]										
Major industrial countries	**-0.6**	**—**	**-0.5**	**0.4**	**—**	**0.1**	**-0.1**	**-0.3**	**—**	**-0.2**
United States[7]	-0.7	—	-0.5	0.7	—	—	-0.6	-0.8	—	—
Japan[7]	-1.3	-0.4	-0.9	—	-0.4	0.9	1.8	1.0	—	—
Germany[3,7]	—	0.7	-1.7	2.0	0.7	-1.6	-1.3	-0.7	—	—
France[7]	-0.9	0.7	0.5	—	—	0.9	—	—	—	-0.6
Italy	—	0.5	—	0.8	-1.3	-1.6	-1.6	—	—	—
United Kingdom	—	-1.0	—	1.1	-0.5	2.0	1.7	—	-2.2	-1.3
Canada	-0.9	-0.5	—	—	—	—	—	-0.5	—	-0.8
Memorandum										
Seven countries except the United States	-0.5	—	-0.5	0.2	-0.2	0.1	0.4	0.2	-0.3	-0.3
Four European countries	-0.1	0.3	-0.4	1.1	-0.2	-0.2	-0.4	-0.2	-0.6	-0.4

[1] On a national income accounts basis.

[2] The structural budget position is defined as the actual budget deficit (or surplus) less the effects of cyclical deviations of output from potential output. Because of the margin of uncertainty that attaches to estimates of cyclical gaps and to tax and expenditure elasticities with respect to national income, indicators of structural budget positions should be interpreted as broad orders of magnitude. Moreover, it is important to note that changes in structural budget balances are not necessarily attributable to policy changes but may reflect the built-in momentum of existing expenditure programs. In the period beyond that for which specific consolidation programs exist, it is assumed that the structural deficit remains unchanged.

[3] Data through 1990 apply to west Germany only. The estimate of the fiscal impulse for 1995 is affected by the assumption by the federal government of the debt of the Treuhandanstalt and various other agencies, which were formerly held outside the general government sector. At the public sector level, there would be an estimated withdrawal of fiscal impulse amounting to just over 1 percent of GDP.

[4] Excludes Greece, Iceland, Luxembourg, Portugal, and Switzerland.

[5] Excludes Greece, Luxembourg, and Portugal.

[6] For a definition of the fiscal impulse measure, see *The New Palgrave Dictionary of Money and Finance* edited by Peter Newman, Murray Milgate, and John Eatwell (London: Macmillan, 1992; New York: Stockton, 1992). Impulse estimates equal to or less than ±0.3 percent of GDP are indicated by "—."

[7] For relevant years, the fiscal impulse is calculated on the basis of data adjusted for net international financial transfers related to the 1990–91 regional conflict in the Middle East.

Table A17. Industrial Countries: Monetary Aggregates

(Annual percent change)[1]

	1987	1988	1989	1990	1991	1992	1993	1994
Narrow money[2]								
Industrial countries	**6.9**	**7.2**	**4.1**	**7.0**	**6.5**	**7.9**	**8.2**	**5.6**
Major industrial countries	6.1	6.3	3.1	6.7	6.5	8.2	8.2	5.6
United States	6.3	4.3	0.6	4.2	7.9	14.3	10.5	6.1
Japan	4.8	8.6	2.4	4.5	9.5	3.9	7.0	7.0
Germany[3]	7.4	10.9	5.6	29.6	3.4	10.8	8.5	5.2
France	4.1	4.1	7.7	3.9	–4.7	–0.1	1.7	2.5
Italy	7.8	7.3	10.3	6.6	10.5	0.6	7.4	5.4
United Kingdom	4.8	6.8	5.7	5.2	2.4	2.4	4.9	2.6
Canada	8.2	7.5	3.2	–1.2	5.2	5.4	13.9	4.7
Other industrial countries	12.9	13.4	10.0	8.8	6.7	6.3	8.3	5.8
Memorandum								
European Union	6.8	8.4	8.2	12.3	3.9	4.4	6.2	4.6
Broad money[4]								
Industrial countries	**7.5**	**8.2**	**8.8**	**7.8**	**4.1**	**3.0**	**3.7**	**3.4**
Major industrial countries	7.1	7.9	8.5	7.7	3.8	2.7	3.3	3.1
United States	4.3	5.3	4.8	4.0	2.9	1.9	1.4	3.0
Japan	10.8	10.2	12.0	7.4	2.3	–0.2	2.2	2.2
Germany[3]	5.9	6.9	5.5	19.7	6.3	7.6	10.9	1.6
France	9.9	8.6	9.4	8.9	2.5	5.2	–1.5	3.0
Italy	7.2	7.6	9.9	8.1	9.1	4.5	7.7	2.8
United Kingdom	16.0	18.1	18.9	12.2	5.6	3.1	5.1	6.0
Canada	8.3	12.6	14.3	8.1	4.7	3.2	3.3	4.7
Other industrial countries	10.7	10.2	10.6	7.9	6.4	5.0	5.8	5.4
Memorandum								
European Union	9.4	9.7	10.5	11.8	6.4	5.6	6.2	4.0

[1] Based on end-of-period data.

[2] M1 except for the United Kingdom, where M0 is used here as a measure of narrow money; it comprises notes in circulation plus bankers' operational deposits. M1 is generally currency in circulation plus private demand deposits. In addition, the United States includes traveler's checks of nonbank issues and other checkable deposits and excludes private sector float and demand deposits of banks. Japan includes government demand deposits and excludes float. Germany includes demand deposits at fixed interest rates. Canada excludes private sector float.

[3] Data through 1989 apply to west Germany only. The growth rates for the monetary aggregates in 1990 are affected by the extension of the currency area.

[4] M2, defined as M1 plus quasi-money, except for Japan, Germany, and the United Kingdom, for which the data are based on M2 plus certificates of deposit (CDs), M3, and M4, respectively. Quasi-money is essentially private term deposits and other notice deposits. The United States also includes money market mutual fund balances, money market deposit accounts, overnight repurchase agreements, and overnight Eurodollars issued to U.S. residents by foreign branches of U.S. banks. For Japan, M2 plus CDs is currency in circulation plus total private and public sector deposits and installments of Sogo Banks plus CDs. For Germany, M3 is M1 plus private time deposits with maturities of less than four years plus savings deposits at statutory notice. For the United Kingdom, M4 is composed of non-interest-bearing M1, private sector interest-bearing sterling sight bank deposits, private sector sterling time bank deposits, private sector holdings of sterling bank CDs, private sector holdings of building society shares and deposits, and sterling CDs less building society holdings of bank deposits and bank CDs, and notes and coins.

Table A18. Industrial Countries: Interest Rates

(In percent a year)

	1987	1988	1989	1990	1991	1992	1993	1994	March 1995
Policy-related interest rate[1]									
Major industrial countries	6.4	6.9	8.6	9.0	7.8	6.3	4.9	4.4	5.5
United States	6.7	7.6	9.2	8.1	5.7	3.5	3.0	4.2	6.0
Japan	3.5	3.6	4.9	7.2	7.5	4.6	3.0	2.1	2.1
Germany	3.7	3.8	6.6	8.0	8.9	9.4	7.4	5.3	4.8
France	8.0	7.6	9.4	10.0	9.5	10.7	8.6	5.6	7.7
Italy	11.1	11.2	12.7	12.3	12.7	14.5	10.5	8.8	11.6
United Kingdom	9.6	10.3	13.9	14.8	11.5	9.4	5.9	5.5	6.8
Canada	8.0	9.2	11.9	12.9	9.0	6.6	4.6	5.1	8.1
Short-term interest rate[2]									
Industrial countries	**6.7**	**7.1**	**8.8**	**9.2**	**8.0**	**6.8**	**5.2**	**4.8**	...
Major industrial countries	6.7	7.2	8.7	9.2	7.8	6.4	4.9	4.6	5.6
United States	6.9	7.7	9.1	8.2	5.8	3.7	3.2	4.6	6.1
Japan	4.1	4.4	5.3	7.6	7.2	4.3	2.8	2.1	2.0
Germany	4.0	4.3	7.1	8.4	9.2	9.5	7.2	5.3	5.0
France	8.2	7.9	9.3	10.3	9.7	10.4	8.4	5.8	7.9
Italy	11.1	11.2	12.7	12.3	12.7	14.5	10.5	8.8	11.6
United Kingdom	9.7	10.3	13.9	14.8	11.5	9.6	5.9	5.5	6.6
Canada	8.4	9.6	12.2	13.0	9.0	6.7	5.0	5.6	8.3
Other industrial countries	9.4	9.0	10.8	11.4	10.8	10.5	8.3	6.5	...
Memorandum									
European Union	8.1	8.2	10.3	11.1	10.7	11.0	8.3	6.4	...
Long-term interest rate[3]									
Industrial countries	**8.4**	**8.5**	**8.7**	**9.6**	**8.7**	**8.0**	**6.6**	**7.2**	...
Major industrial countries	8.0	8.1	8.1	9.0	8.3	7.5	6.2	6.8	5.5
United States	8.4	8.8	8.5	8.6	7.9	7.0	5.9	7.1	6.0
Japan	5.0	4.8	5.1	7.0	6.3	5.1	4.0	4.2	2.1
Germany	6.2	6.5	7.0	8.7	8.5	7.9	6.5	6.9	4.8
France	9.4	9.1	8.8	10.0	9.0	8.6	6.9	7.4	7.7
Italy[4]	11.6	12.0	13.3	13.6	13.1	13.1	11.3	10.3	11.6
United Kingdom	9.6	9.7	10.2	11.8	10.1	9.1	7.5	8.2	6.8
Canada	9.9	10.2	9.9	10.8	9.8	8.8	7.9	8.6	8.1
Other industrial countries	10.9	10.3	11.2	12.2	10.9	10.4	8.6	8.5	...
Memorandum									
European Union	9.4	9.3	10.0	11.3	10.4	10.0	8.3	8.3	...

[1]For the United States, federal funds rate; for Japan, overnight call rate; for Germany, repurchase rate; for France, day-to-day money rate; for Italy, three-month treasury bill rate; for the United Kingdom, base lending rate; and for Canada, overnight money market financing rate.

[2]For the United States, three-month certificates of deposit (CDs) in secondary markets; for Japan, three-month CDs; for Germany, France, and the United Kingdom, three-month interbank deposits; for Italy, three-month treasury bills; and for Canada, three-month prime corporate paper.

[3]For the United States, yield on ten-year treasury bonds; for Japan, over-the-counter sales yield on ten-year government bonds with longest residual maturity; for Germany, yield on government bonds with maturities of nine to ten years; for France, long-term (seven- to ten-year) government bond yield (Emprunts d'Etat à long terme TME); for Italy, secondary market yield on fixed-coupon (BTP) government bonds with two to four years' residual maturity; for the United Kingdom, yield on medium-dated (ten-year) government stock; and for Canada, average yield on government bonds with residual maturities of over ten years.

[4]March 1995 data refer to yield on ten-year government bonds.

Table A19. Industrial Countries: Exchange Rates

	1987	1988	1989	1990	1991	1992	1993	1994	March[1] 1995
	National currency units per U.S. dollar								
U.S. dollar nominal exchange rates									
Japanese yen	144.6	128.2	138.0	144.8	134.7	126.7	111.2	102.2	91.3
Deutsche mark	1.80	1.76	1.88	1.62	1.66	1.56	1.65	1.62	1.41
French franc	6.01	5.96	6.38	5.45	5.64	5.29	5.66	5.55	5.00
Pound sterling[2]	1.63	1.78	1.64	1.78	1.76	1.76	1.50	1.53	1.60
Italian lira	1296	1302	1372	1198	1241	1232	1574	1612	1684
Canadian dollar	1.33	1.23	1.18	1.17	1.15	1.21	1.29	1.37	1.41
Spanish peseta	123.5	116.5	118.4	101.9	103.9	102.4	127.3	134.0	128.5
Dutch guilder	2.03	1.98	2.12	1.82	1.87	1.76	1.86	1.82	1.58
Belgian franc	37.3	36.8	39.4	33.4	34.1	32.1	34.6	33.5	29.1
Swedish krona	6.34	6.13	6.45	5.92	6.05	5.82	7.78	7.72	7.25
Austrian schilling	12.6	12.3	13.2	11.4	11.7	11.0	11.6	11.4	9.9
Danish krone	6.84	6.73	7.31	6.19	6.40	6.04	6.48	6.36	5.66
Finnish markka	4.40	4.18	4.29	3.82	4.04	4.48	5.71	5.22	4.38
Greek drachma	135.4	141.9	162.4	158.5	182.3	190.6	229.2	242.6	229.1
Portuguese escudo	140.9	144.0	157.5	142.6	144.5	135.0	160.8	166.0	148.3
Irish pound	0.67	0.66	0.71	0.60	0.62	0.59	0.68	0.67	0.63
Swiss franc	1.49	1.46	1.64	1.39	1.43	1.41	1.48	1.37	1.18
Norwegian krone	6.74	6.52	6.90	6.26	6.48	6.21	7.09	7.06	6.28
Icelandic krona	38.7	43.0	57.0	58.3	59.0	57.5	67.6	69.9	64.4
Australian dollar	1.43	1.28	1.26	1.28	1.28	1.36	1.47	1.37	1.36
New Zealand dollar	1.69	1.53	1.67	1.68	1.73	1.86	1.85	1.69	1.55
	Annual percent change								
Real effective exchange rates									
United States	−13.2	−6.2	3.0	−4.9	−1.7	−1.9	4.6	−0.9	. . .
Japan	5.0	5.4	−6.1	−10.4	6.1	3.5	17.3	6.8	. . .
Germany	6.8	0.1	−2.0	5.4	−0.9	2.6	7.9	−1.1	. . .
France	−1.9	−2.9	−2.5	3.1	−4.1	1.4	2.6	1.4	. . .
United Kingdom	1.1	5.9	3.5	−6.0	4.4	−2.1	−8.6	0.6	. . .
Italy	0.9	−0.9	3.8	3.6	1.0	−1.5	−16.4	−4.0	. . .
Canada	4.4	9.4	6.3	1.6	2.5	−5.5	−8.6	−6.0	. . .
Spain	1.8	4.6	7.7	6.1	1.7	1.0	−7.9	−7.3	. . .
Netherlands	3.3	−3.1	−5.6	1.1	−1.3	4.3	2.7	1.0	. . .
Belgium	1.0	−2.9	−1.5	4.1	−0.4	1.3	−1.2	2.8	. . .
Sweden	—	3.6	6.3	0.2	−0.9	−0.1	−24.5	−2.9	. . .
Austria	2.3	−4.9	−2.9	−0.5	−2.1	1.4	1.7	−2.1	. . .
Denmark	9.7	−0.2	−1.6	6.6	−3.4	0.6	2.7	0.7	. . .
Finland	−0.8	2.7	4.6	3.3	−7.9	−17.5	−15.8	6.4	. . .
Ireland	−6.3	−5.3	−7.9	1.7	−6.3	−1.6	−7.2	—	. . .
Switzerland	2.5	−0.8	−6.8	5.2	−1.0	−2.4	−0.7	5.3	. . .
Norway	4.2	1.8	−2.3	−0.9	−2.4	0.4	−2.2	0.3	. . .

[1]March data refer to the average for March 1–24, the reference period for the exchange rate assumptions. See "Assumptions" in the introduction to this Statistical Appendix.
[2]Expressed in U.S. dollars per pound.

Table A20. Developing Countries: Central Government Fiscal Balances
(In percent of GDP)

	1987	1988	1989	1990	1991	1992	1993	1994	1995	1996
Developing countries	**−6.0**	**−5.4**	**−4.5**	**−3.3**	**−3.3**	**−2.8**	**−3.0**	**−2.7**	**−1.9**	**−1.6**
By region										
Africa	−6.7	−6.3	−4.8	−3.5	−4.6	−7.1	−8.9	−6.7	−5.0	−3.6
Asia	−3.9	−3.6	−3.1	−2.8	−2.7	−2.6	−2.4	−2.4	−1.8	−1.7
Middle East and Europe	−11.5	−12.1	−9.0	−9.7	−11.3	−5.2	−6.9	−4.9	−3.5	−2.6
Western Hemisphere	−6.8	−5.3	−5.2	−0.7	0.1	−0.5	0.1	−0.6	0.1	−0.2
Sub-Saharan Africa	−9.7	−7.2	−7.2	−7.6	−7.2	−10.4	−8.9	−7.6	−6.5	−5.2
Four newly industrializing Asian economies	0.8	2.0	1.5	1.1	—	0.1	0.7	−0.5	−0.2	0.1
By predominant export										
Fuel	−10.0	−9.3	−5.0	−3.6	−4.7	−2.2	−4.1	−3.2	−1.3	−0.9
Nonfuel exports	−4.8	−4.3	−4.4	−3.2	−2.9	−3.0	−2.6	−2.5	−2.0	−1.8
Manufactures	−3.9	−3.3	−3.5	−2.1	−2.1	−2.4	−2.2	−2.1	−1.5	−1.4
Primary products	−5.4	−5.1	−5.7	−3.5	−3.2	−3.9	−2.9	−2.4	−2.2	−1.9
Agricultural products	−4.9	−6.1	−7.1	−3.9	−3.5	−4.5	−3.3	−3.2	−2.3	−2.3
Minerals	−6.9	−1.9	−1.2	−2.1	−2.2	−1.6	−1.4	0.3	−1.7	−0.8
Services, income, and private transfers	−11.4	−11.4	−11.2	−11.8	−8.9	−6.6	−5.8	−5.6	−5.0	−4.0
Diversified export base	−4.0	−3.6	−3.2	−3.3	−2.6	−3.2	−3.3	−3.3	−3.2	−2.9
By financial criteria										
Net creditor countries	−8.5	−7.4	−2.8	−5.2	−11.0	−4.3	−5.9	−4.4	−1.8	−1.1
Net debtor countries	−5.8	−5.3	−4.7	−3.1	−2.6	−2.7	−2.7	−2.5	−1.9	−1.6
Market borrowers	−4.3	−3.3	−3.0	−0.7	−0.5	−0.9	−0.7	−1.0	−0.2	−0.3
Diversified borrowers	−6.6	−6.7	−6.0	−5.3	−4.6	−4.3	−4.8	−4.2	−4.1	−3.5
Official borrowers	−10.1	−10.0	−8.5	−8.0	−7.1	−6.9	−7.2	−6.0	−5.0	−3.8
Countries with recent debt-servicing difficulties	−8.5	−7.6	−6.9	−3.5	−2.3	−2.7	−2.5	−2.4	−1.6	−1.3
Countries without debt-servicing difficulties	−3.9	−3.7	−3.2	−2.9	−2.8	−2.7	−2.8	−2.5	−2.0	−1.8
Other groups										
Small low-income economies	−9.1	−9.0	−7.7	−7.9	−7.5	−8.5	−7.2	−6.3	−5.8	−4.8
Least developed countries	−10.5	−10.1	−8.7	−8.9	−7.7	−9.4	−8.2	−8.5	−8.2	−7.5
Fifteen heavily indebted countries	−6.5	−5.3	−4.9	−0.9	−0.4	−1.2	−1.1	−1.2	−0.4	−0.5
Memorandum										
Median										
Developing countries	−5.4	−5.8	−4.9	−4.4	−4.4	−4.2	−4.9	−4.3	−3.3	−2.8
By region										
Africa	−6.7	−6.8	−6.7	−5.7	−6.1	−7.2	−6.9	−6.2	−5.2	−4.2
Asia	−5.1	−2.6	−3.5	−6.2	−4.6	−3.7	−3.7	−4.7	−3.4	−3.1
Middle East and Europe	−11.9	−9.1	−5.1	−4.5	−6.6	−4.4	−6.2	−5.0	−4.0	−3.5
Western Hemisphere	−2.9	−4.4	−4.1	−2.5	−2.1	−1.8	−1.8	−1.0	−1.0	−0.8

Table A21. Developing Countries: Broad Money Aggregates

(Annual percent change)

	1987	1988	1989	1990	1991	1992	1993	1994	1995	1996
Developing countries	**46.5**	**67.7**	**81.5**	**77.5**	**59.2**	**66.6**	**70.8**	**56.1**	**19.0**	**16.5**
By region										
Africa	19.3	25.3	16.4	17.9	30.1	34.2	27.9	27.8	17.8	14.0
Asia	27.5	25.0	23.5	21.3	21.7	20.1	19.1	21.0	17.2	16.2
Middle East and Europe	16.4	18.5	19.9	20.2	24.2	24.0	28.5	28.4	27.6	22.0
Western Hemisphere	141.5	311.0	500.6	438.5	223.3	289.2	305.3	177.7	17.2	14.6
Sub-Saharan Africa	23.6	25.9	23.4	21.4	52.5	63.6	49.3	48.3	20.2	12.4
Four newly industrializing Asian economies	23.1	20.0	18.8	15.9	19.3	15.4	15.4	15.7	14.8	14.4
By predominant export										
Fuel	33.4	22.8	22.0	24.0	22.7	20.1	24.8	18.6	23.7	17.3
Nonfuel exports	53.3	93.4	113.9	106.4	78.4	94.8	96.3	73.7	17.4	16.2
Manufactures	57.0	98.7	105.3	108.0	94.2	132.1	144.0	109.8	19.3	16.6
Primary products	89.9	191.6	345.4	257.6	88.8	56.4	43.1	28.6	12.5	14.1
Agricultural products	95.7	198.6	364.1	218.2	73.7	47.6	37.9	21.9	10.5	13.5
Minerals	66.4	164.2	276.9	443.8	151.8	93.1	66.3	62.0	21.6	16.5
Services, income, and private transfers	16.1	12.8	18.4	22.1	23.8	24.4	21.9	22.1	21.2	26.8
Diversified export base	12.5	19.7	20.4	16.5	14.9	11.4	13.2	13.2	13.3	12.8
By financial criteria										
Net creditor countries	14.6	15.3	13.7	15.3	19.4	18.6	21.9	12.7	11.8	10.4
Net debtor countries	53.8	81.4	101.1	95.9	70.9	83.3	85.7	66.2	19.9	17.2
Market borrowers	78.6	130.2	180.6	166.1	105.1	128.4	134.6	91.6	17.5	15.3
Diversified borrowers	23.6	23.9	26.9	20.2	25.5	24.2	24.4	32.6	26.5	21.9
Official borrowers	37.4	63.2	42.4	42.7	37.8	40.5	32.4	27.7	18.9	17.5
Countries with recent debt-servicing difficulties	91.2	176.5	246.0	230.5	142.7	180.8	186.7	118.4	20.0	16.7
Countries without debt-servicing difficulties	23.9	21.0	22.1	22.1	24.6	23.5	22.2	27.3	19.8	17.8
Other groups										
Small low-income economies	55.2	58.0	46.1	29.8	48.2	53.7	41.5	33.9	19.2	17.7
Least developed countries	28.2	32.8	31.2	32.6	57.0	65.4	51.3	40.8	23.7	21.3
Fifteen heavily indebted countries	126.1	261.0	497.5	341.2	197.1	390.8	259.7	151.8	17.9	15.7
Memorandum										
Median										
Developing countries	16.2	18.4	16.5	17.4	17.7	15.3	14.0	15.0	11.9	11.6
By region										
Africa	13.9	14.6	12.8	11.5	16.1	13.5	12.5	15.0	11.9	11.7
Asia	18.9	19.5	19.2	19.3	19.8	15.4	16.9	16.3	15.1	14.3
Middle East and Europe	9.7	9.1	13.0	14.4	14.5	10.7	9.0	9.7	10.1	9.5
Western Hemisphere	19.5	23.6	17.4	28.4	30.9	19.9	13.7	14.5	9.3	10.0

Table A22. Summary of World Trade Volumes and Prices[1]

(Annual percent change)

	Average 1977–86	1987	1988	1989	1990	1991	1992	1993	1994	1995	1996
World trade[2]											
Volume	3.7	6.4	8.7	6.8	4.5	2.9	5.1	3.8	9.4	8.0	6.8
Unit value											
In U.S. dollars	4.2	10.7	5.2	1.2	8.3	–1.0	1.2	–4.6	2.1	5.6	1.9
In SDRs	4.0	0.4	1.2	6.1	2.3	–1.9	–1.7	–3.8	–0.5	–0.7	1.1
World trade prices[3]											
Manufactures	5.0	12.3	6.3	–0.2	9.3	–0.3	3.6	–5.8	2.8	4.0	2.0
Oil	...	28.7	–20.4	21.5	28.2	–17.0	–0.5	–11.5	–4.1	9.4	–0.1
Nonfuel primary commodities	0.6	8.3	22.8	–0.5	–7.8	–4.4	–0.2	–3.7	12.3	8.0	–1.1
Volume of trade											
Exports											
Industrial countries	4.4	4.1	8.3	7.2	5.4	2.8	4.2	1.5	8.6	8.0	4.8
Developing countries	1.1	15.3	11.4	7.8	6.2	7.1	9.6	9.0	10.4	9.1	10.7
Fuel exporters	–3.5	6.4	9.0	9.4	4.0	0.4	6.2	5.5	3.9	5.6	12.4
Nonfuel exporters	6.2	19.2	12.3	7.2	7.1	9.7	10.8	10.2	12.2	10.0	10.2
Imports											
Industrial countries	4.8	6.0	8.3	7.6	4.7	2.1	4.3	1.5	10.5	7.8	5.0
Developing countries	2.7	9.4	11.8	7.1	8.1	10.5	12.6	10.4	8.7	8.6	11.2
Fuel exporters	0.4	–1.2	6.2	5.8	6.1	8.0	12.6	–1.9	–1.4	–6.5	19.0
Nonfuel exporters	3.7	13.1	13.5	7.4	8.7	11.1	12.6	13.8	11.2	11.9	9.8
Unit value of trade in SDRs											
Exports											
Industrial countries	4.1	1.8	2.3	4.7	2.9	–1.9	–0.5	–4.1	0.1	0.4	1.3
Developing countries	4.4	–1.6	–0.5	9.5	0.9	–2.9	–3.2	–1.1	–1.0	–2.8	0.6
Fuel exporters	2.2	5.4	–11.8	17.2	13.5	–8.5	–3.9	–4.2	–3.8	–0.6	1.3
Nonfuel exporters	4.2	–4.4	3.8	7.0	–3.6	–0.6	–2.9	–0.1	–0.1	–3.4	0.5
Imports											
Industrial countries	3.3	1.0	1.0	5.7	3.5	–3.2	–2.2	–6.2	–1.1	0.4	1.0
Developing countries	4.4	–2.9	2.4	8.1	–1.3	0.2	–2.5	—	–0.6	–3.4	1.0
Fuel exporters	3.4	–3.8	1.8	7.7	–0.2	2.7	–1.6	0.5	0.4	–2.2	1.1
Nonfuel exporters	4.9	–2.6	2.5	8.3	–1.6	–0.5	–2.7	–0.1	–0.9	–3.7	0.9
Terms of trade											
Industrial countries	0.7	0.8	1.3	–0.9	–0.6	1.3	1.7	2.3	1.2	0.1	0.3
Developing countries	—	1.3	–2.8	1.2	2.2	–3.1	–0.7	–1.1	–0.3	0.6	–0.3
Fuel exporters	–1.1	9.5	–13.4	8.9	13.7	–10.9	–2.3	–4.6	–4.1	1.6	0.1
Nonfuel exporters	–0.7	–1.9	1.2	–1.2	–2.0	–0.1	–0.2	0.1	0.7	0.3	–0.5

[1]Data in this table and the tables that follow refer to trade in goods only unless otherwise indicated.

[2]Average of annual percent change for world exports and imports. The estimates of world trade comprise, in addition to trade of industrial and developing countries (which is summarized in the table), trade of countries in transition, except that trade among the states of the former U.S.S.R. is not included.

[3]In U.S. dollars. As represented, respectively, by the export unit value index for the manufactures of the industrial countries; the average of U.K. Brent, Dubai, and Alaska North Slope crude oil spot prices; and the average of world market prices for nonfuel primary commodities weighted by their 1979–81 shares in world commodity exports.

Table A23. Industrial Countries: Export Volumes, Import Volumes, and Terms of Trade[1]
(Annual percent change)

	Average 1977–86	1987	1988	1989	1990	1991	1992	1993	1994	1995	1996
Export volume											
Industrial countries	**4.4**	**4.1**	**8.3**	**7.2**	**5.4**	**2.8**	**4.2**	**1.5**	**8.6**	**8.0**	**4.8**
Major industrial countries	4.2	3.5	9.0	7.7	5.3	2.6	3.9	1.1	8.6	8.1	4.3
United States	2.5	10.0	19.3	11.8	7.3	7.6	7.4	4.6	11.4	10.4	4.6
Japan	6.2	0.4	4.4	4.2	5.8	2.4	1.6	−1.1	1.0	3.4	—
Germany[2]	4.3	0.9	6.2	9.7	2.2	−1.7	0.6	−6.0	8.9	6.6	5.9
France	3.7	3.7	9.0	9.0	5.3	3.9	4.9	−0.9	4.4	6.0	6.8
Italy	4.1	4.2	6.0	8.0	4.4	1.6	4.2	8.4	11.0	10.0	6.5
United Kingdom	3.8	5.9	2.1	5.8	6.2	1.2	2.5	2.6	11.1	8.2	6.2
Canada	7.2	3.6	9.3	1.2	4.6	1.5	8.3	10.7	15.1	15.2	1.8
Other industrial countries	5.0	5.8	6.4	5.8	5.5	3.5	4.9	3.0	8.6	7.6	6.5
Memorandum											
European Union	4.3	4.0	6.5	7.6	4.7	1.4	3.3	−0.1	10.0	7.7	6.2
Import volume											
Industrial countries	**4.8**	**6.0**	**8.3**	**7.6**	**4.7**	**2.1**	**4.3**	**1.5**	**10.5**	**7.8**	**5.0**
Major industrial countries	5.0	5.6	8.7	7.2	4.7	2.3	4.8	2.5	11.4	7.6	4.5
United States	7.0	4.2	4.0	4.4	2.4	0.7	10.4	11.7	15.0	6.4	2.4
Japan	3.0	9.0	16.7	7.9	5.6	3.8	−0.7	4.2	13.5	13.6	5.3
Germany[2]	3.4	4.6	5.9	9.7	10.8	12.3	2.0	−8.5	6.7	5.2	5.9
France	3.3	7.7	8.8	8.1	5.7	2.7	0.7	−3.9	5.9	6.0	6.7
Italy	3.6	9.3	6.5	6.7	5.3	4.7	3.4	−9.2	12.2	8.5	6.5
United Kingdom	4.2	7.7	13.5	8.2	0.1	−5.3	6.6	3.4	6.0	4.9	5.4
Canada	7.8	6.2	14.2	5.4	0.4	3.0	7.3	11.0	13.1	12.8	1.8
Other industrial countries	4.3	7.0	7.1	9.1	4.3	1.7	2.9	−0.8	7.8	8.3	6.6
Memorandum											
European Union	3.8	7.9	8.3	8.5	6.0	3.8	3.0	−4.3	8.5	6.7	6.2
Terms of trade											
Industrial countries	**0.7**	**0.8**	**1.3**	**−0.9**	**−0.6**	**1.3**	**1.7**	**2.3**	**1.2**	**0.1**	**0.3**
Major industrial countries	0.7	1.1	1.2	−1.5	−0.7	2.0	2.3	2.9	1.6	0.1	0.3
United States	0.1	−3.7	1.1	−0.8	−2.4	1.7	−0.4	0.7	0.2	−2.3	−0.5
Japan	1.7	0.6	3.1	−4.4	−6.6	10.2	7.3	8.5	7.9	4.8	3.1
Germany[2]	0.1	5.1	0.5	−2.5	1.7	−1.3	3.2	2.1	0.2	0.5	—
France	0.6	0.4	0.1	−1.9	0.1	0.4	0.9	1.4	0.5	−0.8	−0.2
Italy	1.0	—	—	−1.9	2.7	2.7	0.8	0.8	0.1	−0.2	−0.2
United Kingdom	0.6	0.4	0.5	2.1	0.9	0.9	1.9	1.8	−1.9	−1.6	−0.3
Canada	0.9	3.2	1.8	1.8	−2.3	−2.0	0.8	1.3	1.0	−0.1	0.2
Other industrial countries	0.5	−0.1	1.5	0.9	—	−0.6	−0.1	0.4	—	0.1	0.2
Memorandum											
European Union	0.7	1.5	0.5	−0.9	1.0	0.2	1.6	1.3	−0.4	−0.1	−0.1
Memorandum											
Non-oil trade											
Industrial countries											
Export volume	4.3	5.5	7.9	7.8	5.3	2.5	4.3	1.6	8.3	8.0	4.8
Import volume	6.7	8.8	7.9	8.2	4.8	2.3	4.7	1.4	10.6	8.2	5.1
Terms of trade	1.3	1.9	−0.3	0.1	0.6	0.3	1.6	1.9	0.9	0.3	0.2

[1] Data refer to trade in goods only.
[2] Data through June 1990 apply to west Germany only.

Table A24. Developing Countries—By Region: Total Trade in Goods

(Annual percent change)

	Average 1977–86	1987	1988	1989	1990	1991	1992	1993	1994	1995	1996
Developing countries											
Value in U.S. dollars											
Exports	5.7	25.0	15.2	12.6	13.4	4.9	9.3	7.0	12.1	12.7	12.3
Imports	7.4	17.2	19.0	10.4	12.9	11.6	13.0	9.5	10.8	11.5	13.2
Volume											
Exports	1.1	15.3	11.4	7.8	6.2	7.1	9.6	9.0	10.4	9.1	10.7
Imports	2.7	9.4	11.8	7.1	8.1	10.5	12.6	10.4	8.7	8.6	11.2
Unit value in U.S. dollars											
Exports	4.5	8.4	3.4	4.4	6.8	–2.1	–0.3	–1.9	1.5	3.3	1.5
Imports	4.6	7.1	6.4	3.1	4.5	1.0	0.4	–0.9	1.9	2.7	1.8
Terms of trade	—	1.3	–2.8	1.2	2.2	–3.1	–0.7	–1.1	–0.3	0.6	–0.3
Memorandum											
Real GDP growth in developing country trading partners	4.0	5.1	5.5	3.9	3.6	2.6	3.0	2.9	4.0	4.0	3.9
Market prices of nonfuel commodities exported by developing countries	0.8	3.4	17.2	–2.2	–7.2	–3.2	–2.2	–4.1	19.7	10.0	–2.2
By region											
Africa											
Value in U.S. dollars											
Exports	4.1	11.7	2.7	7.0	16.4	–3.9	–1.7	–4.1	0.4	9.0	8.9
Imports	3.8	6.4	12.1	4.7	8.5	–1.5	5.7	–3.4	5.1	11.9	5.1
Volume											
Exports	0.4	3.1	–6.8	1.8	6.5	2.3	1.0	4.2	0.1	2.4	5.2
Imports	–1.5	–1.7	2.4	3.2	3.6	1.0	1.8	–0.2	–2.9	6.1	1.5
Unit value in U.S. dollars											
Exports	3.7	8.4	10.2	5.1	9.2	–6.1	–2.7	–8.1	0.3	6.5	3.6
Imports	5.3	8.2	9.5	1.5	4.7	–2.5	3.9	–3.2	8.2	5.5	3.6
Terms of trade	–1.6	0.2	0.7	3.6	4.3	–3.7	–6.3	–5.0	–7.3	0.9	—
Asia											
Value in U.S. dollars											
Exports	12.6	31.6	23.2	11.5	10.9	14.0	13.2	10.9	15.3	13.9	12.6
Imports	12.2	24.5	27.1	13.5	13.5	14.6	13.1	13.4	14.6	14.3	14.6
Volume											
Exports	7.9	23.9	17.2	9.5	7.8	12.8	12.3	11.0	13.4	11.1	11.3
Imports	6.8	17.2	20.1	10.9	9.4	13.8	13.3	13.8	13.1	11.8	12.9
Unit value in U.S. dollars											
Exports	4.3	6.2	5.1	1.8	2.9	1.1	0.8	—	1.7	2.5	1.2
Imports	5.0	6.2	5.9	2.3	3.7	0.7	–0.2	–0.4	1.3	2.3	1.6
Terms of trade	–0.7	—	–0.7	–0.5	–0.8	0.4	1.0	0.4	0.4	0.2	–0.4

Table A24 *(concluded)*

	Average 1977–86	1987	1988	1989	1990	1991	1992	1993	1994	1995	1996
Middle East and Europe											
Value in U.S. dollars											
Exports	−2.3	26.4	2.1	21.3	22.4	−9.6	6.1	0.2	3.5	7.2	16.1
Imports	5.2	9.5	6.0	7.2	14.3	5.8	10.1	2.9	−5.0	9.2	16.3
Volume											
Exports	−5.8	7.1	10.1	9.8	1.8	−4.1	8.3	4.4	4.3	2.6	13.6
Imports	1.8	1.4	0.8	1.9	6.4	0.4	8.9	4.2	−6.6	5.7	13.8
Unit value in U.S. dollars											
Exports	3.7	18.1	−7.3	10.5	20.2	−5.7	−2.0	−4.1	−0.8	4.5	2.1
Imports	3.3	8.0	5.2	5.1	7.4	5.3	1.1	−1.2	1.6	3.2	2.2
Terms of trade	0.4	9.3	−11.8	5.1	12.0	−10.5	−3.0	−2.9	−2.4	1.2	−0.1
Western Hemisphere											
Value in U.S. dollars											
Exports	7.5	15.5	14.9	10.2	9.8	−1.4	4.7	4.9	13.9	14.7	9.0
Imports	3.3	13.9	14.2	7.1	12.2	16.2	21.0	8.6	15.3	2.0	7.8
Volume											
Exports	4.6	11.1	8.4	3.9	6.8	4.3	6.2	8.9	9.4	10.1	7.8
Imports	−1.3	5.9	6.2	2.0	8.4	17.6	21.4	9.8	13.7	−0.6	5.9
Unit value in U.S. dollars											
Exports	2.8	4.0	6.0	6.1	2.9	−5.4	−1.4	−3.7	4.2	4.2	1.1
Imports	4.6	7.6	7.5	5.0	3.5	−1.2	−0.3	−1.1	1.5	2.6	1.8
Terms of trade	−1.8	−3.4	−1.4	1.1	−0.7	−4.3	−1.1	−2.6	2.7	1.5	−0.7
Sub-Saharan Africa											
Value in U.S. dollars											
Exports	4.7	4.7	3.5	3.9	5.5	−4.1	−3.8	−3.1	5.7	14.2	9.4
Imports	5.3	11.9	8.3	1.5	8.0	−0.1	0.5	−4.1	2.0	10.9	7.3
Volume											
Exports	−0.6	−0.8	−1.7	2.8	2.7	−2.5	−3.6	2.6	−3.2	4.2	6.0
Imports	−1.8	−0.9	0.8	−2.0	−0.9	−2.0	−5.0	−2.1	−9.8	5.2	3.0
Unit value in U.S. dollars											
Exports	5.4	5.6	5.2	1.1	2.8	−1.6	−0.2	−5.6	9.3	9.6	3.3
Imports	7.3	12.9	7.5	3.6	9.0	2.0	5.8	−2.0	13.1	5.4	4.2
Terms of trade	−1.7	−6.5	−2.1	−2.3	−5.7	−3.5	−5.7	−3.6	−3.4	4.1	−0.9
Four newly industrializing Asian economies											
Value in U.S. dollars											
Exports	15.7	34.7	26.0	10.2	7.8	14.3	12.1	10.4	11.7	11.6	11.2
Imports	12.9	35.0	32.6	12.8	13.8	16.5	12.7	9.8	14.2	12.6	11.7
Volume											
Exports	10.6	28.8	20.2	8.1	6.2	12.9	13.0	11.0	10.9	10.6	10.2
Imports	7.3	28.8	25.8	10.2	12.1	16.5	14.5	10.7	13.2	11.3	10.2
Unit value in U.S. dollars											
Exports	4.6	4.6	4.9	1.9	1.6	1.3	−0.8	−0.5	0.7	0.9	1.0
Imports	5.3	4.9	5.4	2.3	1.5	—	−1.6	−0.8	1.0	1.2	1.3
Terms of trade	−0.6	−0.2	−0.5	−0.4	0.1	1.2	0.9	0.2	−0.3	−0.3	−0.4

Table A25. Developing Countries—By Predominant Export: Total Trade in Goods

(Annual percent change)

	Average 1977–86	1987	1988	1989	1990	1991	1992	1993	1994	1995	1996
Fuel											
Value in U.S. dollars											
Exports	−1.1	23.6	−0.1	22.3	24.9	−7.3	5.1	0.2	2.5	11.6	14.7
Imports	4.0	4.8	12.4	8.7	12.1	11.9	14.0	−2.2	1.5	−2.8	21.3
Volume											
Exports	−3.5	6.4	9.0	9.4	4.0	0.4	6.2	5.5	3.9	5.6	12.4
Imports	0.4	−1.2	6.2	5.8	6.1	8.0	12.6	−1.9	−1.4	−6.5	19.0
Unit value in U.S. dollars											
Exports	2.4	16.1	−8.4	11.8	20.1	−7.7	−1.0	−5.0	−1.3	5.7	2.1
Imports	3.6	6.1	5.8	2.7	5.6	3.6	1.3	−0.4	2.9	4.0	2.0
Terms of trade	−1.1	9.5	−13.4	8.9	13.7	−10.9	−2.3	−4.6	−4.1	1.6	0.1
Nonfuel exports											
Value in U.S. dollars											
Exports	10.8	25.6	21.1	9.4	9.3	9.9	10.7	9.2	14.9	13.0	11.7
Imports	8.9	21.5	21.0	10.9	13.2	11.5	12.7	12.7	13.0	14.6	11.8
Volume											
Exports	6.2	19.2	12.3	7.2	7.1	9.7	10.8	10.2	12.2	10.0	10.2
Imports	3.7	13.1	13.5	7.4	8.7	11.1	12.6	13.8	11.2	11.9	9.8
Unit value in U.S. dollars											
Exports	4.4	5.4	7.8	2.0	2.0	0.2	−0.1	−0.9	2.4	2.7	1.3
Imports	5.1	7.4	6.5	3.3	4.1	0.3	0.1	−1.0	1.6	2.4	1.8
Terms of trade	−0.7	−1.9	1.2	−1.2	−2.0	−0.1	−0.2	0.1	0.7	0.3	−0.5
Manufactures											
Value in U.S. dollars											
Exports	13.3	31.5	24.4	9.4	8.4	12.4	12.5	10.1	15.5	12.3	11.9
Imports	11.3	25.2	26.0	12.6	13.4	12.6	12.6	14.4	13.2	15.7	12.7
Volume											
Exports	8.6	25.2	17.4	7.4	5.9	11.1	12.6	11.0	13.9	10.1	10.6
Imports	5.8	16.9	18.2	9.0	9.2	12.5	13.4	15.7	11.8	13.4	10.9
Unit value in U.S. dollars											
Exports	4.3	5.0	6.0	1.9	2.4	1.2	−0.1	−0.8	1.4	2.0	1.2
Imports	5.3	7.1	6.6	3.3	3.9	0.1	−0.7	−1.2	1.2	2.0	1.6
Terms of trade	−0.9	−2.0	−0.6	−1.3	−1.4	1.2	0.6	0.4	0.2	−0.1	−0.4
Primary products											
Value in U.S. dollars											
Exports	7.1	3.7	13.6	9.6	9.8	0.3	3.3	3.7	14.5	16.7	7.7
Imports	4.7	14.5	4.1	2.8	9.3	10.2	22.1	9.7	12.8	7.9	7.9
Volume											
Exports	3.4	−0.1	4.3	6.2	13.1	2.6	5.3	5.5	5.6	9.4	6.0
Imports	−0.8	4.3	−2.2	0.5	1.7	8.5	19.3	10.1	7.1	4.2	4.9
Unit value in U.S. dollars											
Exports	3.6	3.8	8.9	3.2	−2.9	−2.3	−1.9	−1.7	8.4	6.6	1.6
Imports	5.5	9.7	6.5	2.3	7.5	1.5	2.4	−0.3	5.3	3.6	2.9
Terms of trade	−1.8	−5.4	2.3	0.8	−9.7	−3.7	−4.2	−1.4	2.9	3.0	−1.2

Table A25 (concluded)

	Average 1977–86	1987	1988	1989	1990	1991	1992	1993	1994	1995	1996
Agricultural products											
Value in U.S. dollars											
Exports	8.0	−0.9	11.8	6.5	15.6	1.1	3.5	8.2	14.3	17.4	7.7
Imports	5.0	13.1	2.1	−0.2	8.8	14.8	25.3	13.1	15.5	6.0	7.1
Volume											
Exports	3.5	−0.1	6.3	4.8	19.4	2.8	6.8	7.9	4.8	9.6	5.6
Imports	−1.0	2.9	−3.4	−1.9	1.1	11.5	20.9	12.5	8.6	2.3	3.8
Unit value in U.S. dollars											
Exports	4.3	−0.9	5.2	1.6	−3.2	−1.7	−3.1	0.3	9.0	7.1	2.0
Imports	6.1	9.8	5.7	1.7	7.6	2.9	3.7	0.6	6.3	3.5	3.2
Terms of trade	−1.7	−9.7	−0.5	−0.1	−10.0	−4.5	−6.5	−0.3	2.6	3.4	−1.1
Minerals											
Value in U.S. dollars											
Exports	5.4	14.5	17.3	15.6	−0.6	−1.5	2.9	−6.1	15.0	15.0	7.7
Imports	3.9	18.3	9.2	10.2	10.4	0.5	14.3	0.8	5.0	14.3	10.2
Volume											
Exports	3.1	0.1	0.9	8.9	2.0	2.1	2.3	−0.1	7.6	9.0	7.1
Imports	−0.3	8.1	0.7	6.2	2.9	1.9	15.1	3.5	2.4	10.2	8.1
Unit value in U.S. dollars											
Exports	2.2	14.4	16.3	6.1	−2.5	−3.4	0.5	−6.0	6.9	5.5	0.5
Imports	4.2	9.5	8.5	3.8	7.2	−1.4	−0.7	−2.6	2.5	3.7	1.9
Terms of trade	−1.8	4.5	7.2	2.3	−9.1	−2.1	1.2	−3.5	4.3	1.7	−1.4
Services, income, and private transfers											
Value in U.S. dollars											
Exports	5.2	16.2	12.5	11.2	10.7	1.8	1.9	−0.9	10.6	12.1	11.1
Imports	8.4	11.4	9.9	2.4	12.0	4.1	6.5	3.8	3.9	6.8	5.7
Volume											
Exports	0.9	16.0	0.8	8.2	2.6	3.0	2.8	−2.1	7.4	8.5	9.3
Imports	3.8	3.8	3.3	−4.7	5.4	2.2	4.0	4.4	3.5	4.1	3.3
Unit value in U.S. dollars											
Exports	4.3	0.2	11.7	2.8	7.9	−1.1	−0.9	1.2	3.0	3.3	1.7
Imports	4.5	7.2	6.3	7.4	6.3	1.8	2.4	−0.6	0.3	2.6	2.3
Terms of trade	−0.1	−6.6	5.0	−4.4	1.5	−2.9	−3.2	1.8	2.6	0.7	−0.6
Diversified export base											
Value in U.S. dollars											
Exports	7.4	21.5	12.9	8.8	13.7	6.0	8.2	9.7	12.8	14.7	13.3
Imports	4.8	17.5	18.7	14.5	15.5	10.7	10.2	10.5	16.9	17.1	11.9
Volume											
Exports	2.9	10.5	−2.1	7.0	10.8	9.1	6.3	11.6	8.8	10.3	11.4
Imports	0.2	10.4	11.6	13.2	13.9	10.9	8.2	11.1	14.9	13.2	9.7
Unit value in U.S. dollars											
Exports	4.4	10.0	15.4	1.7	2.7	−2.9	1.8	−1.7	3.7	4.0	1.7
Imports	4.6	6.5	6.4	1.2	1.5	−0.2	1.8	−0.5	1.7	3.4	2.0
Terms of trade	−0.2	3.3	8.4	0.5	1.2	−2.7	−0.1	−1.2	2.0	0.6	−0.3

Table A26. Developing Countries: Nonfuel Commodity Prices[1]

(Annual percent change; U.S. dollar terms)

	Average 1977–86	1987	1988	1989	1990	1991	1992	1993	1994	1995	1996
Nonfuel primary commodities	**0.8**	**3.4**	**17.2**	**−2.2**	**−7.2**	**−3.2**	**−2.2**	**−4.1**	**19.7**	**10.0**	**−2.2**
By commodity group											
Food	−0.6	7.5	26.1	0.3	−6.9	1.6	−0.8	−2.2	9.6	−1.8	−0.6
Beverages	1.9	−28.7	0.3	−17.0	−13.3	−6.8	−12.7	6.9	74.6	18.5	−5.1
Agricultural raw materials	1.7	32.6	5.4	−2.4	−3.5	−0.3	1.8	0.5	11.5	12.1	−0.3
Minerals and metals	0.2	14.4	37.9	5.2	−7.5	−8.6	−2.5	−15.6	10.8	13.8	−3.4
By region											
Africa	0.7	0.2	13.1	−2.0	−5.1	−6.5	−3.8	−5.7	23.6	12.2	−2.8
Asia	0.5	16.8	16.8	−2.7	−9.7	0.2	4.1	−3.8	16.9	9.8	−0.5
Middle East and Europe	—	15.5	13.9	2.5	−2.2	−4.3	−6.7	−5.9	15.8	8.9	−4.0
Western Hemisphere	0.9	−7.4	20.4	−2.5	−7.0	−5.2	−6.3	−3.0	23.8	11.3	−3.6
Sub-Saharan Africa	1.0	−0.5	11.3	−3.3	−6.4	−6.5	−3.9	−3.9	27.5	13.6	−3.9
Four newly industrializing Asian economies	0.8	17.3	10.9	−4.6	−9.6	3.2	7.4	−1.3	14.4	7.7	−0.9
By predominant export											
Fuel	1.5	7.6	11.9	−6.9	−8.8	−3.1	—	−1.8	22.0	16.3	−1.1
Nonfuel exports	0.6	1.3	18.2	−1.6	−7.1	−3.8	−2.5	−4.3	20.9	10.1	−2.5
Manufactures	0.6	−4.1	12.2	−1.2	−5.1	−0.3	−3.0	−1.8	16.2	6.1	−0.7
Primary products	0.9	−3.1	20.1	−1.3	−7.3	−6.8	−4.8	−5.0	25.8	12.1	−4.3
Agricultural products	1.1	−11.5	11.5	−5.5	−8.3	−4.4	−7.0	1.8	31.4	11.8	−3.4
Minerals	0.3	18.0	36.2	5.1	−6.0	−9.9	−1.6	−14.2	17.0	12.5	−6.0
Services, income, and private transfers	−0.1	0.2	22.8	−1.8	−7.7	−6.5	−9.8	−2.9	32.8	11.2	−4.4
Diversified export base	0.2	21.2	21.0	−2.7	−9.1	−1.2	4.0	−6.1	15.1	10.8	−0.7
By financial criteria											
Net creditor countries	0.5	18.6	27.3	−2.0	−6.9	−6.7	−3.8	−5.8	19.7	8.0	−2.3
Net debtor countries	0.7	2.1	17.3	−2.3	−7.4	−3.7	−2.2	−3.9	21.0	10.9	−2.3
Market borrowers	0.4	6.1	19.7	−2.0	−7.3	−3.0	−0.3	−4.0	16.4	8.4	−1.8
Diversified borrowers	1.2	−1.6	13.5	−2.9	−7.5	−2.5	−2.7	−2.7	23.6	13.2	−2.1
Official borrowers	0.7	−0.7	18.0	−2.1	−7.2	−7.0	−6.2	−5.9	28.8	13.1	−4.1
Countries with recent debt-servicing difficulties	0.6	−0.1	19.5	−1.5	−6.4	−5.2	−4.3	−5.2	20.3	10.8	−3.0
Countries without debt-servicing difficulties	0.9	5.8	13.9	−3.7	−9.1	−1.0	1.3	−1.9	22.1	11.0	−1.4
Other groups											
Small low-income economies	0.6	1.6	17.5	−0.7	−6.5	−8.0	−5.1	−6.4	29.8	11.5	−5.2
Fifteen heavily indebted countries	0.7	−2.7	18.1	−2.0	−7.3	−4.3	−3.2	−4.5	20.2	10.5	−2.6
Memorandum											
Average oil spot price[2]	...	28.7	−20.4	21.5	28.2	−17.0	−0.5	−11.5	−4.1	9.3	—
In U.S. dollars a barrel	...	17.79	14.15	17.19	22.05	18.30	18.22	16.13	15.47	16.90	16.90
Export unit value of manufactures[3]	5.0	12.3	6.3	−0.2	9.3	−0.3	3.6	−5.8	2.8	6.6	2.0

[1]Averages of prices weighted by 1979–81 commodity shares in exports of developing countries or groups.
[2]Average of U.K. Brent, Dubai, and Alaska North Slope crude oil spot prices.
[3]For the manufactures exported by the industrial countries.

Table A27. Summary of Payments Balances on Current Account
(In billions of U.S. dollars)

	1987	1988	1989	1990	1991	1992	1993	1994	1995	1996
Industrial countries	**−73.2**	**−65.4**	**−96.6**	**−117.1**	**−35.6**	**−41.4**	**23.3**	**−10.1**	**−18.4**	**−20.0**
United States	−167.1	−128.2	−102.8	−91.7	−6.9	−67.9	−103.9	−155.7	−178.3	−179.4
European Union	25.5	5.9	−11.4	−35.3	−81.9	−74.7	10.9	28.5	39.0	40.5
Japan	87.0	79.6	57.2	35.8	72.9	117.6	131.4	129.3	129.5	127.7
Other industrial countries	−21.5	−27.1	−49.3	−40.4	−32.6	−28.7	−18.6	−13.2	−6.0	−2.7
Developing countries	**−4.4**	**−20.1**	**−9.7**	**−3.0**	**−83.6**	**−73.5**	**−98.3**	**−91.0**	**−85.4**	**−90.8**
By region										
Africa	−4.4	−9.7	−7.5	−3.0	−4.3	−9.1	−9.1	−12.6	−14.2	−12.7
Asia	23.4	13.1	4.7	1.2	1.6	1.2	−14.4	−11.2	−20.4	−28.7
Middle East and Europe	−12.2	−12.1	−1.0	0.8	−63.2	−30.6	−29.9	−19.2	−19.6	−18.8
Western Hemisphere	−11.1	−11.5	−5.9	−2.0	−17.7	−35.1	−44.9	−47.9	−31.2	−30.6
By analytical criteria										
Fuel exporters	−12.6	−27.7	−9.9	3.4	−76.9	−57.8	−46.8	−43.8	−19.7	−18.2
Nonfuel exporters	8.2	7.6	0.1	−6.4	−6.7	−15.8	−51.5	−47.2	−65.7	−72.6
Net creditor countries	14.1	6.1	14.7	19.8	−49.0	−18.4	−10.2	−4.6	−3.7	−2.2
Net debtor countries	−18.5	−26.2	−24.4	−22.8	−34.6	−55.1	−88.1	−86.4	−81.7	−88.6
Countries with recent debt-servicing difficulties	−23.0	−28.3	−19.1	−13.8	−24.7	−44.6	−56.3	−60.1	−43.2	−41.5
Countries without debt-servicing difficulties	4.5	2.1	−5.3	−9.0	−9.9	−10.5	−31.8	−26.2	−38.5	−47.1
Countries in transition	**8.2**	**2.4**	**−8.9**	**−26.4**	**−8.5**	**−6.7**	**−7.5**	**−12.3**	**−13.0**	**−16.5**
Central and eastern Europe	...	...	...	...	−12.2	−1.0	−8.9	−9.4	−10.7	−10.3
Excluding Belarus and Ukraine	...	...	...	...	−3.9	−0.5	−8.0	−7.5	−8.3	−10.0
Russia	...	...	...	...	4.1	−4.2	2.8	−1.0	0.6	−2.0
Transcaucasus and central Asia	...	...	...	...	−0.4	−1.5	−1.0	−2.0	−3.0	−4.1
Total[1]	**−69.5**	**−83.1**	**−115.2**	**−146.4**	**−127.7**	**−121.6**	**−82.5**	**−113.4**	**−116.8**	**−127.3**
In percent of sum of world exports and imports of goods and services	−1.1	−1.2	−1.5	−1.7	−1.4	−1.3	−0.9	−1.1	−1.0	−1.0

[1]Reflects errors, omissions, and asymmetries in balance of payments statistics on current account, as well as the exclusion of data for international organizations and a limited number of countries. See "Classification of Countries" in the introduction to this Statistical Appendix.

Table A28. Industrial Countries: Balance of Payments on Current Account

	1987	1988	1989	1990	1991	1992	1993	1994	1995	1996
Balance on current account					*In billions of U.S. dollars*					
Industrial countries	**−73.2**	**−65.4**	**−96.6**	**−117.1**	**−35.6**	**−41.4**	**23.3**	**−10.1**	**−18.4**	**−20.0**
Major industrial countries	−64.3	−55.9	−64.5	−91.4	−21.4	−34.5	−6.2	−44.6	−55.5	−59.8
United States	−167.1	−128.2	−102.8	−91.7	−6.9	−67.9	−103.9	−155.7	−178.3	−179.4
Japan	87.0	79.6	57.2	35.8	72.9	117.6	131.4	129.3	129.5	127.7
Germany[1]	45.9	50.6	57.3	46.9	−19.2	−21.0	−14.8	−22.6	−26.1	−33.4
France	−8.0	−4.8	−4.6	−9.7	−5.9	3.9	10.5	9.6	10.1	10.5
Italy	−2.2	−6.3	−11.8	−17.0	−23.6	−27.8	12.1	13.5	23.2	28.0
United Kingdom	−8.2	−29.6	−36.9	−34.0	−14.5	−17.4	−17.7	−0.6	−2.7	−2.4
Canada	−11.8	−17.2	−22.8	−21.6	−24.1	−21.9	−23.8	−18.1	−11.1	−10.7
Other industrial countries	−8.9	−9.5	−32.1	−25.6	−14.3	−6.9	29.4	34.5	37.1	39.8
Spain	—	−3.7	−11.5	−16.9	−16.7	−18.4	−4.0	−1.4	−2.8	−3.5
Netherlands	3.2	5.3	8.3	10.5	7.9	7.3	9.9	11.5	13.0	12.6
Belgium-Luxembourg	2.8	3.7	3.6	3.6	4.9	6.6	11.3	12.3	16.3	18.1
Sweden	−0.1	−0.7	−3.4	−7.9	−4.8	−6.0	−0.8	0.1	3.0	5.5
Austria	−1.1	−1.0	−0.7	0.2	−1.4	−1.3	−1.7	−2.1	−2.5	−1.3
Denmark	−3.0	−1.3	−1.1	1.4	2.1	4.8	5.5	4.2	3.6	3.7
Finland	−1.7	−2.7	−5.7	−6.9	−6.6	−4.9	−0.8	1.1	1.9	1.9
Greece	−2.5	−2.6	−4.5	−5.4	−4.7	−2.8	−1.8	−0.7	−2.1	−2.6
Portugal	0.5	−1.1	0.1	−0.2	−0.7	—	−0.4	0.4	−0.2	−0.8
Ireland	−0.1	0.1	−0.5	0.1	1.5	2.4	3.6	3.2	4.2	4.4
Switzerland	7.6	9.0	7.0	8.6	10.6	15.1	18.3	19.2	19.9	20.3
Norway	−4.1	−3.9	−4.1	3.9	5.1	2.9	2.4	3.3	4.1	3.5
Iceland	−0.2	−0.2	−0.1	−0.1	−0.3	−0.2	—	−0.1	−0.1	−0.1
Australia	−7.3	−10.0	−17.4	−14.9	−9.9	−10.6	−10.4	−14.6	−19.8	−20.0
New Zealand	−2.9	−0.5	−2.2	−1.6	−1.2	−1.6	−1.7	−2.1	−1.6	−1.7
Memorandum										
European Union	25.5	5.9	−11.4	−35.3	−81.9	−74.7	10.9	28.5	39.0	40.5
Balance on current account					*In percent of GDP*					
United States	−3.7	−2.6	−2.0	−1.7	−0.1	−1.1	−1.6	−2.3	−2.5	−2.4
Japan	3.6	2.7	2.0	1.2	2.2	3.2	3.1	2.8	2.5	2.3
Germany[1]	4.1	4.2	4.8	2.9	−1.1	−1.1	−0.8	−1.1	−1.1	−1.3
France	−0.9	−0.5	−0.5	−0.8	−0.5	0.3	0.8	0.7	0.7	0.7
Italy	−0.3	−0.8	−1.4	−1.6	−2.1	−2.3	1.2	1.3	2.2	2.5
United Kingdom	−1.2	−3.5	−4.4	−3.5	−1.4	−1.6	−1.9	−0.1	−0.2	−0.2
Canada	−2.8	−3.5	−4.1	−3.8	−4.1	−3.8	−4.3	−3.3	−2.0	−1.8
Spain	—	−1.1	−3.0	−3.4	−3.2	−3.2	−0.8	−0.3	−0.5	−0.6
Netherlands	1.5	2.3	3.6	3.7	2.7	2.3	3.2	3.5	3.6	3.3
Belgium-Luxembourg	2.0	2.4	2.3	1.9	2.5	3.0	5.4	5.4	6.0	6.3
Sweden	−0.1	−0.4	−1.8	−3.4	−2.0	−2.4	−0.4	—	1.4	2.5
Austria	−0.9	−0.8	−0.5	0.1	−0.9	−0.7	−1.0	−1.1	−1.1	−0.5
Denmark	−2.9	−1.2	−1.1	1.1	1.7	3.4	4.1	2.9	2.2	2.2
Finland	−1.9	−2.6	−5.1	−5.1	−5.4	−4.6	−1.0	1.1	1.6	1.4
Greece	−4.4	−4.0	−6.8	−6.5	−5.4	−3.0	−2.0	−0.7	−1.9	−2.2
Portugal	1.5	−2.2	0.3	−0.3	−0.9	—	−0.5	0.5	−0.2	−0.8
Ireland	−0.3	0.3	−1.4	0.1	3.3	4.8	7.6	6.1	7.2	7.0
Switzerland	4.4	4.9	4.0	3.8	4.6	6.3	7.9	7.4	7.0	6.9
Norway	−4.9	−4.3	−4.6	3.7	4.8	2.6	2.3	3.1	3.5	2.8
Iceland	−3.4	−3.5	−1.4	−2.2	−4.8	−3.2	−0.8	−1.1	−1.5	−1.4
Australia	−3.7	−4.0	−6.2	−5.0	−3.3	−3.6	−3.7	−4.5	−5.4	−5.2
New Zealand	−8.3	−1.2	−5.2	−3.7	−2.8	−4.0	−3.8	−4.0	−2.6	−2.8

[1]Data through June 1990 apply to west Germany only.

Table A29. Industrial Countries: Current Account Transactions
(In billions of U.S. dollars)

	1987	1988	1989	1990	1991	1992	1993	1994	1995	1996
Exports	1,692.2	1,949.1	2,086.9	2,396.9	2,436.3	2,598.7	2,507.9	2,796.1	3,223.4	3,452.4
Imports	1,724.5	1,960.5	2,127.9	2,440.0	2,432.3	2,555.6	2,412.7	2,704.7	3,110.7	3,328.2
Trade balance	−32.3	−11.4	−41.0	−43.1	4.0	43.1	95.2	91.4	112.8	124.2
Services, credits	512.1	573.7	628.7	773.0	812.1	897.2	875.3	941.2	1,060.8	1,142.8
Services, debits	492.4	567.5	624.5	771.3	798.6	890.7	860.8	917.2	1,030.4	1,104.0
Balance on services	19.7	6.2	4.2	1.7	13.5	6.5	14.5	24.0	30.5	38.9
Balance on goods and services	−18.8	−9.7	−37.8	−43.9	10.9	39.5	102.8	80.1	84.2	88.3
Factor income, net	−6.2	−4.5	−0.9	−2.5	−6.6	−10.1	−6.9	−35.4	−59.0	−74.7
Current transfers, net	−54.4	−55.7	−58.9	−73.1	−46.6	−80.9	−79.5	−90.2	−102.5	−108.3
Current account balance	**−73.2**	**−65.4**	**−96.6**	**−117.1**	**−35.6**	**−41.4**	**23.3**	**−10.1**	**−18.4**	**−20.0**
Balance on goods and services										
Industrial countries	**−12.6**	**−5.2**	**−36.9**	**−41.5**	**17.9**	**49.6**	**110.0**	**114.6**	**142.8**	**162.8**
Major industrial countries	−24.2	−18.9	−30.8	−50.1	−2.0	20.7	52.3	43.5	64.4	78.7
United States	−152.0	−114.8	−90.3	−78.8	−28.5	−40.4	−75.7	−106.4	−109.0	−96.0
Japan	74.0	62.7	37.9	18.0	58.7	86.0	96.2	95.9	89.9	82.7
Germany[1]	58.1	63.5	64.1	52.6	−1.9	−3.4	4.5	9.5	17.3	18.3
France	2.0	3.4	3.5	1.7	6.5	21.8	25.5	28.9	33.8	35.5
Italy	−1.3	−4.9	−9.2	−14.7	−17.7	−22.2	17.5	20.0	28.8	34.0
United Kingdom	−8.8	−31.2	−35.0	−27.0	−11.6	−15.9	−12.3	−8.8	−7.1	−6.8
Canada	3.7	2.4	−1.8	−2.0	−7.4	−5.2	−3.3	4.5	10.5	11.0
Other industrial countries	11.6	13.7	−6.1	8.6	19.9	28.9	57.6	71.1	78.4	84.1
Memorandum										
European Union	56.1	34.3	15.5	4.7	−31.0	−17.9	63.8	92.6	124.3	136.2
Factor income, net										
Industrial countries	**−6.2**	**−4.5**	**−0.9**	**−2.5**	**−6.6**	**−10.1**	**−6.9**	**−35.4**	**−59.0**	**−74.7**
Major industrial countries	18.8	26.2	33.7	41.0	38.6	38.1	30.8	11.1	−10.6	−23.3
United States	7.9	11.6	13.7	20.7	14.8	4.5	3.9	−15.2	−33.2	−45.5
Japan	16.7	21.0	23.4	23.2	26.7	36.2	41.4	40.9	47.1	53.2
Germany[1]	3.9	5.2	11.1	16.8	17.9	14.4	11.9	1.9	−3.0	−8.9
France	−1.6	−1.5	−0.6	−3.2	−5.1	−9.1	−8.9	−11.2	−12.9	−13.6
Italy	1.2	1.7	1.7	1.4	1.3	1.2	0.7	1.2	1.1	1.2
United Kingdom	6.2	7.9	5.6	1.8	−0.4	7.6	2.4	16.9	12.8	12.8
Canada	−15.4	−19.8	−21.2	−19.6	−16.6	−16.8	−20.7	−23.4	−22.4	−22.4
Other industrial countries	−25.0	−30.7	−34.6	−43.6	−45.3	−48.2	−37.7	−46.4	−48.5	−51.5
Memorandum										
European Union	−4.2	−2.6	1.8	−7.1	−10.9	−14.9	−14.1	−18.4	−29.1	−36.4

[1]Data through June 1990 apply to west Germany only.

Table A30. Developing Countries: Payments Balances on Current Account[1]

	1987	1988	1989	1990	1991	1992	1993	1994	1995	1996
	In billions of U.S. dollars									
Developing countries	**-4.4**	**-20.1**	**-9.7**	**-3.0**	**-83.6**	**-73.5**	**-98.3**	**-91.0**	**-85.4**	**-90.8**
By region										
Africa	-4.4	-9.7	-7.5	-3.0	-4.3	-9.1	-9.1	-12.6	-14.2	-12.7
Asia	23.4	13.1	4.7	1.2	1.6	1.2	-14.4	-11.2	-20.4	-28.7
Middle East and Europe	-12.2	-12.1	-1.0	0.8	-63.2	-30.6	-29.9	-19.2	-19.6	-18.8
Western Hemisphere	-11.1	-11.5	-5.9	-2.0	-17.7	-35.1	-44.9	-47.9	-31.2	-30.6
Sub-Saharan Africa	-6.4	-7.8	-6.9	-8.7	-8.4	-9.7	-9.0	-6.8	-7.1	-7.1
Four newly industrializing Asian economies	32.8	30.7	27.0	17.0	12.7	12.8	18.0	11.2	12.1	16.0
By predominant export										
Fuel	-12.6	-27.7	-9.9	3.4	-76.9	-57.8	-46.8	-43.8	-19.7	-18.2
Nonfuel exports	8.2	7.6	0.1	-6.4	-6.7	-15.8	-51.5	-47.2	-65.7	-72.6
Manufactures	23.7	23.0	14.8	5.9	12.1	13.8	-12.0	-1.8	-20.1	-25.3
Primary products	-15.3	-11.6	-7.8	-5.7	-8.9	-19.0	-23.7	-24.5	-21.3	-23.6
Agricultural products	-11.4	-8.4	-5.9	-2.1	-5.2	-13.7	-17.3	-19.5	-15.8	-17.8
Minerals	-3.9	-3.2	-1.9	-3.6	-3.8	-5.3	-6.4	-5.0	-5.5	-5.9
Services, income, and private transfers	-4.9	-6.9	-6.1	-6.4	-5.9	-6.8	-9.8	-10.2	-10.8	-9.8
Diversified export base	4.8	3.1	-0.9	-0.3	-3.9	-3.7	-6.0	-10.7	-13.6	-13.9
By financial criteria										
Net creditor countries	14.1	6.1	14.7	19.8	-49.0	-18.4	-10.2	-4.6	-3.7	-2.2
Net debtor countries	-18.5	-26.2	-24.4	-22.8	-34.6	-55.1	-88.1	-86.4	-81.7	-88.6
Market borrowers	9.4	6.0	6.2	12.3	-12.7	-27.5	-48.8	-52.9	-40.5	-45.3
Diversified borrowers	-15.1	-17.4	-17.6	-26.1	-13.3	-15.9	-23.3	-18.0	-27.1	-29.6
Official borrowers	-12.8	-14.8	-13.0	-9.0	-8.5	-11.7	-15.9	-15.5	-14.0	-13.7
Countries with recent debt-servicing difficulties	-23.0	-28.3	-19.1	-13.8	-24.7	-44.6	-56.3	-60.1	-43.2	-41.5
Countries without debt-servicing difficulties	4.5	2.1	-5.3	-9.0	-9.9	-10.5	-31.8	-26.2	-38.5	-47.1
Other groups										
Small low-income economies	-8.2	-9.0	-8.7	-10.1	-9.0	-9.5	-10.8	-9.8	-10.7	-11.6
Least developed countries	-5.2	-6.1	-5.6	-7.2	-7.4	-8.0	-7.7	-7.1	-7.5	-8.3
Fifteen heavily indebted countries	-8.9	-9.7	-4.4	-3.3	-18.6	-33.8	-47.6	-51.1	-34.1	-32.7

Table A30 (concluded)

	Average 1977–86	1987	1988	1989	1990	1991	1992	1993	1994	1995	1996
	In percent of exports of goods and services										
Developing countries	**–4.4**	**–0.7**	**–2.6**	**–1.1**	**–0.3**	**–8.1**	**–6.5**	**–8.1**	**–6.7**	**–5.5**	**–5.3**
By region											
Africa	–14.5	–5.7	–12.0	–8.7	–3.1	–4.5	–9.6	–9.8	–13.6	–13.7	–11.4
Asia	–4.5	6.9	3.2	1.0	0.2	0.3	0.2	–1.9	–1.3	–2.1	–2.6
Middle East and Europe	4.1	–9.2	–8.8	–0.7	0.4	–34.0	–15.4	–15.0	–9.2	–8.7	–7.3
Western Hemisphere	–17.4	–9.7	–8.8	–4.0	–1.2	–10.9	–20.5	–24.8	–23.4	–13.4	–12.3
Sub-Saharan Africa	–28.2	–22.1	–26.3	–22.3	–26.4	–26.5	–31.9	–29.6	–21.4	–19.6	–18.1
Four newly industrializing Asian economies	1.3	15.8	11.8	9.3	5.4	3.5	3.2	4.0	2.2	2.2	2.6
By predominant export											
Fuel	1.2	–7.3	–16.1	–4.7	1.3	–31.0	–22.1	–17.8	–16.2	–6.5	–5.3
Nonfuel exports	–10.7	1.7	1.3	—	–0.9	–0.8	–1.8	–5.4	–4.3	–5.3	–5.3
Manufactures	–7.1	7.0	5.5	3.2	1.2	2.1	2.1	–1.7	–0.2	–2.2	–2.5
Primary products	–22.2	–27.2	–18.4	–11.2	–7.4	–11.4	–23.2	–27.6	–25.0	–19.0	–19.7
Agricultural products	–20.7	–29.5	–19.6	–12.8	–4.0	–9.5	–23.8	–27.9	–27.5	–19.4	–20.4
Minerals	–27.0	–22.2	–15.7	–8.2	–14.9	–15.7	–21.6	–26.9	–18.5	–17.9	–17.9
Services, income, and private transfers	–21.8	–15.2	–20.0	–16.6	–15.2	–13.6	–14.6	–20.8	–20.0	–19.0	–16.4
Diversified export base	–9.0	7.2	4.2	–1.1	–0.3	–4.0	–3.5	–5.2	–8.2	–9.0	–8.2
By financial criteria											
Net creditor countries	13.9	10.5	4.3	8.9	10.0	–24.3	–8.5	–4.6	–2.1	–1.5	–0.8
Net debtor countries	1.3	–3.5	–4.2	–3.5	–2.9	–4.1	–6.0	–8.8	–7.6	–6.3	–6.1
Market borrowers	–9.3	2.7	1.4	1.3	2.3	–2.2	–4.2	–6.7	–6.3	–4.2	–4.2
Diversified borrowers	–14.3	–11.9	–12.6	–11.5	–15.6	–8.1	–8.9	–12.2	–8.4	–11.3	–10.5
Official borrowers	–25.9	–21.7	–23.0	–18.6	–10.9	–10.2	–13.7	–18.7	–17.1	–13.7	–12.6
Countries with recent debt-servicing difficulties	–18.5	–11.9	–13.3	–8.1	–5.3	–9.9	–17.0	–20.7	–20.0	–12.7	–10.7
Countries without debt-servicing difficulties	–20.7	1.4	0.5	–1.2	–1.7	–1.7	–1.6	–4.4	–3.1	–4.0	–4.4
Other groups											
Small low-income economies	–38.2	–32.7	–34.2	–30.9	–32.3	–27.6	–27.9	–30.6	–24.9	–23.9	–23.3
Least developed countries	–40.5	–32.0	–34.5	–30.2	–37.4	–39.6	–43.8	–40.1	–33.6	–30.7	–31.3
Fifteen heavily indebted countries	–16.5	–6.6	–6.3	–2.5	–1.7	–9.8	–17.0	–23.1	–22.1	–13.0	–11.4
Memorandum											
Median											
Developing countries	–17.9	–11.8	–12.8	–10.4	–12.1	–10.9	–13.1	–14.8	–13.7	–12.2	–11.0

[1]Including official transfers.

Table A31. Developing Countries—By Region: Current Account Transactions

(In billions of U.S. dollars)

	1987	1988	1989	1990	1991	1992	1993	1994	1995	1996
Developing countries										
Exports	550.4	634.0	713.5	809.4	848.9	927.8	992.3	1,112.1	1,253.3	1,407.6
Imports	507.5	603.8	666.8	753.1	840.2	949.5	1,039.6	1,151.8	1,284.6	1,454.7
Trade balance	42.9	30.2	46.7	56.3	8.8	−21.7	−46.8	−39.5	−28.6	−45.4
Services, net	−27.7	−25.2	−32.9	−31.1	−50.3	−41.4	−29.4	−26.3	−18.3	−23.8
Balance on goods and services	15.2	5.0	13.9	25.2	−41.5	−63.1	−76.2	−65.7	−46.9	−69.2
Factor income, net	−43.6	−50.0	−51.9	−54.5	−45.2	−46.2	−52.7	−57.7	−70.3	−54.2
Current transfers, net	24.1	24.9	28.4	26.1	3.1	35.7	31.2	32.8	34.4	35.5
Current account balance	**−4.4**	**−20.1**	**−9.7**	**−3.0**	**−83.6**	**−73.5**	**−98.3**	**−91.0**	**−85.4**	**−90.8**
Memorandum										
Exports of goods and services	663.8	761.7	856.3	979.2	1,035.5	1,138.8	1,219.9	1,367.8	1,543.4	1,721.4
Interest payments	74.0	79.0	84.6	92.5	87.6	87.9	88.5	97.6	110.3	115.0
Oil trade balance	83.2	77.4	103.0	135.1	112.0	112.0	101.3	92.2	95.5	113.0
By region										
Africa										
Exports	65.7	67.5	72.2	84.0	80.7	79.4	76.1	76.4	83.3	90.7
Imports	58.1	65.1	68.2	73.9	72.8	77.0	74.3	78.1	87.4	91.9
Trade balance	7.6	2.4	4.0	10.1	8.0	2.4	2.2	−1.5	−1.4	0.6
Services, net	−7.1	−7.6	−8.4	−9.0	−9.4	−9.7	−9.7	−9.7	−9.1	−9.5
Balance on goods and services	0.5	−5.2	−4.4	1.0	−1.4	−7.3	−7.5	−11.2	−10.5	−8.9
Factor income, net	−14.2	−15.2	−15.0	−17.3	−16.1	−15.2	−13.8	−13.9	−14.6	−15.0
Current transfers, net	9.4	10.7	12.0	13.2	13.2	13.3	12.7	12.7	13.2	13.7
Current account balance	**−4.4**	**−9.7**	**−7.5**	**−3.0**	**−4.3**	**−9.1**	**−9.1**	**−12.6**	**−14.2**	**−12.7**
Memorandum										
Exports of goods and services	77.7	80.5	85.8	99.5	95.6	95.1	92.5	92.7	103.6	111.3
Interest payments	12.6	13.9	14.5	15.6	15.4	15.1	14.4	14.3	14.9	15.2
Oil trade balance	10.3	9.9	15.0	23.6	21.3	20.6	18.5	14.6	16.2	17.0
Asia										
Exports	283.8	349.6	389.9	432.2	492.6	557.7	618.8	713.4	812.7	915.0
Imports	266.6	339.0	384.6	436.4	500.0	565.2	641.0	734.2	839.4	962.2
Trade balance	17.2	10.6	5.3	−4.1	−7.3	−7.5	−22.2	−20.9	−26.8	−47.2
Services, net	5.0	4.4	3.5	6.6	6.0	3.3	3.9	1.5	7.9	4.8
Balance on goods and services	22.2	15.0	8.7	2.5	−1.3	−4.2	−18.2	−19.3	−18.8	−42.4
Factor income, net	−8.8	−11.4	−11.3	−9.6	−7.2	−5.9	−7.7	−5.0	−14.9	0.2
Current transfers, net	10.1	9.4	7.3	8.3	10.2	11.4	11.6	13.3	13.6	13.9
Current account balance	**23.4**	**13.1**	**4.7**	**1.2**	**1.6**	**1.2**	**−14.4**	**−11.2**	**−20.4**	**−28.7**
Memorandum										
Exports of goods and services	337.6	413.0	463.3	520.2	592.1	674.3	746.1	861.3	982.4	1,104.9
Interest payments	19.3	19.9	21.4	22.1	23.9	26.0	26.3	30.8	35.2	39.9
Oil trade balance	−5.6	−6.6	−9.1	−12.9	−14.7	−18.6	−18.9	−20.2	−24.5	−27.4

Table A31 (concluded)

	1987	1988	1989	1990	1991	1992	1993	1994	1995	1996
Middle East and Europe										
Exports	109.0	111.4	135.1	165.4	149.5	158.7	159.0	164.6	176.4	204.7
Imports	109.0	115.5	123.8	141.6	149.8	164.9	169.8	161.2	176.0	204.8
Trade balance	—	−4.2	11.2	23.8	−0.3	−6.3	−10.8	3.3	0.4	—
Services, net	−24.1	−20.4	−28.2	−28.7	−44.9	−33.6	−23.4	−19.6	−20.7	−22.4
Balance on goods and services	−24.1	−24.6	−17.0	−4.9	−45.2	−39.9	−34.2	−16.3	−20.3	−22.4
Factor income, net	11.3	11.9	13.2	10.8	12.5	9.3	7.2	0.6	4.4	6.8
Current transfers, net	0.6	0.6	2.8	−5.1	−30.5	—	−2.9	−3.6	−3.6	−3.1
Current account balance	**−12.2**	**−12.1**	**−1.0**	**0.8**	**−63.2**	**−30.6**	**−29.9**	**−19.2**	**−19.6**	**−18.8**
Memorandum										
Exports of goods and services	133.6	137.1	160.7	196.0	185.9	198.3	199.8	208.5	225.2	256.1
Interest payments	8.9	10.0	11.7	12.4	10.0	10.0	10.3	12.4	13.5	11.3
Oil trade balance	65.1	63.0	82.6	104.1	88.8	94.6	88.3	83.1	89.1	107.2
Western Hemisphere										
Exports	91.9	105.6	116.4	127.8	126.1	132.0	138.5	157.7	180.9	197.2
Imports	73.8	84.2	90.2	101.2	117.6	142.3	154.5	178.2	181.7	195.9
Trade balance	18.1	21.4	26.2	26.6	8.5	−10.4	−16.0	−20.4	−0.8	1.3
Services, net	−1.5	−1.6	0.3	0.1	−2.0	−1.4	−0.3	1.5	3.7	3.2
Balance on goods and services	16.7	19.8	26.5	26.7	6.4	−11.8	−16.3	−18.9	2.9	4.6
Factor income, net	−31.9	−35.4	−38.7	−38.4	−34.4	−34.3	−38.4	−39.4	−45.2	−46.2
Current transfers, net	4.1	4.2	6.3	9.7	10.3	11.1	9.8	10.4	11.2	11.0
Current account balance	**−11.1**	**−11.5**	**−5.9**	**−2.0**	**−17.7**	**−35.1**	**−44.9**	**−47.9**	**−31.2**	**−30.6**
Memorandum										
Exports of goods and services	114.9	131.0	146.6	163.5	161.9	171.0	181.5	205.2	232.1	249.2
Interest payments	33.3	35.3	36.9	42.4	38.2	36.9	37.5	40.2	46.8	48.5
Oil trade balance	13.4	11.1	14.5	20.3	16.5	15.5	13.5	14.7	14.7	16.2
Four newly industrializing Asian economies										
Exports	175.5	221.1	243.7	262.8	300.5	336.9	372.0	415.4	463.4	515.3
Imports	150.0	198.9	224.3	255.3	297.5	335.2	368.2	420.7	473.7	528.9
Trade balance	25.5	22.2	19.3	7.5	3.0	1.7	3.8	−5.3	−10.4	−13.6
Services, net	7.7	7.8	6.8	6.3	5.8	7.1	12.8	13.9	17.2	21.2
Balance on goods and services	33.2	30.0	26.1	13.8	8.8	8.8	16.7	8.6	6.8	7.6
Factor income, net	−0.6	1.5	3.1	4.1	4.8	4.6	2.6	3.3	6.0	9.3
Current transfers, net	0.3	−0.8	−2.2	−0.9	−0.9	−0.6	−1.3	−0.7	−0.8	−0.9
Current account balance	**32.8**	**30.7**	**27.0**	**17.0**	**12.7**	**12.8**	**18.0**	**11.2**	**12.1**	**16.0**
Memorandum										
Exports of goods and services	208.3	260.8	289.9	315.6	359.2	403.8	446.6	501.3	560.6	624.5
Interest payments	4.9	4.5	4.9	4.8	4.7	4.6	4.3	4.4	4.9	5.3
Oil trade balance	−7.6	−7.2	−9.0	−11.7	−12.0	−14.5	−13.5	−14.1	−15.7	−16.6

Table A32. Developing Countries—By Analytical Criteria: Current Account Transactions

(In billions of U.S. dollars)

	1987	1988	1989	1990	1991	1992	1993	1994	1995	1996
By predominant export										
Fuel										
Exports	154.2	154.0	188.4	235.2	217.9	229.1	229.5	235.3	262.7	301.5
Imports	117.6	132.1	143.6	160.9	180.1	205.4	200.8	203.7	198.0	240.2
Trade balance	36.6	21.9	44.8	74.3	37.8	23.7	28.7	31.7	64.7	61.2
Services, net	−38.1	−36.6	−41.9	−45.1	−62.5	−54.9	−43.8	−41.5	−36.8	−44.6
Balance on goods and services	−1.5	−14.6	3.0	29.2	−24.7	−31.2	−15.0	−9.9	27.9	16.7
Factor income, net	0.1	−1.7	−4.1	−7.4	−5.7	−11.6	−14.5	−18.5	−32.5	−19.5
Current transfers, net	−11.2	−11.4	−8.7	−18.4	−46.5	−15.0	−17.3	−15.4	−15.0	−15.4
Current account balance	**−12.6**	**−27.7**	**−9.9**	**3.4**	**−76.9**	**−57.8**	**−46.8**	**−43.8**	**−19.7**	**−18.2**
Memorandum										
Exports of goods and services	173.0	172.5	209.5	261.0	248.1	261.0	262.8	270.0	304.1	344.1
Interest payments	24.3	25.5	29.3	32.5	28.5	29.6	30.3	33.4	35.9	37.2
Oil trade balance	105.5	97.4	125.2	164.6	141.3	145.0	134.0	126.5	134.6	155.1
Nonfuel exports										
Exports	396.2	479.9	525.2	574.2	631.0	698.7	762.8	876.7	990.5	1,106.2
Imports	389.9	471.7	523.3	592.2	660.1	744.1	838.8	948.1	1,086.6	1,214.5
Trade balance	6.3	8.2	1.9	−18.0	−28.9	−45.4	−75.5	−71.1	−93.3	−106.6
Services, net	10.4	11.4	9.0	14.0	12.2	13.5	14.3	15.3	18.6	20.8
Balance on goods and services	16.7	19.6	10.9	−4.0	−16.8	−31.9	−61.2	−55.9	−74.8	−85.8
Factor income, net	−43.7	−48.4	−47.8	−47.0	−39.6	−34.6	−38.2	−39.2	−37.7	−34.7
Current transfers, net	35.4	36.3	37.1	44.5	49.6	50.7	48.5	48.2	49.4	50.9
Current account balance	**8.2**	**7.6**	**0.1**	**−6.4**	**−6.7**	**−15.8**	**−51.5**	**−47.2**	**−65.7**	**−72.6**
Memorandum										
Exports of goods and services	490.8	589.1	646.8	718.2	787.5	877.8	957.1	1,097.7	1,239.2	1,377.3
Interest payments	49.7	53.5	55.3	60.0	59.0	58.3	58.2	64.3	74.4	77.8
Oil trade balance	−22.3	−20.0	−22.2	−29.5	−29.3	−32.9	−32.7	−34.3	−39.1	−42.1
Manufactures										
Exports	281.3	349.9	382.9	415.1	466.8	525.3	578.6	668.2	750.4	839.6
Imports	259.6	327.1	368.1	417.5	469.9	529.0	605.0	684.9	792.4	892.9
Trade balance	21.7	22.8	14.7	−2.4	−3.1	−3.8	−26.2	−16.6	−41.9	−53.3
Services, net	11.4	12.6	11.3	13.7	13.6	12.5	14.8	15.1	17.5	18.4
Balance on goods and services	33.1	35.4	26.0	11.3	10.5	8.7	−11.4	−1.6	−24.5	−34.9
Factor income, net	−20.5	−22.6	−21.4	−19.2	−15.1	−12.3	−17.2	−18.2	−14.5	−10.0
Current transfers, net	11.1	10.2	10.3	13.8	16.6	17.4	17.0	18.2	19.0	19.6
Current account balance	**23.7**	**23.0**	**14.8**	**5.9**	**12.1**	**13.8**	**−12.0**	**−1.8**	**−20.1**	**−25.3**
Memorandum										
Exports of goods and services	336.1	417.3	459.6	506.4	567.5	642.0	708.2	818.1	919.8	1,028.0
Interest payments	22.4	24.7	26.5	27.1	26.9	28.8	29.8	34.1	40.5	41.7
Oil trade balance	−15.1	−14.5	−18.0	−24.8	−24.9	−28.4	−29.0	−30.5	−36.0	−38.9

Table A32 (continued)

	1987	1988	1989	1990	1991	1992	1993	1994	1995	1996
Primary products										
Exports	45.2	51.3	56.2	61.7	61.9	64.0	66.3	75.9	88.6	95.4
Imports	47.3	49.3	50.7	55.4	61.1	74.6	81.8	92.3	99.6	107.5
Trade balance	−2.2	2.0	5.5	6.3	0.9	−10.6	−15.4	−16.5	−11.0	−12.0
Services, net	−7.5	−7.2	−7.6	−7.6	−6.8	−6.9	−7.0	−5.5	−6.6	−6.7
Balance on goods and services	−9.7	−5.2	−2.0	−1.3	−5.9	−17.5	−22.4	−21.9	−17.6	−18.8
Factor income, net	−12.4	−13.7	−13.6	−13.0	−12.9	−11.9	−10.7	−12.1	−13.4	−14.3
Current transfers, net	6.8	7.3	7.9	8.5	9.8	10.3	9.5	9.3	9.7	9.5
Current account balance	**−15.3**	**−11.6**	**−7.8**	**−5.7**	**−8.9**	**−19.0**	**−23.7**	**−24.5**	**−21.3**	**−23.6**
Memorandum										
Exports of goods and services	56.3	63.2	69.4	76.8	78.4	82.1	85.8	97.8	111.8	120.1
Interest payments	13.7	15.0	14.1	16.9	16.8	15.5	14.2	15.5	17.6	18.3
Oil trade balance	−4.9	−3.9	−3.4	−3.8	−4.4	−4.0	−3.2	−3.5	−2.8	−3.3
Services, income, and **private transfers**										
Exports	14.3	16.1	17.9	19.8	20.2	20.6	20.4	22.6	25.3	28.1
Imports	35.6	39.1	40.0	44.8	46.7	49.7	51.6	53.6	57.2	60.5
Trade balance	−21.3	−23.0	−22.1	−25.0	−26.5	−29.1	−31.2	−31.0	−31.9	−32.4
Services, net	8.2	7.9	7.0	9.5	8.2	10.2	10.6	11.6	13.1	14.5
Balance on goods and services	−13.1	−15.0	−15.1	−15.5	−18.3	−18.9	−20.6	−19.4	−18.8	−17.9
Factor income, net	−3.8	−4.7	−4.4	−6.0	−4.0	−3.9	−4.5	−4.8	−5.3	−5.7
Current transfers, net	12.0	12.8	13.5	15.1	16.4	16.1	15.4	14.1	13.7	14.3
Current account balance	**−4.9**	**−6.9**	**−6.1**	**−6.4**	**−5.9**	**−6.8**	**−9.8**	**−10.2**	**−10.8**	**−9.8**
Memorandum										
Exports of goods and services	32.3	34.4	36.5	41.9	43.6	46.4	47.4	51.2	56.9	59.6
Interest payments	6.0	6.0	6.5	7.7	7.6	6.7	6.9	7.2	7.8	8.1
Oil trade balance	−3.3	−3.1	−2.6	−3.2	−3.0	−3.1	−3.2	−2.8	−2.7	−2.3
Diversified export base										
Exports	55.5	62.6	68.2	77.5	82.2	88.9	97.5	110.1	126.2	143.0
Imports	47.4	56.3	64.4	74.4	82.4	90.8	100.4	117.3	137.3	153.6
Trade balance	8.1	6.4	3.7	3.1	−0.3	−1.9	−2.8	−7.0	−8.4	−8.9
Services, net	−1.7	−1.9	−1.7	−1.5	−2.8	−2.3	−4.0	−6.0	−5.5	−5.4
Balance on goods and services	6.4	4.5	2.1	1.6	−3.1	−4.2	−6.8	−13.0	−13.9	−14.2
Factor income, net	−7.1	−7.4	−8.4	−8.9	−7.6	−6.4	−5.8	−4.0	−4.5	−4.7
Current transfers, net	5.5	6.0	5.5	7.1	6.8	6.9	6.7	6.6	7.1	7.5
Current account balance	**4.8**	**3.1**	**−0.9**	**−0.3**	**−3.9**	**−3.7**	**−6.0**	**−10.7**	**−13.6**	**−13.9**
Memorandum										
Exports of goods and services	66.1	74.3	81.3	93.1	98.0	107.3	115.8	130.6	150.7	169.6
Interest payments	7.6	7.9	8.1	8.3	7.8	7.3	7.2	7.4	8.6	9.7
Oil trade balance	1.0	1.5	1.8	2.3	3.0	2.7	2.8	2.5	2.4	2.3

Table A32 *(continued)*

	1987	1988	1989	1990	1991	1992	1993	1994	1995	1996
By financial criteria										
Net debtor countries										
Exports	429.8	507.8	566.0	629.6	665.9	732.6	795.4	909.0	1,033.4	1,175.6
Imports	423.8	503.9	558.9	634.3	698.1	789.8	880.3	991.8	1,110.1	1,269.3
Trade balance	6.0	4.0	7.0	−4.7	−32.1	−57.2	−84.4	−82.6	−74.1	−92.0
Services, net	0.7	1.3	−0.2	6.6	6.8	8.9	9.1	11.8	22.9	19.7
Balance on goods and services	6.7	5.3	6.8	2.0	−25.3	−48.3	−75.2	−70.9	−51.1	−72.3
Factor income, net	−62.9	−71.8	−74.8	−76.4	−64.3	−62.9	−66.5	−68.9	−83.7	−70.7
Current transfers, net	37.8	40.3	43.6	51.5	55.0	56.0	54.3	53.8	55.7	57.3
Current account balance	**−18.5**	**−26.2**	**−24.4**	**−22.8**	**−34.6**	**−55.1**	**−88.1**	**−86.4**	**−81.7**	**−88.6**
Memorandum										
Exports of goods and services	529.3	620.1	691.1	781.9	833.6	923.0	999.9	1,141.1	1,298.2	1,462.6
Interest payments	70.9	75.6	80.1	88.2	83.6	83.4	84.2	92.3	104.9	109.9
Oil trade balance	29.7	26.8	38.0	41.9	25.9	20.0	14.6	10.5	8.3	23.4
Market borrowers										
Exports	282.9	347.9	386.5	433.8	478.4	537.1	591.7	686.2	782.8	880.2
Imports	254.3	319.1	359.7	409.4	479.8	552.5	623.0	720.2	812.4	914.1
Trade balance	28.6	28.9	26.8	24.4	−1.3	−15.4	−31.3	−34.0	−29.6	−33.9
Services, net	9.7	8.2	10.5	13.6	11.2	9.0	10.1	10.2	19.4	19.2
Balance on goods and services	38.3	37.0	37.4	38.0	9.9	−6.5	−21.2	−23.8	−10.2	−14.7
Factor income, net	−37.4	−40.1	−42.1	−39.6	−36.7	−36.7	−43.0	−45.8	−47.8	−48.7
Current transfers, net	8.4	9.1	10.9	13.9	14.1	15.8	15.4	16.7	17.5	18.0
Current account balance	**9.4**	**6.0**	**6.2**	**12.3**	**−12.7**	**−27.5**	**−48.8**	**−52.9**	**−40.5**	**−45.3**
Memorandum										
Exports of goods and services	343.2	417.4	467.4	532.9	585.3	659.0	723.7	837.1	955.9	1,072.1
Interest payments	39.1	41.2	43.0	48.8	46.2	47.4	48.4	54.0	63.3	67.3
Oil trade balance	17.5	13.4	16.5	25.7	21.2	16.3	14.5	12.9	11.0	12.0
Official borrowers										
Exports	42.9	45.8	51.9	60.6	59.5	59.7	58.2	61.6	69.9	76.0
Imports	63.0	68.4	71.0	79.5	81.4	86.6	87.6	90.2	97.8	104.4
Trade balance	−20.2	−22.6	−19.1	−18.9	−21.8	−26.9	−28.9	−28.4	−27.4	−27.7
Services, net	−0.6	−0.1	−2.8	−1.1	−1.8	0.1	−0.5	0.7	1.6	2.4
Balance on goods and services	−20.7	−22.7	−21.9	−20.1	−23.7	−26.8	−29.4	−27.8	−25.7	−25.2
Factor income, net	−12.1	−13.1	−12.8	−14.8	−12.3	−11.5	−11.3	−11.3	−11.7	−12.2
Current transfers, net	20.1	21.0	21.7	25.8	27.5	26.5	25.4	23.9	24.3	25.2
Current account balance	**−12.8**	**−14.8**	**−13.0**	**−9.0**	**−8.5**	**−11.7**	**−15.9**	**−15.5**	**−14.0**	**−13.7**
Memorandum										
Exports of goods and services	59.1	64.3	70.1	82.1	83.0	85.7	85.3	90.3	102.3	108.2
Interest payments	12.1	13.3	14.2	15.4	15.1	14.1	13.9	14.2	14.7	15.1
Oil trade balance	1.2	2.2	6.2	9.0	7.3	7.4	6.3	4.6	5.0	4.7

Table A32 (concluded)

	1987	1988	1989	1990	1991	1992	1993	1994	1995	1996
Countries with recent debt-servicing difficulties										
Exports	160.1	178.1	198.4	212.7	197.7	204.3	210.9	233.2	262.9	306.3
Imports	144.0	161.8	170.5	185.1	194.5	224.5	236.7	265.2	277.4	316.7
Trade balance	16.1	16.3	27.9	27.5	3.3	−20.1	−25.5	−31.8	−11.9	−8.6
Services, net	−10.3	−12.6	−13.9	−12.7	−11.5	−8.7	−11.3	−9.8	−6.0	−8.3
Balance on goods and services	5.8	3.7	14.0	14.9	−8.2	−28.9	−36.8	−41.6	−17.9	−16.9
Factor income, net	−45.9	−50.5	−54.5	−56.5	−45.1	−44.6	−46.4	−45.2	−50.7	−50.1
Current transfers, net	17.2	18.5	21.5	27.8	28.6	28.8	27.0	26.7	27.5	28.1
Current account balance	**−23.0**	**−28.3**	**−19.1**	**−13.8**	**−24.7**	**−44.6**	**−56.3**	**−60.1**	**−43.2**	**−41.5**
Memorandum										
Exports of goods and services	192.9	212.4	236.6	259.7	250.3	262.3	272.0	300.8	341.2	386.3
Interest payments	48.2	51.6	54.8	61.3	54.3	51.3	51.7	53.8	61.1	62.3
Oil trade balance	27.5	27.2	39.0	42.2	27.2	26.4	23.4	22.7	22.2	39.5
Countries without debt-servicing difficulties										
Exports	269.7	329.8	367.6	417.0	468.2	528.2	584.5	675.8	770.5	869.3
Imports	279.8	342.1	388.4	449.2	503.6	565.3	643.6	726.7	832.7	952.6
Trade balance	−10.1	−12.3	−20.8	−32.2	−35.4	−37.1	−58.8	−50.8	−62.2	−83.3
Services, net	11.0	13.9	13.7	19.3	18.3	17.6	20.5	21.6	29.0	28.0
Balance on goods and services	0.9	1.6	−7.1	−12.9	−17.1	−19.5	−38.4	−29.3	−33.2	−55.3
Factor income, net	−17.0	−21.3	−20.3	−19.9	−19.2	−18.3	−20.2	−23.7	−33.0	−20.6
Current transfers, net	20.6	21.8	22.1	23.8	26.4	27.3	27.2	27.1	28.2	29.2
Current account balance	**4.5**	**2.1**	**−5.3**	**−9.0**	**−9.9**	**−10.5**	**−31.8**	**−26.2**	**−38.5**	**−47.1**
Memorandum										
Exports of goods and services	336.3	407.7	454.5	522.2	583.3	660.7	727.9	840.3	957.0	1,076.3
Interest payments	22.7	23.9	25.2	26.9	29.3	32.1	32.4	38.5	43.7	47.7
Oil trade balance	2.2	−0.4	−1.0	−0.3	−1.3	−6.4	−8.9	−12.1	−13.9	−16.1
Other groups										
Least developed countries										
Exports	12.5	14.2	15.2	15.5	14.9	14.4	14.8	16.7	19.2	21.1
Imports	21.3	23.1	23.4	25.1	24.8	25.5	25.6	26.8	29.6	32.3
Trade balance	−8.8	−8.9	−8.2	−9.6	−9.8	−11.1	−10.6	−10.0	−10.4	−11.2
Services, net	−2.1	−2.8	−3.9	−3.6	−3.4	−3.5	−4.0	−4.2	−4.3	−4.2
Balance on goods and services	−10.8	−11.7	−12.1	−13.2	−13.2	−14.6	−14.6	−14.3	−14.7	−15.4
Factor income, net	−3.3	−3.5	−3.1	−3.4	−3.5	−3.4	−2.9	−2.9	−3.1	−3.2
Current transfers, net	9.0	9.1	9.6	9.3	9.3	9.9	9.8	10.0	10.2	10.3
Current account balance	**−5.2**	**−6.1**	**−5.6**	**−7.2**	**−7.4**	**−8.0**	**−7.7**	**−7.1**	**−7.5**	**−8.3**
Memorandum										
Exports of goods and services	16.2	17.8	18.5	19.4	18.8	18.4	19.2	21.2	24.4	26.5
Interest payments	3.0	3.3	4.1	3.4	3.6	3.9	3.8	4.0	4.4	4.5
Oil trade balance	−5.4	−3.7	−2.8	−3.8	−4.2	−4.3	−4.2	−4.0	−4.2	−4.7

Table A33. Summary of External Financing
(In billions of U.S. dollars)

	1987	1988	1989	1990	1991	1992	1993	1994	1995	1996
Developing countries										
Balance on current account	–4.4	–20.1	–9.7	–3.0	–83.6	–73.5	–98.3	–91.0	–85.4	–90.8
Change in reserves (– = increase)[1]	–44.3	–4.5	–33.0	–53.3	–76.0	–54.4	–64.6	–51.2	–34.8	–37.3
Asset transactions, including net errors and omissions[2]	2.1	–23.2	–12.7	–35.0	39.8	–17.0	–32.3	6.4	0.4	–4.6
Total, net external financing[3]	**46.6**	**47.8**	**55.4**	**91.4**	**119.8**	**145.0**	**195.6**	**136.0**	**121.8**	**134.0**
Non-debt-creating flows, net	11.9	19.3	17.6	35.4	28.9	36.7	59.1	58.9	51.7	48.6
Capital transfers	–1.3	0.8	0.2	16.0	–0.1	–0.7	6.8	2.7	4.5	4.7
Direct investment	13.2	18.4	17.4	19.4	29.0	37.4	52.3	56.2	47.2	43.9
Net credit and loans from IMF[4]	–4.7	–4.1	–1.5	–1.9	1.1	–0.2	–0.2	–0.8	...	...
Net external borrowing[5]	39.2	32.5	39.3	57.7	89.8	108.7	136.7	77.7	61.6	88.5
Memorandum										
Net capital flows	39.5	24.2	29.0	39.3	158.7	131.3	159.2	131.2	113.8	116.1
Balance on goods and services in percent of GDP[6]	0.5	0.2	0.4	0.7	–1.1	–1.5	–1.6	–1.3	–0.8	–1.1
Scheduled amortization of external debt	97.6	98.6	90.9	100.2	101.4	115.0	118.4	132.1	120.5	126.5
Gross external financing[7]	144.3	146.4	146.3	191.6	221.3	260.0	314.0	268.0	242.3	260.5
Gross external borrowing[8]	136.8	131.1	130.2	157.9	191.2	223.7	255.1	209.8	182.1	215.0
Exceptional financing	43.2	28.4	45.4	57.8	39.7	40.7	51.4	62.7	12.8	10.8
Arrears on debt service	9.2	12.8	19.0	30.4	7.9	21.6	14.0	–6.4	...	...
Rescheduling of debt service	35.8	22.0	17.7	16.2	16.1	13.0	8.1	49.1	...	...
Net borrowing from official creditors[9]	20.2	17.4	22.2	21.0	23.9	11.3	18.4	10.5	37.5	7.0
Net borrowing from commercial banks[10]	20.2	0.9	1.8	26.8	18.1	8.1	6.4	–34.6	11.7	18.7
Countries in transition										
Balance on current account	8.2	2.4	–8.9	–26.4	–8.5	–6.7	–7.5	–12.3	–13.0	–16.5
Change in reserves (– = increase)[1]	–0.6	–4.2	–4.4	5.8	7.0	–3.6	–10.3	–2.6	–7.7	–3.5
Asset transactions, including net errors and omissions[2]	9.2	10.7	14.7	17.6	–4.2	–0.2	–4.6	2.0	1.0	3.0
Total, net external financing[3]	**–16.8**	**–8.9**	**–1.4**	**3.0**	**9.1**	**11.1**	**22.9**	**13.8**	**20.8**	**16.9**
Non-debt-creating flows, net	—	1.2	1.4	–0.5	4.4	6.5	14.2	9.7	12.3	14.3
Capital transfers	0.2	0.7	1.1	–0.5	2.0	2.2	8.5	4.2	4.3	4.3
Direct investment	–0.2	0.5	0.2	—	2.4	4.3	5.7	5.5	8.0	10.1
Net credit and loans from IMF[4]	–1.1	–0.9	–0.9	0.1	3.5	1.7	2.1	2.4	...	...
Net external borrowing[5]	–15.7	–9.2	–1.8	3.4	1.2	2.8	6.7	1.8	1.5	3.0

Table A33 (concluded)

	1987	1988	1989	1990	1991	1992	1993	1994	1995	1996
Memorandum										
Net capital flows	−17.3	−11.6	−4.0	3.4	5.4	9.3	15.0	10.2	16.8	14.4
Balance on goods and services in percent of GDP[6]	0.2	0.1	−0.1	−0.4	−0.3	−2.3	−1.8	−2.0	−1.6	−1.9
Scheduled amortization of external debt	20.3	23.3	17.4	31.6	27.8	0.2	−4.4	−1.3	1.2	1.3
Gross external financing[7]	3.5	14.3	16.0	34.6	36.9	11.3	18.5	12.4	22.0	18.2
Gross external borrowing[8]	4.6	14.1	15.6	35.0	29.0	3.1	2.3	0.5	2.7	4.3
Exceptional financing	6.1	6.7	5.8	14.7	9.7	4.7	3.8	2.9	1.4	0.9
Arrears on debt service	−3.1	−0.2	0.8	9.0	6.1	0.3	1.5	0.7	. . .	. . .
Rescheduling of debt service	5.8	6.5	1.5	8.3	7.5	2.3	2.2	2.4	. . .	. . .
Net borrowing from official creditors[9]	−1.1	−3.1	−1.0	10.9	24.3	16.3	3.7	6.2	12.7	6.0
Net borrowing from commercial banks[10]	1.7	5.6	11.1	−3.1	−5.7	−1.8	3.5	5.0	0.6	0.9

Note: Except where footnoted, estimates are based on national balance of payments statistics. These flows are not always reconcilable with year-to-year changes in either debtor- or creditor-reported debt statistics, in part because the latter are affected by changes in valuation.

[1] Positioned here to reflect the discretionary nature of many countries' reserve transactions.

[2] Includes export credit, recorded changes in private foreign assets, the collateral for debt-reduction operations, and unrecorded capital transactions.

[3] Equals, with opposite sign, the sum of transactions listed above. It is the amount required to finance the deficit on goods and services, factor income, and current transfers; the increase in the official reserve level; the net asset transactions; and the transactions underlying the net errors and omissions.

[4] Includes use of IMF resources under the General Resources Account, Trust Fund, structural adjustment facility (SAF), and enhanced structural adjustment facility (ESAF). Further detail is given in Table A37.

[5] Residually derived. Includes disbursements of short- and long-term credits as well as exceptional financing from both official and private creditors.

[6] This is often referred to as the "resource balance" and, with opposite sign, as the "net resource transfer."

[7] Defined as total net financing (see footnote 3 above) plus amortization due on external debt.

[8] Defined as net borrowing (see footnote 5 above) plus amortization due on external debt.

[9] Estimates of net disbursements by official creditors (other than monetary authorities) based on directly reported flows and flows derived from statistics on debt stocks. The estimates include the increase in official claims caused by the transfer of officially guaranteed claims to the guarantor agency in the creditor country, usually in the context of debt rescheduling. When possible, the impact of debt forgiveness is excluded.

[10] Estimates based on directly reported flows or on cross-border lending by banks derived from claims data reported in the IMF's International Banking Statistics data base, after adjustment for valuation changes resulting from exchange rate movements, and the impact of debt-reduction operations. Excludes seven offshore banking centers (The Bahamas, Bahrain, the Cayman Islands, Hong Kong, the Netherlands Antilles, Panama, and Singapore).

Table A34. Developing Countries—By Region: External Financing[1]

(In billions of U.S. dollars)

	1987	1988	1989	1990	1991	1992	1993	1994	1995	1996
Africa										
Balance on current account	−4.4	−9.7	−7.5	−3.0	−4.3	−9.1	−9.1	−12.6	−14.2	−12.7
Change in reserves (− = increase)	−1.9	1.7	−2.5	−4.2	−6.4	6.5	0.9	−1.8	−0.6	−2.0
Asset transactions, including										
net errors and omissions	6.4	5.5	3.8	3.1	5.9	−2.4	6.6	2.3	3.5	2.7
Total, net external financing	**−0.1**	**2.5**	**6.3**	**4.1**	**4.8**	**5.1**	**1.9**	**12.3**	**13.2**	**13.2**
Non-debt-creating flows, net	−1.2	0.3	2.7	4.5	0.9	2.3	2.0	3.7	2.5	3.3
Net credit and loans from IMF	−1.1	−0.3	0.1	−0.6	0.2	−0.2	0.2	0.9	. . .	. . .
Net external borrowing	2.1	2.4	3.5	0.1	3.7	3.1	−0.2	7.7	9.4	9.8
Memorandum										
Net capital flows	2.5	3.4	6.7	1.9	5.2	5.0	1.5	12.9	11.8	12.5
Exceptional financing	14.6	7.7	17.0	12.8	11.5	12.2	8.8	11.8	9.5	7.6
Net borrowing from official creditors	5.9	6.2	4.5	4.2	6.5	−0.1	3.3	7.4	5.4	2.8
Net borrowing from commercial banks	−1.7	−2.5	−3.8	−0.2	−2.2	−4.5	−1.3	−2.2	0.4	1.0
Asia										
Balance on current account	−4.4	−9.7	−7.5	−3.0	−4.3	−9.1	−9.1	−12.6	−14.2	−12.7
Change in reserves (− = increase)	−40.0	−16.5	−18.0	−26.2	−45.1	−32.3	−49.3	−63.7	−47.2	−42.9
Asset transactions, including										
net errors and omissions	−3.9	−19.0	−16.0	−18.8	−17.3	−23.3	−33.3	−16.8	−12.7	−14.0
Total, net external financing	**20.5**	**22.4**	**29.2**	**43.9**	**60.8**	**54.4**	**97.0**	**91.7**	**80.3**	**85.6**
Non-debt-creating flows, net	7.3	9.7	6.7	12.1	14.4	19.2	41.0	39.1	29.6	29.1
Net credit and loans from IMF	−2.4	−2.4	−1.1	−2.4	1.9	1.3	0.6	−0.8	. . .	. . .
Net external borrowing	15.6	15.2	23.7	34.1	44.4	33.9	55.5	53.4	51.9	57.5
Memorandum										
Net capital flows	17.3	9.8	11.9	25.6	50.9	39.3	72.2	73.4	61.7	66.8
Exceptional financing	2.1	1.9	1.8	2.2	2.4	2.1	1.6	1.1	—	—
Net borrowing from official creditors	−3.3	4.0	5.4	3.4	12.3	10.3	10.5	9.6	7.9	9.1
Net borrowing from commercial banks	10.6	6.6	5.2	12.4	18.8	11.2	13.7	8.6	15.1	14.7
Middle East and Europe										
Balance on current account	−12.2	−12.1	−1.0	0.8	−63.2	−30.6	−29.9	−19.2	−19.6	−18.8
Change in reserves (− = increase)	0.7	9.4	−10.7	−5.8	−8.0	−7.3	5.1	8.3	4.8	8.4
Asset transactions, including										
net errors and omissions	−1.7	−5.6	−0.3	−8.7	58.0	10.9	1.9	17.7	12.8	8.3
Total, net external financing	**13.3**	**8.2**	**12.1**	**13.8**	**13.2**	**27.0**	**22.9**	**−6.8**	**2.1**	**2.1**
Non-debt-creating flows, net	1.0	1.3	1.2	12.0	1.8	2.2	1.8	1.3	—	2.8
Net credit and loans from IMF	−0.4	−0.5	−0.2	−0.1	—	0.4	—	0.4	. . .	. . .
Net external borrowing	12.6	7.4	11.0	1.9	11.4	24.4	21.0	−8.5	1.8	−0.5
Memorandum										
Net capital flows	10.2	0.2	7.9	−3.0	74.1	44.9	23.0	7.5	18.7	11.2
Exceptional financing	0.3	—	1.1	14.3	7.0	6.4	12.0	3.2	1.5	1.5
Net borrowing from official creditors	11.2	2.2	3.8	2.0	3.0	3.3	4.3	−3.7	−2.1	−2.2
Net borrowing from commercial banks	6.4	8.7	−0.6	0.5	5.8	7.3	−5.2	−7.2	1.1	4.5

Table A34 *(concluded)*

	1987	1988	1989	1990	1991	1992	1993	1994	1995	1996
Western Hemisphere										
Balance on current account	−11.1	−11.5	−5.9	−2.0	−17.7	−35.1	−44.9	−47.9	−31.2	−30.6
Change in reserves (− = increase)	−3.1	0.9	−1.8	−17.1	−16.5	−21.4	−21.4	6.0	8.2	−0.9
Asset transactions, including										
net errors and omissions	1.2	−4.1	−0.1	−10.6	−6.9	−2.1	−7.5	3.2	−3.3	−1.7
Total, net external financing	**13.0**	**14.7**	**7.8**	**29.6**	**41.1**	**58.5**	**73.8**	**38.7**	**26.2**	**33.1**
Non-debt-creating flows, net	4.8	8.0	7.0	6.8	11.7	12.9	14.4	14.8	19.6	13.4
Net credit and loans from IMF	−0.8	−0.9	−0.2	1.2	−1.0	−1.6	−0.9	−1.3	. . .	. . .
Net external borrowing	8.9	7.5	1.0	21.6	30.3	47.4	60.3	25.1	−1.5	21.7
Memorandum										
Net capital flows	9.4	10.8	2.4	14.9	28.5	42.1	62.5	37.5	21.5	25.6
Exceptional financing	26.3	18.7	25.6	28.5	18.7	20.0	29.0	46.5	1.8	1.7
Net borrowing from official creditors	6.4	5.0	8.6	11.4	2.1	−2.2	0.3	−2.9	26.2	−2.7
Net borrowing from commercial banks	4.9	−11.9	1.0	14.1	−4.2	−5.9	−0.8	−33.8	−5.0	−1.4
Sub-Saharan Africa										
Balance on current account	−6.4	−7.8	−6.9	−8.7	−8.4	−9.7	−9.0	−6.8	−7.1	−7.1
Change in reserves (− = increase)	−0.8	0.3	−0.8	−0.1	−3.6	3.9	−0.1	−1.9	−0.1	−0.6
Asset transactions, including										
net errors and omissions	3.9	4.2	3.6	4.6	7.7	1.4	4.4	3.0	3.0	3.2
Total, net external financing	**3.2**	**3.3**	**4.1**	**4.1**	**4.5**	**4.5**	**4.7**	**5.6**	**4.3**	**4.5**
Non-debt-creating flows, net	—	0.2	0.9	0.7	0.7	0.7	0.3	1.3	0.1	1.0
Net credit and loans from IMF	−0.5	−0.2	−0.4	−0.3	—	—	−0.2	0.5	. . .	. . .
Net external borrowing	3.7	3.3	3.5	3.7	3.8	3.8	4.6	3.9	2.9	3.4
Memorandum										
Net capital flows	4.2	4.0	4.2	4.9	4.5	4.9	4.5	6.4	4.7	5.0
Exceptional financing	5.4	6.2	7.3	7.2	7.6	8.5	8.8	7.0	6.1	4.9
Net borrowing from official creditors	5.9	5.3	4.2	7.3	7.9	1.6	3.9	4.9	4.2	2.8
Net borrowing from commercial banks	−0.6	−0.6	−0.3	0.3	−1.3	0.1	0.5	—	0.7	0.8
Four newly industrializing Asian economies										
Balance on current account	32.8	30.7	27.0	17.0	12.7	12.8	18.0	11.2	12.1	16.0
Change in reserves (− = increase)	−36.0	−14.5	−13.1	−7.0	−18.8	−17.5	−21.5	−16.1	−18.2	−20.9
Asset transactions, including										
net errors and omissions	−0.7	−11.7	−14.5	−17.3	−12.5	−16.1	−23.1	−16.7	−12.3	−12.6
Total, net external financing	**3.9**	**−4.4**	**0.7**	**7.3**	**18.7**	**20.7**	**26.5**	**21.6**	**18.4**	**17.5**
Non-debt-creating flows, net	3.1	1.1	−3.0	−0.1	2.4	2.8	1.9	−0.1	−1.5	−3.0
Net credit and loans from IMF	−1.2	−0.5	—	—	—	—	—	—	. . .	. . .
Net external borrowing	2.0	−5.0	3.7	7.4	16.2	17.9	24.6	21.6	19.9	20.5
Memorandum										
Net capital flows	1.9	−14.7	−14.4	−6.8	7.5	4.7	7.8	5.3	6.6	5.5
Exceptional financing	—	—	—	—	—	—	—	—	—	—
Net borrowing from official creditors	−7.0	−2.5	−1.7	−0.8	0.2	−0.6	−1.9	−0.6	−0.5	−0.5
Net borrowing from commercial banks	7.5	−1.8	−0.3	−0.6	4.3	0.5	1.3	−2.1	−0.6	−0.6

[1]For definitions, see footnotes to Table A33.

Table A35. Developing Countries—By Analytical Criteria: External Financing[1]

(In billions of U.S. dollars)

	1987	1988	1989	1990	1991	1992	1993	1994	1995	1996
By predominant export										
Fuel										
Balance on current account	−12.6	−27.7	−9.9	3.4	−76.9	−57.8	−46.8	−43.8	−19.7	−18.2
Change in reserves (− = increase)	−1.6	22.1	−6.6	−15.6	−16.0	−0.4	0.8	29.0	4.2	−3.8
Asset transactions, including net errors and omissions	−0.7	−4.1	4.3	−19.8	52.5	22.0	0.3	4.7	9.5	7.4
Total, net external financing	**14.9**	**9.7**	**12.1**	**32.0**	**40.4**	**36.1**	**45.7**	**10.1**	**5.9**	**14.5**
Non-debt-creating flows, net	2.5	2.7	5.7	4.7	9.2	7.4	7.8	12.4	9.6	6.7
Net credit and loans from IMF	1.0	—	2.0	2.7	0.3	−1.3	−2.0	−0.6	. . .	. . .
Net external borrowing	11.5	6.9	4.5	24.5	30.9	30.1	40.0	−1.8	−10.2	9.1
Memorandum										
Net capital flows	10.3	−0.4	8.2	15.1	101.7	57.5	46.4	15.8	16.7	16.9
Exceptional financing	11.1	2.7	13.8	12.2	10.0	14.9	12.1	12.4	3.4	3.1
Net borrowing from official creditors	7.9	9.3	6.3	9.3	5.1	5.0	−2.1	−3.1	24.4	−1.9
Net borrowing from commercial banks	4.7	−1.7	−0.1	10.8	10.4	1.0	3.1	−10.1	0.2	9.5
Nonfuel exports										
Balance on current account	8.2	7.6	0.1	−6.4	−6.7	−15.8	−51.5	−47.2	−65.7	−72.6
Change in reserves (− = increase)	−42.7	−26.6	−26.4	−37.7	−60.0	−54.1	−65.4	−80.2	−39.1	−33.6
Asset transactions, including net errors and omissions	2.8	−19.1	−17.0	−15.3	−12.7	−39.0	−32.5	1.7	−9.1	−12.0
Total, net external financing	**31.7**	**38.1**	**43.3**	**59.4**	**79.4**	**108.8**	**149.9**	**125.9**	**115.9**	**119.5**
Non-debt-creating flows, net	9.4	16.6	11.9	30.7	19.7	29.3	51.3	46.5	42.1	41.8
Net credit and loans from IMF	−5.6	−4.1	−3.5	−4.6	0.8	1.2	1.8	−0.2	. . .	. . .
Net external borrowing	27.7	25.6	34.8	33.2	59.0	78.6	96.7	79.5	71.8	79.4
Memorandum										
Net capital flows	29.2	24.6	20.8	24.2	57.0	73.8	112.8	115.4	97.1	99.2
Exceptional financing	32.1	25.6	31.5	45.5	29.7	25.9	39.3	50.3	9.5	7.7
Net borrowing from official creditors	12.3	8.1	15.9	11.6	18.8	6.3	20.5	13.6	13.1	8.9
Net borrowing from commercial banks	15.5	2.6	1.9	16.0	7.7	7.2	3.4	−24.5	11.5	9.2
By financial criteria										
Net creditor countries										
Balance on current account	14.1	6.1	14.7	19.8	−49.0	−18.4	−10.2	−4.6	−3.7	−2.2
Change in reserves (− = increase)	−23.0	11.3	−1.7	5.2	−11.0	−0.7	8.7	8.1	2.7	2.3
Asset transactions, including net errors and omissions	−3.3	−12.0	−7.7	−23.5	53.2	6.1	−5.3	2.3	4.5	—
Total, net external financing	**12.2**	**−5.5**	**−5.2**	**−1.4**	**6.8**	**13.1**	**6.7**	**−5.8**	**−3.5**	**−0.1**
Non-debt-creating flows, net	−0.5	−3.5	−6.1	−3.9	−0.2	−1.5	−1.9	−2.0	−5.4	−2.9
Net credit and loans from IMF	—	—	—	—	—	—	—	—	. . .	. . .
Net external borrowing	12.7	−2.0	0.8	2.4	7.0	14.6	8.6	−3.8	1.9	2.8
Memorandum										
Net capital flows	9.5	−18.4	−13.3	−19.3	66.1	27.8	0.2	−2.2	3.9	−0.1
Exceptional financing	—	—	—	—	—	2.2	7.8	1.5	—	—
Net borrowing from official creditors	−0.9	−0.1	0.5	0.2	0.6	4.6	−1.3	−3.5	−1.4	−1.7
Net borrowing from commercial banks	9.4	−1.2	−0.1	−2.5	10.9	5.3	2.5	−8.7	0.3	3.2

Table A35 *(continued)*

	1987	1988	1989	1990	1991	1992	1993	1994	1995	1996
Net debtor countries										
Balance on current account	−18.5	−26.2	−24.4	−22.8	−34.6	−55.1	−88.1	−86.4	−81.7	−88.6
Change in reserves (− = increase)	−21.3	−15.8	−31.3	−58.5	−64.9	−53.7	−73.3	−59.3	−37.6	−39.6
Asset transactions, including										
net errors and omissions	5.3	−11.2	−5.0	−11.5	−13.5	−23.0	−27.0	4.1	−4.1	−4.6
Total, net external financing	**34.5**	**53.3**	**60.7**	**92.8**	**113.0**	**131.9**	**188.9**	**141.8**	**125.3**	**134.0**
Non-debt-creating flows, net	12.4	22.8	23.6	39.3	29.1	38.1	61.0	60.9	57.1	51.5
Net credit and loans from IMF	−4.7	−4.1	−1.5	−1.9	1.1	−0.2	−0.2	−0.8	. . .	. . .
Net external borrowing	26.5	34.5	38.4	55.3	82.8	94.2	128.1	81.6	59.7	85.6
Memorandum										
Net capital flows	30.0	42.5	42.3	58.6	92.6	103.5	159.0	133.4	109.8	116.2
Exceptional financing	43.2	28.4	45.4	57.8	39.7	38.6	43.6	61.2	12.8	10.8
Net borrowing from official creditors	21.2	17.4	21.7	20.7	23.3	6.7	19.7	14.0	38.9	8.7
Net borrowing from commercial banks	10.9	2.1	1.9	29.3	7.3	2.8	3.9	−25.9	11.4	15.5
Market borrowers										
Balance on current account	9.4	6.0	6.2	12.3	−12.7	−27.5	−48.8	−52.9	−40.5	−45.3
Change in reserves (− = increase)	−19.3	−17.0	−22.5	−45.0	−41.8	−42.3	−59.8	−45.3	−30.4	−34.8
Asset transactions, including										
net errors and omissions	−2.8	−16.0	−11.7	−22.8	−27.0	−27.3	−36.0	−10.8	−10.7	−13.2
Total, net external financing	**12.6**	**27.0**	**28.0**	**55.5**	**81.5**	**97.1**	**144.6**	**108.9**	**81.5**	**93.4**
Non-debt-creating flows, net	9.4	16.9	14.5	17.7	20.6	26.8	49.3	47.0	39.4	34.8
Net credit and loans from IMF	−1.8	−1.4	0.2	0.7	−1.2	−1.6	−1.2	−0.7	. . .	. . .
Net external borrowing	4.9	11.4	13.3	37.0	62.1	72.1	96.4	62.5	33.8	60.2
Memorandum										
Net capital flows	7.1	16.9	10.7	35.9	64.7	70.9	117.4	98.0	69.6	75.1
Exceptional financing	22.6	15.2	21.5	25.4	15.4	17.6	26.1	48.9	4.8	3.8
Net borrowing from official creditors	−4.3	1.5	5.9	7.1	5.0	−0.8	3.2	5.3	30.8	1.5
Net borrowing from commercial banks	9.2	−3.9	3.9	20.7	3.3	2.4	6.1	−28.6	7.0	10.4
Diversified borrowers										
Balance on current account	−15.1	−17.4	−17.6	−26.1	−13.3	−15.9	−23.3	−18.0	−27.1	−29.6
Change in reserves (− = increase)	−0.4	1.3	−7.3	−7.2	−14.6	−11.0	−9.6	−9.4	−5.1	−4.4
Asset transactions, including										
net errors and omissions	3.0	0.5	6.2	8.3	7.1	2.8	2.9	11.4	4.6	5.3
Total, net external financing	**12.5**	**15.7**	**18.7**	**25.0**	**20.8**	**24.1**	**30.0**	**16.0**	**29.2**	**29.5**
Non-debt-creating flows, net	0.7	3.1	3.1	4.3	3.4	5.2	5.4	7.5	11.0	10.6
Net credit and loans from IMF	−2.2	−1.9	−1.5	−1.5	2.0	1.1	1.4	−0.5	. . .	. . .
Net external borrowing	13.8	14.4	17.0	22.2	15.5	17.8	23.2	9.0	19.1	20.1
Memorandum										
Net capital flows	15.1	16.0	20.8	27.1	21.9	22.4	29.6	20.1	28.9	31.5
Exceptional financing	5.2	6.3	7.3	5.2	6.3	5.7	5.0	3.3	1.0	1.6
Net borrowing from official creditors	14.3	4.7	5.8	8.1	11.6	6.8	11.2	2.5	4.0	3.7
Net borrowing from commercial banks	2.6	7.3	−0.1	9.5	5.4	3.2	−0.3	2.6	3.1	4.9

Table A35 *(continued)*

	1987	1988	1989	1990	1991	1992	1993	1994	1995	1996
Official borrowers										
Balance on current account	−12.8	−14.8	−13.0	−9.0	−8.5	−11.7	−15.9	−15.5	−14.0	−13.7
Change in reserves (− = increase)	−1.6	−0.1	−1.4	−6.3	−8.6	−0.4	−4.0	−4.7	−2.1	−0.4
Asset transactions, including net errors and omissions	5.1	4.3	0.5	3.0	6.5	1.5	6.0	3.5	2.0	3.4
Total, net external financing	**9.4**	**10.6**	**14.0**	**12.3**	**10.7**	**10.7**	**14.3**	**16.9**	**14.5**	**11.2**
Non-debt-creating flows, net	2.4	2.8	6.0	17.2	5.1	6.1	6.2	6.3	6.7	6.1
Net credit and loans from IMF	−0.7	−0.8	−0.2	−1.1	0.3	0.3	−0.3	0.4	. . .	. . .
Net external borrowing	7.7	8.6	8.1	−3.8	5.2	4.3	8.4	10.1	6.7	5.3
Memorandum										
Net capital flows	7.8	9.7	10.8	−4.4	6.0	10.2	12.0	15.4	11.3	9.7
Exceptional financing	15.4	6.9	16.6	27.2	17.9	15.3	12.6	9.0	7.1	5.4
Net borrowing from official creditors	11.2	11.2	10.0	5.5	6.7	0.7	5.2	6.2	4.1	3.5
Net borrowing from commercial banks	−0.9	−1.3	−1.8	−0.9	−1.5	−2.7	−1.9	0.1	1.3	0.1
Countries with recent debt-servicing difficulties										
Balance on current account	−23.0	−28.3	−19.1	−13.8	−24.7	−44.6	−56.3	−60.1	−43.2	−41.5
Change in reserves (− = increase)	−8.4	1.9	−9.0	−25.7	−25.1	−24.3	−22.8	2.6	9.3	−1.2
Asset transactions, including net errors and omissions	9.4	2.6	5.8	−3.3	−4.6	−0.4	−2.1	6.7	−2.4	1.4
Total, net external financing	**22.1**	**23.7**	**22.3**	**42.8**	**54.5**	**69.3**	**81.4**	**50.9**	**38.2**	**42.4**
Non-debt-creating flows, net	4.7	9.8	10.7	22.4	13.7	16.6	17.6	16.8	22.4	15.2
Net credit and loans from IMF	−1.8	−1.3	−0.5	0.4	−1.0	−1.8	−0.3	−1.1	. . .	. . .
Net external borrowing	19.0	15.2	12.1	20.0	41.8	54.7	64.2	35.0	6.7	29.1
Memorandum										
Net capital flows	21.6	22.7	17.8	15.0	40.2	54.0	69.3	50.0	29.8	33.6
Exceptional financing	43.2	28.3	45.3	57.6	39.2	38.3	43.0	56.1	8.5	7.7
Net borrowing from official creditors	20.9	14.4	17.1	15.7	6.5	−0.4	7.6	1.9	28.9	−0.5
Net borrowing from commercial banks	3.7	−10.4	−5.2	12.7	−7.7	−10.9	−3.9	−33.6	−3.1	0.2
Countries without debt-servicing difficulties										
Balance on current account	4.5	2.1	−5.3	−9.0	−9.9	−10.5	−31.8	−26.2	−38.5	−47.1
Change in reserves (− = increase)	−12.9	−17.8	−22.3	−32.8	−39.8	−29.4	−50.6	−61.9	−46.9	−38.5
Asset transactions, including net errors and omissions	−4.0	−13.9	−10.8	−8.2	−8.9	−22.7	−24.9	−2.6	−1.7	−6.0
Total, net external financing	**12.4**	**29.6**	**38.3**	**50.0**	**58.5**	**62.6**	**107.4**	**90.8**	**87.1**	**91.6**
Non-debt-creating flows, net	7.7	13.0	12.9	16.9	15.4	21.5	43.4	44.0	34.7	36.3
Net credit and loans from IMF	−2.9	−2.8	−1.0	−2.3	2.1	1.6	0.2	0.3	. . .	. . .
Net external borrowing	7.5	19.3	26.3	35.3	41.0	39.4	63.9	46.5	53.0	56.5
Memorandum										
Net capital flows	8.5	19.9	24.5	43.6	52.4	49.5	89.7	83.5	80.0	82.7
Exceptional financing	—	—	0.1	0.1	0.5	0.3	0.6	5.1	4.3	3.0
Net borrowing from official creditors	0.3	3.0	4.6	5.0	16.8	7.1	12.1	12.1	10.0	9.1
Net borrowing from commercial banks	7.1	12.5	7.2	16.6	15.0	13.7	7.8	7.8	14.5	15.2

Table A35 *(concluded)*

	1987	1988	1989	1990	1991	1992	1993	1994	1995	1996
Other groups										
Small low-income countries										
Balance on current account	-8.2	-9.0	-8.7	-10.1	-9.0	-9.5	-10.8	-9.8	-10.7	-11.6
Change in reserves (– = increase)	-0.3	0.4	-0.7	1.4	-4.0	2.8	-1.8	-3.8	-1.8	-1.5
Asset transactions, including										
net errors and omissions	1.0	-0.9	0.4	0.3	5.7	-0.9	3.0	2.6	3.1	2.9
Total, net external financing	**7.5**	**9.5**	**9.0**	**8.4**	**7.5**	**7.6**	**9.9**	**11.1**	**9.5**	**10.2**
Non-debt-creating flows, net	0.3	0.8	1.3	1.5	1.8	2.0	2.1	2.9	1.9	2.7
Net credit and loans from IMF	-0.6	-0.3	—	-0.6	0.4	0.2	-0.1	0.7	. . .	. . .
Net external borrowing	7.8	9.0	7.6	7.3	5.3	5.4	7.9	7.4	6.3	7.4
Memorandum										
Net capital flows	7.3	8.3	7.4	7.2	6.2	6.2	8.2	10.0	8.4	9.2
Exceptional financing	4.2	4.5	5.3	4.9	5.8	5.6	6.5	5.7	4.5	4.1
Net borrowing from official creditors	4.4	5.2	7.9	9.0	9.4	3.3	5.9	6.7	6.7	6.6
Net borrowing from commercial banks	0.4	0.3	0.1	0.9	-1.1	0.1	0.1	-0.4	—	—
Least developed countries										
Balance on current account	-5.2	-6.1	-5.6	-7.2	-7.4	-8.0	-7.7	-7.1	-7.5	-8.3
Change in reserves (– = increase)	-1.6	0.2	-0.5	0.4	-3.7	3.2	-0.5	-1.3	0.1	-0.2
Asset transactions, including										
net errors and omissions	1.8	0.6	0.5	0.9	6.0	-1.0	2.8	1.3	1.8	2.4
Total, net external financing	**5.0**	**5.4**	**5.6**	**5.9**	**5.2**	**5.9**	**5.5**	**7.2**	**5.7**	**6.0**
Non-debt-creating flows, net	—	0.4	0.6	1.0	1.6	2.1	2.1	1.9	0.9	1.6
Net credit and loans from IMF	—	-0.1	-0.3	-0.4	0.1	0.2	-0.1	0.2	. . .	. . .
Net external borrowing	4.9	5.1	5.3	5.3	3.6	3.5	3.6	5.1	3.8	4.5
Memorandum										
Net capital flows	1.0	0.8	—	0.6	-0.8	-1.0	-1.7	0.6	0.3	0.9
Exceptional financing	3.9	4.3	4.9	5.2	5.8	6.4	6.6	6.5	5.2	5.0
Net borrowing from official creditors	4.7	4.8	5.2	6.4	7.5	1.8	3.9	4.7	4.7	5.1
Net borrowing from commercial banks	0.3	-0.5	0.8	0.8	-1.0	-0.2	—	-0.7	0.1	0.1
Fifteen heavily indebted countries										
Balance on current account	-8.9	-9.7	-4.4	-3.3	-18.6	-33.8	-47.6	-51.1	-34.1	-32.7
Change in reserves (– = increase)	-3.3	-0.7	-5.1	-20.6	-14.0	-17.7	-22.8	4.6	6.6	-3.0
Asset transactions, including										
net errors and omissions	1.7	-1.1	2.9	-6.9	-10.2	-7.2	-8.4	5.2	-2.1	-0.5
Total, net external financing	**10.5**	**11.5**	**6.7**	**30.7**	**42.7**	**58.7**	**78.9**	**41.2**	**29.9**	**36.7**
Non-debt-creating flows, net	5.3	8.9	9.6	10.1	11.7	13.4	14.1	14.9	20.6	14.1
Net credit and loans from IMF	-1.3	-1.4	-0.8	0.6	-1.4	-1.8	-0.9	-1.3	. . .	. . .
Net external borrowing	6.5	3.9	-2.2	20.0	32.4	47.4	65.7	27.4	1.1	24.3
Memorandum										
Net capital flows	7.2	7.8	1.1	13.4	31.6	43.2	67.5	40.7	24.7	28.6
Exceptional financing	37.3	21.3	35.2	36.8	25.2	25.2	29.4	46.1	1.5	2.0
Net borrowing from official creditors	7.7	5.4	8.6	9.1	0.3	-4.3	-0.7	-4.6	23.9	-6.3
Net borrowing from commercial banks	2.6	-12.9	-2.6	9.7	-5.0	-11.7	-2.3	-34.2	-4.9	-0.5

[1]For definitions, see footnotes to Table A33.

Table A36. Developing Countries: Reserves[1]

	1987	1988	1989	1990	1991	1992	1993	1994	1995	1996
					In billions of U.S. dollars					
Developing countries	**253.6**	**247.2**	**270.1**	**317.9**	**389.7**	**413.0**	**476.6**	**519.8**	**547.0**	**574.7**
By region										
Africa	11.0	10.4	12.0	16.7	19.7	16.2	16.7	18.8	21.4	24.7
Asia	148.5	158.6	168.6	194.4	238.9	239.8	276.5	331.9	369.5	401.4
Middle East and Europe	55.7	47.0	56.3	58.5	65.1	68.2	74.6	66.3	61.5	53.1
Western Hemisphere	38.3	31.1	33.3	48.3	66.0	88.8	108.8	102.8	94.6	95.5
Sub-Saharan Africa	6.0	6.2	6.5	7.7	8.4	7.7	7.8	9.7	9.9	10.5
Four newly industrializing Asian economies	102.8	111.4	117.7	126.3	143.6	152.7	166.6	174.4	183.0	193.0
By predominant export										
Fuel	69.3	50.2	56.4	66.2	80.2	74.5	82.9	53.9	49.7	53.4
Nonfuel exports	184.2	197.0	213.8	251.7	309.5	338.5	393.7	465.9	497.4	521.3
Manufactures	145.7	156.7	169.1	193.0	230.4	235.7	269.4	326.2	346.5	361.7
Primary products	17.1	19.7	20.5	28.2	36.1	44.5	50.8	58.9	62.3	66.2
Agricultural products	10.5	12.5	11.8	16.1	21.2	26.7	31.5	34.9	36.7	39.1
Minerals	6.6	7.2	8.7	12.1	14.9	17.8	19.3	24.0	25.6	27.1
Services, income, and private transfers	8.9	8.5	8.7	10.8	14.4	19.6	23.3	26.5	26.5	25.0
Diversified export base	12.6	12.1	15.5	19.8	28.7	38.8	50.2	54.4	62.0	68.4
By financial criteria										
Net creditor countries	116.9	106.7	106.1	101.0	111.0	107.8	109.9	101.7	99.0	96.8
Net debtor countries	136.6	140.4	164.0	217.0	278.7	305.2	366.7	418.1	448.0	477.9
Market borrowers	94.6	99.2	113.0	154.8	196.6	211.7	260.5	297.5	318.3	342.1
Diversified borrowers	27.2	26.4	34.7	39.6	53.1	61.2	71.1	80.5	87.1	92.3
Official borrowers	14.9	14.8	16.3	22.5	29.0	32.3	35.1	40.1	42.6	43.5
Countries with recent debt-servicing difficulties	44.9	36.7	45.8	68.1	95.0	120.4	142.9	140.5	133.1	135.6
Countries without debt-servicing difficulties	91.8	103.8	118.2	148.9	183.7	184.8	223.8	277.6	314.8	342.4
Other groups										
Small low-income economies	5.5	5.3	5.0	5.6	7.2	8.1	9.4	13.3	15.2	16.7
Least developed countries	7.2	7.1	6.9	8.3	9.5	9.3	9.7	11.1	11.2	11.4
Fifteen heavily indebted countries	38.7	32.9	38.1	57.2	74.5	93.8	114.4	109.7	103.4	106.9

Table A36 *(concluded)*

	1987	1988	1989	1990	1991	1992	1993	1994	1995	1996
	Ratio of reserves to imports of goods and services[2]									
Developing countries	**39.1**	**32.7**	**32.1**	**33.3**	**36.2**	**34.4**	**36.8**	**36.3**	**34.4**	**32.1**
By region										
Africa	14.3	12.2	13.3	17.0	20.4	15.8	16.7	18.1	18.8	20.5
Asia	47.1	39.8	37.1	37.5	40.3	35.3	36.2	37.7	36.9	35.0
Middle East and Europe	35.3	29.1	31.7	29.1	28.2	28.6	31.9	29.5	25.0	19.1
Western Hemisphere	39.0	28.0	27.8	35.3	42.4	48.6	55.0	45.9	41.3	39.0
Sub-Saharan Africa	16.8	16.0	16.3	17.9	19.7	17.7	18.4	23.1	21.3	21.5
Four newly industrializing Asian economies	58.7	48.2	44.6	41.8	41.0	38.7	38.8	35.4	33.0	31.3
By predominant export										
Fuel	39.7	26.8	27.3	28.6	29.4	25.5	29.8	19.3	18.0	16.3
Nonfuel exports	38.9	34.6	33.6	34.9	38.5	37.2	38.7	40.4	37.9	35.6
Manufactures	48.1	41.0	39.0	39.0	41.4	37.2	37.4	39.8	36.7	34.0
Primary products	25.9	28.7	28.7	36.1	42.8	44.7	47.0	49.2	48.2	47.6
Agricultural products	22.0	25.7	23.7	29.7	35.3	36.8	39.3	38.6	38.3	38.3
Minerals	36.3	36.3	40.3	50.6	61.9	65.5	68.9	81.4	76.4	73.7
Services, income, and private transfers	19.5	17.2	16.8	18.8	23.3	30.0	34.2	37.5	35.0	32.2
Diversified export base	21.0	17.4	19.6	21.6	28.4	34.8	41.0	37.9	37.7	37.2
By financial criteria										
Net creditor countries	92.8	75.3	67.1	58.0	50.9	46.7	49.7	45.9	41.1	37.8
Net debtor countries	26.1	22.8	24.0	27.8	32.5	31.4	34.1	34.5	33.2	31.1
Market borrowers	31.0	26.1	26.3	31.3	34.2	31.8	35.0	34.6	32.9	31.5
Diversified borrowers	19.7	17.9	21.4	21.7	30.0	31.7	33.0	34.5	34.1	29.3
Official borrowers	18.7	17.0	17.7	22.1	27.2	28.7	30.6	33.9	33.3	32.6
Countries with recent debt-servicing difficulties	24.0	17.6	20.6	27.8	36.7	41.3	46.3	41.0	37.1	33.6
Countries without debt-servicing difficulties	27.4	25.5	25.6	27.8	30.6	27.2	29.2	31.9	31.8	30.3
Other groups										
Small low-income economies	13.9	12.6	11.4	11.8	14.9	15.7	17.4	23.5	24.1	24.4
Least developed countries	26.7	24.0	22.6	25.5	29.6	28.1	28.7	31.5	28.6	27.1
Fifteen heavily indebted countries	32.5	24.3	25.4	31.7	40.2	44.6	50.3	42.6	38.6	36.8

[1] In this table, official holdings of gold are valued at SDR 35 an ounce. This convention results in a marked underestimate of reserves for countries that have substantial gold holdings.

[2] Reserves at year-end in percent of imports of goods and services for the year indicated.

Table A37. Net Credit and Loans from IMF[1]

(In billions of U.S. dollars)

	1987	1988	1989	1990	1991	1992	1993	1994
Developing countries	**-4.7**	**-4.1**	**-1.5**	**-1.9**	**1.1**	**-0.2**	**-0.2**	**-0.8**
By region								
Africa	-1.1	-0.3	0.1	-0.6	0.2	-0.2	0.2	0.9
Asia	-2.4	-2.4	-1.1	-2.4	1.9	1.3	0.6	-0.8
Middle East and Europe	-0.4	-0.5	-0.2	-0.1	—	0.4	—	0.4
Western Hemisphere	-0.8	-0.9	-0.2	1.2	-1.0	-1.6	-0.9	-1.3
Sub-Saharan Africa	-0.5	-0.2	-0.4	-0.3	—	—	-0.2	0.5
By predominant export								
Fuel	1.0	—	2.0	2.7	0.3	-1.3	-2.0	-0.6
Nonfuel exports	-5.6	-4.1	-3.5	-4.6	0.8	1.2	1.8	-0.2
Manufactures	-4.0	-2.9	-2.6	-2.6	1.3	1.1	-0.1	-1.0
Primary products	-0.3	-0.4	-1.0	-0.9	-0.8	-0.4	1.0	0.6
Services, income, and private transfers	-0.5	-0.6	0.2	-0.4	0.3	0.3	0.1	0.4
Diversified export base	-0.8	-0.3	-0.1	-0.7	0.1	0.1	0.8	-0.3
By financial criteria								
Net creditor countries	—	—	—	—	—	—	—	—
Net debtor countries	-4.7	-4.1	-1.5	-1.9	1.1	-0.2	-0.2	-0.8
Market borrowers	-1.8	-1.4	0.2	0.7	-1.2	-1.6	-1.2	-0.7
Official borrowers	-0.7	-0.8	-0.2	-1.1	0.3	0.3	-0.3	0.4
Countries with recent debt-servicing difficulties	-1.8	-1.3	-0.5	0.4	-1.0	-1.8	-0.3	-1.1
Countries without debt-servicing difficulties	-2.9	-2.8	-1.0	-2.3	2.1	1.6	0.2	0.3
Other groups								
Small low-income economies	-0.6	-0.3	—	-0.6	0.4	0.2	-0.1	0.7
Least developed countries	—	-0.1	-0.3	-0.4	0.1	0.2	-0.1	0.2
Fifteen heavily indebted countries	-1.3	-1.4	-0.8	0.6	-1.4	-1.8	-0.9	-1.3
Countries in transition	**-1.1**	**-0.9**	**-0.9**	**0.1**	**3.5**	**1.7**	**2.1**	**2.4**
Central and eastern Europe	...	...	...	...	3.5	0.7	0.4	0.5
Excluding Belarus and Ukraine	...	...	...	...	3.5	0.7	0.3	0.2
Russia	...	...	...	...	—	—	—	—
Transcaucasus and central Asia	...	...	...	...	—	—	0.2	0.3
Memorandum								
Total, nonindustrial countries								
Net credit provided under:								
General Resources Account	-5.642	-4.875	-3.121	-2.148	3.606	0.842	1.711	0.594
Trust Fund	-0.711	-0.669	-0.509	-0.365	-0.069	—	-0.060	-0.014
SAF	0.522	0.413	0.902	0.131	0.242	0.024	-0.064	-0.185
ESAF	—	0.138	0.330	0.557	0.804	0.706	0.317	1.139
Disbursements at year-end under:[2]								
General Resources Account	40.267	33.314	29.334	29.503	33.434	32.961	34.609	37.389
Trust Fund	1.946	1.177	0.627	0.296	0.226	0.217	0.157	0.153
SAF	0.688	1.067	1.967	2.403	2.670	2.590	2.524	2.494
ESAF	—	0.138	0.473	0.959	1.805	2.424	2.734	4.068

[1] Excludes industrial countries' net credit from IMF. Includes net disbursements from programs under the General Resources Account, Trust Fund, SAF, and ESAF. The data are on a transaction basis, with conversions to U.S. dollar values at annual average exchange rates.

[2] Converted to U.S. dollar values at end-of-period exchange rates.

Table A38. Summary of External Debt and Debt Service

	1987	1988	1989	1990	1991	1992	1993	1994	1995	1996
External debt					*In billions of U.S. dollars*					
Developing countries	**1,165.9**	**1,181.4**	**1,210.4**	**1,298.7**	**1,371.6**	**1,447.0**	**1,559.2**	**1,623.1**	**1,716.0**	**1,796.7**
By region										
Africa	199.2	203.6	210.9	225.9	235.5	234.2	239.6	245.3	258.7	268.0
Asia	316.2	326.1	335.0	369.1	413.7	455.0	514.6	550.4	604.2	661.8
Middle East and Europe	223.6	235.5	247.1	266.0	270.7	285.2	306.7	303.4	301.9	298.3
Western Hemisphere	426.9	416.1	417.3	437.6	451.8	472.7	498.4	523.9	551.2	568.6
By financial criteria										
Net creditor countries	49.0	48.0	48.2	48.0	55.0	62.4	67.2	62.5	58.3	55.8
Net debtor countries	1,116.9	1,133.4	1,162.1	1,250.7	1,316.6	1,384.6	1,492.0	1,560.5	1,657.7	1,740.9
Market borrowers	539.5	528.8	531.5	569.2	610.9	654.2	722.5	773.9	845.1	906.8
Diversified borrowers	341.1	358.5	376.8	410.9	428.1	450.9	482.8	488.2	503.4	520.3
Official borrowers	236.3	246.1	253.8	270.6	277.6	279.5	286.7	298.5	309.2	313.8
Countries with recent debt-servicing difficulties	712.5	716.6	731.3	774.1	794.2	818.3	853.7	884.6	922.7	945.6
Countries without debt-servicing difficulties	404.4	416.8	430.8	476.6	522.4	566.2	638.3	676.0	735.0	795.4
Countries in transition	**146.8**	**145.1**	**153.1**	**160.5**	**168.9**	**192.4**	**207.8**	**224.7**	**232.9**	**244.1**
Central and eastern Europe	...	...	...	...	101.7	114.4	121.6	127.8	133.3	141.7
Excluding Belarus and Ukraine	...	...	...	...	101.6	113.6	119.8	125.1	127.3	131.5
Russia	...	...	...	...	67.0	77.7	83.7	93.4	96.2	98.8
Transcaucasus and central Asia	...	...	...	...	0.2	0.3	2.6	3.6	3.4	3.6
Debt-service payments[1]										
Developing countries	**133.0**	**145.0**	**144.1**	**155.0**	**178.8**	**175.1**	**180.0**	**216.0**	**220.2**	**214.4**
By region										
Africa	20.1	20.6	23.7	26.4	26.4	27.1	22.8	23.6	27.9	22.2
Asia	44.4	46.2	50.7	55.2	60.1	62.7	65.6	81.8	81.6	94.9
Middle East and Europe	18.9	20.1	21.8	26.6	22.6	19.4	17.6	37.3	23.7	20.8
Western Hemisphere	49.5	58.0	47.9	46.8	69.8	65.8	73.9	73.3	87.0	76.6
By financial criteria										
Net creditor countries	5.3	5.6	5.4	5.4	5.3	5.8	6.9	23.5	9.7	8.5
Net debtor countries	127.7	139.3	138.7	149.6	173.6	169.3	173.1	192.5	210.5	205.9
Market borrowers	74.7	84.1	77.5	79.7	107.7	102.6	110.4	115.7	122.7	130.6
Diversified borrowers	35.5	41.8	44.9	47.6	43.6	47.3	47.0	57.3	66.8	60.3
Official borrowers	17.5	13.5	16.3	22.2	22.2	19.4	15.7	19.5	20.9	15.1
Countries with recent debt-servicing difficulties	69.2	75.1	69.2	73.6	91.2	84.5	88.6	92.6	111.1	95.4
Countries without debt-servicing difficulties	58.5	64.3	69.5	75.9	82.4	84.8	84.5	99.9	99.4	110.6
Countries in transition	**24.2**	**27.4**	**24.6**	**17.0**	...	**17.0**	**12.2**	**22.7**	**23.1**	**24.7**
Central and eastern Europe	...	...	...	...	8.0	10.0	9.6	18.3	14.3	14.0
Excluding Belarus and Ukraine	...	...	...	...	8.0	10.0	9.4	17.6	13.3	13.0
Russia	...	...	...	...	...	7.0	2.5	3.6	8.0	9.7
Transcaucasus and central Asia	...	...	...	...	—	0.1	0.1	0.7	0.8	1.0

Table A38 (concluded)

	1987	1988	1989	1990	1991	1992	1993	1994	1995	1996
External debt[2]					*In percent of exports of goods and services*					
Developing countries	**175.6**	**155.1**	**141.3**	**132.6**	**132.5**	**127.1**	**127.8**	**118.7**	**111.2**	**104.4**
By region										
Africa	256.2	252.9	245.9	227.1	246.3	246.2	258.9	264.5	249.7	240.9
Asia	93.7	79.0	72.3	71.0	69.9	67.5	69.0	63.9	61.5	59.9
Middle East and Europe	167.3	171.7	153.8	135.7	145.6	143.8	153.5	145.5	134.0	116.5
Western Hemisphere	371.6	317.7	284.7	267.7	279.0	276.4	274.6	255.3	237.4	228.2
By financial criteria										
Net creditor countries	36.4	33.9	29.2	24.3	27.2	28.9	30.5	27.6	23.8	21.6
Net debtor countries	211.0	182.8	168.2	160.0	157.9	150.0	149.2	136.8	127.7	119.0
Market borrowers	157.2	126.7	113.7	106.8	104.4	99.3	99.8	92.4	88.4	84.6
Diversified borrowers	268.7	259.0	245.2	246.3	258.9	253.0	253.0	228.5	209.7	184.4
Official borrowers	399.8	382.9	362.2	329.5	334.6	326.0	336.0	330.4	302.3	289.9
Countries with recent debt-servicing difficulties	369.3	337.4	309.2	298.1	317.3	312.0	313.8	294.1	270.4	244.8
Countries without debt-servicing difficulties	120.3	102.2	94.8	91.3	89.6	85.7	87.7	80.4	76.8	73.9
Countries in transition	**71.7**	**67.8**	**73.2**	**82.1**	**98.0**	**128.2**	**131.8**	**131.5**	**125.1**	**119.3**
Central and eastern Europe	...	...	...	...	132.0	140.7	155.1	150.4	142.2	139.2
Excluding Belarus and Ukraine	...	...	...	...	152.2	160.2	172.9	162.6	149.8	142.2
Russia	...	...	...	...	108.8	135.3	128.4	128.4	123.7	116.7
Transcaucasus and central Asia	...	...	...	...	0.7	2.7	18.2	27.1	23.3	19.7
Debt-service payments										
Developing countries	**20.0**	**19.0**	**16.8**	**15.8**	**17.3**	**15.4**	**14.8**	**15.8**	**14.3**	**12.5**
By region										
Africa	25.9	25.6	27.7	26.6	27.7	28.5	24.6	25.4	26.9	19.9
Asia	13.2	11.2	10.9	10.6	10.1	9.3	8.8	9.5	8.3	8.6
Middle East and Europe	14.2	14.7	13.5	13.6	12.1	9.8	8.8	17.9	10.5	8.1
Western Hemisphere	43.1	44.3	32.7	28.6	43.1	38.5	40.7	35.7	37.5	30.8
By financial criteria										
Net creditor countries	3.9	4.0	3.3	2.7	2.6	2.7	3.1	10.4	4.0	3.3
Net debtor countries	24.1	22.5	20.1	19.1	20.8	18.3	17.3	16.9	16.2	14.1
Market borrowers	21.8	20.1	16.6	15.0	18.4	15.6	15.3	13.8	12.8	12.2
Diversified borrowers	28.0	30.2	29.2	28.5	26.4	26.6	24.6	26.8	27.8	21.4
Official borrowers	29.6	21.0	23.3	27.1	26.8	22.6	18.4	21.6	20.5	14.0
Countries with recent debt-servicing difficulties	35.9	35.3	29.3	28.4	36.4	32.2	32.6	30.8	32.6	24.7
Countries without debt-servicing difficulties	17.4	15.8	15.3	14.5	14.1	12.8	11.6	11.9	10.4	10.3
Countries in transition	**11.8**	**12.8**	**11.8**	**8.7**	**...**	**11.4**	**7.7**	**13.3**	**12.4**	**12.1**
Central and eastern Europe	...	...	...	...	10.4	12.3	12.2	21.5	15.3	13.8
Excluding Belarus and Ukraine	...	...	...	...	11.9	14.0	13.5	22.9	15.7	14.1
Russia	...	...	...	...	...	12.2	3.8	5.0	10.3	11.5
Transcaucasus and central Asia	...	...	...	...	—	0.6	0.8	5.7	5.7	5.3

[1]Debt-service payments refer to actual payments of interest on total debt plus actual amortization payments on long-term debt. The projections incorporate the impact of exceptional financing items.

[2]Total debt at year-end in percent of exports of goods and services in year indicated.

Table A39. Developing Countries—By Region: External Debt, by Maturity and Type of Creditor

(In billions of U.S. dollars)

	1987	1988	1989	1990	1991	1992	1993	1994	1995	1996
Developing countries										
Total debt	**1,165.9**	**1,181.4**	**1,210.4**	**1,298.7**	**1,371.6**	**1,447.0**	**1,559.2**	**1,623.1**	**1,716.0**	**1,796.7**
By maturity										
Short-term	210.7	218.4	225.1	252.7	262.1	276.5	293.5	317.1	356.1	383.2
Long-term	955.2	963.0	985.2	1,046.0	1,109.5	1,170.6	1,265.7	1,306.0	1,359.9	1,413.5
By type of creditor										
Official	520.2	535.4	556.7	608.1	637.7	653.0	683.5	737.5	784.0	797.8
Commercial banks	482.2	460.3	443.2	421.7	449.9	468.0	467.4	450.0	429.3	440.9
Other private	163.6	185.7	210.5	268.9	284.1	326.1	408.3	435.6	502.7	558.0
By region										
Africa										
Total debt	**199.2**	**203.6**	**210.9**	**225.9**	**235.5**	**234.2**	**239.6**	**245.3**	**258.7**	**268.0**
By maturity										
Short-term	45.8	46.5	43.4	43.7	42.4	39.7	41.2	41.5	44.5	48.0
Long-term	153.4	157.1	167.4	182.3	193.0	194.5	198.4	203.8	214.2	220.0
By type of creditor										
Official	126.0	128.5	135.1	149.2	155.6	156.8	161.9	177.8	188.1	194.0
Commercial banks	59.7	57.4	55.6	58.5	58.3	51.5	46.7	40.3	41.4	42.3
Other private	13.5	17.7	20.2	18.2	21.6	25.9	31.0	27.1	29.2	31.7
Asia										
Total debt	**316.2**	**326.1**	**335.0**	**369.1**	**413.7**	**455.0**	**514.6**	**550.4**	**604.2**	**661.8**
By maturity										
Short-term	53.3	59.7	63.8	73.0	88.7	98.5	117.3	140.0	162.8	185.6
Long-term	262.9	266.4	271.2	296.2	325.1	356.5	397.2	410.5	441.4	476.2
By type of creditor										
Official	176.6	179.3	183.2	197.6	208.4	223.7	242.8	266.3	278.7	288.7
Commercial banks	101.0	104.1	104.4	116.6	139.3	156.1	169.1	181.7	198.1	212.8
Other private	38.7	42.7	47.5	54.9	66.1	75.1	102.7	102.5	127.5	160.4
Middle East and Europe										
Total debt	**223.6**	**235.5**	**247.1**	**266.0**	**270.7**	**285.2**	**306.7**	**303.4**	**301.9**	**298.3**
By maturity										
Short-term	53.1	52.9	55.3	59.2	52.6	56.4	64.2	62.2	65.8	65.4
Long-term	170.5	182.6	191.8	206.8	218.1	228.8	242.4	241.2	236.0	232.9
By type of creditor										
Official	113.5	116.4	119.5	122.9	121.8	118.5	123.6	129.5	130.5	130.0
Commercial banks	56.6	60.0	63.7	65.2	69.9	76.6	65.5	65.2	61.7	59.4
Other private	53.5	59.1	63.9	77.8	79.0	90.1	117.5	108.6	109.7	108.9
Western Hemisphere										
Total debt	**426.9**	**416.1**	**417.3**	**437.6**	**451.8**	**472.7**	**498.4**	**523.9**	**551.2**	**568.6**
By maturity										
Short-term	58.4	59.2	62.6	76.9	78.5	81.8	70.7	73.5	82.9	84.1
Long-term	368.5	356.9	354.7	360.8	373.3	390.9	427.7	450.5	468.2	484.4
By type of creditor										
Official	104.1	111.1	118.9	138.3	151.9	154.0	155.2	163.8	186.8	185.2
Commercial banks	264.9	238.9	219.5	181.3	182.4	183.7	186.1	162.7	128.2	126.4
Other private	57.9	66.1	78.9	118.0	117.5	134.9	157.1	197.4	236.2	257.0
Sub-Saharan Africa										
Total debt	**98.1**	**102.0**	**105.9**	**118.0**	**128.9**	**133.8**	**139.9**	**138.6**	**145.7**	**149.9**
By maturity										
Short-term	30.3	30.4	25.5	27.2	28.4	29.0	31.9	29.9	30.8	32.2
Long-term	67.7	71.6	80.4	90.8	100.5	104.8	108.0	108.7	114.9	117.7
By type of creditor										
Official	77.3	80.6	83.0	93.6	101.6	102.2	106.4	114.0	118.6	121.3
Commercial banks	13.7	13.2	13.4	15.7	16.1	15.8	15.8	10.7	11.6	12.3
Other private	7.1	8.3	9.5	8.8	11.3	15.8	17.7	13.9	15.4	16.2

Table A40. Developing Countries—By Analytical Criteria: External Debt, by Maturity and Type of Creditor
(In billions of U.S. dollars)

	1987	1988	1989	1990	1991	1992	1993	1994	1995	1996
By predominant export										
Fuel										
Total debt	**348.3**	**357.5**	**361.5**	**395.2**	**414.9**	**432.9**	**457.0**	**466.6**	**486.5**	**490.7**
By maturity										
Short-term	54.2	57.7	58.6	59.3	49.5	49.2	48.1	50.9	64.7	71.7
Long-term	294.1	299.7	302.9	335.9	365.4	383.7	409.0	415.6	421.7	419.1
By type of creditor										
Official	108.8	117.6	124.7	143.7	151.1	160.9	172.1	188.5	212.5	217.0
Commercial banks	178.4	166.6	166.0	138.3	150.1	155.8	161.9	170.6	136.3	138.8
Other private	61.1	73.3	70.8	113.2	113.6	116.1	123.0	107.4	137.7	134.9
Nonfuel exports										
Total debt	**817.6**	**823.9**	**848.8**	**903.5**	**956.8**	**1,014.2**	**1,102.2**	**1,156.5**	**1,229.5**	**1,306.0**
By maturity										
Short-term	156.5	160.6	166.5	193.4	212.7	227.3	245.4	266.1	291.3	311.5
Long-term	661.1	663.3	682.3	710.1	744.1	786.9	856.8	890.4	938.1	994.5
By type of creditor										
Official	411.3	417.7	432.0	464.3	486.6	492.1	511.4	549.0	571.5	580.8
Commercial banks	303.8	293.8	277.2	283.4	299.7	312.2	305.5	279.3	293.0	302.1
Other private	102.5	112.4	139.6	155.8	170.4	210.0	285.3	328.2	365.0	423.1
Manufactures										
Total debt	**368.3**	**370.0**	**382.7**	**419.4**	**454.0**	**491.6**	**556.6**	**571.5**	**611.6**	**652.9**
By maturity										
Short-term	75.4	75.5	82.0	104.9	121.3	128.9	148.9	161.2	177.2	190.5
Long-term	292.8	294.4	300.8	314.5	332.7	362.7	407.8	410.3	434.4	462.3
By type of creditor										
Official	132.5	133.2	137.5	147.2	161.7	166.1	172.5	183.0	187.7	188.7
Commercial banks	172.6	169.8	156.5	166.2	185.1	198.9	199.7	173.6	181.8	187.4
Other private	63.2	66.9	88.7	106.1	107.1	126.6	184.4	214.9	242.1	276.8
Primary products										
Total debt	**222.0**	**226.1**	**235.0**	**248.7**	**256.6**	**267.9**	**276.8**	**298.0**	**313.0**	**333.3**
By maturity										
Short-term	51.6	55.7	54.7	61.1	64.6	68.9	63.5	65.1	67.8	71.3
Long-term	170.4	170.4	180.3	187.5	192.0	198.9	213.2	232.9	245.3	262.0
By type of creditor										
Official	115.4	120.5	125.9	142.4	150.7	152.2	156.0	167.4	177.6	182.4
Commercial banks	78.2	73.6	72.1	69.4	67.7	67.5	66.3	63.8	63.3	62.5
Other private	28.4	31.9	37.0	36.9	38.3	48.1	54.5	66.8	72.2	88.4
Agricultural products										
Total debt	**155.6**	**158.3**	**168.2**	**174.4**	**180.9**	**186.5**	**191.4**	**207.9**	**219.2**	**234.4**
By maturity										
Short-term	20.3	22.4	24.2	27.1	31.0	32.4	26.0	27.1	29.3	32.3
Long-term	135.2	135.9	144.1	147.3	149.9	154.1	165.4	180.9	189.9	202.0
By type of creditor										
Official	80.6	83.1	87.2	95.5	101.6	102.8	104.4	112.6	120.9	124.8
Commercial banks	57.4	55.3	56.4	52.9	51.3	50.6	48.8	45.3	46.9	46.5
Other private	17.6	19.9	24.7	26.0	28.0	33.0	38.2	50.0	51.4	63.1
Minerals										
Total debt	**66.4**	**67.7**	**66.7**	**74.2**	**75.8**	**81.4**	**85.4**	**90.1**	**93.9**	**98.9**
By maturity										
Short-term	31.3	33.3	30.5	34.0	33.7	36.5	37.5	38.1	38.5	39.0
Long-term	35.1	34.4	36.2	40.2	42.1	44.8	47.8	52.1	55.4	60.0
By type of creditor										
Official	34.9	37.3	38.7	46.9	49.0	49.4	51.6	54.8	56.7	57.7
Commercial banks	20.8	18.3	15.7	16.4	16.4	16.9	17.5	18.5	16.3	16.0
Other private	10.8	12.1	12.3	10.9	10.3	15.1	16.3	16.8	20.8	25.3

Table A40 (continued)

	1987	1988	1989	1990	1991	1992	1993	1994	1995	1996
Services, income, and private transfers										
Total debt	**102.5**	**105.3**	**108.9**	**113.9**	**116.2**	**118.0**	**121.8**	**129.7**	**134.8**	**137.9**
By maturity										
Short-term	10.2	10.3	9.9	8.5	7.0	7.1	9.3	13.0	14.4	12.9
Long-term	92.3	95.0	99.0	105.4	109.2	110.8	112.5	116.7	120.5	125.0
By type of creditor										
Official	79.2	82.9	86.4	88.5	87.5	84.2	87.5	95.2	98.6	100.4
Commercial banks	13.8	13.9	14.2	15.2	15.1	15.5	13.2	14.0	14.9	14.5
Other private	9.5	8.4	8.2	10.1	13.6	18.3	21.0	20.6	21.4	23.1
Diversified export base										
Total debt	**124.8**	**122.6**	**122.2**	**121.5**	**130.0**	**136.7**	**147.0**	**157.3**	**170.0**	**181.9**
By maturity										
Short-term	19.2	19.1	19.9	18.8	19.8	22.3	23.7	26.9	32.0	36.7
Long-term	105.6	103.5	102.3	102.7	110.2	114.4	123.3	130.4	138.0	145.1
By type of creditor										
Official	84.2	81.1	82.1	86.2	86.7	89.5	95.4	103.4	107.7	109.3
Commercial banks	39.3	36.4	34.3	32.7	31.8	30.3	26.2	28.0	33.0	37.7
Other private	1.4	5.1	5.8	2.6	11.5	16.9	25.4	25.9	29.3	34.9
By financial criteria										
Net creditor countries										
Total debt	**49.0**	**48.0**	**48.2**	**48.0**	**55.0**	**62.4**	**67.2**	**62.5**	**58.3**	**55.8**
By maturity										
Short-term	39.1	38.0	37.2	36.3	35.4	35.9	37.9	37.9	40.8	43.8
Long-term	9.9	10.0	11.0	11.6	19.6	26.5	29.3	24.7	17.5	12.0
By type of creditor										
Official	5.1	5.0	4.5	4.7	4.9	4.8	4.8	4.5	4.2	4.2
Commercial banks	39.2	38.2	38.5	36.2	45.6	50.4	52.2	49.3	44.7	41.2
Other private	4.7	4.8	5.3	7.1	4.5	7.3	10.2	8.8	9.4	10.3
Net debtor countries										
Total debt	**1,116.9**	**1,133.4**	**1,162.1**	**1,250.7**	**1,316.6**	**1,384.6**	**1,492.0**	**1,560.5**	**1,657.7**	**1,740.9**
By maturity										
Short-term	171.6	180.4	187.9	216.4	226.8	240.5	255.6	279.2	315.3	339.4
Long-term	945.3	953.0	974.2	1,034.4	1,089.9	1,144.1	1,236.4	1,281.3	1,342.3	1,401.5
By type of creditor										
Official	515.0	530.3	552.2	603.4	632.8	648.2	678.7	733.0	779.8	793.6
Commercial banks	443.0	422.2	404.7	385.5	404.3	417.6	415.2	400.7	384.6	399.7
Other private	158.9	180.9	205.2	261.8	279.6	318.8	398.1	426.8	493.3	547.6
Market borrowers										
Total debt	**539.5**	**528.8**	**531.5**	**569.2**	**610.9**	**654.2**	**722.5**	**773.9**	**845.1**	**906.8**
By maturity										
Short-term	84.3	89.4	97.4	120.0	134.3	143.7	146.0	168.9	197.5	214.9
Long-term	455.2	439.4	434.1	449.3	476.6	510.5	576.5	605.0	647.6	691.9
By type of creditor										
Official	128.3	129.8	136.8	156.2	172.8	176.5	187.2	205.0	235.6	238.3
Commercial banks	321.4	297.2	273.8	242.7	258.3	271.8	282.6	267.6	246.6	256.7
Other private	89.8	101.9	120.9	170.3	179.8	205.8	252.7	301.3	362.9	411.9
Diversified borrowers										
Total debt	**341.1**	**358.5**	**376.8**	**410.9**	**428.1**	**450.9**	**482.8**	**488.2**	**503.4**	**520.3**
By maturity										
Short-term	46.1	49.4	52.9	59.7	57.8	63.9	73.0	72.4	79.9	88.8
Long-term	295.0	309.1	323.9	351.2	370.3	387.1	409.8	415.8	423.4	431.5
By type of creditor										
Official	194.6	198.5	204.9	221.8	233.0	242.8	258.7	276.9	283.7	288.1
Commercial banks	92.6	96.0	102.3	112.6	116.6	121.4	111.2	111.8	115.2	120.1
Other private	53.9	64.0	69.6	76.5	78.6	86.8	112.9	99.5	104.4	112.1

Table A40 (concluded)

	1987	1988	1989	1990	1991	1992	1993	1994	1995	1996
Official borrowers										
Total debt	**236.3**	**246.1**	**253.8**	**270.6**	**277.6**	**279.5**	**286.7**	**298.5**	**309.2**	**313.8**
By maturity										
Short-term	41.2	41.5	37.7	36.7	34.7	33.0	36.6	37.9	37.9	35.7
Long-term	195.1	204.5	216.1	233.9	242.9	246.5	250.1	260.6	271.3	278.1
By type of creditor										
Official	192.2	202.1	210.5	225.4	227.0	228.8	232.9	251.1	260.5	267.2
Commercial banks	29.0	29.0	28.6	30.2	29.4	24.4	21.4	21.3	22.8	22.9
Other private	15.2	15.0	14.7	15.0	21.2	26.2	32.5	26.1	25.9	23.7
Countries with recent debt-servicing difficulties										
Total debt	**712.5**	**716.6**	**731.3**	**774.1**	**794.2**	**818.3**	**853.7**	**884.6**	**922.7**	**945.6**
By maturity										
Short-term	117.7	118.3	118.2	130.9	129.8	131.2	121.4	126.4	138.3	138.7
Long-term	594.8	598.3	613.1	643.3	664.4	687.1	732.3	758.1	784.4	806.9
By type of creditor										
Official	293.1	306.1	324.3	360.0	373.5	379.0	389.8	416.1	448.3	452.1
Commercial banks	326.2	297.9	278.2	240.1	239.7	233.6	225.9	197.9	165.5	165.4
Other private	93.1	112.6	128.8	174.1	181.0	205.8	238.0	270.5	308.9	328.1
Countries without debt-servicing difficulties										
Total debt	**404.4**	**416.8**	**430.8**	**476.6**	**522.4**	**566.2**	**638.3**	**676.0**	**735.0**	**795.4**
By maturity										
Short-term	53.9	62.1	69.7	85.5	97.0	109.3	134.2	152.8	177.0	200.8
Long-term	350.5	354.7	361.1	391.1	425.4	456.9	504.1	523.2	557.9	594.6
By type of creditor										
Official	221.9	224.2	227.9	243.4	259.3	269.2	288.9	317.0	331.5	341.5
Commercial banks	116.8	124.3	126.5	145.4	164.5	184.1	189.3	202.7	219.1	234.3
Other private	65.8	68.3	76.4	87.8	98.6	113.0	160.2	156.3	184.4	219.5
Other groups										
Small low-income economies										
Total debt	**115.4**	**118.7**	**124.0**	**134.2**	**145.6**	**150.5**	**157.7**	**166.3**	**176.6**	**184.3**
By maturity										
Short-term	27.8	28.0	24.0	25.8	26.7	27.5	29.6	30.1	31.1	32.1
Long-term	87.6	90.6	100.0	108.5	118.8	123.0	128.1	136.2	145.5	152.2
By type of creditor										
Official	97.6	102.3	107.2	117.4	125.5	126.5	133.1	145.9	153.0	159.8
Commercial banks	9.7	9.7	9.9	11.0	10.7	10.2	10.1	10.0	10.1	10.1
Other private	8.1	6.7	6.8	5.9	9.3	13.8	14.5	10.3	13.5	14.5
Least developed countries										
Total debt	**89.2**	**93.8**	**98.1**	**109.2**	**118.5**	**120.2**	**125.7**	**131.2**	**138.8**	**143.9**
By maturity										
Short-term	27.1	27.2	22.5	24.1	25.1	26.0	27.2	27.4	28.5	29.6
Long-term	62.1	66.6	75.5	85.1	93.4	94.3	98.4	103.8	110.4	114.3
By type of creditor										
Official	76.3	80.5	84.6	96.3	103.2	102.4	106.9	116.1	120.9	126.1
Commercial banks	6.9	6.9	7.3	8.2	8.0	7.5	7.4	6.9	7.0	7.1
Other private	6.0	6.3	6.2	4.6	7.3	10.3	11.3	8.2	10.9	10.7
Fifteen heavily indebted countries										
Total debt	**493.4**	**481.0**	**481.7**	**504.1**	**522.4**	**540.6**	**571.1**	**596.2**	**626.3**	**645.8**
By maturity										
Short-term	63.4	63.1	67.1	81.2	83.2	85.5	73.9	77.1	88.4	91.0
Long-term	430.0	417.9	414.6	422.9	439.2	455.1	497.1	519.1	537.9	554.8
By type of creditor										
Official	138.7	141.4	153.7	178.7	190.5	194.8	204.3	217.3	243.1	241.2
Commercial banks	290.7	263.6	241.7	201.7	203.2	197.6	196.0	167.8	133.5	132.7
Other private	63.9	76.1	86.4	123.7	128.7	148.2	170.8	211.0	249.7	271.9

Table A41. Developing Countries: Ratio of External Debt to GDP[1]

	1987	1988	1989	1990	1991	1992	1993	1994	1995	1996
Developing countries	**41.0**	**37.8**	**35.9**	**34.8**	**35.2**	**33.7**	**33.0**	**31.3**	**29.4**	**27.5**
By region										
Africa	61.9	60.0	62.6	60.7	64.2	60.6	63.5	65.7	61.2	63.2
Asia	26.8	23.8	21.9	22.9	24.0	23.7	23.8	23.9	22.5	21.8
Middle East and Europe	39.6	41.8	44.7	41.4	40.3	37.5	37.3	33.7	28.0	23.1
Western Hemisphere	55.0	49.0	43.6	39.6	40.0	38.5	36.5	32.6	33.1	31.7
Sub-Saharan Africa	83.9	79.9	83.8	87.5	93.4	93.6	101.6	113.2	102.7	97.1
Four newly industrializing Asian economies	18.3	12.8	10.2	9.3	10.2	9.8	11.7	10.5	11.2	11.8
By predominant export										
Fuel	49.3	48.3	45.8	44.7	44.2	40.6	39.7	37.0	35.6	31.6
Nonfuel exports	38.3	34.6	32.9	31.7	32.4	31.4	30.9	29.5	27.5	26.2
Manufactures	27.6	23.6	20.8	21.2	23.0	23.3	23.6	22.1	20.5	19.6
Primary products	54.9	57.7	66.3	56.9	49.1	43.8	40.4	39.1	36.2	34.5
Agricultural products	48.0	51.1	64.7	52.0	44.1	38.2	34.4	33.1	30.7	29.5
Minerals	83.2	82.2	70.9	73.1	67.0	66.3	66.6	67.0	61.7	58.3
Services, income, and private transfers	62.2	56.2	82.5	80.1	75.3	69.9	68.6	66.7	61.8	56.7
Diversified export base	53.2	51.1	47.7	42.0	42.3	40.4	42.4	41.9	40.9	39.8
By financial criteria										
Net creditor countries	13.9	12.9	11.7	10.7	11.3	11.3	12.7	11.4	10.0	9.0
Net debtor countries	44.9	41.2	39.2	38.1	38.6	37.0	35.6	33.7	31.5	29.4
Market borrowers	39.7	33.1	29.3	28.5	29.1	28.1	27.5	26.9	26.6	25.7
Diversified borrowers	45.7	46.8	45.8	44.4	46.8	45.9	44.1	39.8	34.4	30.2
Official borrowers	61.3	64.0	77.8	75.0	70.2	63.9	60.3	56.5	49.7	46.2
Countries with recent debt-servicing difficulties	58.3	55.7	54.1	50.0	49.7	46.1	42.5	37.1	34.8	31.4
Countries without debt-servicing difficulties	31.9	28.5	26.7	27.5	28.9	28.7	29.2	30.1	28.2	27.3
Other groups										
Small low-income economies	56.7	59.1	63.0	61.6	60.1	54.4	51.7	49.7	44.7	40.1
Least developed countries	79.8	74.6	71.0	70.7	67.8	58.1	52.8	48.8	42.5	36.4
Fifteen heavily indebted countries	57.7	50.3	43.7	38.4	36.1	41.0	38.1	32.9	31.8	30.7

[1]Debt at year-end in percent of GDP in year indicated.

Table A42. Developing Countries: Debt-Service Ratios[1]

(In percent of exports of goods and services)

	1987	1988	1989	1990	1991	1992	1993	1994	1995	1996
Interest payments[2]										
Developing countries	**9.8**	**9.5**	**8.1**	**7.1**	**7.5**	**6.3**	**6.6**	**6.1**	**6.5**	**5.6**
By region										
Africa	11.1	10.5	11.3	10.5	10.4	9.3	8.7	11.3	12.4	8.7
Asia	5.4	4.8	4.5	4.1	3.8	3.7	3.5	3.5	3.6	3.6
Middle East and Europe	7.6	7.1	6.9	6.7	5.9	4.6	4.3	4.6	5.0	3.4
Western Hemisphere	24.4	26.1	19.1	15.2	21.2	16.8	20.6	16.2	17.8	15.5
Sub-Saharan Africa	8.7	8.7	7.8	7.8	7.7	6.3	4.7	11.3	15.6	5.1
Four newly industrializing Asian economies	2.4	1.7	1.7	1.5	1.3	1.1	1.0	0.9	0.9	0.9
By predominant export										
Fuel	12.2	12.8	12.1	9.7	8.9	8.4	8.3	9.8	10.3	8.9
Nonfuel exports	9.0	8.5	6.9	6.2	7.1	5.7	6.1	5.2	5.6	4.8
Manufactures	6.6	7.2	5.3	4.4	4.6	4.4	4.1	4.1	4.4	4.1
Primary products	18.7	15.0	13.1	11.6	20.6	11.6	18.6	10.4	11.7	6.5
Agricultural products	20.6	15.8	14.4	12.2	13.9	11.4	21.9	10.6	8.4	6.9
Minerals	14.6	13.2	10.7	10.2	36.1	12.2	10.0	9.7	20.4	5.4
Services, income, and private transfers	13.4	8.4	9.8	14.1	15.2	12.8	13.6	12.7	12.4	12.0
Diversified export base	10.6	10.0	9.3	8.0	7.0	6.0	5.8	5.7	5.7	5.7
By financial criteria										
Net creditor countries	1.8	1.9	2.0	1.5	1.3	1.2	1.2	1.3	1.5	1.2
Net debtor countries	11.8	11.2	9.6	8.6	9.0	7.5	7.7	7.1	7.5	6.4
Market borrowers	10.8	10.4	7.9	6.4	7.6	6.3	7.0	5.9	6.2	5.9
Diversified borrowers	13.9	14.4	14.0	13.4	12.7	11.2	10.6	11.4	12.0	9.6
Official borrowers	13.6	9.6	11.4	12.6	11.6	8.9	7.5	8.3	8.2	3.1
Countries with recent debt-servicing difficulties	19.9	20.2	16.6	14.6	17.9	13.9	16.5	14.3	15.7	12.0
Countries without debt-servicing difficulties	7.2	6.5	6.0	5.6	5.2	4.9	4.5	4.5	4.5	4.4
Other groups										
Small low-income economies	11.3	11.9	10.5	9.5	8.7	9.2	8.4	11.0	17.2	8.2
Least developed countries	8.6	8.8	7.6	6.3	7.7	7.2	6.3	6.9	19.6	2.5
Fifteen heavily indebted countries	23.8	24.7	19.3	15.1	20.2	16.6	20.5	16.7	18.8	16.9

Table A42 *(concluded)*

	1987	1988	1989	1990	1991	1992	1993	1994	1995	1996
Amortization[2]										
Developing countries	**10.2**	**9.6**	**8.7**	**8.7**	**9.8**	**9.1**	**8.2**	**9.7**	**7.7**	**6.8**
By region										
Africa	14.8	15.1	16.4	16.1	17.3	19.2	16.0	14.1	14.5	11.2
Asia	7.7	6.4	6.4	6.5	6.3	5.6	5.3	5.9	4.7	5.0
Middle East and Europe	6.5	7.6	6.7	6.9	6.2	5.2	4.5	13.3	5.5	4.7
Western Hemisphere	18.7	18.2	13.6	13.4	21.9	21.7	20.2	19.5	19.7	15.3
Sub-Saharan Africa	12.6	12.8	13.9	11.7	11.7	13.2	9.3	15.1	19.1	11.4
Four newly industrializing Asian economies	5.2	3.9	3.5	4.4	5.1	3.8	2.8	4.0	2.4	2.4
By predominant export										
Fuel	11.6	12.5	9.0	8.5	9.9	12.5	11.7	18.5	12.9	9.6
Nonfuel exports	9.7	8.7	8.6	8.8	9.7	8.1	7.2	7.5	6.5	6.1
Manufactures	8.2	6.9	6.8	6.7	7.5	6.6	5.8	6.2	5.1	4.9
Primary products	13.1	17.2	18.0	16.9	24.5	17.7	18.4	17.4	17.8	13.6
Agricultural products	17.3	22.9	24.3	22.5	19.5	20.4	19.9	20.6	16.8	15.1
Minerals	3.9	5.2	5.6	4.5	35.9	11.3	14.4	9.2	20.6	9.5
Services, income, and private transfers	16.3	10.9	10.9	17.7	17.4	11.6	7.9	8.7	4.5	8.7
Diversified export base	11.3	10.8	9.9	9.0	7.5	8.1	7.3	7.5	7.4	7.6
By financial criteria										
Net creditor countries	2.1	2.1	1.3	1.2	1.3	1.4	2.0	9.1	2.5	2.1
Net debtor countries	12.3	11.3	10.5	10.6	11.8	10.9	9.6	9.8	8.7	7.7
Market borrowers	11.0	9.7	8.7	8.5	10.8	9.3	8.2	7.9	6.6	6.3
Diversified borrowers	14.1	15.8	15.2	15.2	13.7	15.4	14.1	15.5	15.8	11.8
Official borrowers	16.0	11.4	11.9	14.5	15.2	13.8	10.9	13.3	12.3	10.8
Countries with recent debt-servicing difficulties	15.9	15.1	12.7	13.8	18.5	18.3	16.1	16.5	16.9	12.7
Countries without debt-servicing difficulties	10.2	9.3	9.3	9.0	8.9	7.9	7.1	7.4	5.8	5.9
Other groups										
Small low-income economies	17.6	17.1	16.8	14.5	14.7	15.1	13.5	14.1	19.9	12.1
Least developed countries	11.8	11.0	14.1	11.9	15.1	15.2	11.8	10.6	23.0	10.7
Fifteen heavily indebted countries	17.7	17.6	14.4	13.7	20.3	21.0	19.7	18.9	19.5	15.5

[1]Excludes service payments to the IMF.
[2]Interest payments on total debt and amortization on long-term debt. Estimates through 1994 reflect debt-service payments actually made. The estimates for 1995 and 1996 take into account projected exceptional financing items, including accumulation of arrears and rescheduling agreements. In some cases amortization on account of debt-reduction operations is included.

Table A43. IMF Charges and Repurchases to the IMF[1]
(In percent of exports of goods and services)

	1987	1988	1989	1990	1991	1992	1993	1994
Developing countries	**1.7**	**1.2**	**1.0**	**1.0**	**0.8**	**0.6**	**0.6**	**0.4**
By region								
Africa	2.9	2.1	2.1	1.6	1.3	1.2	1.2	0.9
Asia	1.2	0.8	0.5	0.5	0.4	0.2	0.1	0.2
Middle East and Europe	0.4	0.4	0.2	0.1	0.1	—	—	—
Western Hemisphere	3.8	3.1	3.0	3.2	3.0	2.7	2.6	1.5
Sub-Saharan Africa	4.7	4.5	4.8	3.5	2.6	2.2	1.7	1.2
By predominant export								
Fuel	0.5	0.7	0.7	0.9	1.1	1.0	1.0	0.8
Nonfuel exports	2.1	1.4	1.1	1.0	0.8	0.5	0.4	0.3
By financial criteria								
Net creditor countries	—	—	—	—	—	—	—	—
Net debtor countries	2.1	1.5	1.3	1.2	1.0	0.8	0.7	0.5
Market borrowers	1.5	1.0	0.9	1.0	0.9	0.7	0.7	0.4
Official borrowers	4.1	3.3	3.0	2.6	1.9	1.4	1.2	0.7
Countries with recent debt-servicing difficulties	3.5	2.7	2.6	2.6	2.5	2.2	2.1	1.4
Countries without debt-servicing difficulties	1.3	0.9	0.6	0.5	0.4	0.2	0.2	0.2
Other groups								
Small low-income economies	7.1	5.9	5.9	4.9	3.1	2.5	1.9	1.0
Least-developed countries	5.0	3.6	4.9	4.0	2.9	1.8	1.5	1.1
Fifteen heavily indebted countries	3.9	3.3	3.1	3.0	2.9	2.4	2.4	1.5
Countries in transition	**0.7**	**0.7**	**0.5**	**0.4**	**0.3**	**0.7**	**0.5**	**1.4**
Central and eastern Europe	...	...	...	...	0.6	1.2	0.9	2.6
Excluding Belarus and Ukraine	...	...	...	...	0.7	1.4	1.0	2.9
Russia	...	...	...	...	—	—	—	—
Transcaucasus and central Asia	...	...	...	...	—	—	—	0.1
Memorandum								
Total, in billions of U.S. dollars								
General Resources Account	12.580	10.890	10.000	10.538	9.010	8.348	7.671	8.348
Charges	2.673	2.428	2.422	2.596	2.525	2.427	2.341	1.804
Repurchases	9.907	8.462	7.578	7.941	6.485	5.921	5.330	6.544
Trust Fund	0.708	0.673	0.513	0.367	0.070	—	0.063	0.015
Interest	0.005	0.004	0.004	0.002	0.001	—	0.003	—
Repayments	0.703	0.669	0.509	0.365	0.069	—	0.060	0.014
SAF	0.001	0.003	0.006	0.010	0.014	0.045	0.138	0.314
Interest	0.001	0.003	0.006	0.010	0.014	0.012	0.012	0.010
Repayments	—	—	—	—	—	0.033	0.126	0.304
ESAF	—	—	0.001	0.003	0.007	0.010	0.013	0.016
Interest	—	—	0.001	0.003	0.007	0.010	0.013	0.014
Repayments	—	—	—	—	—	—	—	0.002

[1] Excludes industrial countries. Charges on, and repurchases (or repayments of principal) for, use of IMF credit.

Table A44. Summary of Sources and Uses of World Saving
(In percent of GDP)

	Averages		1988	1989	1990	1991	1992	1993	1994	1995	1996
	1973–80	1981–87									
World											
Saving	24.8	22.4	23.5	23.7	23.1	22.7	21.8	21.9	22.8	23.1	23.2
Investment	25.0	23.3	24.1	24.6	23.9	23.5	22.9	23.0	23.7	24.0	24.3
Industrial countries											
Saving	23.4	20.8	21.3	21.5	20.8	20.4	19.5	19.3	19.7	20.0	20.2
Private	21.6	20.7	19.8	19.2	19.2	19.8	19.9	20.0	19.9	19.7	19.7
Public	1.8	0.1	1.5	2.3	1.6	0.7	−0.4	−0.7	−0.1	0.2	0.5
Investment	23.3	21.2	21.7	22.2	21.6	20.7	20.0	19.5	20.0	20.3	20.5
Private	18.8	17.5	18.2	18.5	17.8	17.1	16.3	15.7	16.4	16.8	16.9
Public	4.5	3.8	3.5	3.6	3.7	3.6	3.7	3.8	3.6	3.6	3.6
Net lending	0.1	−0.4	−0.4	−0.7	−0.8	−0.3	−0.5	−0.2	−0.2	−0.4	−0.3
Private	2.8	3.2	1.6	0.7	1.3	2.7	3.6	4.3	3.5	3.0	2.8
Public	−2.6	−3.6	−2.0	−1.4	−2.1	−2.9	−4.1	−4.5	−3.7	−3.3	−3.1
Current transfers	−0.4	−0.4	−0.4	−0.4	−0.4	−0.2	−0.4	−0.4	−0.4	−0.4	−0.4
Factor income	0.6	0.2	0.4	0.2	0.1	—	−0.1	−0.1	−0.1	−0.3	−0.4
Resource balance	−0.1	−0.2	−0.4	−0.4	−0.5	−0.1	—	0.3	0.3	0.4	0.5
United States											
Saving	20.3	17.6	16.5	16.4	15.3	15.4	14.2	14.6	15.5	15.3	15.3
Private	18.6	18.4	16.4	15.6	15.5	16.4	16.3	15.8	15.4	15.2	15.4
Public	1.6	−0.7	0.1	0.8	−0.3	−1.0	−2.1	−1.2	0.1	0.1	−0.1
Investment	20.0	19.4	18.3	18.1	16.8	15.3	15.3	16.1	17.4	17.6	17.3
Private	17.4	17.2	16.2	15.8	14.6	13.0	13.1	13.9	15.3	15.6	15.3
Public	2.6	2.2	2.1	2.2	2.2	2.3	2.2	2.2	2.0	2.0	2.0
Net lending	0.3	−1.8	−1.8	−1.7	−1.6	0.1	−1.1	−1.5	−1.9	−2.3	−2.0
Private	1.2	1.2	0.2	−0.2	0.9	3.4	3.2	1.9	0.1	−0.3	0.1
Public	−1.0	−2.9	−2.0	−1.5	−2.5	−3.2	−4.3	−3.4	−2.0	−1.9	−2.1
Current transfers	−0.3	−0.5	−0.5	−0.5	−0.6	0.1	−0.5	−0.5	−0.5	−0.5	−0.5
Factor income	1.1	1.0	1.0	0.5	0.5	0.5	0.1	0.2	0.2	−0.2	−0.3
Resource balance	−0.6	−2.2	−2.3	−1.7	−1.4	−0.5	−0.7	−1.2	−1.6	−1.5	−1.3
European Union											
Saving	23.4	20.2	21.4	21.9	21.3	20.0	19.1	18.7	19.4	20.2	20.7
Private	22.2	20.8	21.0	20.9	21.2	21.0	21.1	21.7	22.0	21.9	21.5
Public	1.2	−0.6	0.4	1.0	0.1	−1.0	−2.0	−3.0	−2.6	−1.6	−0.9
Investment	23.2	20.0	21.2	22.0	21.8	21.2	20.2	18.6	19.0	19.6	20.1
Private	18.2	16.1	17.5	18.0	17.8	17.8	16.7	15.2	15.9	16.6	17.1
Public	5.0	3.9	3.7	3.9	4.0	3.4	3.5	3.4	3.0	3.0	3.0
Net lending	0.2	0.2	0.2	—	−0.4	−1.2	−1.0	0.1	0.5	0.6	0.5
Private	4.1	4.7	3.5	2.9	3.5	3.3	4.4	6.5	6.1	5.3	4.5
Public	−3.8	−4.5	−3.3	−2.9	−3.9	−4.4	−5.5	−6.4	−5.6	−4.7	−3.9
Current transfers	−0.8	−0.3	−0.4	−0.4	−0.4	−0.5	−0.4	−0.4	−0.5	−0.5	−0.5
Factor income	0.6	−0.1	0.2	0.3	0.1	−0.1	−0.2	−0.3	−0.2	−0.3	−0.4
Resource balance	0.4	0.5	0.4	0.1	−0.2	−0.6	−0.4	0.8	1.1	1.4	1.4
Japan											
Saving	33.2	31.2	33.3	33.7	33.9	34.6	34.3	33.1	31.7	31.4	31.1
Private	29.1	26.7	25.5	24.1	23.5	24.9	25.5	26.2	25.9	25.7	25.7
Public	4.1	4.5	7.9	9.6	10.4	9.7	8.7	6.9	5.8	5.7	5.4
Investment	33.3	28.8	30.6	31.8	32.8	32.5	31.1	29.9	28.9	28.9	28.8
Private	23.9	21.0	24.0	25.3	26.1	25.8	23.5	21.3	19.8	20.0	20.1
Public	9.4	7.8	6.6	6.5	6.6	6.7	7.6	8.6	9.0	8.9	8.7
Net lending	−0.1	2.4	2.7	1.9	1.1	2.1	3.2	3.1	2.8	2.5	2.3
Private	5.2	5.7	1.5	−1.2	−2.6	−0.9	2.0	4.9	6.0	5.7	5.6
Public	−5.3	−3.3	1.2	3.1	3.8	3.1	1.2	−1.8	−3.2	−3.2	−3.3
Current transfers	−0.1	−0.1	−0.1	−0.1	−0.2	−0.4	−0.1	−0.1	−0.2	−0.1	−0.1
Factor income	−0.2	0.3	0.7	0.7	0.7	0.7	1.0	1.0	0.9	0.9	1.0
Resource balance	0.1	2.2	2.2	1.3	0.6	1.8	2.4	2.3	2.1	1.7	1.5

Table A44 *(continued)*

	Averages		1988	1989	1990	1991	1992	1993	1994	1995	1996
	1973–80	1981–87									
Developing countries											
Saving	25.7	22.5	25.0	25.5	25.6	24.3	24.9	25.5	27.5	27.6	27.7
Investment	25.7	24.0	26.4	26.9	26.2	26.3	26.5	27.9	29.0	29.1	29.3
Net lending	—	−2.0	−1.3	−1.4	−0.6	−1.9	−1.6	−2.4	−1.6	−1.5	−1.6
Current transfers	0.9	0.5	1.2	1.5	1.5	0.9	1.5	1.3	1.2	1.2	1.2
Factor income	−1.1	−1.7	−1.9	−2.1	−1.9	−1.5	−1.4	−1.3	−1.2	−1.5	−1.2
Resource balance	0.2	−0.6	−0.6	−0.8	−0.2	−1.4	−1.8	−2.5	−1.6	−1.2	−1.6
Memorandum											
Acquisition of foreign assets	3.2	0.8	0.6	0.8	2.4	1.2	1.2	1.6	1.7	0.9	0.7
Change in reserves	1.8	0.1	—	0.7	1.8	2.2	1.1	1.4	1.9	0.8	0.6
By region											
Africa											
Saving	26.5	18.8	17.0	17.7	18.7	18.3	15.1	15.7	16.8	18.3	18.4
Investment	31.7	23.4	20.9	21.8	21.3	23.2	21.0	19.7	22.6	23.2	23.0
Net lending	−5.2	−5.3	−3.9	−4.1	−2.6	−4.9	−5.9	−3.9	−5.8	−4.9	−4.6
Current transfers	2.0	2.0	4.2	4.9	5.2	5.1	5.1	5.2	5.4	5.1	5.0
Factor income	−4.5	−4.9	−4.9	−5.7	−5.8	−7.5	−6.8	−4.6	−4.8	−4.3	−5.2
Resource balance	−2.7	−1.8	−3.3	−3.3	−1.9	−2.4	−4.2	−4.5	−6.3	−5.7	−4.4
Memorandum											
Acquisition of foreign assets	1.9	−1.2	−2.2	−0.4	0.2	−0.3	−2.4	−2.3	−1.2	−1.4	−0.4
Change in reserves	1.0	−0.5	−0.5	0.6	1.4	1.6	−2.6	−0.4	−0.3	−0.5	0.3
Asia											
Saving	25.5	27.4	30.4	30.4	30.5	30.2	30.5	31.7	33.9	33.6	33.1
Investment	26.0	27.8	31.0	31.8	30.8	30.4	30.6	33.0	34.6	34.5	34.4
Net lending	−0.5	−0.9	−0.5	−1.3	−0.3	−0.1	—	−1.4	−0.6	−0.9	−1.3
Current transfers	1.1	0.9	0.9	0.8	0.7	0.9	0.9	0.9	0.8	0.7	0.7
Factor income	−0.3	−0.6	−1.1	−1.4	−0.8	−0.8	−0.3	−0.4	−0.3	−0.7	—
Resource balance	−1.3	−0.7	−0.4	−0.8	−0.2	−0.2	−0.6	−1.9	−1.2	−0.9	−2.0
Memorandum											
Acquisition of foreign assets	1.5	1.9	1.7	1.3	2.6	3.4	2.1	2.9	4.0	2.0	1.5
Change in reserves	1.2	1.4	0.7	0.7	1.9	2.6	1.2	1.9	3.6	1.7	1.1
Middle East and Europe											
Saving	34.5	21.6	18.8	19.5	22.1	15.3	20.1	19.0	20.6	21.1	21.9
Investment	24.4	23.5	21.5	21.6	22.9	23.8	24.0	23.6	20.8	21.8	22.7
Net lending	10.1	−4.1	−2.7	−2.1	−0.8	−8.6	−3.9	−4.6	−0.2	−0.7	−0.7
Current transfers	1.0	−1.1	0.6	3.0	2.6	−2.2	2.6	1.8	1.2	1.1	1.3
Factor income	0.5	1.2	0.8	—	—	3.1	0.3	−0.1	0.2	0.4	0.3
Resource balance	8.6	−4.2	−4.2	−5.2	−3.4	−9.4	−6.8	−6.4	−1.6	−2.2	−2.4
Memorandum											
Acquisition of foreign assets	11.1	1.1	−0.6	1.3	2.3	−8.0	0.3	−1.0	−2.9	−1.0	−1.8
Change in reserves	5.8	−1.4	−1.3	1.7	1.5	1.9	2.6	0.5	−0.6	−0.4	−1.3
Western Hemisphere											
Saving	20.5	19.0	20.6	21.2	19.4	18.2	18.0	17.4	18.3	18.4	19.2
Investment	23.8	20.2	21.9	21.5	19.7	19.6	20.5	20.7	21.5	20.5	21.2
Net lending	−3.3	−1.2	−1.3	−0.3	−0.2	−1.4	−2.6	−3.3	−3.1	−2.1	−2.0
Current transfers	0.2	0.3	0.7	0.8	1.1	1.1	1.1	0.9	0.8	0.9	0.9
Factor income	−1.5	−3.9	−3.9	−3.6	−3.7	−3.1	−2.8	−2.9	−2.8	−3.5	−3.6
Resource balance	−1.9	2.5	2.0	2.5	2.4	0.6	−0.9	−1.3	−1.1	0.5	0.7
Memorandum											
Acquisition of foreign assets	1.1	0.1	0.1	−0.1	2.9	1.8	1.2	1.3	−0.7	−0.3	0.2
Change in reserves	0.5	−0.3	−0.4	0.2	1.8	1.8	1.7	1.5	−0.5	−0.5	0.2

Table A44 (continued)

	Averages		1988	1989	1990	1991	1992	1993	1994	1995	1996
	1973–80	1981–87									
By predominant export											
Fuel											
Saving	31.6	22.1	19.8	22.2	23.8	19.4	21.5	21.0	23.1	23.5	23.9
Investment	26.8	24.3	23.5	24.1	24.4	26.4	26.9	25.2	25.8	24.8	25.5
Net lending	4.7	–2.2	–3.7	–1.9	–0.6	–7.0	–5.4	–4.2	–2.7	–1.3	–1.6
Current transfers	–1.4	–1.0	–0.8	–0.2	–0.6	–3.5	–0.4	–0.6	–0.5	–0.4	–0.3
Factor income	–2.5	–1.4	–1.7	–2.3	–2.8	–1.2	–2.6	–2.2	–2.3	–4.2	–3.2
Resource balance	8.6	0.2	–1.3	0.7	2.9	–2.4	–2.4	–1.4	0.1	3.3	1.8
Memorandum											
Acquisition of foreign assets	8.1	–0.3	–2.4	–0.3	4.2	–3.0	–1.6	–0.2	–2.3	–0.4	0.4
Change in reserves	4.2	–1.2	–2.8	0.7	2.2	1.8	0.1	0.5	–2.2	—	0.7
Nonfuel exports											
Saving	23.1	22.8	26.6	26.5	26.1	25.8	25.9	26.8	28.7	28.7	28.7
Investment	25.2	24.7	27.2	27.8	26.7	26.2	26.4	28.7	29.9	30.2	30.3
Net lending	–2.0	–1.9	–0.6	–1.3	–0.6	–0.4	–0.5	–1.9	–1.2	–1.5	–1.7
Current transfers	1.8	2.1	1.7	2.0	2.1	2.2	2.1	1.9	1.7	1.6	1.5
Factor income	–0.5	–1.8	–2.0	–2.1	–1.6	–1.5	–1.0	–1.0	–0.9	–0.8	–0.7
Resource balance	–3.3	–2.2	–0.4	–1.2	–1.1	–1.1	–1.6	–2.8	–2.1	–2.3	–2.5
Memorandum											
Acquisition of foreign assets	1.2	0.8	1.5	1.1	1.8	2.5	2.1	2.1	2.8	1.2	0.8
Change in reserves	0.8	0.7	0.9	0.7	1.6	2.3	1.5	1.7	2.9	1.0	0.6
By financial criteria											
Net creditor countries											
Saving	41.5	27.1	23.5	24.7	27.1	14.5	22.0	21.1	23.5	24.2	24.1
Investment	25.3	23.3	20.9	22.2	23.3	25.5	26.1	24.8	22.6	23.4	23.3
Net lending	16.2	3.8	2.6	2.5	3.8	–11.0	–4.0	–3.7	0.9	0.8	0.8
Current transfers	–4.4	–3.5	–3.8	–3.1	–4.4	–11.8	–2.9	–3.2	–3.0	–2.9	–2.8
Factor income	0.4	4.3	7.1	5.3	4.9	7.1	2.7	1.5	1.5	2.0	2.2
Resource balance	20.2	3.0	–0.7	0.3	3.3	–6.3	–3.8	–1.9	2.4	1.6	1.4
Memorandum											
Acquisition of foreign assets	15.4	5.1	–0.2	1.3	3.5	–13.4	–2.0	–2.3	–2.3	–0.8	–0.2
Change in reserves	5.0	2.3	–2.9	0.6	–1.2	1.6	–0.1	–0.9	–1.4	—	–0.3
Net debtor countries											
Saving	23.9	22.2	25.1	25.5	25.5	25.2	25.2	25.9	27.8	27.9	28.0
Investment	25.7	24.8	26.8	27.3	26.4	26.4	26.6	28.2	29.6	29.6	29.8
Net lending	–1.8	–2.6	–1.7	–1.8	–0.9	–1.1	–1.4	–2.3	–1.8	–1.6	–1.8
Current transfers	1.5	1.7	1.6	1.9	2.0	2.1	1.9	1.7	1.6	1.5	1.5
Factor income	–1.3	–2.3	–2.7	–2.8	–2.4	–2.2	–1.7	–1.5	–1.4	–1.8	–1.4
Resource balance	–2.0	–1.9	–0.6	–0.9	–0.5	–1.0	–1.6	–2.6	–2.0	–1.4	–1.9
Memorandum											
Acquisition of foreign assets	1.8	0.1	0.7	0.7	2.3	2.5	1.5	2.0	2.0	1.0	0.8
Change in reserves	1.4	–0.1	0.3	0.7	2.0	2.3	1.3	1.6	2.1	0.9	0.7
Market borrowers											
Saving	25.6	25.8	29.7	29.9	29.0	28.5	28.5	30.2	33.1	32.7	32.2
Investment	28.1	26.9	30.0	30.2	28.3	28.6	29.4	32.2	34.4	33.8	33.7
Net lending	–2.6	–1.0	–0.3	–0.3	0.7	—	–0.8	–2.1	–1.3	–1.1	–1.5
Current transfers	0.5	0.4	0.4	0.5	0.5	0.5	0.5	0.5	0.5	0.5	0.5
Factor income	–1.2	–2.7	–2.3	–2.1	–1.9	–1.6	–1.5	–1.3	–1.2	–1.3	–1.4
Resource balance	–1.8	1.2	1.6	1.3	2.1	1.1	0.1	–1.3	–0.6	–0.3	–0.5
Memorandum											
Acquisition of foreign assets	1.4	1.0	1.6	1.2	3.8	3.7	2.4	3.0	3.5	1.7	1.5
Change in reserves	0.8	0.4	0.6	0.9	2.6	2.4	1.3	1.8	2.8	1.2	1.0

Table A44 *(concluded)*

	Averages		1988	1989	1990	1991	1992	1993	1994	1995	1996
	1973–80	1981–87									
Official borrowers											
Saving	19.2	15.1	14.2	14.8	16.2	16.1	14.6	13.1	13.7	15.1	16.3
Investment	25.2	21.0	18.8	19.4	19.3	20.5	19.5	18.4	18.9	19.8	20.5
Net lending	–6.0	–5.9	–4.6	–4.7	–3.1	–4.4	–4.9	–5.3	–5.2	–4.7	–4.2
Current transfers	4.7	6.6	6.4	8.4	9.4	9.4	8.5	7.9	7.0	6.5	6.6
Factor income	–3.8	–3.5	–3.8	–4.1	–4.8	–5.6	–5.1	–4.4	–3.8	–3.9	–4.3
Resource balance	–6.9	–9.0	–7.3	–9.0	–7.7	–8.2	–8.3	–8.8	–8.5	–7.4	–6.6
Memorandum											
Acquisition of foreign assets	1.8	–0.9	–1.3	0.2	1.2	1.1	–0.1	–0.4	—	–0.4	–0.9
Change in reserves	1.1	–0.2	—	—	2.1	2.6	1.0	1.3	1.0	–0.1	–0.4
Countries with recent debt-servicing difficulties											
Saving	23.0	17.8	18.6	19.5	18.5	17.7	17.2	16.3	17.3	17.8	18.8
Investment	25.6	21.2	21.0	21.1	19.9	20.2	20.3	19.9	20.9	20.4	21.3
Net lending	–2.6	–3.4	–2.4	–1.6	–1.4	–2.5	–3.2	–3.6	–3.6	–2.6	–2.5
Current transfers	1.2	1.6	1.8	2.7	3.3	3.2	3.0	2.6	2.4	2.4	2.4
Factor income	–2.1	–3.7	–4.1	–4.0	–4.5	–4.0	–3.4	–3.1	–2.7	–3.2	–3.5
Resource balance	–1.7	–1.3	–0.1	–0.3	–0.2	–1.7	–2.8	–3.2	–3.3	–1.7	–1.4
Memorandum											
Acquisition of foreign assets	2.1	–0.8	–0.6	—	2.2	1.9	1.0	0.7	–0.7	–0.4	–0.3
Change in reserves	1.6	–0.6	–0.4	0.5	2.2	2.0	1.6	1.3	–0.2	–0.6	—
Countries without debt-servicing difficulties											
Saving	24.9	25.8	29.5	29.3	29.6	29.6	29.6	30.9	33.1	32.8	32.3
Investment	25.8	27.6	30.7	31.2	30.3	29.9	30.0	32.5	33.9	34.0	33.8
Net lending	–1.0	–1.8	–1.2	–1.9	–0.7	–0.3	–0.4	–1.7	–0.8	–1.2	–1.5
Current transfers	1.8	1.7	1.4	1.3	1.2	1.4	1.3	1.3	1.2	1.1	1.0
Factor income	–0.4	–1.1	–1.7	–2.0	–1.2	–1.2	–0.8	–0.7	–0.7	–1.1	–0.5
Resource balance	–2.4	–2.4	–0.9	–1.3	–0.7	–0.6	–1.0	–2.2	–1.3	–1.2	–2.1
Memorandum											
Acquisition of foreign assets	1.5	0.8	1.5	1.2	2.3	2.9	1.9	2.6	3.4	1.7	1.2
Change in reserves	1.3	0.4	0.7	0.8	1.9	2.5	1.0	1.8	3.3	1.6	1.0
Countries in transition											
Central and eastern Europe excluding Belarus and Ukraine											
Saving	29.8	29.8	31.4	28.8	27.3	22.9	20.8	17.3	16.6	15.6	15.4
Investment	34.2	31.3	31.5	30.3	30.0	25.0	20.4	20.5	20.4	20.5	21.4
Net lending	–4.4	–1.5	–0.2	–1.5	–2.7	–2.1	0.4	–3.2	–3.8	–4.9	–6.0
Current transfers	1.7	1.8	2.1	1.8	2.3	0.6	1.7	1.3	1.3	1.0	0.9
Factor income	–1.0	–2.7	–2.3	–2.2	–2.2	–1.9	1.3	–0.2	–2.0	–2.7	–3.9
Resource balance	–5.1	–0.7	—	–1.1	–2.8	–0.9	–2.6	–4.2	–3.1	–3.2	–3.0
Memorandum											
Acquisition of foreign assets	–3.0	–1.4	–1.4	–1.7	–2.2	2.6	2.3	4.1	2.4	1.3	0.5
Change in reserves	0.4	0.2	0.9	0.9	1.1	1.4	2.0	2.4	2.2	1.1	0.7

Note: The estimates in this table are based on individual countries' national accounts and balance of payments statistics. For many countries, the estimates of national saving are built up from national accounts data on gross domestic investment and from balance-of-payments-based data on net foreign investment. The latter, which is equivalent to the current account balance, comprises three components: current transfers, net factor income, and the resource balance. The mixing of data sources, which is dictated by availability, implies that the estimates for national saving that are derived incorporate the statistical discrepancies. Furthermore, errors, omissions, and asymmetries in balance of payments statistics affect the estimates for net lending; at the global level, net lending, which in theory would be zero, equals the world current account discrepancy. Notwithstanding these statistical shortcomings, flow of funds estimates, such as those presented in this table, provide a useful framework for analyzing development in saving and investment, both over time and across regions and countries. Country group composites are weighted by GDP valued at purchasing power parities (PPPs) as a share of total world GDP.

Table A45. Summary of Medium-Term Baseline Scenario

	Eight-Year Averages		Four-Year Average 1993–96	1993	1994	1995	1996	Four-Year Average 1997–2000
	1977–84	1985–92						
	Annual percent change, unless otherwise noted							
Industrial countries								
Real GDP	2.6	2.7	2.5	1.2	3.0	3.0	2.7	2.7
Real total domestic demand	2.4	2.8	2.4	1.0	3.2	2.9	2.7	2.7
GDP deflator	7.9	3.9	2.4	2.5	1.9	2.3	2.7	2.5
Real six-month LIBOR (in percent)[1]	4.4	3.7	3.1	1.2	3.0	4.3	3.9	3.7
World prices (in U.S. dollars)								
Manufactures	4.0	6.0	0.7	–5.8	2.8	4.0	2.0	1.6
Oil	...	...	–1.9	–11.5	–4.1	9.4	–0.1	1.6
Nonfuel primary commodities	3.0	–0.3	3.7	–3.7	12.3	8.0	–1.1	1.4
Developing countries								
Real GDP	4.5	5.0	6.0	6.1	6.3	5.6	6.1	6.3
Export volume	0.7	7.8	9.8	9.0	10.4	9.1	10.7	8.9
Terms of trade	2.4	–2.6	–0.3	–1.1	–0.3	0.6	–0.3	–0.1
Import volume	4.0	6.7	9.7	10.4	8.7	8.6	11.2	8.4
World trade, volume	**3.7**	**5.2**	**7.0**	**3.8**	**9.4**	**8.0**	**6.8**	**6.0**
World real GDP	**3.3**	**3.2**	**3.5**	**2.5**	**3.7**	**3.8**	**4.2**	**4.4**

	Four-Year Average 1985–88	1988	1992	1993	1994	1995	1996	2000
	In percent of exports of goods and services							
Current account balance	–4.3	–2.6	–6.5	–8.1	–6.7	–5.5	–5.3	–1.8
Total external debt	167.1	155.1	127.1	127.8	118.7	111.2	104.4	85.3
Debt-service payments[2]	21.0	19.0	15.4	14.8	15.8	14.3	12.5	10.0
Interest	11.4	9.5	6.3	6.6	6.1	6.5	5.6	4.1
Amortization	9.6	9.6	9.1	8.2	9.7	7.7	6.8	6.0
Memorandum								
Net debtor countries								
Current account balance	–7.0	–4.2	–6.0	–8.8	–7.6	–6.3	–6.1	–2.9
Total external debt	203.5	182.8	150.0	149.2	136.8	127.7	119.0	95.3
Debt-service payments[2]	25.7	22.5	18.3	17.3	16.9	16.2	14.1	11.3
Interest	14.0	11.2	7.5	7.7	7.1	7.5	6.4	4.6
Amortization	11.7	11.3	10.9	9.6	9.8	8.7	7.7	6.7

[1]London interbank offered rate on U.S. dollar deposits less percent change in U.S. GDP deflator.
[2]Interest payments on total debt, plus amortization payments on long-term debt only. Projections incorporate the impact of exceptional financing items. Excludes service payments to the IMF.

Table A46. Developing Countries—Medium-Term Baseline Scenario: Selected Economic Indicators

	Averages			1993	1994	1995	1996	Average 1997–2000
	1977–84	1985–92	1993–96					
	Annual percent change							
Developing countries								
Real GDP	4.5	5.0	6.0	6.1	6.3	5.6	6.1	6.3
Export volume	0.7	7.8	9.8	9.0	10.4	9.1	10.7	8.9
Terms of trade	2.4	−2.6	−0.3	−1.1	−0.3	0.6	−0.3	−0.1
Import volume	4.0	6.7	9.7	10.4	8.7	8.6	11.2	8.4
By region								
Africa								
Real GDP	1.7	2.6	3.1	0.7	2.7	3.7	5.3	4.4
Export volume	−1.3	2.8	3.0	4.2	0.1	2.4	5.2	3.8
Terms of trade	1.3	−3.4	−2.9	−5.0	−7.3	0.9	—	0.3
Import volume	−0.7	0.1	1.1	−0.2	−2.9	6.1	1.5	3.7
Asia								
Real GDP	6.9	7.2	8.1	8.7	8.6	7.6	7.3	7.4
Export volume	8.2	12.0	11.7	11.0	13.4	11.1	11.3	10.6
Terms of trade	0.1	−1.0	0.2	0.4	0.4	0.2	−0.4	−0.2
Import volume	8.2	10.8	12.9	13.8	13.1	11.8	12.9	10.1
Middle East and Europe								
Real GDP	2.6	2.8	3.0	3.7	0.7	2.9	4.7	4.5
Export volume	−6.5	3.3	6.2	4.4	4.3	2.6	13.6	4.2
Terms of trade	5.4	−4.8	−1.1	−2.9	−2.4	1.2	−0.1	0.1
Import volume	5.2	−0.4	4.0	4.2	−6.6	5.7	13.8	3.5
Western Hemisphere								
Real GDP	3.1	2.5	3.5	3.2	4.6	2.3	3.7	4.9
Export volume	6.6	4.2	9.1	8.9	9.4	10.1	7.8	7.6
Terms of trade	−0.3	−3.2	0.2	−2.6	2.7	1.5	−0.7	−0.2
Import volume	−1.9	7.8	7.0	9.8	13.7	−0.6	5.9	6.6
By financial criteria								
Countries with recent debt-servicing difficulties								
Real GDP	2.9	2.5	3.4	2.7	4.1	2.6	4.1	4.9
Export volume	1.8	3.0	9.8	8.4	7.6	8.3	14.9	6.8
Terms of trade	1.2	−3.7	−0.8	−4.0	0.5	0.9	−0.6	0.1
Import volume	−0.4	2.5	7.2	6.2	9.6	1.4	11.9	6.3
Countries without debt-servicing difficulties								
Real GDP	6.3	6.8	7.6	8.3	7.8	7.3	7.2	7.2
Export volume	6.3	10.3	11.5	11.0	13.6	10.3	11.0	10.4
Terms of trade	0.9	−1.0	0.2	0.8	−0.1	0.6	−0.3	−0.2
Import volume	7.4	8.8	12.4	15.1	10.8	11.5	12.2	9.7

Table A46 (concluded)

	1984	1988	1992	1993	1994	1995	1996	2000
				In percent of exports of goods and services				
Developing countries								
Current account balance	−5.6	−2.6	−6.5	−8.1	−6.7	−5.5	−5.3	−1.8
Total external debt	145.8	155.1	127.1	127.8	118.7	111.2	104.4	85.3
Debt-service payments[1]	20.4	19.0	15.4	14.8	15.8	14.3	12.5	10.0
Interest payments	11.9	9.5	6.3	6.6	6.1	6.5	5.6	4.1
Amortization	8.4	9.6	9.1	8.2	9.7	7.7	6.8	6.0
By region								
Africa								
Current account balance	−11.4	−12.0	−9.6	−9.8	−13.6	−13.7	−11.4	−5.7
Total external debt	179.8	252.9	246.2	258.9	264.5	249.7	240.9	195.8
Debt-service payments[1]	28.9	25.6	28.5	24.6	25.4	26.9	19.9	19.6
Interest payments	11.6	10.5	9.3	8.7	11.3	12.4	8.7	7.1
Amortization	17.3	15.1	19.2	16.0	14.1	14.5	11.2	12.5
Asia								
Current account balance	−1.5	3.2	0.2	−1.9	−1.3	−2.1	−2.6	−0.9
Total external debt	96.5	79.0	67.5	69.0	63.9	61.5	59.9	56.0
Debt-service payments[1]	12.4	11.2	9.3	8.8	9.5	8.3	8.6	7.3
Interest payments	6.7	4.8	3.7	3.5	3.5	3.6	3.6	3.1
Amortization	5.8	6.4	5.6	5.3	5.9	4.7	5.0	4.3
Middle East and Europe								
Current account balance	−12.3	−8.8	−15.4	−15.0	−9.2	−8.7	−7.3	−0.8
Total external debt	89.2	171.7	143.8	153.5	145.5	134.0	116.5	93.7
Debt-service payments[1]	9.1	14.7	9.8	8.8	17.9	10.5	8.1	4.9
Interest payments	5.4	7.1	4.6	4.3	4.6	5.0	3.4	2.6
Amortization	3.6	7.6	5.2	4.5	13.3	5.5	4.7	2.3
Western Hemisphere								
Current account balance	−1.0	−8.8	−20.5	−24.8	−23.4	−13.4	−12.3	−5.9
Total external debt	301.1	317.7	276.4	274.6	255.3	237.4	228.2	177.0
Debt-service payments[1]	46.4	44.3	38.5	40.7	35.7	37.5	30.8	24.4
Interest payments	31.5	26.1	16.8	20.6	16.2	17.8	15.5	9.3
Amortization	14.8	18.2	21.7	20.2	19.5	19.7	15.3	15.1
By financial criteria								
Countries with recent debt-servicing difficulties								
Current account balance	−10.7	−13.3	−17.0	−20.7	−20.0	−12.7	−10.7	−4.8
Total external debt	276.4	337.4	312.0	313.8	294.1	270.4	244.8	189.6
Debt-service payments[1]	39.5	35.3	32.2	32.6	30.8	32.6	24.7	20.0
Interest payments	24.5	20.2	13.9	16.5	14.3	15.7	12.0	7.8
Amortization	15.0	15.1	18.3	16.1	16.5	16.9	12.7	12.2
Countries without debt-servicing difficulties								
Current account balance	−6.0	0.5	−1.6	−4.4	−3.1	−4.0	−4.4	−2.3
Total external debt	114.7	102.2	85.7	87.7	80.4	76.8	73.9	65.1
Debt-service payments[1]	15.9	15.8	12.8	11.6	11.9	10.4	10.3	8.5
Interest payments	8.2	6.5	4.9	4.5	4.5	4.5	4.4	3.5
Amortization	7.6	9.3	7.9	7.1	7.4	5.8	5.9	5.0

[1]Interest payments on total debt plus amortization payments on long-term debt only. Projections incorporate the impact of exceptional financing items. Excludes service payments to the IMF.

World Economic and Financial Surveys

This series (ISSN 0258-7440) contains biannual, annual, and periodic studies covering monetary and financial issues of importance to the global economy. The core elements of the series are the *World Economic Outlook* report, usually published in May and October, and the annual report on *International Capital Markets*. Other studies assess international trade policy, private market and official financing for developing countries, exchange and payments systems, export credit policies, and issues raised in the *World Economic Outlook.*

World Economic Outlook: A Survey by the Staff of the International Monetary Fund

The *World Economic Outlook,* published twice a year in English, French, Spanish, and Arabic, presents IMF staff economists' analyses of global economic developments during the near and medium term. Chapters give an overview of the world economy; consider issues affecting industrial countries, developing countries, and economies in transition to the market; and address topics of pressing current interest.

ISSN 0256-6877.
$34.00 (academic rate: $23.00; paper).
1995 (May). ISBN 1-55775-468-3. **Stock #WEO-195.**
1994 (May). ISBN 1-55775-381-4. **Stock #WEO-194.**
1994 (Oct.). ISBN 1-55775-385-7. **Stock #WEO-294.**

International Capital Markets: Developments, Prospects, and Policy Issues
by an IMF Staff Team led by Morris Goldstein and David Folkerts-Landau

This annual report reviews developments in international capital markets, including recent bond market turbulence and the role of hedge funds, supervision of banks and nonbanks and the regulation of derivatives, structural changes in government securities markets, recent developments in private market financing for developing countries, and the role of capital markets in financing Chinese enterprises.

$20.00 (academic rate: $12.00; paper).
1994. ISBN 1-55775-426-8. **Stock #WEO-694.**

1993. *Part I: Exchange Rate Management and International Capital Flows,* by Morris Goldstein, David Folkerts-Landau, Peter Garber, Liliana Rojas-Suarez, and Michael Spencer.
ISBN 1-55775-290-7. **Stock #WEO-693.**

1993. *Part II: Systemic Issues in International Finance,* by an IMF Staff Team led by Morris Goldstein and David Folkerts-Landau.
ISBN 1-55775-335-0. **Stock #WEO-1293.**

Staff Studies for the World Economic Outlook
by the IMF's Research Department

These studies, supporting analyses and scenarios of the *World Economic Outlook,* provide a detailed examination of theory and evidence on major issues currently affecting the global economy.

$20.00 (academic rate: $12.00; paper).
1995. ISBN 1-55775-499-3. **Stock #WEO-395.**
1993. ISBN 1-55775-337-7. **Stock #WEO-393.**

Issues in International Exchange and Payments Systems
by a Staff Team from the IMF's Monetary and Exchange Affairs Department

The global trend toward liberalization in countries' international exchange and payments systems has been widespread in both industrial and developing countries and most dramatic in Central and Eastern Europe. Countries in general have brought their exchange systems more in line with market principles and moved toward more flexible exchange rate arrangements in recent years.

$20.00 (academic rate: $12.00; paper).
1995. ISBN 1-55775-480-2. **Stock #WEO-895.**

Private Market Financing for Developing Countries
by a Staff Team from the IMF's Policy Development and Review Department

This study surveys recent trends in private market financing for developing countries, including flows to developing countries through banking and securities markets; the restoration of access to voluntary market financing for some developing countries; and the status of commercial bank debt in low-income countries.

$20.00 (academic rate: $12.00; paper).
1995. ISBN 1-55775-456-X. **Stock #WEO-994.**
1993. ISBN 1-55775-361-X. **Stock #WEO-993.**

International Trade Policies
by a Staff Team led by Naheed Kirmani

The study reviews major issues and developments in trade and their implications for the work of the IMF. Volume I, *The Uruguay Round and Beyond: Principal Issues,* gives and overview of the principal issues and developments in the world trading system. Volume II, *The Uruguay Round and Beyond: Background Papers,* presents detailed background papers on selected trade and trade-related issues. This study updates previous studies published under the title *Issues and Developments in International Trade Policy.*

$20.00 (academic rate: $12.00; paper).
1994. *Volume I. The Uruguay Round and Beyond: Principal Issues*
ISBN 1-55775-469-1. **Stock #WEO-1094.**
1994. *Volume II. The Uruguay Round and Beyond: Background Papers*
ISBN 1-55775-457-8. **Stock #WEO-1494.**
1992. ISBN 1-55775-311-1. **Stock #WEO-1092.**

Official Financing for Developing Countries
by a Staff Team from the IMF's Policy Development and Review Department led by Michael Kuhn

This study provides information on official financing for developing countries, with the focus on low- and lower-middle-income countries. It updates and replaces *Multilateral Official Debt Rescheduling: Recent Experience* and reviews developments in direct financing by official and multilateral sources.

$20.00 (academic rate: $12.00; paper)
1994. ISBN 1-55775-378-4. **Stock #WEO-1394.**

Officially Supported Export Credits: Recent Developments and Prospects
by Michael G. Kuhn, Balazs Horvath, Christopher J. Jarvis

This study examines export credit and cover policies in major industrial countries.

$20.00 (academic rate: $12.00; paper).
1995. ISBN 1-55775-448-9. **Stock #WEO-595.**

Available by series subscription or single title (including back issues); academic rate available only to full-time university faculty and students.

Please send orders and inquiries to:
International Monetary Fund, Publication Services, 700 19th Street, N.W.
Washington, D.C. 20431, U.S.A.
Tel.: (202) 623-7430   Telefax: (202) 623-7201
Internet: publications@imf.org